# The Last Word

**Law and Society Series**
**W. Wesley Pue, General Editor**

The Law and Society Series explores law as a socially embedded phenomenon. It is premised on the understanding that the conventional division of law from society creates false dichotomies in thinking, scholarship, educational practice, and social life. Books in the series treat law and society as mutually constitutive and seek to bridge scholarship emerging from interdisciplinary engagement of law with disciplines such as politics, social theory, history, political economy, and gender studies.

*A list of the books in this series appears at the end of this book.*

LAW AND
SOCIETY

# The Last Word

## Media Coverage of the Supreme Court of Canada

By Florian Sauvageau,
David Schneiderman,
David Taras

with Ruth Klinkhammer and Pierre Trudel

**UBC** Press · Vancouver · Toronto

15 14 13 12 11 10 09 08 07 06    5 4 3 2 1

Printed in Canada on ancient-forest-free paper (100% post-consumer recycled) that is processed chlorine- and acid-free, with vegetable-based inks.

**Library and Archives Canada Cataloguing in Publication**

Sauvageau, Florian, 1941-
   The last word : media coverage of the Supreme Court of Canada / by Florian Sauvageau, David Schneiderman, David Taras ; with Ruth Klinkhammer and Pierre Trudel.

(Law and society, ISSN 1496-4953)
Includes bibliographical references and index.
ISBN-13: 978-0-7748-1243-6 (bound); 978-0-7748-1244-3 (pbk.)
ISBN-10: 0-7748-1243-5 (bound); 0-7748-1244-3 (pbk.)

   1. Canada. Supreme Court – Press coverage.   2. Judgements – Canada – Press coverage.   3. Judicial process – Canada – Press coverage.   4. Journalism, Legal – Canada.   5. Reporters and reporting – Canada.   6. Press and politics – Canada.   I. Schneiderman, David, 1958-   II. Taras, David, 1950-   III. Title.   IV. Series: Law and society series (Vancouver, B.C.)

KE8244.S39 2005        347.71'035       C2005-905462-X
KF8764.ZA2S29 2005

# Canadä

UBC Press gratefully acknowledges the financial support for our publishing program of the Government of Canada through the Book Publishing Industry Development Program (BPIDP), and of the Canada Council for the Arts, and the British Columbia Arts Council.

This book has been published with the help of a grant from the Canadian Federation for the Humanities and Social Sciences, through the Aid to Scholarly Publications Programme, using funds provided by the Social Sciences and Humanities Research Council of Canada.

UBC Press
The University of British Columbia
2029 West Mall
Vancouver, BC V6T 1Z2
604-822-5959 / Fax: 604-822-6083
**www.ubcpress.ca**

# Contents

# Acknowledgments

WE WOULD LIKE to thank the Social Sciences and Humanities Research Council of Canada and the Max Bell Foundation for providing the funding for this study. We are grateful to Dean Kathleen Scherf of the Faculty of Communication and Culture at the University of Calgary for giving the project much needed office space and for her enthusiastic support. The Department of Information and Communication at Laval University also supplied office space and provided great encouragement. The Faculty of Law at the University of Toronto provided meeting space and encouragement throughout the project. Our research manager, Ruth Klinkhammer, was the linchpin that kept the project going. Her tremendous energy, diligence, and professionalism are deeply appreciated and made all the difference. Valérie Langlois and Marie-Julie Fortin, with their backgrounds in both law and communications, also provided invaluable help. Numerous students (graduate and undergraduate in law and communications) lent their support to the project, including Aliza Craimer, Karen Dawson, Melissa Hogg, Melissa Kluger, Gérard Leclerc, Kate Morrison, Amnon Reichman, Shannon Sampert, Christine Shalaby, and Samantha Thrift.

We would like to thank those current and former justices of the Supreme Court of Canada who agreed to be interviewed for this study. Similarly, we are grateful to the journalists and news managers whom we interviewed and who, in some cases, allowed us to look over their shoulders while they worked. One of the great pleasures in conducting such a study is that it is a great learning experience for those who are conducting it. We can only hope that we did justice to the insights and perspectives that we gained from those who participated in our study.

We also received help from colleagues and friends. Some read chapters. Some provided advice. Some were just there when we needed someone to talk to about the project. In this regard, we would like to acknowledge the special effort made by Allan Tupper of the University of British Columbia. We also would like to thank Sujit Choudhry, Richard Davis, Michael Keren, Rainer Knopff, Joan Paul, Tamara Seiler, and Lionel Smith. Wes Pue was enthusiastic about placing this study in the Law and Society series, and we thank him. Peter Milroy, Randy Schmidt, and Darcy Cullen at UBC Press also must be thanked for their encouragement and professionalism. It was a pleasure working with them. We would also like to thank the reviewers for their insights and suggestions. Their strong endorsements mean a great deal to us.

Collaborative efforts are not necessarily easy, especially ones that span a wide country, distinct language communities, and different disciplinary backgrounds. Yet we all benefited enormously from our collaboration. The best part of the project for each of us was that we got to share the journey with each other.

# Judgment Day: A Vignette

FOR CHRISTINE ST-PIERRE, a television reporter in the parliamentary bureau of Radio-Canada, CBC's French-language network, judgment day promised to be nerve-racking and chaotic. The case of John Robin Sharpe, an older man caught in possession of child pornography, had stirred a great deal of publicity and controversy. The decisions rendered by the lower courts had made headlines across the country. Police associations, parental groups, civil libertarians, feminists, and clerics had staked out their positions on the case. What made St-Pierre's job so difficult was that she would have to go on air at noon – almost the same time the judgment was being handed down. She had done as much preparation as she could prior to the decision. She had read a resumé of the *Sharpe* case that had been prepared by the Supreme Court of Canada, she had reviewed press clippings about lower court decisions, and attended briefings given by the Department of Justice and by the court's executive legal officer, James O'Reilly. Although she sometimes speaks to experts, she hadn't had time to phone or consult with anyone beforehand.[1]

The court handed down three decisions on Friday, 26 January 2001. Two of the judgments, a case in administrative law from Ontario (whether principles that had guided a particular set of labour relations board consultations had violated the rules of natural justice) and a criminal case from Newfoundland (whether a mentally challenged complainant had to be called as a witness), received no media coverage, evaporating from public view as soon as they were released. From a media perspective, these cases were dead on arrival. But the *Sharpe* case, which dealt with the possession of child pornography, had all the ingredients of a major news story. Sharpe, a retired city planner who lived in Vancouver and who had won some recognition as a writer, fit the popular conception of what a sex deviant might look like: old and dishevelled, and a bit decrepit. Far from being embarrassed by his perverse behaviour, Sharpe seemed to revel in it. For most Canadians, the case was primarily about ensuring that children are protected from the exploitation of pornographers. Emotions ran deep.

For others, the *Sharpe* case was about freedom of expression. Of particular concern was whether creating diaries or drawings or visual materials for one's own use constituted criminal behaviour. However repugnant Sharpe's behaviour might be, his rights had to be protected. There was also the overhang of partisan politics. The Alliance Party had made the *Sharpe* case into a *cause célèbre*. Pressure had mounted on the Liberal government to react strongly if the court ruled in

Sharpe's favour and struck down the pornography law. In fact, 150,000 people had signed a petition asking the government to overturn the lower court judgments that had found the sections of the pornography law dealing with possession to be too broad, too sweeping.

## The Briefing

For the court's executive legal officer (ELO), James O'Reilly, who was responsible for briefing journalists and announcing the decision, judgment day had really begun at 10 p.m. the night before, when he received the final version of the judgment. Although he had seen previous drafts of the decision and had conducted a "day before" briefing attended by approximately fifteen journalists, care had to be taken to ensure that there were no major errors in the text. Translators had worked feverishly through the previous weekend and there had been concern that the decision would not be ready for Friday. As it was, the schedule was pushed back so that the decision would be released at noon instead of at the usual time of 9:45 a.m. This upset some of the radio and TV reporters, including St-Pierre, who would have almost no time to read or digest the judgment before having to go on air with their stories.

O'Reilly, who had come to the court from private practice in 1997, had briefed the press countless times before. But the *Sharpe* case would not be routine. He felt that coverage of the lower court cases had been marred by suggestions that the entire pornography law could be struck down – not just the prohibitions concerning possession – because of concerns over freedom of expression. He now wanted to ensure that journalists understood the details – the subtleties of the case – and to hammer home the point that "no matter what the court did a large part of the child pornography law was going to be completely untouched and a lot of protections would still be available" (O'Reilly 2001).

By the time St-Pierre arrived at the Supreme Court Building for the briefing at about 10:45 a.m., the west side of the building was jammed with TV trucks. Thick, brightly coloured TV cables lay like dead snakes in the solemn and majestic lobby. Ten to fifteen camera crews had jostled with each other for the best positions and were setting up behind a red velvet security rope. Journalists were connecting their feeds to a single unidirectional mic, behind which those who wished to make statements or be interviewed could stand. A small army of legal experts and spokespeople for interested parties such as Focus on the Family and Victims of Violence mingled in the lobby.

Approximately forty journalists were in the Media and Barristers Room when O'Reilly arrived at 11:30 a.m. All the chairs were occupied; some journalists were standing and a number were sitting on a window ledge. Tape recorders were neatly aligned on the table in front of where O'Reilly sat. The room was noisy and tense.

Cellphones rang constantly and the door opened and closed frequently as journalists came and went. The room was also awash with rumours and predictions. St-Pierre overheard another journalist tell a colleague that "they're supposed to strike down and amend the law."

Adding to the tension was that the Department of Justice was also worried about how to control the story. One department spokesperson was described by a newspaper journalist as having "freaked out." The spokesperson had warned reporters that "speculating in the media is really not in our best interest. I'd really prefer it if you did not write stories until the decision comes out."

O'Reilly's briefing, as was the case with all his briefings, was strictly off the record. He began by distributing copies of the relevant sections of the Criminal Code in both French and English. He reviewed the definitions of pornography and the history of the case. He then described the options that were available to the judges. St-Pierre listened intently. Others were scribbling. A number were repeating O'Reilly's words into cellphones. But even as he briefed reporters, cellphones continued to clamour and the door continued to swing open as reporters came in and out of the room.

As noon approached, the scramble began. One female TV reporter put on her makeup much like a warrior putting on war paint before a battle. The door finally opened and a trolley with a hundred copies of the decision was wheeled in. O'Reilly announced the decision at exactly twelve o'clock. The court had unanimously upheld the sections of the Criminal Code that dealt with possession of child pornography, but had carved out two narrow exceptions. Although he encouraged journalists to take time to read the decision, he provided a shortcut for those who were under severe deadline pressure by noting the key paragraphs in the judgment. He pointed out, for instance, that a particular paragraph was a very good summary of the decision. Again, some journalists were repeating his words into cellphones. Although O'Reilly would spend the next twenty minutes reviewing the judgment and its reasons, St-Pierre had to leave immediately. While she found the briefing helpful, that it was only in English was a problem. Now she had only a minute or so to read the decision before going on air.

## Constructing the Story
Amid the frenzy, an English-language reporter fell down the stairs while rushing to the lobby. To make matters worse, she had audio trouble and would soon be forced to conduct interviews in a silent void – that is, without instructions or prompting from the main studio. Even while she was reporting, she seemed unclear about the details of the decision.

After her live hit, St-Pierre stayed in the lobby for another ten minutes to listen to interviews with the experts and interveners. She then had to leave to prepare a more complete story for the news at 5 p.m. A producer and a researcher from her bureau stayed behind to tape statements and interviews so that St-Pierre could view them later.

It is interesting to note that for all the talk about pack journalism and pressures on journalists to conform to the prevailing mood of the pack, journalists had little time to talk to each other amid the chaos. There was no opportunity for any group dynamic or consensus to develop. Most reporters were under severe deadline pressure, they were all involved in negotiations of some kind or another with their desks or bureaus, and they pursued their own sources and angles, making individual choices about which perspectives were important and what constituted balance. One can argue that the breakup of the pack enhanced the ability of O'Reilly and the court to set the agenda and establish a particular angle.

Much of St-Pierre's story would be built around reactions to the decision first by Sharpe himself and then by government leaders, opposition politicians, and spokespeople for various interest groups. Her job was to keep track from Ottawa of what amounted to a patchwork quilt of statements that were being made across the country at different times. Vic Toews, the Alliance Party justice critic, held a news conference in Ottawa at 1:30 p.m. Sharpe's lawyer, Richard Peck, spoke to the press from Vancouver at 2:45. His remarks were transmitted to newsrooms directly via the Internet. The government's response came at 3:15 when Justice Minister Anne McLellan appeared at a news conference in Edmonton.

Most of these events were carried live on CBC *Newsworld,* which had begun broadcasting soon after the decision was handed down. The cable channel joined what amounted to a series of rolling news conferences that were occurring across the country, and also had a panel of legal experts providing instant analysis. *Newsworld* had the capacity to set the agenda for other news organizations and for groups that wished to react to what others were saying. *Newsworld* both reported the news and helped in making it.

Kirk Makin, the *Globe and Mail*'s legal affairs reporter who had been assigned the front-page story, decided to avoid the Ottawa maelstrom entirely. Makin believed that he had all the tools he needed in Toronto. At his desk he had a small TV, which was tuned to *Newsworld,* a copy of the decision was on his desk within minutes of its release, and he could phone O'Reilly or anyone else that he had to if he had questions. Most importantly, he could remain at a comfortable and dispassionate distance from the "sense of electricity" that pervaded the court and the swirl of events and players. As Makin reasoned, "It's counterproductive to go, I can do a better job reading the judgment calmly and coolly in my office and then using the phones. I think that the people who cover Ottawa probably feel compelled to go. You know it's a block away, so you sort of gravitate there and you become part of the TV scrum scenario. I mean it's rare that I've gotten quotes I needed or even used at those scrums. But it's one-stop shopping for some people. If you've got short deadlines, you just take your mic around and record five interviews and then go back and get your quote" (Makin 2002). Another *Globe* reporter had been assigned to cover the Ottawa angle, and there would be another story filed from Vancouver.

The *Globe*'s game plan was finalized at a 10 a.m. editorial meeting presided over by editor-in-chief Richard Addis. Angus Frame, the paper's webmaster, told those at the meeting that Sharpe would be the main story on the website. In fact, a story about the decision, written by Makin, was posted soon after its release. There would be even heavier coverage on Monday, with three opinion pieces – two by regular *Globe* columnists and one by a guest contributor who would analyze the *Sharpe* decision from a Christian perspective.

## Two Minutes and Two Seconds

Not surprisingly, Robin Sharpe was at the centre of the media storm. Much of the coverage seemed to hinge on whether Sharpe would be available to the press. If he did make an appearance, that would provide the main visual material – the backbone – around which the story might be constructed. Sharpe, however, feared for his safety. He had changed his appearance and had moved to a new address. The last thing he wanted was the glare and exposure of TV cameras. Nonetheless, camera crews from VTV, CTV, CBC, and BCTV were soon camped in the hallway outside his apartment. In the rush to get the story, the issue of whether journalists might be endangering Sharpe's safety seemed to be of little concern.

Sharpe was living in a windowless room in a dingy walk-up across the street from a fish market. Used condoms and needles were strewn in front of the building. The hallway where the journalists were assembled was cramped, dirty, and had a noxious stench. One person who was there described the hallway as smelling like a combination of old sweat, dirty socks, and desperation. Although Sharpe refused to come out, he spoke to reporters over the phone, in effect conducting a news conference from behind his apartment door. When it became clear after several hours that there would be no visuals of Sharpe, the camera crews departed. There would be no opportunity for what scholar K.T. Erikson might describe as the parading of the deviant (cited in Ericson, Baranek, and Chan 1987, 7).

At her office in the National Press Building, St-Pierre, her producer, and two technicians were frantically trying to patch together a report for the five o'clock news on Réseau de l'information (RDI). They had been told that the Sharpe story would be the lead item but that they had only two minutes and two seconds. All the day's activities and complexities had to fit inside a very small box. Parts of the piece had been easy to assemble. The story began with an image of the Supreme Court, there was stock footage of Sharpe, a graphic with the salient parts of the decision had been prepared, and St-Pierre had taped a sign off from the Supreme Court Building lobby. The story also included clips or sound bites from Sharpe's lawyer, Richard Peck; Mark Hecht from the child advocacy group Beyond Borders; and Justice Minister Anne McLellan.

But there were problems. Sharpe's reluctance to come on camera meant they had to improvise quickly. One of the technicians had created a visual depicting Sharpe as he was speaking on the phone. The producer tried to create another visual of a man leafing through a private journal. St-Pierre warned him that the police had not seized such a journal and that the images they used had to correspond exactly with what Sharpe was arrested for. Compounding the problem was that although a research assistant had been able to conduct a phone interview with Sharpe just before 4 p.m., St-Pierre had not had time to listen to the tape. It was too late to use the Sharpe interview for the five o'clock show. Finally, the story was sent from Ottawa at 5 p.m. St-Pierre had not had time to see the complete report before it was broadcast.

St-Pierre now had a short time to catch her breath before the six o'clock news broadcast. She finally had a chance to listen to the Sharpe interview. She decided to insert a clip from the interview and drop the sound bites from Sharpe's lawyer. She did a voice-over paraphrasing in French Sharpe's words. Again, the story had to be exactly two minutes and two seconds long.

Although the Sharpe story was one of the lead items on most of Radio-Canada's 6 p.m. local news shows, other news stations made different decisions. At some of them, the court's decision to uphold the pornography law, Sharpe's reluctance to appear on camera, and a large earthquake in India knocked the story from the lead position in the newscast. Had the child pornography law been struck down and Sharpe been allowed to avoid the "justice" that much of the public thought he deserved, their decisions might have been different. The political fallout from the judgment might have lasted for days if not weeks. The brewing political tempest had been stilled by the court's decision.

But it was also the case that earthquakes make good television and dramatic pictures were available. As John Gibb, a producer for CBC's *Canada Now* show in Vancouver, explained, "I felt conflicted about what to lead with. On almost any other day, it would have been a no-brainer for sure and we would have led with Sharpe. But things like earthquakes trump other kinds of stories and we have a large Indian community involved. The lead should be the story that is most likely to stop people from turning the channel. So we went with the pictures that we had of the earthquake." In Winnipeg, local Shriners had been caught with prostitutes. The earthquake had not been the lead story.

After a frantic day, St-Pierre could finally go home. The story that aired at 6 p.m. was broadcast on *Le Téléjournal* at 10 p.m. On Monday, she would be back

covering Parliament Hill with its daily diet of question period, scrums, news conferences, and partisan political attacks. She would remember covering the *Sharpe*
decision as being an exciting but gruelling experience.

## Note

1  This vignette was compiled from direct observations and interviews conducted on 26
   January 2001 by Ruth Klinkhammer (Ottawa), Melissa Kruger (Ottawa), Valérie Langlois (Ottawa), Shannon Sampert (Vancouver), and David Schneiderman (Toronto).

## References

Ericson, Richard, Patricia Baranek, and Janet Chan. 1987. *Visualizing deviance: A study of
   news organization.* Toronto: University of Toronto Press.

Makin, Kirk. 2002. Interview by authors. Toronto, 13 September.

O'Reilly, James. 2001. Interview by authors. Ottawa, 26 January.

# Introduction: The Supreme Court under the Media Lens

*The Last Word* is about the relationship between arguably two of the most important institutions in Canadian life: the Supreme Court of Canada and the Canadian news media. The relationship is critical for the court, for journalists, and for the public. While Supreme Court justices operate within a seemingly self-enclosed world of legal procedures and precedents, they exercise extraordinary political, social, and moral authority. Yet the court cannot function unless its decisions, and the reasons and spirit behind them, are conveyed to the public and to elected officials in an accurate manner. For this, the court relies on journalists. As Peter Russell (2002) observes, "Journalists are the managers of the political life of judicial decisions."

The adoption of the Charter of Rights and Freedoms in 1982 transformed Canadian political life. It placed the Supreme Court at the nexus of societal power and change. Judges had to give life to the Charter, and in doing so it can be argued that they redefined and reordered much of the Canadian social contract. Their increased role, however, brought both increased scrutiny and controversy. Judges often find themselves in what some describe as a "dialogue" with Parliament, and they are sometimes the subject of intense criticism in the news media.

News organizations have their own motivations and agendas and their own institutional logics. Most important, they play a gate-keeping role. Journalists have the power to decide which Supreme Court rulings will be covered and which will not, whether stories will appear at the beginning or end of the newscast or the front or back of the newspaper, which parts of decisions will be highlighted and which will be downplayed, and which sources they will look to for comments. Journalists write the editorials and choose who will write the op-ed pieces. Simply put, once judges hand down rulings, they lose control of the message. They are dependent on and at the mercy of the journalists who report on, interpret, and place their own meanings on judicial rulings. Thus, journalists, it can be argued, have the last word.

Media coverage has emerged as a critical factor not only in how the public but how the other institutions view the court. It is true that Parliament will sometimes respond to judicial decisions by enacting new laws, but without the questions, criticisms, and controversies generated by an attentive press, Parliament might not be galvanized into action. Journalists and news organizations maintain a vigil at the key crossroads of political power – where the key decisions of a society are made. Journalists must explain, probe, ask questions, provide meaning, and be the eyes and ears of the public. "Good journalism," write Leonard Downie Jr. and Robert Kaiser (2002, 4), "makes possible the cooperation among citizens that is critical to a civilized society. Citizens cannot function together as a community unless they share a common body of information ... The best journalism digs into it, makes sense of it and makes it accessible to everyone."

Not surprisingly, judges are not always satisfied with how the court and its decisions are portrayed. Judgments are sometimes misinterpreted, sensationalized, and even lampooned. On more than a few occasions, judges have been both surprised and stung by the sharpness of media criticism. Antonio Lamer, former chief justice of the Supreme Court of Canada, expressed concern about attacks that he believed went "beyond acceptable criticism" and threatened "to undermine public confidence in the judicial system" (Stewart 1998, A1). Yves Boisvert of *La Presse* advised us that part of the problem may be that judges have been sheltered from criticism for too long and have had a difficult time adjusting to the new world in which they now find themselves. According to Boisvert (2002b), judges have been the subject of legitimate criticism but "in ways that were hard, unexpected and surprising for judges because it hadn't been done before."

Not only have Supreme Court of Canada justices felt the sharp end of the stick of media criticism, but there has been a sizable increase in media attention since the early 1990s. The glare of the media spotlight has meant increased scrutiny of their public and private lives. The authority of judges, their views and convictions as expressed through their rulings, even disputes among judges, are now exposed to public view in a way that was inconceivable just a short time ago. The "monastic view of the judiciary is no longer acceptable," notes Stephen Bindman, a former reporter and now an advisor to the Department of Justice (Canadian Judicial Council 1999, 5).

Frustrating, perhaps, for some judges is the fact that they are expected to refrain from commenting on the cases that they have decided. This code of silence sometimes has left judges feeling vulnerable and without the means to respond when media and academic critics attack their decisions. Yet at the same time, this new world requires judges to reach out, be visible, explain their points of view, and convince the public that their decisions are fair and independent. The justices of the Supreme Court cannot hide behind a protective wall of distant and dignified authority. They must, in their own way, campaign for public favour.

Former justice Frank Iacobucci (2001) acknowledges that the legitimacy of the court, and indeed of the democratic process, is dependent, at least to some degree, on the court's ability to get its message out. "The danger," he warns, "is that if the media are inaccurate in conveying the information to the public, you are dealing with a misinformed public. What is worse: a misinformed public or an uninformed public? I don't know. They can both lead to the same results and that is an inadequate way of understanding, of dealing with problems, and that is not good." According to Iacobucci, "Decisions are enforced because people accept the decisions as the law. If confidence is eroded, then we worry about the legitimacy of the court and the role of the court to settle disputes through the rule of law in our country and that's an absolutely priceless commodity in a constitutional democracy. So those are the stakes."

*The Last Word* has two major tasks. The first is to describe a genre of news reporting that has seldom before been examined in any detail in Canada. To our knowledge, there have been only three studies of media coverage of Supreme Courts: two of the American Supreme Court and one on the Canadian court (Davis 1994; Slotnick and Segal 1998; Miljan and Cooper 2003). Ours is the most comprehensive study yet undertaken of media coverage of the Canadian Supreme Court. There are many unanswered questions: Is there a difference between coverage in Quebec and English Canada? Does reporting vary among news organizations or is there a single flavour that can be found in all the reporting? Is the court depicted in a positive or negative light? What are the contingencies that determine how a decision or event will be framed? Do certain kinds of judgments receive the lion's share of coverage while other kinds of cases are underreported or missing in action?

One of the most contentious debates in media studies is whether media coverage reinforces the power of the powerful by celebrating and sanctifying the established interests and values in society. The notion is that the news media are inherently conservative and are a part of the governing structure of authority (Gans 1980; Gitlin 1980; McChesney 2000). Other scholars argue that media coverage can undermine and subvert governing elites and values and that reporting is contingent on the factors at play in a given event (Cook 1998; Page 1996; Wolfsfeld 1997). News is a contested ground where a variety of forces and factors can determine the nature of reporting. In this regard, the Supreme Court of Canada constitutes an ideal case. If there is any institution that upholds and symbolizes the hard crust of tradition and hierarchy, it is the Supreme Court. The court stands at the apex of societal and political power and has enjoyed an almost automatic authority and deference. How the court is depicted by the news media will tell us a great deal about the nature of media power generally.

The relationship between the Supreme Court and the journalists who cover it constitutes a distinct world of Canadian journalism. Our second task is to examine this relationship. Many of the operating assumptions that apply to general political reporting operate less successfully in this milieu. Our goal is to explore this world, to peer inside for the first time, and to describe how it operates. To this end we have interviewed most of the journalists who are covering or have covered the court, former and current justices of the Supreme Court, and former and the current executive legal officers (see Appendix A for a list of the interview questions). We are grateful to them for their cooperation and their candour. As part of this effort we also had members of our team present at the Supreme Court and in newsrooms across Canada when a particularly controversial judgment was handed down – the *Sharpe* decision on child pornography.

In order to examine how the Supreme Court has appeared under the media spotlight, we have analyzed the English- and French-language media's portrayal of the court using two probes. We evaluated news coverage for the period from 1 September 2000 to 31 August 2001 to identify the major trends in how the Supreme Court and its judgments were covered (see Appendix B). Reporting in *La Presse, Le Devoir, Le Journal de Montréal,* the *Globe and Mail, National Post,* and the *Toronto Sun,* as well as broadcasts on Radio-Canada, TVA, CBC, and CTV, were scrutinized. The second probe took a more in-depth approach. Media reporting of four significant cases – *Vriend,* the *Quebec Secession Reference, Marshall,* and *Sharpe* – were investigated in detail. These cases were selected because they dealt with issues that were critical for society and in which the legitimacy and integrity of the court were at stake. We do not pretend that these cases were the only important cases or that they were typical in any way. We believe, however, that they each provide unique vantage points from which to view the media's coverage of the court.

*Vriend* pitted the Alberta government against a gay teacher who had been fired from his job and was seeking protection under Alberta's human rights legislation. This was a case in which the legitimacy of the court was at stake. On one level, the judgment was about human rights. On another level, however, it was about federal and provincial powers and applying the values of the Charter to a resistant Alberta. Alberta's popular premier, Ralph Klein, had been a forceful critic of the power of the judges and was under pressure from his caucus to use the notwithstanding clause to override court decisions. Our study found that coverage in the national media differed considerably from coverage in Alberta. Albertans saw the case through an entirely different media lens.

The *Quebec Secession Reference* dealt with the rules and obligations that would govern any attempt by Quebec to pursue political independence unilaterally. Indeed, the *Secession Reference* may have been the most important case ever decided by the court. The judges had to walk a dangerous political path knowing that their own credibility was at stake. All the major political parties in Quebec had opposed the decision by the federal government to refer the issue to the court and had been stoking the fires of doubt for months about whether the court could make a fair decision. All the old ghosts about a one-sided federalist court blind to Quebec's needs and to basic fairness were dragged out before Quebec public opinion.

The contentious *Marshall* case dealt with Aboriginal treaty rights in Atlantic Canada and the resulting outbreak of violence over access to the Atlantic fisheries. Following in the wake of several landmark decisions on Aboriginal rights, including *Delgamuukw v. British Columbia,* the judgment both refined and limited Aboriginal rights. Our study suggests that poor and inaccurate media coverage of the decision may have contributed to the outbreak of violence.

The *Sharpe* case concerned the child pornography law and called on the Supreme Court to weigh issues of freedom of speech and privacy against the dangers of child pornography. Lower court decisions in British Columbia that had found the existing law to be too broad had ignited a brushfire of controversy and media criticism. The case was hotly debated in Parliament, and interest groups, particularly those who wanted tougher laws against pedophiles, had moved into high gear. While the news media largely framed the story in terms of whether the pornography laws would protect children from predators, others tended to see *Sharpe* as a freedom of expression case. Again, the legitimacy of the court was at stake.

## Lifting the Curtain

The decision to enter the world of public and media relations was made incrementally and in slow, hesitating steps. When Chief Justice Bora Laskin gave his first interview to the press in the mid-1970s, he was beginning a process that would evolve considerably over time. Some credit Brian Dickson, who was chief justice between 1984 and 1990, with doing the most to create a new relationship between the court and the news media. It was under Chief Justice Dickson that the position of executive legal officer (ELO), the person who has the job of briefing and dealing with journalists, was established. Dickson also began the practice of meeting with newspaper editorial boards, conducting interviews, and releasing texts of speeches in advance. In a bold step, he invited a documentary camera crew into the court's inner sanctum: the hallways, offices, and conference rooms from which the public had previously been denied access.

Chief Justice Dickson's colleague, John Sopinka, undoubtedly played a critical role in breaking some of the old taboos and lifting the curtain that had hidden judges from public view for so long. Justice Sopinka saw judges as public figures who should be free to comment in public about their work. He believed that the best way of dispelling the mystery around the judiciary was "to loosen the restraints that many judges feel bind them in their public statements ... A judge can and ought to speak on the work of the court. It is absolutely essential that the workings of the court be demystified. Otherwise how can the public have confidence in it?" Sopinka was of the view that there should be no "absolute rule that prevents a judge from explaining his or her decision to the public if failure to do so has led or may lead to confusion or misunderstanding" (Canadian Judicial Council 1999, 11).

Chief Justice Antonio Lamer opened the court up to even greater scrutiny. Under Lamer's tenure, cameras were invited into the courtroom and oral arguments were televised live on the Canadian Parliamentary Affairs Channel (CPAC), the public affairs cable channel. In addition, broadcasters were allowed to use short clips or sound bites for their newscasts. The court, under Chief Justice Lamer, also decided that, when a nest of decisions was scheduled to be handed down during a particular week, judgments would be released over a two-day period so that journalists would not be overwhelmed.

Today, Supreme Court judges speak out frequently in public forums and to a variety of audiences. When Beverley McLachlin was named chief justice in January 2000, she conducted what amounted to a media tour, giving interviews and accepting a host of speaking invitations. "I did it more than any other chief justice has," she admitted to us. "These are the people's courts and the people are entitled to know who's been named to that court and who is chief justice responsible for the administration of that court" (McLachlin 2002).

There is now a conscious effort by the court to better organize, and some would argue orchestrate, its relationship with the press. The ELO briefs reporters before sessions begin and before important rulings are issued. The court floods subscribers with e-mails containing press releases about leaves to appeal, hearings, and upcoming or just-released judgments. More recently, the court has agreed to allow lock-ups, which prohibit reporters from leaving the room to contact their newsrooms, so that journalists can have time to read important judgments before their release to the parties and the public. While the court does not engage in image management to nearly the same degree as other institutions, it has developed its own communications system with its own rules and special understandings. There is no doubt that the decision to enter the world of media relations, to explain and consciously promote its public role, has altered the nature and role of the court (Canadian Judicial Council 1999, 7).

Reporting from the court is also a vital test for journalists. Journalists must enter a world with which they are largely unfamiliar. Judgments are highly complex, containing abstract and subtle arguments that often are difficult to explain in a few paragraphs or seconds. Dry legal reasoning does not translate easily into the stories that journalists most covet. Moreover, the assumptions that normally govern political reporting don't readily apply to legal judgments. There are few exciting visuals, and judges don't leak stories, appear at news conferences, or attack their critics. It is also sometimes difficult to find heroes and villains in the carefully crafted judgments that often give something to both sides in a dispute.

As vital societal decisions are being made at the Supreme Court, journalists and the news organizations that they work for have had to face new challenges. Some would argue that the frames used by journalists, the narratives that journalists invariably depend on, are unsuited to reporting on the court and its rulings. Others contend that judicial reporting will always take a back seat to the acrimony, accusations, and compelling visuals provided by party politics and parliamentary debates. In addition, while the court has come a long way in opening itself up to journalists, it can be argued that there are few settings that erect as many barriers and pose as many challenges to good reporting as does the Supreme Court. As this study demonstrates, the rules that govern the relationship between the court and the journalists who cover it are decidedly different from those found in other milieus. This sometimes makes it difficult for journalists to do the job expected of them. There is also the question of whether news organizations have acquired the expertise and devoted the resources needed to explain court rulings and the realities of judicial power to the public. As Frank Iacobucci noted, the stakes are high.

## Judicial Authority and Media Power

Among the most important developments of the past few decades in Canadian society has been the growth of judicial authority, the extraordinary and enhanced power of the mass media to shape societal values, and the advent of a new societal consciousness of rights and freedoms. Each of these forces has roots in social and technological change and has emerged, to some degree, independently of the other. Yet, together, they have shaped and altered much of the landscape of Canadian society.

The origins of the rights revolution are complex and multidimensional. The horrors of the Holocaust, the fight for civil rights in the American South, the growth of the women's movement, and the emergence of post-materialist values that have spawned demands for more and greater rights are all part of a vast tapestry. There is, in Charles Epp's view, "a cultural-centred explanation" for why the courts have become a locus of power (Epp 1998, 15). The courts have had to respond to the changing nature of society – in this regard, they have been followers rather than leaders.[1]

Some observers believe that the relationship between at least some social groups and the Supreme Court has been mutually reinforcing. They contend that while social groups may have used the court to gain political ground, the court needed these groups to enhance its own legitimacy. This is because the case for enhanced judicial authority rests to some degree on the proposition that there are important constituencies that cannot be served by legislatures and cabinets. While the proverbial upper dogs, those with financial clout and electoral muscle, have always enjoyed access to the cabinet, top bureaucrats, and parliamentarians, the underdogs have had to depend on the courts. Hence, the role of the judges and their claim to power are implicitly linked to the existence of these groups (Brodie 2002, 123).

Most interesting, perhaps, has been the role the media have played in reflecting and inspiring rights consciousness. According to Justice Ian Binnie, it is the media that have "been responsible for this so-called rights revolution" (Schmitz 2001). People can read about, see, hear, and correspond with those who are fighting similar battles in other jurisdictions. The battles for enhanced rights for women, Aboriginal peoples, and gays and lesbians are played out on the television screens and in the newspapers as much as in the courtrooms.

The expanded authority of judges must be seen against the backdrop of another major development, a new kind of activism with regard to the court by reporters and news organizations. During the 1970s and 1980s, the Supreme Court of Canada was at the periphery, at the outer edges, of political reporting in Ottawa. Today, the court has moved closer to centre stage. Court proceedings are broadcast live on CPAC, important judgments are covered extensively on CBC *Newsworld* and on Réseau de l'information (RDI), and reporting, particularly by national newspapers such as the *National Post, Le Devoir,* and the *Globe and Mail,* has increased substantially. In 1999, *Time* Canada had chosen the Supreme Court as the most important newsmaker of the year (Tibbetts 1999).

In an attempt to measure the quantity of reporting over time, we conducted a simple, though impressionistic, exercise. We counted all stories about the court reported in *Le Devoir* and the *Globe and Mail* during the first year of each decade since 1970. We tabulated all stories that ran from 1 September 1970 to 31 August 1971, including features, editorials, and commentaries, as well as regular news stories. The results are startling. In 1970-71, there were a total of 33 stories reported in *Le Devoir*. The number increased to 55 stories in 1980-81 and then to 79 in 1990-91. By 2000-01 the number of stories in *Le Devoir* had increased to 90 articles. The rise in the number of stories appearing in the *Globe and Mail* was even more dramatic. There were 40 in 1970-71, 102 in 1980-81, 113 in 1990-91, and 145 in 2000-01. By this admittedly primitive measure, coverage of the Supreme Court has at least tripled since the early 1970s.

This seems to be part of a wider trend. In the United States, newspapers such as the *New York Times* and the *Washington Post,* as well as broadcasters such as NBC, have legal reporters who are permanently stationed at the US court. Important decisions receive extensive coverage and the *Washington Post* even maintains an extensive archive on its website chronicling all the decisions of the US Supreme Court during each session and the articles that have been written about each decision.

Another important factor in the placing of a larger and more glaring media spotlight on the court was the creation by Conrad Black of the *National Post* in

1998. In its early years, particularly from 1998 to 2000 when the paper was owned by Black, the *Post* waged a fierce ideological crusade against what it saw as the power of unelected judges. The paper attacked judgments with relish and questioned the assumptions upon which the authority of the court rests. It also gave the court more coverage than any other single news organization. In a striking departure, it assigned Luiza Chwialkowska, a young journalist, to cover the court. She was allowed to write long articles on individual cases and multipage spreads such as the one commemorating the 125th anniversary of the court. In our study of newspaper and TV coverage of the court during 2000-01, the *Post* accounted for over 27 percent of the articles in a sample of six newspapers.

The following editorial is typical of the salvos against judicial supremacy launched by the *National Post* (2000):

> There is a battle afoot between the people and the judiciary over who makes the laws in this country ... Canadians have been outraged as the courts have used the Charter to tweak or abolish dozens of laws, the Lord's Day Act, restrictions on pornography and voluntary school prayer, and laws that kept incompetents from fighting fires ... When challenged on slapping down legislators in this manner, the judges have bristled, and claimed simply to be engaged in a "dialogue" with Parliament ... Apart from having no authority to legislate in this manner, judges are ill-equipped to do so. Since they address policy questions only as they happen to arise in litigation, judges often have little feeling for the broader issues at stake. After all, they are not politicians.

The extraordinary attention given to the court by the *Post* stemmed from a number of factors. The then editor-in-chief Kenneth Whyte was a Charter skeptic who wanted the paper to be different from what he saw as the "grey and bland" *Globe and Mail*. Crusading against the power of judges was one way in which the *Post* could make its mark. The editorial board included John O'Sullivan, a British-born conservative who believed in parliamentary supremacy. O'Sullivan had also worked in Washington for William F. Buckley's *National Review* and so brought with him the more aggressive and critical stance that American journalists have toward the US Supreme Court. Other members of the board included Ezra Levant, now the publisher of the *Western Standard* magazine, and Neil Seeman, now with the right-wing Fraser Institute. According to Levant (2002), the members of the board shared the conviction that "Canadian public policy is no longer made in our legislatures but rather by the courts. We were unwilling to accept the law as if it would be handed down from Mount Sinai or Mount Olympus. But rather we would treat it as if it was just as politically charged as a parliamentary bill and we would treat the judges as human beings with all of the flaws, frailties, and biases of politicians."

Chwialkowska (2003) believes that the *Post*'s critique rested on three propositions: the need to sound an alarm about the enhanced power of the court, the use of the court by liberal and left-leaning interest groups, and the unchecked power of the prime minister to appoint judges. These were themes that would be repeated, indeed pounded on, regularly in the *Post*'s early years. Again, as our study will show, the paper devoted considerable space to exposing and dissecting judgments that offended or violated its moral and political code.

There is little doubt that the *Post*'s coverage sent shock waves through the journalistic community and set a new tone in coverage of the court. Kirk Makin (2002c), the principal legal reporter for the *Globe and Mail,* described the reaction the *Globe* had to the *Post*'s coverage:

> I do remember that I was quite taken aback at their early approach of basically bashing the court. They seemed to set out from the premise that these were bad people who had to be thrashed because they had the temerity to make decisions. There was a period, I have to admit, where I felt some pressure, subtle pressure, to sort of be on board with the bashing brigade. But you know I had a number of talks with editors that just went: "As far as I'm concerned, they're making a mistake. I don't want to make the same one. We should continue covering the court the way that we have been."

Some would argue that since the sale of the *National Post* to CanWest Global in 2000, the departure from the editorial board of anti-court crusaders, and recent financial cutbacks, the high tide of court reporting at the *Post* has receded at least to some degree. Chwialkowska left the *Post* in 2003.

In recent years, there has been no equivalent in Quebec to the campaign against judicial activism waged by the *National Post* in English Canada. In fact, our review of coverage of the court in *La Presse* and *Le Devoir* found little concern over judicial activism. Yves Boisvert (2002a) perhaps best summed up attitudes in Quebec generally when he wrote on the twentieth anniversary of the Charter that "There is no doubt that justices are political actors. They make decisions that have a profound effect on public life. At first, this created astonishment and seemed almost scandalous. Now it seems to be accepted."[2] Judicial activism does have vehement critics, however. For instance, Marc Chevrier (1999) condemned what he called "le papisme légal" in the journal *Argument*. But such attacks have not been given prominence in the Quebec media.

Another reason for the increase in media attention to the courts may be the extent to which films, TV programs, and novels about law and justice have become a mainstay of popular culture. From *To Kill a Mockingbird* to *CSI,* from *Law and Order* to the Michael Jackson trial, from *Judge Judy* to Court TV, a twenty-four-hour cable channel in the United States (now available in Canada) devoted exclusively to showing ongoing trials, crime and its punishment are deeply embedded in the public imagination. As Richard Sherwin (2000, 17) has observed, "Just a flip of the channel: another case, another cast, another reality, another outcome." One can watch justice being rendered in TV dramas, reality shows, or TV movies from early morning to late at night practically without interruption.

As Elayne Rapping (2003, 51) points out, "Crime drama has an important social function: it is the nightly ritual through which we collectively experience the dread of the chaos that violence symbolizes, and the reassurance that comes when the violent are captured and restrained." Indeed, Rapping has argued that while early TV dramas such as *Perry Mason* and *Owen Marshall* emphasized crusading attorneys who fought on behalf of the innocent, today's programs stress crime control, with lawyers and police battling to keep the streets safe from the alien and depraved.

In the fall of 2002, CBS and ABC even aired prime-time dramas about the US Supreme Court: *First Monday* and *The Court.* And this is not just an American phenomenon. *Street Legal* dominated English-Canadian TV screens in the 1980s, as has our peculiar obsession with heroic coroners as seen on *Wojek* and *Da Vinci's Inquest.*

In Quebec, there is a long tradition of public affairs programs on the law. In the 1950s, *C'est la loi* was hosted by the popular TV personality Alban Flamand. Produced with the cooperation of the Montreal bar, the show explained and dramatized legal issues. Fifty years later, the tradition continues. Radio-Canada is still programming a weekly show called *Justice,* explaining court decisions and legal issues. Most recently, Canal D, a specialty channel, broadcast *Dossiers Justice,* hosted by *La Presse* journalist Yves Boisvert, and Télévision Quatre Saisons (TQS) aired *Auger enquête,* an inquiry into organized crime in Canada featuring journalist Michel Auger, the target of a murder attempt by the Hell's Angels – a program that attracted large audiences. Indeed, the trials of the Hell's Angels have become a staple of Quebec reporting and public fascination – some would even say obsession – for almost a decade. Canadian public affairs programming also stresses legal issues. *The Docket,* which aired on CBC *Newsworld,* took an in-depth look at controversial cases and issues. *History's Courtroom* hosted by Kirk Makin of the *Globe and Mail* revisited Canada's great trials for History TV.

Another aspect of popular culture is that crime reporting has become the steady diet of evening newscasts and tabloid newspapers, a process that sometimes has had the perverse effect of turning criminals into celebrities. Notorious trials have always held a certain fascination. The parading and bringing to justice of the villains, the pain and suffering of the victims, the grizzly nature of the crime itself, all are part of public spectacle and, arguably, public catharsis. Grotesque personalities such as Paul Bernardo, Maurice ("Mom") Boucher, and, of course, O.J. Simpson have become inscribed in the general culture. One study of local television in the United States conducted by the Project for Excellence in Journalism, affiliated with Columbia University's School of Journalism, found that crime was the most popular news topic in 2002, accounting for a quarter of all reporting. Close to 40 percent of news stations maintained a full-time crime and courts reporter (Dean and Brady 2002, 94-95).

While it may be argued that coverage of the Canadian Supreme Court hardly ranks with the reporting of shocking murders, the court has had its share of riveting and even spectacular cases. In a study that we conducted of media reporting of the Supreme Court for the year from 1 September 2000 to 31 August 2001, celebrity villains such as Robin Sharpe and celebrity "victims" such as Robert Latimer dominated the headlines.

Aside from the public's seemingly insatiable appetite for the human drama of crime and punishment, a number of other factors have led to an increase in coverage of the court. The cable and digital revolutions and the emergence of what has been called the perpetual news cycle have changed the landscape considerably. The proliferation of twenty-four-hour news channels and a torrent of local breakfast, noon-hour, and supper-hour newscasts have created an insatiable appetite for news. Stories that once may have been given only passing coverage, relegated to a minute and thirty seconds on the main evening newscasts, are now recycled throughout the day. So, depending on the other news stories that are breaking, court stories may receive extensive coverage. It is no coincidence that cameras were allowed in the foyer of the Supreme Court of Canada soon after CBC *Newsworld* started broadcasting.

## The Supreme Court and Its Publics

Most Canadians have never been to the Supreme Court. The court is housed in a formidable and majestic building that sits on a high bluff overlooking the Ottawa River. It lies just to the west of the Parliament buildings. The building, designed by the eminent Montreal architect Ernest Cormier, was completed in 1941. The façade is a mass of cut stone. A copper roof sits atop a towering entrance that probably makes most people who enter the building feel small and insignificant. Statues stand on either side of the entrance: a statue symbolizing Truth is to the west; Justice is to the east. The main hall is cast in marble, there are cascading stairways, and shards of light pour in from seven giant windows. It is a breathtaking sight. The main courtroom is simple but imposing. The judges sit in high-backed burgundy leather chairs that resemble thrones, and the courtroom is embossed in walnut panelling. The Great Seal of Canada hangs above the judges. The setting radiates splendour, decorum, and a sense of dignified order.

One can argue that the grand physical setting, the symbolic rituals, and the particular styles that are used to communicate with the public are part of a larger message (Davis 1994, 12-13). Everything is done to convey a sense of continuity and established order and, above all, deference to authority. When the court is in session, the chief justice, Beverley McLachlin, sits at the centre, while the other justices are seated around her according to their seniority on the court. They wear black robes; on special ceremonial occasions they wear archaic tri-cornered hats and scarlet robes trimmed with Canadian mink. Court procedure is encased in formality and lawyers plead their cases from a point below where the judges are sitting: they have to look up at the judges. Though oral arguments and questions are televised live on CPAC, after they have been made, the judges retire to a conference room that is, in effect, an intimate but ornate library. Their deliberations are private, and their decisions are kept private until they are handed down.

The late sociologist Pierre Bourdieu (1987) argues that the power of courts lies in their ability to name winners and losers. "Control of the legal text is the prize to be won in interpretive struggles," writes Bourdieu, in which the judges are the "authorized interpreters" (818). Their judgments "consecrate the established order" through the symbolic power of "naming" reality (838). What is at stake in legal disputes, then, is a struggle over the power to certify that reality.

The symbolic power of the courts in Canada, their ability to name and constitute reality, has been under threat. As Bourdieu notes, symbolic power "can be exercised only through the complicity of those who are dominated by it" (844). If the act of "faith" that attends the exercise of symbolic power is questioned – if the belief in the neutrality and autonomy of law and judges is shaken – then presumably the authority of the courts is at risk.

Richard Davis (1994, 111) in his study of the US Supreme Court has argued that the American court is involved in an elaborate but deceptive game, a ruse meant to conceal the real nature and extent of its power. The justices participate in what Davis has called a "sweet fabrication." The basis of the deception is that the court presents itself as being above and removed from politics. The entire ambience of the court – its language, procedures, and demeanour – convey the impression that the judges are nonpartisan, independent, and exercise a wise and disinterested counsel. Their expertise and their decisions are presumably grounded only in the law and in the precedents established by a long line of previous cases. Above all, they claim not to pay attention to the press, to the pleadings of interest groups, to the reactions of politicians, or to the tides and currents of public opinion.

There is no shortage of Canadian observers who believe that the "sweet fabrication" applies here as well. There can be little doubt, however, that the justices see their power as highly circumscribed and that they exercise only limited discretion. Justice John C. Major, for instance, believes that the Supreme Court operates under significant constraints. He expressed what is almost certainly an opinion shared by a majority of justices: "This notion of power has always escaped me. We are not gunslingers with no restraint. If we reach a certain decision on a certain law, Parliament can fix it. We don't have the freedom to act on whim. We have to be careful in the extreme; we have to think about what courts have done previously. The only power we have taken away from Parliament is the power not to act contrary to the Charter of Rights" (Makin 2002a).

The picture, admittedly, is complex. Undoubtedly, the justices are bound by rules of the game that constrain them in ways that politicians are not constrained. Judges, for one, do not seek out problems for legal resolution; rather, they resolve only those disputes brought to them by particular parties. Justices are expected to lay down the law in accordance with statutory or constitutional texts and judicial precedent. Judges, moreover, must provide convincing and defensible reasons justifying a legal decision addressed to the parties and to the world at large (Hart 1994, 272-75). So, in some significant ways, the Supreme Court of Canada is not, as some would have it, engaged merely in partisan political decision making. Nevertheless, the judiciary has a great deal of room to manoeuvre around these constraints. Certainly, the court's "purposive" approach to constitutional interpretation entitles judges to fill in the vague and indeterminate language of the Charter using a variety of sources and techniques (Lajoie 1997).

But the Supreme Court is by any standard an intensely political institution. Through its power of judicial review, the court can invalidate laws that have been passed by the federal Parliament or provincial legislatures. Supreme Court justices have the power to declare the winners and losers in important societal conflicts and to redistribute resources (legal, fiscal, or political) accordingly. Their judgments uphold and celebrate some societal values and practices while downplaying or denigrating others. The court has the power to construct both a real and a symbolic universe and to impose that universe on the wider society. While Alexis de Tocqueville (1969, 270) could observe in mid-nineteenth-century America that there "is hardly a political question ... which does not sooner or later turn into a judicial one," Chief Justice Beverley McLachlin could observe in early-twenty-first-century Canada that, increasingly, "the headlines of our newspapers are concerned with judicial decisions. More and more, courts are being called upon to decide questions of central importance to great numbers of people in our society." Like de Tocqueville, she sees an "increasing tendency" to transform social and political issues into legal questions, "thus placing the task of their resolution on the shoulders of the courts" (Gall and Sober 2000, 28).

Unlike other institutions in the Canadian political constellation, though, the Supreme Court is largely unaccountable. Its members are appointed by the prime minister, sometimes without any consultation with provincial premiers even though the federal government and the provinces share legislative authority in many areas of Canadian life over which the court has jurisdiction. Moreover, appointments to the Supreme Court do not have to be approved by Parliament nor are nominees made to appear before a parliamentary committee. They do not have to undergo the intense scrutiny, the ordeal of public exhibition, which is required of judges in the United States. A new and controversial procedure, however, was adopted in August 2004 with the nominations of Louise Charron and Rosalie Abella to the Supreme Court of Canada. An ad hoc Committee of the House of Commons, together with a representative from the Canadian Bar Association and from the Canadian Judicial Council, were given the opportunity to question Justice Minister Irwin Cotler about the prime minister's appointments. The proceedings were broadcast live on CPAC (Lunman and Laghi 2004).

On the occasion of the tenth anniversary of the Canadian Charter of Rights and Freedoms, Chief Justice Antonio Lamer observed that the Charter had produced "a revolution on the scale of the introduction of the metric system, the great discoveries of Louis Pasteur, and the invention of penicillin and the laser" (Morton and Knopff 2000, 13). While not everyone would agree with Lamer's exuberant description, there is little doubt that there has been a significant shift of authority from Parliament and legislatures to the Supreme Court. After all, prior to 1982, Canada had no entrenched constitutional regime for the general protection of rights and freedoms. But it is critical to note that Canada has a long tradition of judges reviewing laws for their conformity to constitutional text under the division of legislative powers. In this context, the Supreme Court of Canada had been developing a new rights-oriented jurisprudence (Dickson 1994, 4-5). Judges now exercise supervisory authority over a vastly expanded number of rights (Strauss 1985). The volume of rights litigation really has been turned up considerably in the Charter era. As Chief Justice Lamer admitted to *Time* magazine, "Our decisions hit harder because they hit wider" (Handelman 1999).

This transformation in Canadian public life is the product of a number of factors. Some observers argue that politicians have abdicated their responsibility by passing "hot potato" issues to the courts. Wary of offending powerful interests and alienating key constituencies, political leaders know that making tough, painful decisions and unsatisfying compromises, especially on issues where feelings run deep and essential rights are at stake, can shorten political careers. They have often been more than happy to hand difficult "no win" political issues to the court. Everything from the rules governing Quebec secession to abortion, from Aboriginal rights to gay marriage, and from a parent's right to spank his or her children to the extent of freedom of expression in cases involving pornography, hate, and advertising have been bounced to and ultimately decided by the Supreme Court.

Former justice Charles Gonthier is among those who have charged politicians with ducking their responsibilities. He told a conference in October 2002, "We can often notice a lack of will on the part of political power to tackle certain issues that are raised. The effect of this reticence is often to push toward the courts certain fundamental questions that members of Parliament could have better resolved themselves through a large debate ... The result, definitely, is to avoid this often necessary public debate and provoke accusations of judicial activism on the part of the media and the public" (Gambrill 2002).

Some believe that this abdication of political responsibility helps to tear the fabric of the civic culture that is the basis for a healthy society. In particular, there is concern that the sharp decline in voting and in involvement in all forms of political activity that occurred during the 1980s and 1990s — some would say with the establishment of the Charter — was due at least in part to the realization by the public that judges rather than politicians had the stronger voice. While citizens may be increasingly conscious of their rights, their lack of involvement in civic life is corrosive to democracy (Hutchinson 1995).

Others, such as Kent Roach, believe that elected officials haven't been the ineffective and helpless bystanders they are sometimes made out to be. Instead, there is a dialogue of sorts between the Supreme Court and elected officials (Roach 2001, 14-15; also Hiebert 2002). First, Parliament and the provincial legislatures have the ability to nullify the court's decisions by using section 33 of the Charter, the notwithstanding clause. While the clause has come to be seen in some circles as "the equivalent of dropping a nuclear bomb in a war," it does provide legislatures with a potent weapon if their interests are really being threatened or ignored (Leeson 2001, 321). Second, Parliament has on more than a few occasions delivered what Roach calls an "in your face" response to court decisions (277). Parliament was not only able to answer the court with stronger and more focused legislation but it can be argued that the court's decisions pressured Parliament into producing better laws — hence the notion of a dialogue.

Admittedly, court rulings have long shaped Canada's political history (Saywell 2002; McCormick 2000). The decisions of the Judicial Committee of the Privy Council (JCPC) sitting in London, Canada's final court of appeal until 1949, structured Canada's constitutional order in a direction that favoured provincial rights and disfavoured centralized political authority (Vipond 1991). This prompted those who adhered to a highly centralized vision of the federation, such as Bora Laskin, later chief justice of the Supreme Court of Canada, to accuse the JCPC of practising a jurisprudence based on "rigid abstractions" having "a sense of unreality" (Laskin 1964, 73).

If the decisions of the JCPC created some suspicion and bitterness, the Supreme Court of Canada has stirred similar controversy within Quebec. Governments and nationalists within Quebec have traditionally viewed the court as a leaning Tower of Pisa that always leans in the same direction, a centralist one (Lajoie, Mulazzi, and Gamache 1986). The court has been viewed as distant and threatening, with the primary mission of preserving and enhancing Ottawa's power. For instance, André Laurendeau (1973, 132), one of Quebec's great public intellectuals of the postwar period, wrote in 1949 when the power over final appeals was finally transferred from the JCPC to the Supreme Court, that the court would be Ottawa's "bird in the hand." He noted simply that "since the Supreme Court, a tribunal, will be our ultimate judicial resort – even in constitutional matters – Ottawa has been provided with a powerful means of action against the provincial state, perhaps even of weighting the constitution in its favour" (130).

This suspicion was reinforced by rulings issued after the patriation of the constitution in 1982, particularly those judgments striking down parts of Quebec's controversial language law, Bill 101. For these reasons, Guy Laforest (1995, 180-81) saw the creation of the Charter of Rights and Freedoms in 1982 as nothing less than "an updating of the Conquest" and an attempt "to break the spine of the Quebecois community." He argued that the "primary condition for a genuine partnership between Quebec and Canada" was that primacy be given to Quebec's own Charter of Human Rights and Freedoms and that the Supreme Court exercise no authority whatsoever in Quebec (191).

Laforest's account reflects the profound sense of betrayal that was felt throughout Quebec society when the constitution was patriated in 1982 without Quebec's consent. Premier René Lévesque ordered flags to be flown at half-mast – even the federalist Liberal Party of Quebec joined the Parti québécois in opposing patriation in Quebec's National Assembly. To some degree, the wound remains unhealed. On the twentieth anniversary of the patriation of the constitution, in April 2002, both *Le Devoir* and *La Presse* published special sections of eight and ten pages respectively. The main article in *Le Devoir*'s supplement was entitled "The day Canada repudiated Quebec" (Cornellier 2002). Henri Brun, a professor of constitutional law at Laval University, was quoted by *La Presse* as saying that Canada's Charter of Rights was born with a "congenital defect" (Côté 2002).

A critique of the Supreme Court has emerged from western Canada, as well. The populist movements that were produced by the frontier and egalitarian spirit of western Canada – the Progressives, the Cooperative Commonwealth Federation (CCF), the Social Credit, and the Reform/Alliance Party – shared certain assumptions about "the West as a victimized region." A hotbed of civic boosterism, republican individualism, evangelical fervour, and radical social experiments, the West feared Ottawa's encroachments on its natural resources and autonomy. It is a fear that is deeply embedded – part of the DNA of the western Canadian experience. Roger Gibbins (1980, 168), president and CEO of the Canada West Foundation, observed that "On the prairies an almost conspiratorial view of national politics has existed ... The West consistently [sees itself as getting] shortchanged, exploited and ripped off."

To western populists, the Supreme Court remains a symbol of the entrenched power of the East. Among the long litany of complaints against the high court that has festered in the consciousness of western Canadians was the blocking of attempts by Alberta's Social Credit government to control the banks and monetary system during the Dirty Thirties. Decisions that limited Alberta's control over natural resources during the energy wars of the early 1980s are also part of this legacy of distrust. This skepticism was reflected in the policies of the Reform and Alliance parties and in the positions taken by the Klein government in Alberta. Conservative leader Stephen Harper has also been a vigorous opponent of judicial activism and at one point even accused the Chrétien government of "stacking" the court so that it could get the decisions that it wanted. During the 2004 federal election he charged the court with acting "unconstitutionally" and suggested that a Conservative government might use the notwithstanding clause to override court decisions.

Limiting the power of the court and the Charter has become a major objective of a phalanx of right-wing politicians, journalists, and thinkers. Although the chorus has been led by the *National Post,* the *Sun* chain, and editorial opinion in western Canada, they are hardly alone. Right-wing critics have vented their anger against the "robed dictators," "the imperial arrogance of judges," and the dangers of "an aristocratic jurocracy" (Roach 2001, 99). A former federal minister of justice, John Crosbie went so far as to attack the "Godzilla" judges, whom he contrasted with the "Mickey Mouses" of government, the legislatures, and cabinets (Bindman 1998). Alliance activist and political scientist Ted Morton described the *Vriend* decision, a case that will be discussed in some detail in this book, as a "naked power grab which culminates a decade and a half of ever-bolder assertions of judicial policymaking" (Makin 2002b).

The court has faced the energetic critique of academic commentators. These broadsides come from a variety of sources. First, the legitimacy of the Canadian Supreme Court has been challenged by academic commentators from Quebec who, as we noted above, argue that the court's decisions lean in favour of the federal government (Lajoie, Mulazzi, and Gamache 1986). Second, following the entrenchment of the Charter, there was an early and vigorous assault on the Charter from the academic left in English Canada. Their concern was that the constitutionalizing of rights would deflate the power of the state and simultaneously shield private power from public scrutiny (Mandel 1994; Hutchinson 1995).

A third phalanx in the academic assault emanates from conservative scholars. The "Court Party" thesis articulated principally by University of Calgary political scientists F.L. (Ted) Morton and Rainer Knopff (2000, 113) contends that a cohort of liberal post-materialist groups has been able to secure political advantages through the courts rather than in legislatures. They have bypassed legitimate political processes and formed an alliance with the judiciary. In supporting these groups the judges have ventured into the unfamiliar terrain of public policy. As there is little in the text of Canada's constitution that would produce results favourable to these social movements, the Canadian judiciary is simply putting into effect the preferences of well-organized cadres of professional litigants and legal academics.

If judges have succumbed, as Morton and Knopff (2000, 22) claim, "to the seduction of power," it is also difficult to resist the notion that the Charter is by its nature a transformative document. The Charter created a new symbolic universe. It sparked and sustained a new rights consciousness and made the courts the centre of gravity in determining and awarding rights. This was, some would argue, Pierre Trudeau's most enduring legacy. His grand political design was to create countervailing forces that would challenge and ultimately break down the old loyalties and identities that were rooted in the provinces and regions. With the Charter, citizens would have to turn to the courts and hence to Ottawa to secure their rights. Lorraine Weinrib (2001) makes precisely this claim when she writes that the Charter "was designed to transform the Canadian legal system." Hence, judges have been required to put flesh on the bones of the Charter, elaborating, interpreting, refining, and embellishing what is a vague and amorphous legal text. At times, they have been required to make law as much as interpret it.

To some degree, the court sits precariously on top of a volcano of political distrust and conflict. Although there have been long periods during which the volcano has remained dormant, there are times when the volcano threatens to erupt. During the political and constitutional battles over the Meech Lake and Charlottetown accords, the court's role as a centralizing institution came under fierce attack. Provincial governments made a concerted effort to change the method by which judges were appointed, to in effect change the face of the court. Although both accords were defeated because of widespread suspicion about the elitist nature of the process and discontent over other parts of both deals, reforming the Supreme Court had been high on the agenda.

Despite these challenges to its authority, the Supreme Court has dominated the Canadian political landscape in terms of credibility and prestige. Surveys indicate that while the faith that Canadians place in political institutions has plummeted since the mid-1980s, the Supreme Court and, in particular, the Charter of Rights and Freedoms over which it is the guardian have become pillars of trust and identity. According to a Gallup poll released in 2001, Canadians had greater respect for and confidence in the Supreme Court than they did in almost all other Canadian institutions, including churches, newspapers, banks, large corporations, the federal government, the House of Commons, and provincial governments (Mazzuca 2001). Most crucial, perhaps, is that Canadians appear to trust the courts far more than legislatures. When asked whether courts or legislatures should have the final say on the key questions in public life, Canadians supported the courts by a margin of two to one. Support for the courts was slightly higher among francophones (Fletcher and Howe 2001, 260-64).

Some of the results of surveys, however, must also be disturbing to judges. Despite efforts to appear independent and nonpartisan, the public views the Supreme Court as being deeply enmeshed in politics. In a poll conducted by Ipsos-Reid in 2001, seven out of ten of those surveyed believed that the court was influenced by partisan politics (Makin 2001). A similar poll taken by the same firm in 2003 asked a harsher and more straightforward question: whether respondents felt that "party politics" played a role in judicial decisions. An astonishing two-thirds of those surveyed believed that party politics either always or sometimes played a role (Tibbetts 2003).

There may be cause for worry on yet another front. While nine out of ten of those interviewed in a 2001 survey approved of the court's performance, that number had slipped to just 65 percent in 2003. Indeed, less than 20 percent of those who were surveyed in 2003 expressed strong confidence in the court.

There are at least two schools of thought about the popularity and prestige of the Supreme Court. One position is that approval for the court rests on solid and unshakable ground. Fletcher and Howe (2001, 287) found in their study that there was "a considerable reservoir of diffuse support" even among those who were consistently opposed to the Supreme Court's rulings. Peter Russell (2002) described the diffuse support argument to us:

> No matter how rough a ride a judicial decision gets, and they get real rough rides all over the place, public support, what we call diffuse support for the courts, is still very high. It is way higher than it is for Parliament or political leaders or journalists. They're doing real well despite the judge bashing that goes on and there's a kind of disconnect to some extent between what we talk about as specific support for a specific decision or specific opposition and diffuse general support for the court. If you ask people about whether there should be a Supreme Court interpreting the Charter; they say oh, yeah, yeah, yeah. But that *Vriend* decision was a real bummer.

But others would suggest that public support is far more fragile and precarious than adherents of the "solid ground" or "diffuse" position would have us believe. The public's support for the court, and the Charter over which it is the trustee, rests on slippery footing, footing that can easily give way under pressure. Paul

Sniderman and his colleagues (Sniderman et al. 1996) found that while there was broad and even deep support for Charter values, opinion can be volatile and shift dramatically depending on the issue or situation. Citizens often hold more than one opinion on a particular question. The drama and publicity that surround a high-profile decision can give prominence to one perspective over another and the public can be persuaded to rethink its position. "Sudden gusts of political passion" can overturn what was thought to be deep popular support for particular rights and freedoms (Sniderman et al. 1996, 28). Sniderman and his colleagues were disturbed by the degree to which majorities could be made and unmade.[3]

Some scholars believe that support for the court is predicated on the "good behaviour" of the judges. The court cannot be on the wrong side of public opinion or offend public sensibilities too often without risking the goodwill that it enjoys and which is both the key to and the great limitation on its power. For instance, Fletcher and Howe (2001, 268) asked respondents whether the Supreme Court should be abolished if it "started making a lot of decisions that most people disagreed with." They found that while in Canada as a whole 53 percent of respondents strongly disagreed, the results in Quebec were reversed – 53 percent would support the abolition of the court.

There is more volatility here than might be expected. Two out of three people surveyed in a 2002 Environics poll were opposed to the current method of appointing judges to the court and wanted Supreme Court judges to be elected. The figure in western Canada was, not surprisingly, even higher – 71 percent (Cobb 2002). It would seem that many westerners would like to see elected judges checking elected politicians.

One can argue that much of the court's success has rested on the judges' ability to gauge the public mood. The judges are, with the exception of reference cases, able to pick and choose the cases that they will hear from among a small avalanche of appeals. The judges have known which fights to pick, when to tread gingerly, and when to speak loudly. Of course, there is only so much room to manoeuvre, and not all the difficult cases can be avoided or delayed.

It might be said that the court has been saved by the integrity, talent, and ingenuity of the judges who have been appointed to the bench. Despite charges by its critics, prime ministers have generally not used the highest court to reward friends or pursue party politics by other means. The court was not allowed to become a political football. Judges such as Brian Dickson, Antonio Lamer, Bertha Wilson, Gérald La Forest, Peter Cory, and Frank Iacobucci, among others, have created a standard of excellence that has brought great distinction to the court. Had the standard of appointment or conduct been lower, had the court not developed the aura that it now has, the political volcano on which it rests might have erupted.

## Media Agenda Setting

The place reserved for reporters by the court has none of the splendour of the judges' chambers, conference rooms, or the courtroom itself. The Media and Barristers Room is on the second floor, next to the female barristers' change room. When we visited the room, the floor was covered by an ordinary reddish carpet, it held two long tables and about fifteen chairs. The window overlooked the parking lot. A large garbage can had been placed against one of the walls. A coat rack built into a cabinet jutted up against another wall. There was also a TV set. The atmosphere was informal as reporters mingled, came and went, bantered with each other and with the executive legal officer.

Despite their informal and less than majestic surroundings, these reporters exercise considerable power. First, as we've mentioned, they, together with editors and producers, decide which cases will be covered and which will not. Lydia Miljan and Barry Cooper (2003) have gone so far as to argue that media coverage supports the court's judicial activism. They contend that by covering only the most sensational cases and giving the court little regular coverage, media organizations signal that there is little reason to be concerned about the decisions that are being made. The relative absence of coverage serves as an endorsement of the court's power.

Second, and just as importantly, reporters choose the "frames" or angles that will be used in reporting those cases. Journalistic repertoires typically highlight some themes and downplay others. Stories that feature sharp conflict, can be easily explained and condensed, involve people in positions of authority or who are compelling in some way either as villains or victims, and have eye-catching visuals are the stories that contain the ingredients most sought after by journalists. Media frames are imposed on almost every event journalists cover. Critics contend that the stories that fit media frames tend to be given a great deal of play regardless of how trivial they might be for society. Similarly, stories that do not fit a frame are relegated to the sidelines, regardless of how important they might be. In addition, as Doris Graber has observed, journalists "select the sources through whose eyes the public views the world" (Lawrence 2000, 5).

Again, the news values that are the lifeblood of journalism often conflict with the operating principles used by judges and the legal community. Judgments often are complex and involve abstract points of principle and cannot easily be reduced to five paragraphs or ten-second sound bites. Important cases rarely lend themselves to the "hot" visuals that TV producers require. The reasoning behind decisions is sometimes ignored or misunderstood and spokespersons for various interest groups dominate the headlines. As we found from our interviews, Supreme Court justices are sometimes frustrated when their judgments come off the news assembly line looking far different from what they thought had gone in.

Moreover, most television reporting is episodic rather than thematic (Iyengar 1991). News stories tend to focus on a single case or decision rather than on broader themes such as whether judges have too much power or whether the ability of the police to catch criminals has been hampered by the courts. According to Shanto Iyengar, episodic framing leads viewers to blame societal problems on the individuals depicted in the story rather than on larger political or legal issues and patterns. Iyengar argues that television's basic format distorts the way viewers see the courts and criminals.

Much media reporting deals with what can be described as "morality tales." James Carey believes that journalism often involves the construction of common identities and the maintenance of societal and ideological boundaries. Order itself is often on trial, and those who violate societal norms often endure "rituals of shame, degradation and excommunication" (Carey 1998, 42). Media reporting concentrates to a large extent on the exposure of crimes and scandals or is about people who violate moral and societal boundaries in some way. Disgraced politicians, notorious criminals, and people with shocking or controversial views are chased, hounded, and held up to public ridicule. As K.T. Erikson observed, "Newspapers (and now radio and television) offer their readers the same kind of entertainment once supplied by public hangings or the use of the stocks and pillories" (cited in Ericson, Baranek, and Chan 1987, 7-8). Both Michel Foucault (1995) and Roland Barthes (1992) claimed that the notion of spectacle always played a role in the punishment of crime. Today, as Carey (1998) and others have argued, journalists "police" society by producing their own spectacles of reward and punishment.

Todd Gitlin (1980, 2) once wrote that the media have the power to "name the world's parts" and "to certify reality as reality." Gitlin uses the same language to describe the power of the media that Bourdieu uses to describe the power of the judiciary. They both have the power of "naming." That is the capacity to set social parameters, to declare what is acceptable and unacceptable in society, and to inflict penalties on those who violate these norms. The fundamental problem for the justices is that their messages cannot get through to society without being altered by the journalistic lens. In a sense, journalists have the last word. The problem for journalists and news organizations is that their routines and priorities do not always accurately reflect the court and its judgments. Both judges and journalists have begun to realize that a great deal is at stake in this most essential of relationships.

## Outline of the Book

Having laid down the foundation for the research study that follows, we will describe in the next chapter the results of our study of a year in the life of the court. Differences in reporting by French- and English-language news organizations, newspapers and television, broadsheet and tabloid papers, public and private broadcasters, and individual news outlets are analyzed. The chapter also describes the types of cases that received extensive coverage and those that received little or no attention. The chapter presents a broad canvas with many vivid and not so vivid colours. Among our findings is that relatively few cases attracted the lion's share of coverage. These cases invariably involved highly charged moral issues, morality tales, which had the ingredients that journalists need for their news stories.

The next four chapters deal with the controversial cases of *Vriend,* the *Quebec Secession Reference, Marshall,* and *Sharpe.* Here we undertake an in-depth analysis stressing how the court is portrayed; which aspects of each decision are highlighted and which are downplayed; the frames used by journalists in covering the judgments; differences between local, regional, and national coverage; and the sources relied on in news stories. We also ask whether the court was successful in having its "message," namely, the rationale that lay behind its decisions, conveyed to the public. Not all these cases fall neatly into a single pattern. In some instances, the court was successful in setting the agenda – the reasoning behind its decisions got through loud and clear via the news media. In other instances, the court's message did not penetrate through the media's own logic or was contested by journalists.

Chapter 6 describes the relationship between the court and the journalists who cover it. We argue that the court has carefully constructed a system which ensures that not only are its points of view clearly communicated to the public but that it can play a role in setting the agenda and enhancing its prestige. While the court is engaged in what is clearly an important public service, it is also a political institution that is attempting to ensure that its judgments are understood by journalists. We will examine the ways in which Supreme Court reporting differs from political reporting and the special pressures on and concerns of the journalists who cover the court. Again, our study will examine the degree to which the relationship between the court and the journalists who cover it constitutes a unique political world.

*The Last Word* also sheds light on what ordinary Canadians learn about the court and its decisions, and hence about their rights as citizens, from the mass media. To this extent, we maintain, the book tells us a great deal about the nature of the society in which we live.

## Notes

1 This fits well Antonio Lamer's view of the court. The court did not ask for this expanded judicial role; rather, the edict "came from the elected (Parliament). We're heeding the command of the elected ... That's their doing, that's not ours." See Morton and Knopff (2000, 23) and Bertha Wilson, "We Didn't Volunteer" (Howe and Russell 2001, 73-79).

2 Author's translation. In French it was: "Il ne fait plus de doute que les juges sont des acteurs politiques. C'est-à-dire qu'ils prennent des décisions qui affectent la vie dans la cité, et profondément. Après l'étonnement – et le scandale, même – que cette découverte a provoqué dans les premières années, la chose semble acceptée."

3 It is interesting to note that a survey conducted by Ipsos-Reid in 2003 found that 71 percent of Canadians thought that Parliament and not the courts should make the laws. This was a complete reversal from the results of polls taken just two years earlier (Sallot 2003).

## References

Barthes, Roland. 1992. *Mythologies.* New York: Noonday Press.

Bindman, Stephen. 1998. Minister to bar: Put an end to court-bashing. Montreal *Gazette,* 27 August, p. A10.

Boisvert, Yves. 2002a. Les vingt ans de la Charte canadienne des droits et liberte. Le monde allait changer sans elle! *La Presse,* 13 April, p. B3.

—. 2002b. Comments. Media-Supreme Court Research Workshop, 7 November, Ottawa.

Bourdieu, Pierre. 1987. The force of law: Toward a sociology of the judicial field. *Hastings Law Journal* 38: 805-53.

Brodie, Ian. 2002. *Friends of the court: The privileging of interest group litigants in Canada.* Albany: State University of New York Press.

Canadian Judicial Council. 1999. *The judicial role in public information.* Canadian Judicial Council, September 1999, 5.

Carey, James. 1998. Political ritual on television. In *Media, ritual and identity,* ed. Tamar Liebes and James Curran, 42-70. New York: Routledge.

Chevrier, Marc. 1999. Le papisme legal. *Argument* 1 (2): 73-92.

Cobb, Chris. 2002. Canadians want to elect court. *National Post,* 4 February, p. A1.

Cook, Timothy. 1998. *Governing with the news: The news media as a political institution.* Chicago: University of Chicago Press.

Cornellier, Manon. 2002. Le jour où Canada a renié le Québec. *Le Devoir,* 13 April, p. G1.

Côté, Charles. 2002. Contre la tyrannie. *La Presse,* 13 April, p. B9.

Davis, Richard. 1994. *Decisions and images: The Supreme Court and the press.* Englewood Cliffs, NJ: Prentice Hall.

Dean, Wally, and Lee Ann Brady. 2002. After 9/11, has anything changed? Washington, DC: Project for Excellence in Journalism.

*Delgamuukw v. British Columbia,* [1997] 1 S.C.R. 1010.

Dickson, Chief Justice Brian. 1994. The Canadian Charter of Rights and Freedoms: Dawn of a new era? *Review of Constitutional Studies* 2: 1-19.

Downie Jr., Leonard, and Robert Kaiser. 2002. *The news about the news: American journalism in peril.* New York: Alfred A. Knopf.

Epp, Charles. 1998. *The rights revolution.* Chicago: University of Chicago Press.

Ericson, Richard, Patricia Baranek, and Janet Chan. 1987. *Visualizing deviance: A study of news organization.* Toronto: University of Toronto Press.

Fletcher, Joseph, and Paul Howe. 2001. Public opinion and Canada's courts. In Howe and Russell, 255-96.

Foucault, Michel. 1995. *Discipline and punish: The birth of the prison.* 2nd ed. New York: Vintage.

Gall, Gerald, and Rebecca Sober. 2000. The Supreme Court of Canada: Judges speak out! *Canadian Issues* (Spring): 26-29.

Gambrill, David. 2002. Politicians leaving complex issues to courts: Gonthier. *Law Times* (28 October): 3.

Gans, Herbert. 1980. *Deciding what's news.* New York: Vintage.

Gibbins, Roger. 1980. *Prairie politics and society: Regionalism in decline.* Toronto: Butterworths.

Gitlin, Todd. 1980. *The whole world is watching.* Berkeley: University of California Press.

Handelman, Stephen. 1999. Canadian Supreme Court. *Time* Canada, 27 December, pp. 110-11.

Hart, H.L.A. 1994. *The concept of law.* 2nd ed. Oxford: Clarendon Press.

Hiebert, Janet. 2002. *Charter conflicts: What is Parliament's role.* Montreal and Kingston: McGill-Queen's University Press.

Howe, Paul, and Peter Russell, eds. 2001. *Judicial power and Canadian democracy.* Montreal and Kingston: McGill-Queen's University Press.

Hutchinson, Allan C. 1995. *Waiting for CORAF: A critique of law and rights.* Toronto: University of Toronto Press.

Iacobucci, Justice Frank. 2001. Interview by authors. Calgary, 26 October.

Iyengar, Shanto. 1991. *Is anyone responsible? How television frames political issues.* Chicago: University of Chicago Press.

Laforest, Guy. 1995. *Trudeau and the end of a Canadian dream.* Montreal and Kingston: McGill-Queen's University Press.

Lajoie, Andrée. 1997. *Jugements de valeurs: Le discours judiciaire et le droit.* Coll. Les voies du droit. Paris: PUF.

Lajoie, Andrée, Pierrette Mulazzi, and Michèle Gamache. 1986. Political ideas in Quebec and the evolution of Canadian constitutional law. In *The Supreme Court of Canada as an instrument of political change,* ed. Ivan Bernier and Andrée Lajoie, 1-103. Vol. 47. Royal Commission on the Economic Union and the Development Prospects for Canada. Toronto: University of Toronto.

Laskin, Bora. 1964. "Peace, order and good government" re-examined. In *The Courts and the Canadian Constitution,* ed. W.R. Lederman, 66-104. Toronto: McClelland and Stewart.

Laurendeau, André. 1973. *Witness for Quebec.* Toronto: Macmillan.

Lawrence, Regina. 2000. *The politics of force: Media and the construction of police brutality.* Berkeley: University of California Press.

Leeson, Howard. 2001. Section 33, the notwithstanding clause: A paper tiger? In Howe and Russell, 297-323.

Levant, Ezra. 2002. Interview by authors. Calgary, 26 November.

Lunman, Kim, and Brian Laghi. 2004. Commons panel to accept judges, but want stronger vetting process. *Globe and Mail,* 26 August, p. A1.

Makin, Kirk. 2001. Canadians believe Supreme Court rulings are influenced by politics: Poll. *Globe and Mail,* 3 July, p. A1.

—. 2002a. We are not gunslingers with no restraint. *Globe and Mail,* 9 April, p. 4.

—. 2002b. Charting new territory. *Globe and Mail,* 10 April, p. 7.

—. 2002c. Interview by authors. Toronto, 13 September.

Mandel, Michael. 1994. *The Charter of Rights and the legalization of politics in Canada.* Toronto: Thomson Educational Publishing.

Mazzuca, Josephine. 2001. Armed forces, Supreme Court and public schools top institutional list for respect and confidence. *Gallup Poll* 61 (28 May): 30.

McChesney, Robert. 2000. *Rich media, poor democracy: Communication politics in dubious times.* New York: The New Press.

McCormick, Peter. 2000. *Supreme at last: The evolution of the Supreme Court of Canada.* Toronto: Lorimer.

McLachlin, Beverley. 1999. Courts, legislatures and executives in the post-Charter era. *Policy Options* 20 (5): 45-46.

—. 2002. Interview by authors. Ottawa, 7 December.

Miljan, Lydia, and Barry Cooper. 2003. *Hidden agendas: How journalists influence the news.* Vancouver: UBC Press.

Morton, F.L., and Rainer Knopff. 2000. *The Charter revolution and the court party.* Peterborough, ON: Broadview Press.

*National Post.* 2000. Supreme self-restraint. Editorial, 7 April, p. A19.

Newman, Don. 2002. Interview by authors. Ottawa, 7 December.

Page, Benjamin. 1996. *Who deliberates? Mass media in modern democracy.* Chicago: University of Chicago Press.

Rapping, Elayne. 2003. *Law and justice as seen on TV.* New York: New York University Press.

Roach, Kent. 2001. *The Supreme Court on trial: Judicial activism or democratic dialogue.* Toronto: Irwin Law.

Russell, Peter. 1983. The political purposes of the Canadian Charter of Rights and Freedoms. *Canadian Bar Review* 61: 30-54.

—. 2002. Comments. Media-Supreme Court Research Workshop, 7 November, Ottawa.

Sallot, Jeff, 2003. Judges' power too great: Poll. *Globe and Mail,* 11 August, p. A1, 5.

Saywell, John T. 2002. *The Lawmakers: Judicial power and the shaping of Canadian federalism.* Toronto: University of Toronto Press.

Schmitz, Cristin. 2001. Judges their own best ambassadors: CBA media panel. *Lawyers Weekly* (24 August): 23.

Sherwin, Richard. 2000. *When law goes pop: The vanishing line between law and popular culture.* Chicago: University of Chicago Press.

Slotnick, Elliot, and Jennifer Segal. 1998. *Television coverage and the Supreme Court: All the news that's fit to air?* Cambridge: Cambridge University Press.

Sniderman, Paul, Joseph Fletcher, Peter Russell, and Philip Tetlock. 1996. *The clash of rights: Liberty, equality and legitimacy in pluralist democracy.* New Haven: Yale University Press.

Stewart, Edison. 1998. Judges wonder how to right twisted rulings. *Toronto Star,* 24 August, p. A1.

Strauss, Marina. 1985. Scrutiny under Charter called bold step. *Globe and Mail,* 26 April, p. 1.

Tibbetts, Janice. 1999. Top court named newsmaker of 1999. *Ottawa Citizen,* 21 December, p. A7.

—. 2003. High court too partisan: Survey. Canada.com, 12 May.

Tocqueville, Alexis de. 1969. *Democracy in America.* New York: Doubleday/Anchor.

Vipond, Robert C. 1991. *Liberty and community: Canadian federalism and the failure of the constitution.* Albany: State University of New York Press.

Weinrib, Lorraine Eisenstat. 2001. The activist constitution. In Howe and Russell, 80-86.

Wolfsfeld, Gadi. 1997. *Media and political conflict: News from the Middle East.* Cambridge: Cambridge University Press.

# A Year in the Life of the Supreme Court

THE FRENZY THAT television crews went into on the day the decision in the *Sharpe* case was announced lasted no more than a few hours. On that day only, the country's major English and French television networks reported on the ruling and the reactions to it. As for the major newspapers, however, their coverage of the child pornography case lasted almost a week and can be divided into three phases: articles that prepped readers about the forthcoming decision, coverage of the decision and reactions to it, and, finally, analytical pieces.

The Supreme Court had announced on the Monday that the decision would be rendered on Friday, 26 January 2001. On Tuesday, as is common journalistic practice with major decisions, many newspapers prepared their readers for an important piece of news. Montreal's three French-language newspapers, *Le Journal de Montréal, La Presse,* and *Le Devoir,* published the same report by Jules Richer, an Ottawa correspondent for the Presse canadienne, the French news service of the Canadian Press. He wrote that almost one year to the day after hearing the case, the Supreme Court would render a long-awaited ruling on possession of child pornography (Richer, 2001a, 2001b; *La Presse* 2001). The stakes were high and the case was fraught with emotion.

The same day, the headline of an article in the *Globe and Mail* blared: "Top court to rule on child porn. B.C. man's 1999 acquittal on charges of possession sparked outrage across country" (Makin and Matas 2001). Reporters Kirk Makin and Robert Matas summed up the confrontation in a few words: "The Supreme Court of Canada will declare a winner on Friday in a mighty clash between the principle of free expression and the need to suppress child pornography."

Let's briefly review the facts. John Robin Sharpe, of Vancouver, was charged with "simple possession" of child pornography and "possession for the purpose of distribution and sale." Before his trial he had contested the constitutionality of the charge of "simple possession," arguing that it infringed the freedom of expression guaranteed him by the constitution and the Charter of Rights and Freedoms. The trial judge and a majority of the judges (two to one) of the British Columbia Court of Appeal decided that the prohibition on simple possession of child pornography was not justifiable in a free and democratic society. The ruling by the first court and that of the Court of Appeal caused a flood of negative reactions.

The case became a political issue during the 2000 federal election when Canadian Alliance leader Stockwell Day attacked Prime Minister Jean Chrétien for not being tough enough on child pornography. If the Supreme Court upheld the decision by the British Columbia courts, a major political battle was likely to erupt. According to Luiza Chwialkowska (2001b), the *National Post* reporter assigned to cover the Supreme Court, "The decision sets the stage for a potential political showdown when the House of Commons resumes sitting next week."

On the Thursday, the *Toronto Sun* reported that it had learned that the federal Department of Justice was bracing itself for the worst (Rubec 2001b). Amendments to the Criminal Code would be quickly introduced in the House of Commons if the Supreme Court ruled in Sharpe's favour. In this context, the frenzy surrounding the decision is easy to understand. But as we explain in a later chapter, the court's decision nipped the crisis in the bud. With two narrow exceptions, the court confirmed the constitutionality of the contested section of the Criminal Code.

The *Toronto Sun* ended the suspense it had created: "Porn law solid: Top court" (Rubec 2001c). Most of the headlines on page one of the Saturday papers echoed similar themes. *Globe and Mail* reporter Kirk Makin (2001a) summarized the decision as follows: "The Supreme Court of Canada yesterday upheld a law criminalizing the possession of child pornography – but it carved out narrow exceptions to protect private works of the imagination or photographic depictions of oneself." Under the heading "Both sides claim victory" (Mickelburgh and Freeze 2001), the newspaper summarized the main reactions to the decision.

Most newspapers carried lengthy, wide-ranging reports on the reactions of various interest groups but mentioned only in passing the views of the minority of three of the court's nine judges, who would have preferred to maintain the law in its entirety, without the exceptions established by the majority. These legal subtleties, indicative of significantly diverging opinions within the court, were of little interest to journalists. Only the *National Post* reported at length on the minority, under the heading "Freedom of expression not absolute: Three judges" (Chwialkowska 2001c). According to Madam Justice Claire L'Heureux-Dubé, Mr. Justice Charles Gonthier, and Mr. Justice Michel Bastarache (photos of whom appeared in the newspaper), certain forms of expression, such as child pornography, are "inherently harmful," and the balance established by Parliament between the "rights and values at stake" was entirely justifiable.

Most newspapers repeated the comments made by then Justice Minister Anne McLellan, who spoke of a decision that was balanced (it seemed to suit everyone) but at the same time was a great victory for the children of Canada (Makin 2001a). The editorials showed that the newspapers shared her interpretation. Under the heading "Pour l'amour des enfants," Agnès Gruda of La Presse characterized the decision as one of balance and eminent common sense (Gruda 2001). Paule des Rivières wrote in Le Devoir that the court was to be commended for a courageous judgment that recognized the importance of protecting children from sexual exploitation, even if this protection involved restrictions on the right to freedom of expression (des Rivières 2001). Under the heading "For the children," the Toronto Sun (2001b) welcomed a "sensible ruling – not the legal chaos many feared."

The court didn't have much choice, Jeffrey Simpson seemed to say in the Globe and Mail. He chastised critics who said the ruling indicated the judges had become less activist and less inclined to overturn laws and commended the court's realism: "Had it [the court] overturned the Criminal Code provisions against child pornography, the outcry would have reverberated from one end of Canada to the other" (Simpson 2001).

The National Post (2001b) welcomed the decision in an editorial, but its columnist Andrew Coyne (2001) regarded it as "a piece of political footwork." As Coyne argued, "Indeed, so dazzled was the audience that the Court left both sides of the debate convinced they had won, trimming federal child pornography legislation of its worst excesses even as the headlines read 'High court upholds child porn ban.'"

The Sharpe case was one of the Supreme Court decisions that received the most coverage during our study of a year in the life of the court. Our analysis is based on a review of coverage of the Supreme Court from 1 September 2000 to 31 August 2001. Moral issues, which often divide opinion and involve matters of conscience, fascinate the media. Twenty percent of the articles and reports we surveyed during the year were devoted to the Sharpe case (7.7 percent) and to Robert Latimer (12.7 percent), the Saskatchewan farmer who was given a ten-year sentence for the mercy killing of his severely handicapped daughter. In matters of justice, as in other areas, human interest and morality tales are among the foremost criteria that guide the media when they build or construct the news.

## Coverage of Decisions Rather than the Court Itself

How did the media see the Supreme Court from September 2000 to September 2001? Did television and newspapers perceive it differently? Did Quebec's French-language media present the court in a way that was distinctly different from that

**Table 1.1: Articles and reports surveyed (2000-01)**

|  | No. | % |
| --- | :---: | :---: |
| Newspapers | 621 | 87 |
| Television | 96 | 13 |
| **Total** | **717** | **100** |

of the English media? In this chapter we present the results of our analysis. We will begin by providing an overview of how the court and its decisions were portrayed by the media. A careful reading of the year's articles and reports on the court will then enable us to make specific comments and draw conclusions.

We analyzed the content of six newspapers and four television networks. The choices were a given. The two national English-language newspapers, the *Globe and Mail* and the *National Post,* had to be included because of the size of their readership as well as their national reach. Both pay special attention to the court and its activities. At the time of our survey, each had a reporter who devoted a great deal of time to the court, Kirk Makin of the *Globe* and Luiza Chwialkowska of the *Post*. The *Post* also had access to the services of Southam News legal reporter Janice Tibbetts. As for the French language, we chose *Le Devoir,* which is still perceived by many as the French-language newspaper of record and at the time published a regular column by lawyer Alain-Robert Nadeau, and *La Presse,* whose columnist Yves Boisvert has long been keenly interested in legal matters. We also analyzed the country's two largest tabloids (both owned by the Quebecor group), *Le Journal de Montréal* and the *Toronto Sun*. As for television, we chose the largest privately owned English- and French-language networks, CTV and TVA, and the English- and French-language networks of the public broadcaster CBC/Radio-Canada.

The Supreme Court has three sessions a year, in the fall, winter, and spring. The session dates are determined in the fall, and the court traditionally resumes sitting in September. During 2000-01 there were a spate of cases likely to stir the interest of the media. A number of long-awaited decisions were to be rendered during the year, including the controversial *Sharpe* and *Latimer* cases. In September 2000, the court also celebrated its 125th anniversary under the leadership of its new chief justice, Beverley McLachlin, who had succeeded Antonio Lamer in January.

Although certain matters before the court were rather technical, other more politically charged cases would also be heard and would no doubt make headlines, such as the *Trinity Western University* case. It involved a private religious university and the British Columbia College of Teachers, which refused to accredit the institution's teacher-training programs because it obliged its students to abide by a code of conduct that the College of Teachers deemed discriminatory. The code was

**Table 1.2: English- and French-language newspapers (2000-01)**

| Newspapers | Articles | |
|---|---|---|
| | No. | % |
| *La Presse* | 110 | 17.7 |
| *Le Devoir* | 90 | 14.5 |
| *Le Journal de Montréal* | 53 | 8.5 |
| **Total French-language** | **253** | **40.7** |
| *Globe and Mail* | 145 | 23.3 |
| *National Post* | 172 | 27.8 |
| *Toronto Sun* | 51 | 8.2 |
| **Total English-language** | **368** | **59.3** |
| **Total French- and English-language** | **621** | **100** |

based on biblical scriptures and included bans on swearing, drinking, premarital sex, and homosexuality (Chwialkowska 2000a). Undoubtedly the media would also be interested in the case of Richard Therrien, the Quebec Superior Court judge who was removed from the bench for having failed to disclose at the time of his appointment his previous involvement with the notorious Front de libération du Québec (FLQ) in 1970.

Lawyer Alain-Robert Nadeau, whose *Le Devoir* column was devoted mainly to the Supreme Court and its jurisprudence, wrote that, although often technical, the matters to be examined by the Supreme Court involved the fine line between law and morality, sanction and pardon, rehabilitation and ostracism (Nadeau 2000a). The year offered plenty for the media.

The six newspapers published 621 articles devoted either in whole or in part to the Supreme Court, and the television networks broadcast 96 reports (see Table 1.1). It should come as no surprise that the number of newspaper articles far exceeds the number of television reports. Newspapers publish far more news on a daily basis than appears on TV. A twenty-minute newscast covers only about fifteen stories. Moreover, the court's activities lack the visual appeal that television requires, and the complex subjects it deals with are often difficult to explain in a minute and a half.[1] Since most people get their news mainly from television, we can conclude that their knowledge of the Supreme Court's activities is limited.

Table 1.2 and Table 1.3 give the number of articles published by each newspaper we studied and the number of reports broadcast by each television network. Two conclusions can be drawn from Table 1.2. The broadsheet English dailies (the *National Post* and the *Globe and Mail*) were far more interested in the court than

Table 1.3: Television: English- and French-language networks (2000-01)

| Network | Reports | |
|---|---|---|
| | No. | % |
| CBC | 34 | 35.4 |
| CTV | 32 | 33.3 |
| **Total** | **66** | **68.7** |
| Radio-Canada | 15 | 15.6 |
| TVA | 15 | 15.6 |
| **Total** | **30** | **31.3** |
| **Total English- and French-language** | **96** | **100** |

their French-language counterparts, *Le Devoir* and *La Presse*. Slightly more than 50 percent of the articles surveyed were published by these two newspapers. Although most of their readers are in Ontario, especially Toronto, the *Globe* and the *Post* are distributed across Canada.[2] Their choices regarding what to cover must take this factor into account. The French-language newspapers are interested above all in events that take place in or affect Quebec in some way – their readers live in Quebec, after all. It is not surprising that they were more interested in the smaller number of cases originating in Quebec. In 2000-01, seventeen of the court's sixty-eight written decisions dealt with Quebec cases.

Language is not a decisive factor, however, in explaining the tabloids' relative lack of interest in the court. The *Toronto Sun* was scarcely more interested in the court than *Le Journal de Montréal*. The tabloids are fuelled by police matters, crime, and other such news items and less by the larger societal issues that the Supreme Court often deals with.

The French-language television networks were also less interested in the court than the English networks. Table 1.3 shows that more than two-thirds of the television reports were broadcast on CBC and CTV. However, public and private networks, whether in French or in English, gave equal importance to the court.

We have divided the articles and reports into five categories: (1) judicial activities, such as motions for leave to appeal, hearings, and decisions by the court; (2) the court as an institution: articles or reports concerned above all with the institution, how it functions, how it has changed, and who its members are; (3) social matters that go beyond specific cases and deal with major social or moral topics, such as Native rights, euthanasia, and privacy; and analyses of the Supreme Court's jurisprudence; (4) excerpts from judgments; and (5) other.

**Table 1.4: Nature of articles and reports (%): Newspapers and television**

| Nature of reports | Newspapers | Television |
|---|---|---|
| Judicial activities | 82.8 | 98.0 |
| Supreme Court as an institution or its judges | 10.1 | 1.0 |
| Social issues involving the Supreme Court | 4.2 | 0.0 |
| Excerpts from judgments | 0.5 | 0.0 |
| Other | 2.4 | 1.0 |
| Total          % | 100 | 100 |
|                No. | 621 | 96 |

**Table 1.5: Nature of articles (%): Newspapers**

| Nature | Le Devoir | La Presse | Le Journal de Montréal | Globe and Mail | National Post | Toronto Sun |
|---|---|---|---|---|---|---|
| Judicial activities | 88.2 | 82.2 | 84.9 | 75.0 | 82.7 | 96.0 |
| Supreme Court as an institution or its judges | 7.3 | 6.7 | 11.3 | 12.8 | 14.5 | 0.0 |
| Social issues involving the Supreme Court | 0.9 | 6.7 | 1.9 | 7.0 | 2.8 | 4 |
| Excerpts from judgments | 1.8 | 0.0 | 0.0 | 0.6 | 0.0 | 0.0 |
| Other | 1.8 | 4.4 | 1.9 | 4.6 | 0.0 | 0.0 |
| Total          % | 100 | 100 | 100 | 100 | 100 | 100 |
|                No. | 110 | 90 | 53 | 172 | 145 | 51 |

Table 1.4 shows that judicial activities receive by far the most coverage in the media's articles and reports. Television was interested almost exclusively in judicial activities (98 percent), namely "official" news, and specific decisions. This is not surprising. In all areas, the media are interested in specific matters. Their coverage of community life is organized mainly as a function of foreseeable events. They have far more difficulty defining far-reaching issues and major trends. It is simpler for them to cover the court's decisions, as opposed to analyzing what sociologist Guy Rocher (1990) calls "l'emprise du droit," the law's increasing power in our lives and in society.

Fifty-one of the sixty-eight formal (or written) judgments rendered by the court from September 2000 to September 2001 were the subject of articles or reports, with some receiving more coverage than others, as we shall see. Of the seventeen decisions left in the shadows, six involved criminal law, five administrative law, three labour law, and three tax law. Most were minor or technical decisions that were not likely to attract the attention of the major media. About twenty other decisions generated only one or two articles in one or another newspaper.

Some newspapers are more concerned than others about the court as an institution and its broader role. These newspapers – the *Globe and Mail* and the *National Post* – assigned a journalist to cover the Supreme Court closely on a regular basis. In the case of the *Globe and Mail,* the categories "Supreme Court as an institution" and "social issues" together represent 20 percent of that newspaper's total coverage for the year (see Table 1.5). That figure shows clearly that the newspaper took a more proactive approach than did certain other media (television especially), which merely reacted to the court's activities. As was the case with TV networks, the *Toronto Sun* was interested almost exclusively in activities related to cases.

Surprisingly, the French-language tabloid *Le Journal de Montréal* published a higher percentage of articles than its French-language counterparts about the court as an institution. When we look closely, however, those six articles (out of the fifty-three published) had nothing to do with any willingness on the part of the Montreal tabloid to explore the life of the court in any depth. One, published in January 2001, was a routine beginning-of-year summary from the Presse canadienne of the court's activities during the previous year (Presse canadienne 2001a). Another was a report on attacks by then Canadian Alliance leader Stockwell Day on the court's "activists" during the election campaign in the fall of 2000 (Bisson 2000). A third was an article reporting comments by Madam Justice Louise Arbour, who, when receiving an honorary doctorate from Mount Saint Vincent University in Halifax, encouraged young people to cherish democracy (Presse canadienne 2001e).

### A Few Cases Dominate Coverage

Table 1.6 lists the ten cases that received the most media coverage during the year, regardless of their status before the court (motion for leave to appeal, hearing, judgment on appeal, and so on). All the coverage, with the exception of that involving Maurice ("Mom") Boucher of the Quebec Hell's Angels, was based on formal judgments. Boucher's motion for leave to appeal contested the Quebec Court of Appeal ruling that he be tried a second time for the murders of two prison guards after being acquitted the first time.

Almost a third (31.8 percent) of the articles and reports published or broadcast were on only four cases. Three were criminal cases: *Latimer, Sharpe,* and *United States v. Burns* (or the *Burns-Rafay* case), a decision concerning the extradition of two Canadians accused of murder in the United States. The fourth, pertaining to the Town of Hudson, dealt with the environment and municipal law; it addressed the scope of municipalities' regulatory power – in this instance, their power to

**Table 1.6: Overall top ten cases with the most coverage:
Newspapers and television**

| Rank | Case | No. | % (of 717) |
|---|---|---|---|
| 1. | Robert Latimer | 91 | 12.7 |
| 2. | John R. Sharpe | 56 | 7.7 |
| 3. | Burns-Rafay | 43 | 5.9 |
| 4. | Town of Hudson | 40 | 5.5 |
| 5. | Maurice Boucher | 21 | 2.9 |
| 6. | Richard Therrien | 17 | 2.3 |
| 7. | Stephen Harper | 16 | 2.2 |
| 8. | Little Sister's | 15 | 2.1 |
| 9. | Asbestos Corporation | 14 | 1.9 |
| 10. | Red Cross | 14 | 1.9 |
| | **Subtotal** | **327** | **45.1** |
| | **Total** | **717** | **100** |

prohibit the use of pesticides. The top ten cases represent almost half (45.1 percent) of everything published and broadcast about the court from September 2000 to September 2001.

The case of Richard Therrien, the judge who was removed from the bench, and the case of Stephen Harper,[3] on behalf of the National Citizens Coalition, which concerned the federal election law and limits on campaign expenditures by third parties during federal elections, were both heard and the decisions were rendered during the year, as was the case involving the Town of Hudson. The three cases that round out the top ten concerned the importations of gay and lesbian pornographic or erotic materials by Little Sister's bookstore in Vancouver, the Red Cross's tainted blood scandal, and the minority shareholders of Asbestos Corporation, a case heard in December 2000, with the decision rendered in June 2001.

The *Latimer* case, charged with emotion and human interest, was way out in front, having been featured in 91 out of 717 articles and reports. Defying all assumptions based on proximity – the media, one can argue, are interested above all, and increasingly so, in what happens in their own backyard – the Saskatchewan farmer's story enthralled the media and public opinion across Canada, including in Quebec.

Robert Latimer was charged with committing murder in the first degree (with premeditation) after the death of his twelve-year-old daughter Tracy, who suffered from cerebral palsy and had a mental age of four months. After learning that doctors wanted his daughter to undergo an operation he perceived as mutilation (she had already undergone two such surgeries), Latimer decided in October 1993 to put an end to her suffering. He placed her in the cab of his truck and ran a hose from the exhaust pipe to the cab. Tracy died of carbon monoxide inhalation.

Latimer was first found guilty of unpremeditated murder and sentenced to life in prison with no chance of parole for ten years. In 1997, the Supreme Court ordered a new trial because of irregularities in jury selection. During the second trial, the jury once again found him guilty of unpremeditated murder but recommended that he become eligible for parole after one year. The judge granted Latimer a constitutional exemption from the mandatory life sentence, giving him one year in prison and a year of probation to be served on his farm. The Saskatchewan Court of Appeal, however, upheld the mandatory life sentence with no parole eligibility for ten years.

In January 2001, the Supreme Court upheld the decision by the Court of Appeal. In its opinion, nothing justified a constitutional exemption. A life sentence was not disproportionate in view of the crime committed. But in the conclusion of its decision, the Supreme Court pointed out that the government's royal prerogative of mercy was available. The ruling received extensive coverage. The next day, Friday, 19 January, the *Globe and Mail* devoted two pages to the case and the *National Post* four. Beneath a large photo of a "visibly upset" Robert Latimer, who had just learned of the decision, the *Toronto Sun* announced in its pull-no-punches style: "Decade in jail for killer dad" (Rubec 2001a). In an editorial titled "Mercy," the *Toronto Sun* (2001a) said it understood and respected the Supreme Court's decision because Latimer had been found guilty of murder. But the editorial writer reminded readers that the *Sun* had always advocated compassion in his case and hoped that he would receive a royal pardon after a few months in prison: "We call on the federal cabinet to extend the royal prerogative of mercy to Latimer after a short period of incarceration – a few months in prison. Enough."

This heart-rending case transcended the language barrier. Montreal's *La Presse* published nineteen articles on it (see Table 1.7), accounting for 17.3 percent of the newspaper's coverage of the court during the year. As with the *Sharpe* case, the French-language newspapers prepared their readers for the ruling. The decision was to be announced on 18 January. On the preceding Saturday, *La Presse* and *Le Devoir* published a Canadian Press article, translated and transmitted by the Presse canadienne, which summarized the case and pointed out that the Supreme Court would decide the Saskatchewan farmer's fate the following Thursday. The reporter, Sue Bailey, wrote that the decision would put an end to the debate over the sentence to be imposed on Latimer (Presse canadienne 2001b). On the Thursday, *Le Devoir* once again told its readers that Latimer would learn his fate that day. Hélène Buzzetti (2001a) explained that the nature of the constitutional exemption that Latimer's lawyer was seeking arose from an interpretation of section 12 of the Canadian Charter of Rights: "Everyone has the right not to be subjected to any

**Table 1.7: Top ten: Newspapers**

| | Case | Le Devoir | La Presse | Le Journal de Montréal | Globe and Mail | National Post | Toronto Sun | Total (print) |
|---|---|---|---|---|---|---|---|---|
| 1. | Latimer | 10 | 19 | 5 | 14 | 14 | 9 | 71 |
| 2. | Sharpe | 9 | 7 | 5 | 10 | 14 | 6 | 51 |
| 3. | Burns-Rafay | 3 | 5 | 1 | 12 | 7 | 7 | 35 |
| 4. | Hudson | 7 | 8 | 3 | 4 | 8 | 3 | 33 |
| 5. | Boucher | 3 | 5 | 2 | 3 | 2 | 1 | 16 |
| 6. | Therrien | 4 | 3 | 3 | 1 | 3 | 1 | 15 |
| 7. | Asbestos | 3 | 2 | 3 | 4 | 2 | 0 | 14 |
| 8. | Little Sister's | 1 | 2 | 1 | 3 | 5 | 1 | 13 |
| 9. | Harper | 2 | 1 | 2 | 5 | 1 | 1 | 12 |
| 10. | Trinity Western | 1 | 0 | 0 | 5 | 4 | 2 | 12 |

cruel and unusual treatment or punishment." In the circumstances, a life sentence would be "cruel and unusual" punishment.

The day after the decision, the headline on page 1 of *Le Devoir* made it clear there was no mercy for Latimer (Buzzetti 2001b). The *Globe and Mail* used a similar head: "Latimer gets no mercy" (Makin 2001b). Kirk Makin wrote: "The Supreme Court of Canada showed no mercy to Robert Latimer yesterday, ruling unanimously that the Saskatchewan farmer must serve at least 10 years in prison for the murder of his severely disabled daughter." Generally, the English-language media took up the idea of mercy for a father whose tragic fate inspired compassion. Careful analysis of the *Globe and Mail,* the *National Post,* and the national newscasts of the CBC and CTV shows that coverage was mainly sympathetic toward Latimer. The media's emphasis had shifted from murder to mercy. The moral issue had been turned inside out: "suddenly, the focus was on the supposed blindness of the law [the mandatory sentence] and on the courts rather than on Latimer" (Klinkhammer and Taras 2001, 573).

But for the most part, this was not the case in the French press. "A murder" read the heading above Michel Venne's editorial in *Le Devoir* (Venne 2001). He wrote that the murder was the outcome of a tragic love story. Everyone understood that Latimer had acted out of compassion. Venne understood Latimer's motives but did not share them and wondered about the paradox he saw in the public's sympathetic

---

The *Latimer* case, in which a Saskatchewan farmer was charged with murdering his invalid ▶ daughter, transcended the language barrier and captured the interest of the Quebec news media. Pictured here is the treatment given the Supreme Court's decision by Montreal's *La Presse*. Note the front-page column by Yves Boisvert, entitled "Souffrance, droit et politique" (Pain, law, and politics). *Courtesy of La Presse*

# La Presse

cyberpresse.ca

Hockey, page S3

### Visage blanc culture noire
Cahier Actuel, page B1

### Monsieur Madonna
Cahier Cinéma, page C1

Guy Ritchie

MONTRÉAL | VENDREDI 19 JANVIER 2001 | LE PLUS GRAND QUOTIDIEN FRANÇAIS D'AMÉRIQUE | 117ᵉ ANNÉE • NO 98 • 60 PAGES • 6 CAHIERS    60 ¢ TAXES EN SUS | EST ET NORD-OUEST DU QUÉBEC • HULL-OTTAWA • 70¢ | FLORIDE 1,75 $ U.S.

## Clinton vole la vedette à Bush

### Il lui adresse des conseils en guise d'adieu

RICHARD HÉTU
collaboration spéciale

WASHINGTON — Bill Clinton et George W. Bush se sont disputé l'attention des Américains, hier, à deux jours du changement de garde à la Maison-Blanche.

À 20 h, lors d'une allocution télévisée, le président sortant a salué ses concitoyens une dernière fois. Il les remerciait de l'avoir élu à deux reprises et se félicitait des progrès économiques et sociaux réalisés sous son administration.

« Vous, le peuple américain, avez fait de notre passage à l'ère de l'information mondiale une période de renouveau américain », a déclaré Clinton, prononçant son dernier discours à titre de président depuis le bureau Ovale de la Maison-Blanche.

« Notre économie est forte, notre environnement est plus propre et notre monde est plus libre, plus sûr, plus prospère », a ajouté le président sortant.

Deux heures plus tôt, le successeur de Clinton s'était adressé à ses compatriotes à l'occasion d'un spectacle marquant l'ouverture officielle des cérémonies d'intronisation de sa présidence.

Prenant la parole sur les marches extérieures du Lincoln Memorial, Bush a promis aux Américains qu'il se conduirait de façon irréprochable au cours de sa présidence. Personne n'a raté l'allusion aux scandales des années Clinton.

« Je suis honoré de servir comme président et je suis prêt à commencer », a déclaré Bush à la fin d'un spectacle auquel ont participé, sous un ciel menaçant, plusieurs artistes et personnalités, dont Ricky Martin, Sylvester Stallone et Mohammed Ali.

« Je traiterai cette fonction avec respect, a ajouté Bush. Je ne la considérerai jamais comme acquise et je me souviendrai toujours à qui elle appartient. Elle appartient au peuple américain. »

En dépit de la fragilité de son mandat électoral, Bush s'est également engagé à apporter un « changement » et à une nouvelle direction à la tête du pays.

« C'est la promesse que j'ai faite et c'est une promesse que je tiendrai afin de donner à l'Amérique un nouveau départ », a-t-il dit.

*Voir CLINTON en A2*

| LA COUR SUPRÊME LUI REFUSE LA CLÉMENCE |

# Latimer se livre

La Cour suprême du Canada a statué que la peine de prison à vie imposée à Robert Latimer en 1997 pour le meurtre, en 1993, de sa fille Tracy, âgée de 12 ans, atteinte de paralysie cérébrale grave, n'était pas disproportionnée au regard du délit. Le fermier de Wilkie, en Saskatchewan, a répété hier que garder Tracy en vie aurait été barbare.

GILLES TOUPIN

OTTAWA — À l'unanimité, sept juges de la Cour suprême ont trouvé que la peine de prison à vie imposée à Robert Latimer en 1997 n'était pas disproportionnée au regard du délit commis, soit le meurtre de sa fille Tracy, âgée de 12 ans, qui souffrait d'une paralysie cérébrale grave.

Déjà amer et répétant qu'il n'avait aucun remords pour son crime, le fermier de Saskatchewan de 47 ans et père de trois autres enfants, qui célèbre depuis 1993 avoir tué sa fille par amour et compassion, s'est livré hier après-midi au Centre correctionnel provincial de Saskatoon après avoir dit au revoir à son épouse Laura.

Après toutes années de multiples procès et d'appels, une des affaires judiciaires les plus suivies au pays semble devoir s'achever sur le jugement, qualifié par plusieurs de « glacial », de la Cour suprême. Robert Latimer passera au minimum les dix prochaines années derrière les barreaux avant d'être admissible à une libération conditionnelle, à moins — chose rarissime — qu'il bénéficie de la prérogative de clémence royale prévue au Code criminel et même évoquée dans la décision d'hier.

Secoué, Latimer a estimé que le jugement du plus haut tribunal du pays allait à l'encontre du sentiment des Canadiens devant le geste qu'il a fait. Garder Tracy en vie aurait été barbare, a-t-il dit. « C'est prononcer la torture, a-t-il ajouté en parlant du jugement, la mutilation, l'alimentation par la force simplement pour qu'un pauvre petit enfant puisse survivre quelques jours de plus et endure davantage de tortures. C'est illogique. Est-ce que la justice ne devrait pas être logique? Pas aujourd'hui. Mais s'il ne s'agit pas de ce que le mot justice devrait signifier? »

L'avocat de Robert Latimer, Mark Brayford, n'a pas non plus caché son dépit devant le verdict unanime des juges McLachlin, L'Heureux-Dubé, Gonthier, Iacobucci, Major, Binnie et Arbour.

*Voir LATIMER en pages A3 et A6*
*Autres informations en pages A2*

cyberpresse.ca  Lisez le jugement intégral de la Cour suprême dans l'affaire Latimer et une chronologie des événements, vous saurez ce que vous en pensez.
www.cyberpresse.ca

## Souffrance, droit et politique

YVES BOISVERT

Il fallait une Cour suprême solide pour dire tout cela. Dire qu'un père, aussi bon soit-il, ne peut prendre la vie de sa fille, si misérable soit-elle. Qu'un meurtre est un meurtre. Dire aussi, à mots feutrés, qu'il y aurait de l'inhumanité à laisser croupir Robert Latimer en prison 10 ans. Dire enfin que cela relève du gouvernement, pas des tribunaux.

Robert Latimer a souffert autant qu'un père peut souffrir. Le 24 octobre 1993, il a décidé que ce serait le dernier jour de Tracy. Tracy: quatre mois dans sa tête, douze ans dans son corps, mille ans dans sa douleur. Tracy, immobile, que les médecins voulaient opérer jusqu'à la fin des temps, pour lui installer une sonde dans l'estomac, lui tailler les os, l'aider à respirer, le prétendre lui rendre la vie tolérable entre les cinq ou six crises d'épilepsie de tous les jours.

Il a choisi le jour. Sa femme était à la messe avec les autres enfants. Il y a un moment, quand il l'a attachée dans la camionnette pour l'asphyxier, où leurs yeux se sont croisés. « Le dernier jugement signé » la cour « était le Renvoi sur la sécession du Québec, en 1998.

Entre deux enfers sur terre, ce fermier de Saskatchewan a décidé de souffrir celui-là. Mais voilà, la souffrance ne donne pas de droits. Il fallait que la Cour le dise. Implacablement. Mais pas froidement.

« Il faisait face à des difficultés que la plupart des Canadiens ne peuvent qu'imaginer, écrit la cour. Le soin qu'il a pris de sa fille pen-

dant de nombreuses années était admirable. Sa décision de mettre fin aux jours de celle-ci a été une erreur de jugement. Enlever la vie d'une autre personne est le crime le plus grave en droit criminel. »

Un jugement signe solennellement « la cour » et endosse unanimement par les sept juges ayant entendu l'affaire. Le dernier jugement signé « la cour » était le Renvoi sur la sécession du Québec, en 1998.

Ce n'est pas innocent: le plus haut tribunal au Canada, souvent divisé sur les questions délicates, a parlé solennellement d'une seule voix, qui aurait tout aussi bien pu être celle des juges libéraux ou celle des juges conservateurs. Pour dire les limites de la compassion et celles du droit. Et pour une fois, très bien choisie, renvoyer le ballon au Parlement.

*Voir SOUFFRANCE en A2*

## C'est un industriel à la carrière fort mouvementée qui convoite le Canadien

ALEXANDRE PRATT

UN HOMME D'AFFAIRES du Colorado à la carrière fort mouvementée, George Gillett Jr., se trouve à Montréal pour discuter de la vente du Canadien et du Centre Molson avec les Brasseries Molson, a appris La Presse hier.

M. Gillett, qui séjourne dans un hôtel du centre-ville, cherche depuis deux ans à acheter une équipe de sport professionnel. Il a tenté sans succès, en 1999, de s'emparer des partenaires pour mettre la main sur l'Avalanche du Colorado (LNH), les Nuggets de Denver (NBA) et leur aréna, le Pepsi Center. Il s'est également rendu à Miami, en décembre dernier, pour rencontrer les dirigeants des Panthers de la Floride, une autre équipe de la LNH qui cherche un acheteur.

Un informateur américain qui a déjà brassé des affaires avec George Gillett soutient que ce dernier est sérieux dans son intention d'acheter le Canadien et le Centre Molson. « C'est un passionné de sport qui n'hésite pas à mettre le gros prix pour obtenir ce qu'il

veut », indique notre source. M. Gillett avait d'ailleurs déclaré faillite, en 1991, après avoir acheté plusieurs stations de télévision trop au-delà de prix du marché. Il espérait un boom économique, mais il s'est buté à la récession. « Il a tout perdu: ses réseaux de télévision, sa station de ski à Vail, son jet privé et sa compagnie de viande dans le Midwest avec laquelle il a fait fortune », raconte notre informateur.

M. Gillett ne nous a pas rappelé hier. Une entreprise privée et il ne commente pas ses transactions d'affaires », a déclaré sa porte-parole, Pat Peeples. Elle a également refusé de dévoiler les raisons de la présence de son client à Montréal.

De son côté, la direction de Molson nie depuis mardi toutes les rumeurs de vente du Canadien et du Centre Molson à des intérêts américains.

*Voir INDUSTRIEL en page S2*
*Autres informations en page S2*

George Gillett, en 1990, alors propriétaire de la station de ski de Vail, au Colorado.

AUJOURD'HUI DANS LA PRESSE

| | | | |
|---|---|---|---|
| Arts et spectacles | C7-C8 | Loteries | A2, E3 |
| - télévision | B7 | Monde | A7 |
| Bandes dessinées | D12 | Mots croisés | D10, S10 |
| Bridge | D12 | Mot mystère | D10 |
| Décès | E4 | Petites annonces | E4 |
| Éditorial | B8-B9 | - marchandises | E4, E5 |
| Êtes-vous... | A6 | - emploi | E6 |
| observateur? | | - automobile | E5-E7 |
| Feuilleton | A10 | - affaires | E2 |
| Forum | A9 | Politique | A4-A6 |
| Horoscope | D10 | | |

MÉTÉO    Voir S14

Neige
Maximum -1 minimum -15

6  21924  98765  1

**Table 1.8: Top ten: Television**

|  |  | CTV | CBC | TVA | Radio-Canada | Total |
|---|---|---|---|---|---|---|
| 1. | Latimer | 10 | 5 | 2 | 3 | 20 |
| 2. | Burns-Rafay | 2 | 4 | 1 | 1 | 8 |
| 3. | Hudson | 3 | 2 | 1 | 1 | 7 |
| 4. | Van de Perre | 2 | 5 | 0 | 0 | 7 |
| 5. | Boucher | 0 | 1 | 3 | 1 | 5 |
| 6. | Sharpe | 1 | 2 | 1 | 1 | 5 |
| 7. | Harper | 1 | 3 | 0 | 0 | 4 |
| 8. | Red Cross | 1 | 1 | 1 | 1 | 4 |
| 9. | Little Sister's | 1 | 1 | 0 | 0 | 2 |
| 10. | Therrien | 0 | 0 | 1 | 1 | 2 |

reaction to Latimer. He asked what logic people had used to conclude that someone who loves is also someone who is entitled to kill.

*La Presse* editorial writer André Pratte (2001a) asked whether the judges were made of ice. In his opinion, they were not, but they had a duty not to be swayed by emotion. The courts, especially the Supreme Court, must render justice based on reason. Justice of the heart would inevitably get out of hand.

The editorial writers of the *Globe and Mail* (2001a) and the *National Post* (2001a) also welcomed the decision, but the English-language coverage seemed more inclined to leniency. The many interviews that Latimer's wife Laura gave to the English-language media no doubt contributed to the image of a compassionate man and a devoted father. The absence of French-speaking journalists in Saskatchewan[4] to provide coverage of Mrs. Latimer's touching comments and the strong support that the family enjoyed in the community may explain why the French media were in general so clearly in favour of the decision, although their coverage also conveyed compassion and often hoped for mercy.

The *Latimer* case represented 20.8 percent of total TV coverage of the Supreme Court during the year (14.7 percent CBC, 13.3 percent TVA, 20 percent Radio-Canada, and 31.3 percent CTV). Ten of CTV's thirty-two reports on the court concerned the *Latimer* case, which provided what television thrives on above all: emotion (see Table 1.8).

Another case, heard by the court in June 2001, also illustrates the close links between television and emotions, personalities and images. The case concerned custody of a child born of an affair between a black basketball star, who was married and already had two daughters, and Kimberly Van de Perre, a young white former beauty queen living in Vancouver. Theodore ("Blue") Edwards, the American basketball player and former member of the Vancouver Grizzlies, lived in North Carolina with his family.

The judge of the court of first instance did not deem race to be a determining factor when he awarded custody to the mother. But race was a factor at the Court of Appeal, where the court favoured Edwards and his wife, who were seeking joint custody. The father argued that his son had to be reared with his black family, so that he could learn about his racial origins. The interracial aspect was central to the coverage of the Supreme Court hearing. English-language television devoted seven reports to the story, which had almost come to resemble a soap opera.[5]

Table 1.8 shows that only a handful of the cases handled by the court received television coverage. The far smaller amount of news broadcast by television, compared with the number of articles published on the court by newspapers, obviously results in coverage that is not as broad or varied. Two-thirds (sixty-four) of the ninety-six reports broadcast by the four networks were devoted to ten cases: eight formal decisions, Maurice Boucher's appeal, and the hearing of *Van de Perre v. Edwards*.

In contrast, a case involving the minority shareholders of Asbestos Corporation, although the subject of fourteen newspaper articles (eight in French and six in English), was ignored by television, at least by the national newscasts. The case involved a complex business matter. And it is well known that business news does not lend itself well to television coverage. In 1977, the Quebec government decided to take over Asbestos Corporation. About 30 percent of the company's common shares were held by minority shareholders living in Ontario, with control held by General Dynamics Canada, a subsidiary of an American firm. In 1981, the Quebec government and the American parent company concluded an agreement, and Quebec announced it did not intend to make a follow-up offer to the minority shareholders. For twenty years they had been trying to redeem their shares at the price received by General Dynamics.

The minority shareholders turned to several authorities, including the Ontario Securities Commission (OSC). While recognizing that the minority shareholders had been treated in an "abusive" manner by the Quebec government, the commission concluded that its mandate to protect Ontario's financial markets did not call for intervention in this instance. The Supreme Court held that it was reasonable for the OSC to refuse to intervene. In the newspapers, business columnists commented at length on the decision, but television completely ignored it.

## The Two Solitudes of Supreme Court Reporting

Only a small number of cases transcend geographic, linguistic, or cultural barriers. The coverage of the Supreme Court is reminiscent of the comment often made about coverage of Canadian politics in general – that there are "two solitudes." What interests the English-language media does not necessarily interest the French media, and vice versa. One of the most heavily covered cases of the year,

**Table 1.9: Difference in coverage between English- and French-language media (number of articles and reports)**

| Case | French | English | Total | Difference (English-French) |
|---|---|---|---|---|
| Burns-Rafay | 11 | 32 | 43 | + 21 E (49%) |
| Latimer | 39 | 52 | 91 | + 13 E (14%) |
| Van de Perre | 0 | 12 | 12 | + 12 E (100%) |
| Trinity Western | 1 | 12 | 13 | + 11 E (85%) |
| Sharpe | 23 | 33 | 56 | + 10 E (18%) |
| Bernson | 2 | 10 | 12 | + 8 E (67%) |
| Protestant schools | 8 | 0 | 8 | + 8 F (100%) |
| Starr | 1 | 9 | 10 | + 8 E (80%) |
| Boucher | 14 | 7 | 21 | + 7 F (33%) |
| Little Sister's | 4 | 11 | 15 | + 7 E (47%) |
| Therrien | 12 | 5 | 17 | + 7 F (41%) |
| Harper | 5 | 11 | 16 | + 6 E (38%) |
| Musqueam | 0 | 5 | 5 | + 5 E (100%) |
| Ville Sept-Îles | 5 | 0 | 5 | + 5 F (100%) |
| Suresh | 2 | 7 | 9 | + 5 E (56%) |

number three on our top ten list (see Table 1.6), the *Burns-Rafay* case, illustrates this phenomenon.

The court had to rule on the extradition of two young Canadians, from British Columbia, accused in the United States of having murdered Rafay's parents and sister in order to collect an insurance policy. The two young men were arrested in British Columbia and jailed in Vancouver. Allan Rock, who was then justice minister, signed an unconditional extradition order. Under a treaty between the two countries, he was entitled to seek a guarantee that a Canadian extradited to the United States would not face the death penalty. The Supreme Court had to rule on the validity of Rock's decision to extradite the two men without having obtained assurances from the United States that they would not be executed if found guilty. The nine judges ruled that without such guarantees extradition would infringe the Canadian Charter of Rights and Freedoms. The decision sparked considerable controversy in English Canada and heated debate in the House of Commons.

Thirty-two of the forty-three articles and reports surveyed regarding this case were published or broadcast by English-language media (see Table 1.9). The *Globe and Mail* and the *Toronto Sun* published more articles on this subject than on the *Sharpe* case. The CBC aired four reports on the case, CTV two. The court's decision was a page 1 story in both the *Globe and Mail* and the *National Post*. Each published two editorials on the decision. They also reported on how the ruling might affect the deportation of refugees and the extradition of presumed terrorists (Alphonso 2001; Bell 2001; Gatehouse 2001; Makin 2001c).

The opposition Canadian Alliance Party saw it as a political decision "that put out the welcome mat for foreign killers to flock to Canada" (Dunn 2001). Toronto's police chief said that Canada had become a paradise for "international criminals" and that the court's decision "only strengthens the view this country is a refuge" (Godfrey 2001). The *Globe and Mail* also reported reactions gathered in the suburb of Seattle, Washington, where the murders were committed (Alphonso 2001) and published a piece by Neil Seeman, a Canadian lawyer who was then a member of the editorial staff of the *National Review* in New York. Seeman's view (2001) was that "by blocking extradition of two accused killers, Canada's Supreme Court has insulted U.S. courts and the will of U.S. voters."

Montreal's French-language newspapers carried no such coverage. *Le Devoir* published a detailed report on the decision on its front page under the byline of Manon Cornellier, one of its Ottawa correspondents, with a heading that stated that the Supreme Court saw the death penalty as unjust (Cornellier 2001). But *La Presse* only published a two-column Presse canadienne summary of a translation of a much longer and complete piece by Canadian Press journalist Sue Bailey (Bailey 2001b). The French summary (Bailey 2001c) provided little context. It appeared on page A5. As for *Le Journal de Montréal,* it published four short paragraphs from the same Presse canadienne report in its *Politique en bref* section (Presse canadienne 2001c). Here is everything that readers of *Le Journal de Montréal* learned about this case, which created controversy for several days in English Canada and which some perceived as one of the court's major rulings in recent years (Guillemard and Saint-Hilaire 2002) [translation]:

> OTTAWA (CP) – The Supreme Court ruled yesterday that two Canadians accused of murder in the United States cannot be extradited if Canada does not first obtain assurance they will not face the death penalty.
>
> The country's top court hinged its ruling on fundamental constitutional values and the right to liberty and security.
>
> The judgment means Canada's justice minister must seek assurances that Canadians – and others – to be extradited to face trials won't be executed if convicted in countries using the death penalty.
>
> Atif Rafay and Glen Sebastian Burns are wanted in the United States for the slayings of Rafay's father, mother and, sister. All three were found beaten to death in their Bellevue, Wash., home on July 12, 1994.

Well aware of the importance of the decision, which overturned the court's previous jurisprudence, columnist Yves Boisvert returned to it on the following Monday under the headline "A requiem for hangmen" (Boisvert 2001). He wrote that to render justice was sometimes to make history, and that some decisions were milestones in the life of a democracy. Fine. But the French-language press said almost nothing about the reaction in the United States or the controversy caused by the decision in English Canada. In *La Presse,* as in *Le Devoir,* a short review of the English-language press noted the extensive coverage of this Supreme Court ruling (Lortie 2001), which had created a considerable stir in the rest of Canada (Robitaille 2001).

We found many examples of decisions, such as the *Burns-Rafay* case, where there was a pronounced difference between the English- and French-language media in terms of which cases were reported on and the volume and scope of coverage. Table 1.9 gives all cases, regardless of their status before the court, that show a difference of five stories or more, for newspapers and television combined. The *Van de Perre* case is the most striking example. The hearing of this case generated twelve articles and reports in the English-language media, including seven TV reports, but the French media did not cover it. And yet the story of the young woman and the sports star fighting over custody of their child was of universal interest. But although the beauty queen and the basketball star were celebrities in Vancouver, they were unknown in Quebec.

The *Trinity Western University* case shows the same disparity. Eleven articles were published in the English-language press and there was one TV report. In the French-language press, the case got only a brief mention in *Le Devoir* (Nadeau 2000a). Again the case came from distant British Columbia. As mentioned earlier, the British Columbia College of Teachers refused to accredit the teacher-training programs offered by this private university, which is linked to the Evangelical Free Church and obliged members of the academic community to abide by a code of conduct deemed discriminatory. The Supreme Court ruled in favour of Trinity Western.

But the intersection of religion and education is of interest to Quebec media when it has a local and linguistic impact. The case brought by a group of French-speaking Protestant parents who wanted to preserve the system of Protestant schools and were seeking a stay until they had been heard received coverage in the French-language media. The parents were contesting various amendments to the *Education Act* intended to deconfessionalize Quebec's school system. Eight Presse canadienne articles were published from the end of July to the end of August. None of the English-language media reported the case.

High-profile lawyer Guy Bertrand, who acted for the parents, helped attract attention to the case. Indeed, the controversial and flamboyant Bertrand has a habit of becoming the news as soon as he becomes involved in a case. The heading of the news brief in *Le Journal de Montréal* on 26 July announced that Guy Bertrand wanted to maintain Protestant schools (Presse canadienne 2001f). On 20 August, *Le Devoir* and *La Presse* published a Presse canadienne report that reminded readers that the Supreme Court would consider the matter that day, but without hearing the lawyers (Parent 2001a, 2001b). The reporter added that Bertrand would not have to go to Ottawa. Ten days later, the court rendered its decision. It would not hear the case. There would be no stay. The Protestant students would have to attend a secular school in the fall.

The Franco-Protestants' cause was not completely lost, however, since in October the Court of Appeal would hear arguments on the constitutionality of the government's policy. Bertrand, disappointed by the turn of events, pointed out that if the parents won in the fall, the government would have to reopen the schools, whereas it would have been simple to merely postpone the closure for another year (Rodrigue 2001).

Other examples are the *Therrien* and *Little Sisters* cases. The French-language press published only four short articles (the same Presse canadienne text) and nothing was broadcast on television about Little Sister's, the Vancouver bookstore whose materials, intended for a gay and lesbian clientele and imported from the United States, were frequently held up or confiscated by Canada Customs. The Supreme Court concluded that the definition of obscenity had to apply without distinction to homosexual and heterosexual erotic materials. The freedom of expression guaranteed by the Charter and Little Sister's right to equality before the law had been abrogated by customs procedures. Because the bookstore imported gay and lesbian materials, it was treated differently from other stores importing publications of a heterosexual nature. It was not the customs legislation but its application by Canada Customs that was deemed to be a source of discrimination and an infringement on freedom of expression.

The *National Post* devoted an entire page (three articles) to the decision, an editorial, titled "Tolerant Canada, intolerant Customs" (2000), and a wry column by Andrew Coyne (2000). The *Globe and Mail* gave the decision front-page coverage and also published an editorial. Why were the French-language media so unconcerned? The decision, involving fundamental rights, was as important in Quebec as it was in the rest of Canada. But Little Sister's bookstore is in Vancouver. Presumably, the French-language media regarded the case as a regional matter of interest to British Columbia but not to Quebec.

The fate of Judge Richard Therrien, however, interested the French-language press far more. In 1971, Therrien was sentenced to one year in prison for having sheltered members of the Front de libération du Québec (FLQ) during the October Crisis of 1970. After serving his sentence, he continued his legal studies and

---

THE GLOBE AND MAIL • FRIDAY, JUNE 8, 2001

**News** A3

# Court approves judge's removal

## Panel says Therrien's pardon over FLQ affair does not supersede judicial integrity

BY KIRK MAKIN
JUSTICE REPORTER

Thirty years after he harboured four FLQ terrorists who had abducted and killed Quebec cabinet minister Pierre Laporte, Richard Therrien's past has haunted him right off the Quebec Court bench.

In approving his removal yesterday, the Supreme Court of Canada said the integrity of the judiciary must take precedence over the humanitarian generosity that underlies a criminal pardon.

"The issue of confidence governs every aspect of this case — and ultimately dictates the result," Mr. Justice Charles Gonthier wrote for a 7-0 majority. "The appellant's conduct has sufficiently undermined public confidence that he is incapable of performing the duties of his office."

The case represents the first time the Supreme Court has had to deal with the extraordinarily delicate job of removing a sitting judge. The court noted that judges occupy a unique position of trust over the lives and liberty of the vulnerable citizens who appear before them.

"The judicial function is absolutely unique," the court said. "The judge is the pillar of our entire justice system, and of the rights and freedoms which that system is designed to promote and protect.

"The public will demand virtually irreproachable conduct from anyone performing a judicial function. What is demanded of them is something far above what is demanded from their fellow citizens."

Mr. Therrien, a 19-year-old law student at the time his sister hid the four FLQ terrorists in the Montreal apartment he shared with her, was ultimately sentenced to a year in jail under the War Measures Act. He was pardoned in 1987.

After failing in several attempts to become a judge, Mr. Therrien purposely omitted any reference to his conviction and pardon when he applied in 1996. He got the appointment.

Within weeks, the Quebec Judicial Council learned of his omission and recommended his removal. Its decision was upheld in 1998 by the Quebec Court of Appeal.

Mr. Therrien has insisted throughout that the purpose of a pardon is to erase an offence once the offender has paid for his actions and rehabilitated himself.

The court agreed with that proposition yesterday, acknowledging that the case was an unprecedented opportunity for it to show generosity and brotherhood. However, it said that while a pardon eliminates

**'The public will demand virtually irreproachable conduct from anyone performing a judicial function.'**

future consequences, it cannot simply erase the past.

Patrick Monahan, a law professor at York University's Osgoode Hall Law School in Toronto, said yesterday that the ruling affirms both the importance of judicial impartiality and the need for judges to be scrupulously frank.

"There was a certain Clintonesque quality to his [Mr. Therrien's] concept that: 'In my own mind, I believed I was telling the truth because I viewed the procedure as expunging my conviction,'" Prof. Monahan said. "In this case, the

point wasn't so much his conviction, as the fact that he hid it."

The four notorious FLQ fugitives — Jacques Rose, Paul Rose, Francis Simard and Bernard Lortie — lived in the Therrien apartment in Montreal for three weeks commencing on Oct. 17, 1970. Mr. Laporte's body was found in the trunk of a car the same day.

Since he was not an FLQ member, Mr. Therrien steered clear of the apartment for much of the three weeks. He did help the fugitives by obtaining materials for them to build a hideout and by mailing three letters for them.

The procedure for removing him from the bench involved a recommendation from Quebec's judicial council to the federal Minister of Justice. The minister accepted the recommendation, and asked the Quebec Court of Appeal to put its seal of approval on the decision.

Simultaneously, Mr. Therrien launched an application to have the removal procedure declared unconstitutional.

The main questions facing the Supreme Court involved whether Mr. Therrien was given a fair and impartial hearing, and whether he had been truly obliged to volunteer the information about his pardon. It gave a firm yes on both counts.

Richard Therrien, pictured here in 1971, was jailed 30 years ago for helping four FLQ terrorists.

CANADIAN PRESS

Richard Therrien lost his job as a Quebec judge yesterday when the Supreme Court ruled that omitting his conviction for aiding FLQ terrorists on his application was enough to undermine public confidence that he could do his duties. The FLQ abducted and killed Pierre Laporte, top right, and abducted James Cross, right.

CANADIAN PRESS

The body of Quebec labour minister Pierre Laporte was found in the trunk of a car at an airport near Montreal on Oct. 17, 1970, one week after he was kidnapped by FLQ terrorists.

---

Although French-language newspapers took greater interest in it, the *Therrien* case was not neglected by the English media. The *Globe and Mail* devoted a half-page to the court's decision regarding Judge Therrien's removal for failing to disclose his conviction and subsequent pardon for having sheltered members of the FLQ in late 1970. The photos focus on the October Crisis, even including a shot of the car trunk where the body of Pierre Laporte was found – despite the fact that the decision had dealt only with the judge's failure to report his conviction. *Courtesy of the Globe and Mail*

became a lawyer. In 1987, he obtained a pardon from the Governor-in-Council. From 1989 to 1996, he submitted his candidacy for judicial appointments on five occasions. In 1991 and 1993, he disclosed his conviction and pardon. His candidacy was rejected. When in 1996 he made no mention of his conviction or pardon, he was appointed a judge of the Court of Quebec. His record was later made public and, after an inquiry, Quebec's Conseil de la magistrature recommended that removal procedures be initiated against Judge Therrien. In 1998, the Quebec Court of Appeal recommended removal. In June 2001, the Supreme Court upheld the decision by the Court of Appeal.

**Table 1.10: Journalism categories (%): Newspapers**

| Type | Le Devoir | La Presse | Le Journal de Montréal | Globe and Mail | National Post | Toronto Sun | Total |
|---|---|---|---|---|---|---|---|
| News | 46.7 | 68.2 | 64.2 | 66.2 | 73.8 | 70.6 | 65.9 |
| Editorials | 4.4 | 8.2 | 0.0 | 12.4 | 9.3 | 5.9 | 8.1 |
| Analyses | 0.0 | 0.9 | 0.0 | 1.4 | 0.0 | 0.0 | 0.5 |
| Columns, opinions, commentary | 20.0 | 10.9 | 1.9 | 15.2 | 8.1 | 21.6 | 12.9 |
| Excerpts from decisions | 0.0 | 1.8 | 0.0 | 1.4 | 1.7 | 0.0 | 1.1 |
| Briefs | 22.2 | 1.8 | 30.2 | 2.8 | 2.3 | 2.0 | 7.3 |
| Features | 4.4 | 3.6 | 3.8 | 0.7 | 2.9 | 0.0 | 2.5 |
| Other | 2.2 | 4.5 | 0.0 | 0.0 | 1.7 | 0.0 | 1.6 |
| **Total   %** | **100** | **100** | **100** | **100** | **100** | **100** | **100** |
| **No.** | **90** | **110** | **53** | **145** | **172** | **51** | **621** |

*Note:* Due to rounding, percentages do not add up to 100.

French-language newspapers published ten articles on the hearing and the decision, the English-language press five. But a closer look shows that the English-language newspapers did not neglect the story. The *Globe and Mail* devoted half a page to it, with two photos of Richard Therrien, one recent, the other taken in 1971 when he was involved with the FLQ. The article also featured photos of Pierre Laporte, the cabinet minister assassinated in 1970, and of James Richard Cross, the British trade commissioner kidnapped during the October Crisis (Makin 2001d). Astonishingly, if one considers the importance of the case in Quebec, the French-language press published Presse canadienne reports almost exclusively when the case was heard in October as well as when the decision was rendered in June.

This leads us to another noteworthy difference between the English and French newspapers that we analyzed. The French-language newspapers tend to rely more often on the Presse canadienne, as we have seen several times. While our data show that almost a quarter (23.4 percent) of the articles published by the six newspapers we analyzed were stories from the news agency, 80 percent of these reports appeared in French-language newspapers. Most of the articles published by *Le Journal de Montréal* were from the Presse canadienne (thirty-nine out of fifty-three). *Le Devoir* and *La Presse* used the agency almost as much as they did their own journalists. The Canadian Press is rarely used by the *Globe and Mail* and the *National Post,* which were the only news organizations that had journalists covering the court on a regular basis during the period we analyzed.

A content analysis of regional English-language newspapers would no doubt show an equal reliance on Canadian Press wire stories. The agency therefore has a special responsibility as regards the Supreme Court. Jules Richer, who covered the court from 1995 to 2000 as the parliamentary correspondent for the Presse canadienne in Ottawa, was well aware of his role. He said that, as a Presse canadienne journalist, he considered himself the eyes and ears of Quebec newspapers. He knew *La Presse* or *Le Journal de Montréal* would assign a reporter to cover major rulings, but he also knew it was important that he take care of routine coverage (Richer 2003).

We also did a breakdown of the journalistic categories (news, editorials, columns, and so on) used by the various newspapers. In this respect, some of the figures in Table 1.10 are astounding, such as the large percentage of "news briefs" published by *Le Devoir*. The coverage of the Supreme Court and its decisions by the venerable Montreal daily is often similar to that of the tabloid *Le Journal de Montréal*: it relies on Presse canadienne news briefs. The English-language newspapers in our group, as well as *La Presse,* publish few briefs. Although *Le Devoir* leaves routine coverage of the court to the Presse canadienne, it often gives front-page coverage to decisions it considers important. *Le Devoir* also published far more columns and other opinion pieces than the other French-language newspapers. Regular columns by Alain-Robert Nadeau were a case in point.[6]

In English, the high percentage of commentary and editorials published by the *Globe and Mail* were to be expected. Still, some would have thought that opinion in all its forms would be more in evidence in the *National Post*. But this represented slightly more than 17 percent of the articles. The fact that during the year the *Toronto Sun* published a higher percentage of columns than any other newspaper will come as no surprise to the tabloid's regular readers, who are well aware that columns – and the controversy they create – are one of its trademarks. The *Toronto Sun* publishes almost no news briefs concerning the court. It covers very few cases, but when it does take an interest, it can get deeply involved. More than 40 percent of the articles published by the *Sun* during the year dealt with only three decisions: *Latimer, Sharpe,* and *Burns-Rafay*.

## Covering the Supreme Court as an Institution

The coverage of the life of the court, beyond the decisions that it rendered, illustrates the differences between the English- and French-language newspapers even more clearly. We have already noted that the media take a limited interest in the court as an institution, the French-language media even less so. The following examples are telling.

The court celebrated its 125th anniversary in September 2000. A symposium that attracted "an array of distinguished speakers" (the expression used by Chief

Justice Beverley McLachlin) was held to mark the event under the theme "The Supreme Court: Its legacy and its challenges." But no one really covered the event. For instance, the *Globe and Mail* briefly reported the statement of a law professor who deemed the court's approach to the Charter of Rights incoherent (Makin 2000a). To be fair, the media stopped covering most conferences of any kind long ago. Still, the two major English-language newspapers marked the anniversary in their own ways. In a lengthy article published on 16 September in the *Globe and Mail,* Kirk Makin (2000b) assessed the path the court had taken, especially in the past twenty-five years, and pondered the future. He wrote that the court had "far more clout" in the business of the country than its creators ever intended. He reminded readers of the recent debate over judicial activism and forecast the cases that would attract attention in the ensuing months:

> a body, run by a woman, that routinely makes rulings with a profound impact on virtually every aspect of Canadian life and is now so powerful that it stands accused of overshadowing the nation's elected representatives.
>
> In the coming months, the Court will decide cases dealing with such fundamental, politically charged issues as mercy-killing, child pornography and whether Canadians can be sent to face execution in another country.

Makin even predicted the order of the three cases – *Latimer, Sharpe,* and *Burns-Rafay* – that the media would give the most coverage to in the following months.

The *National Post* had published a special section on the 125th anniversary of the court earlier in the year. But on 28 September, in the *Post,* Luiza Chwialkowska took advantage of the presence of the US Supreme Court justice Ruth Bader Ginsburg at the anniversary symposium held by the court to draw a parallel between the two courts by painting appealing, personal portraits of Judge Ginsburg and her colleague and friend Madam Justice Claire L'Heureux-Dubé, two women whose careers and lives have not always been easy in a world dominated by men. One of only nine women enrolled at Harvard Law School in the 1950s, Judge Ginsburg "was asked by the law dean to justify why women should be allowed to occupy seats that could otherwise go to men" (Chwialkowska 2000b). She has been accused of "making up the law" by her more conservative critics (ibid.). As for Judge L'Heureux-Dubé, she has repeatedly come under attack in recent years for her efforts – her opponents would say crusades – in favour of equality. These attacks have always made headlines, especially in the *National Post.*

Luiza Chwialkowska (2000b) wrote that "the women's work in court sheds light on the divergent legal philosophies in Canada and the United States." The American Bill of Rights speaks of "equal protection" when it comes to gender and race, the Canadian Charter of "equal protection and equal benefit without discrimination."

According to Chwialkowska, "That difference, Canadian feminists say, allows their heroine Judge L'Heureux-Dubé more scope to pursue 'substantive' rather than just 'formal' equality." But a woman who was a heroine to some was guilty of activism in the eyes of others.

The French-language press barely mentioned the court's 125th anniversary. *Le Devoir* columnist Alain-Robert Nadeau referred to the symposium held to mark the event twice but did not go into detail. In one column, he reviewed the cases that would be heard during the 125th session (Nadeau 2000a). In another, he discussed the convergence of law and legal systems, and publicized a forthcoming conference at the University of Ottawa (Nadeau 2000b). There was not a word about the court's milestone and, more important, what it had become in the life of the country, in *La Presse, Le Journal de Montréal,* or the *Toronto Sun*. And, of course, there was nothing on television.

Let's take another, even more compelling, example. On 13 January 2001, the *National Post* published under the heading "Supreme Court goes 'too far': Judge," a piece by Cristin Schmitz, a freelance journalist contributing to the *Lawyers Weekly*. Schmitz reported on controversial comments that Mr. Justice Michel Bastarache made in a long interview for the *Lawyers Weekly*. She referred to the interview as "candid."

Judge Bastarache explained that when it came to deciding whether legislation complied with the Charter of Rights, he favoured a more deferential attitude toward Parliament than did some of his colleagues: "'I think that legal principle is distinct from legal policy, and that policy is for Parliament and principle is for the courts,' he said, adding that it's not always easy to distinguish between the two. 'I don't think that we have a mandate to sort of define a whole social policy for Canada,' he said, referring to the Supreme Court's role as guardian of the Constitution" (Schmitz 2001a).

The judge's statements are consistent with the stance taken many times by the *National Post* since it began its campaign against judicial activism. So it's not surprising that the newspaper gave them considerable play. But the interview in and of itself remains important. Two days later, the *National Post* published another piece by Cristin Schmitz based on the same interview. Schmitz (2001b) writes: "The Supreme Court of Canada is not the best forum for resolving disputes over aboriginal land claims and other 'ill-defined' native rights, says Justice Michel Bastarache, who argues such politically complex conflicts are better settled by negotiation." Justice Bastarache also said, in what the journalist called "an exceptionally frank interview," that he disagreed with the court's decision (in which he did not take part) in the 1999 *Marshall* case on Native fishing rights (see Chapter 4).

Judge Bastarache's words sparked controversy in English Canada, including complaints to the Canadian Judicial Council. For instance, the Atlantic Policy

Congress of First Nations Chiefs believed that his "bias" made him incapable of rendering fair decisions involving Natives. The complaints were rejected (the Judicial Council deemed the judge's motives "laudable"), but just the same, the Council's letter urged caution: "It is clearly preferable for judges to exercise restraint when speaking publicly" (Mofina 2001). Although the controversy was spearheaded by the *National Post,* the *Globe and Mail* also weighed in with an editorial, titled "What a judge may say," asserting that the judge had "crossed the line between openness and inappropriate commentary ... It is not helpful for a judge to criticize the work of his colleagues in public, and there is a risk in declaring strong positions on policy matters that will almost surely come before the court again" (*Globe and Mail* 2001b).

We did not find a single line about this controversy in the French-language press. The omission is difficult to explain.

We can cite other examples of coverage requiring research and time, which the French press does not devote to the court. In January 2001, the *National Post* published an in-depth three-page article by reporter Luiza Chwialkowska (2001a). She analyzed the court's decisions during the previous year, looked at majority and dissenting opinions, and concluded that the "new" court led by Beverley McLachlin was difficult to label and was now exempt from accusations of activism since it was no longer overturning laws. It was, in contrast to the United States, difficult to identify "conservative" and "liberal" judges.

According to Chwialkowska, the court had maintained a high level of unanimity during the year: "With two new judges [Louise Arbour and Louis LeBel] and a new Chief Justice, the revamped Supreme Court of Canada has emerged from its first year of decision-making without striking down a single law." Chwialkowska asked whether the new judges, who arrived since 1999, had been "bucking the trend," which one analyst had summarized as follows: "It's conservative on criminals and liberal on social policy."

On 27 August, reviewing the major cases that the court was to hear in the fall of 2001, Janice Tibbetts of Southam News also described how the court might be changing: "The verdicts in these cases will test the assertion by some court analysts that the nine-member bench is becoming more socially conservative under the stewardship of Chief Justice Beverley McLachlin" (Tibbetts 2001b). Ever interested in the life of the court, the *National Post* published along with Tibbetts's article a photo of the judges in their ermine-trimmed robes under the heading: "Has our highest court become socially conservative?" No such overview of the court and its work can be found in the French-language press.

Similarly, the French-language press never paid the same attention to the accusations of judicial activism levelled at the Supreme Court in English Canada, especially by the Canadian Alliance Party. *La Presse* and *Le Journal de Montréal* reported the outburst by former chief justice Antonio Lamer, who denounced the Alliance for its yapping, and said it should stop its improvised criticism of the judges (Presse canadienne 2001d). But the Presse canadienne article quoting Lamer was published without the context and perspective that would allow francophone readers to understand the debate surrounding the life of the court that was taking place in English Canada. The comments by the former chief justice made headlines in the *Post* on 14 April (Tibbetts 2001a), and the reaction from the Canadian Alliance Party filled a large portion of page A6 on 17 April (Greenaway 2001).

Finally, unlike the *Globe and Mail* and, of course, the *National Post,* the French-language newspapers did not say a word about the strong criticism levelled at the media by Judge L'Heureux-Dubé and Mr. Justice Ian Binnie at a conference in August 2001. Judge L'Heureux-Dubé explained that she had been "harmed" by the "savage" attacks on her by certain media in 1999:[7] "I would ask the people in the media to [tell] me what is productive in personal attacks against judges and the pressures that it puts on the judiciary, it is a sliding slope, an attack really, to independence of the judiciary" (Rubin 2001).

As for Judge Binnie, while acknowledging the work accomplished by the media in the previous twenty years in making citizens aware of the rights that the Charter of 1982 granted them, he also criticized their coverage of the court: "What a judge sees bears a passing resemblance to the original ruling," he said, "but it is frequently distorted in the most grotesque ways." In his opinion, the media changed far more than the courts did in those twenty years. Newspapers are now obsessed with marketing the personality of their writers and are "prone to catering to the biases of their audience"; "'Read the *National Post,'* he mocked. 'It thinks just like you'" (Makin 2001f).

## Critics and Supporters of the Court

It is true that the media do not always report, or do not always grasp, all the nuances of the court's decisions. They can't explain everything in a minute and a half. The need for concise headings also leads to certain shortcuts. Do the media distort reality? Let's look at the *Hudson* case, one of the most heavily covered decisions of 2000-01. A simple question involving interpretation of the regulatory power of municipalities led some to see the court as a heroic defender of the environment.

In 1991, the Town of Hudson, west of Montreal, passed a bylaw limiting the use of pesticides within its boundaries. Landscaping and lawn-maintenance companies, which held permits required by the Quebec *Pesticides Act* and had complied with the federal *Pest Control Products Act,* were accused of having used pesticides in violation of the Hudson bylaw. These companies asked the Quebec Superior Court to declare the bylaw invalid. The Superior Court and the Quebec Court of Appeal ruled that the bylaw was indeed valid. The companies took the matter to the Supreme Court.

The case was heard in December 2000. *National Post* reporter Ian Jack (2000) summed up the fairly limited legal issue: "The legal issue is the scope of municipalities to pass bylaws outside their specific powers, using a clause of provincial legislation." The Quebec *Cities and Towns Act* allows municipal councils to pass bylaws "to secure peace, order, good government, health and general welfare in the territory of the municipality." Under the act, a municipal council may also "regulate or prohibit the ... use of ... combustible, explosive, corrosive, toxic, radioactive or other materials that are harmful to public health and safety."

The Supreme Court rendered its decision in June 2001 and concluded that the bylaw was valid and that its objective was to ensure general welfare. The court confirmed that municipalities can intervene in environmental matters, but it did not rule on the merits of the measures taken by the Town of Hudson. But the interpretation of the decision by certain environmental groups and newspaper headlines ("Municipalities can ban pesticides," *Globe and Mail* [Makin 2001e], and "Les municipalités peuvent limiter l'utilisation des pesticides," *Le Devoir* [Francoeur 2001]), although accurate, allow an interpretation that goes beyond the relatively narrow legal issue. An environmental law professor at the University of Victoria, a witness for Greenpeace and the Council of Canadians before the Supreme Court, concluded: "The Supreme Court is quietly emerging as one of Canada's leading environmental watchdogs" (Boyd 2001). Yet the court did not rule that municipalities had an obligation to pass environmental bylaws.

Anyone who does not consult the text of the decision has to read several newspapers to grasp all the nuances of the case and the ruling. On 5 July, the chief editorial writer of *La Presse,* André Pratte (2001b), wrote that the judgment's meaning needed to be clarified, since the court had not said that pesticides were either harmful or had to be eliminated. He said the judgment was essentially an interpretation of municipal law and as such was not terribly exciting. But he added that, almost in passing, the court (or at least four of the seven judges involved in the decision) seemed to have embraced as a rule of interpretation the so-called precautionary principle arising from the philosophy of sustainable development. The precautionary principle, included in several provisions of Canadian legislation, such as the *Canadian Environmental Protection Act* (1999), comes from international law, specifically the Bergen Ministerial Declaration on Sustainable Development (1990), which reads: "In order to achieve sustainable development, policies must be based on the precautionary principle. Environmental measures must anticipate, prevent, and attack the causes of environmental degradation. Where there are threats of serious or irreversible damage, lack of full scientific certainty should not be used as a reason for postponing measures to prevent environmental degradation."

It was not lost on the *Globe and Mail,* which published an editorial (2001c) arguing that, if three judges had limited themselves strictly to interpreting the *Cities
and Towns Act,* the four others had adopted a broader framework: "They put the
Hudson bylaw in the context of the 'precautionary principle,' a concept in international law that it's better to be safe than sorry – that governments may take
measures to protect the health of citizens without definitive scientific proof."

The judges' use of a broad framework and the international context raised the
ire of the *National Post* and its business editor, Terence Corcoran. Once again, the
*Post* saw the case as an example of "judicial activism" that had to be challenged. The
newspaper published two editorials condemning the court's decision, including
one by Corcoran in its business section on 26 July 2001, accompanied by two
lengthy analytical and critical texts written by two lawyers in private practice.

Corcoran (2001) wrote: "Two aspects of the Supreme Court decisions stand
out. One is the court's habit of judicial activism in deciding to create new environmental law by importing fuzzy international agreements into its reasoning. The
second and related issue is the court's precedent-setting adoption of the fuzziest
concept of all – the precautionary principle – as a basis for its decision." According
to Corcoran, the arbitrary importing of these "sham concepts without meaning"
into a decision of the court will in his opinion increase the confusion surrounding
environmental law.

The charge is a harsh one, and Corcoran's interpretation may seem excessive.
But did four of the judges not open themselves up to these attacks, when it would
have been enough for them to limit themselves to a strict interpretation of the
*Cities and Towns Act?* As stated by Justice Louis LeBel, who would have liked a less
comprehensive approach: "Interesting as they may be, reference to international
sources has little relevance."

It was in reference to the *Hudson* decision that *La Presse* editorial writer Pierre
Gravel provided one of the few examples of negative commentary about the court
that appeared in the French-language press during the year. In a piece called "A
good start," Gravel (2001) commented on statements of the chief justice to the effect that the court was swamped with work. He wrote that, no doubt, the court's
effectiveness could be increased if certain members imposed greater self-discipline
on themselves and resisted the natural tendency to treat all matters as if they were
exceptional legal cases requiring lengthy discussions, drawing on examples from
around the world and dwelling on interminable sociological considerations.

As we pointed out in the Introduction, the *National Post* has been, since its in-
ception, a voice for those who oppose judicial power. For instance, when the court
resumed sitting in September 2000, the *Post* published the text of an address given
to the Donner Canadian Foundation by Ted Morton, coauthor with Rainer Knopff
of *The Charter Revolution and the Court Party,* regarded as an essential reference by

**Table 1.11: Tone of references to the court or a final decision by the court: Newspapers**

| Type | Le Devoir | La Presse | Le Journal de Montréal | Globe and Mail | National Post | Toronto Sun | Total (print) |
|---|---|---|---|---|---|---|---|
| Positive | 13.2 | 5.7 | 3.8 | 9.7 | 4.7 | 3.9 | 7.4 |
| Negative | 6.6 | 4.5 | 1.9 | 14.6 | 13.0 | 9.8 | 9.8 |
| Neutral/Mixed | 80.2 | 89.8 | 94.2 | 75.7 | 82.2 | 86.3 | 82.8 |

the court's critics. In his address, Morton reiterated their thesis that liberal pressure groups (the Court Party), such as feminists, environmentalists, and defenders of gay rights, had used the courts rather than Parliament to advance their causes (Morton 2000). However, our analysis of the tone and the references to the court and its decisions from September 2000 to September 2001 shows that the *Post* was no more negative than the *Globe and Mail* (see Table 1.11). In fact, 14.6 percent of the articles that appeared in the *Globe* and 13 percent of those published by the *Post* made negative references to the court. These included editorials, columns, other opinion pieces, and news items in which a clear majority of the comments were negative. The editorial writers at the *Post* were more negative than their *Globe* counterparts, however.

Generally, the tone adopted by the media regarding the court is in the great majority of cases neutral or mixed. The vast majority of articles and reports contained a balance of positive and negative comments. The negative tone (9.8 percent) for the newspapers as a group is not much more pronounced than the positive tone (7.4 percent). In short, the coverage of the court was for the most part factual and balanced and in line with standard journalistic practices.

The English-language newspapers tended to be more negative toward the court than the French press. *La Presse* stood out with a high percentage of positive references, with 13.2 percent of its articles taking a positive tone. Opinion pieces, especially columns by Yves Boisvert, were supportive of the court. Boisvert devoted six columns to the court during the year. Only one was negative: a piece in which he expressed concern that in Canada it is difficult to find a clear definition of "reasonable doubt," one of the central concepts of criminal law (Boisvert 2000). His comments about the decisions that received the most coverage (*Latimer, Sharpe,* and *Burns-Rafay*) were laudatory.

In an interview for this study, Boisvert (2004) said his opinion of the Supreme Court was both favourable and critical. He believed that the court has played its role fairly well in a large number of cases, though about ten years earlier it appeared to be less sure of itself. Its solutions rarely seemed unreasonable to him, even when he disagreed with them, but the result of well-thought-out, high-calibre argument and reflection. He was critical of the court, however, in matters of criminal law, where he often found what he believed were grave errors. But this did not cause him to conclude that the Charter had given too much power to judges. Rather, although in specific instances he disagreed with their decisions, he still found this system preferable to parliamentary absolutism.

## Conclusion

Why does one Supreme Court decision make headlines and keep columnists busy for days, while another is reported on an inside page in the news briefs section or completely ignored? Why does one decision become news while another does not? The question raises another, broader, matter: what is news?

Studies of the selection of news and the production of information are numerous and anything but a new phenomenon. They have evolved a great deal since the 1950s when the first research done on the subject attributed tremendous power to deskmen, or "gatekeepers," who were said to choose news according to their personal interests. But observers soon realized that journalists are merely cogs in a complex system and that various factors, such as the weight of their sources, the priorities and constraints of their media companies, and the presumed expectations of the public, influence the selection of news as much as, if not more than, journalists' interests and beliefs do.

This general analysis also applies to news about the Supreme Court and explains the differences observed between television and the print media, between the so-called quality papers and the tabloids, and between the English- and French-language media. Manon Cornellier (2003), of *Le Devoir,* provides a good explanation of how various influences shape the selection of news. She says journalists' personal interests make them more aware of certain causes but do not dictate coverage. Their bosses' decisions come into play, too. Then there are issues that don't interest her especially but which are of interest to her readers.

Her colleague Hélène Buzzetti (2002) described the role of the news editor and the importance of the editor's appraisal in weighing the news of the day. She may be immersed in a particular story and think that it is the day's most important news, but her editor in Montreal may have spoken to a dozen reporters who have the same view about the stories they are working on. The editor quite rightly weighs the importance of one story against another. That, according to Buzzetti, is how stories end up on page 1 while another story is relegated to the back pages.

Buzzetti's description mirrors our description of how decisions were made during coverage of the *Sharpe* case. An earthquake in India, Sharpe's refusal to appear before the cameras, and the nature of the court's decision in some instances at least bumped the story from the headlines.

Some court decisions are covered automatically because of their general interest or broad scope or because of the way they affect people's lives. They may be decisions that involve societal debates over heart-rending issues such as abortion or euthanasia. They may also be cases that are compelling because they feature morality plays of good versus evil, deviance, and punishment. Sharpe, Latimer, and Boucher could all be described as celebrity villains who attracted prurient interest. Most of the cases that received a great deal of attention had another element. They had attracted the attention of politicians and had become part of the political landscape. *Latimer, Sharpe,* and *Burns-Rafay* had been the subject of sometimes vigorous and contentious debate during question period in the House of Commons. Indeed, the political fallout from decisions often attracted as much of the journalists' attention as the decision itself.

A decision's relevance to the public is also part of the criteria for choice. Quebec journalists are not concerned about common law issues, just as their colleagues in the rest of Canada are not interested in appeals involving Quebec's civil law system. If a case received extensive coverage when heard by the lower courts, it would be surprising if the Supreme Court decision did not make news. Conversely, if cases are specialized, technical, and complex, such as financial matters, and if they concern a small minority of citizens, they receive little newspaper coverage and even less television coverage. Television needs emotion and thrives on images. Supreme Court decisions offer few images. Television is therefore less interested in the Supreme Court, with some exceptions, such as the *Van de Perre* case, which offered all the drama a television report requires.

In the work done by Gaye Tuchman in the 1970s on the standardization of news production, she describes the routine nature of information gathering by the media and its impact on the portrayal of current events (Tuchman 1978). The media regularly assign journalists to specific locations (major capital cities, parliaments), specific organizations, or specific subjects (business, sports). This pre-established information gathering system is a determining factor, and its role is vital to news construction. Naturally, news comes regularly from those places where there are journalists, and the subjects to which journalists are assigned are also those that receive the most coverage.

No journalists are assigned to the Supreme Court exclusively, and the few who cover legal matters (as opposed to the police beat) devote only a portion of their time to the country's highest court. Most often, parliamentary correspondents cover the court and, since they have a great deal to do on Parliament Hill, they are interested only in those decisions that demand coverage. Thus, a small number of decisions receive broad coverage, and the life of the court, its evolution, and analyses of its rulings are absent from most media.

## Notes

1   Not surprisingly, Miljan and Cooper also found in their 1996-97 study of the coverage of the Supreme Court that newspapers gave more attention to the court than television did (Miljan and Cooper 2003).

2   According to data collected in the fall of 2002 by the Audit Bureau of Circulation, the two newspapers' weekday circulation in Vancouver was more than 30,000 copies (more than 10 percent of their circulation).

3   In November 2000, during the federal election campaign, the Supreme Court had upheld the section in the *Elections Act* restricting spending by special interest groups in federal elections. The court set aside an Alberta court injunction that suspended this section of the law. The National Citizens Coalition had challenged the law, and the federal government asked for a stay to the injunction pending the complete constitutional review of the legislation (Canadian Press 2002). On 18 May 2004, before the federal election was called, the Supreme Court upheld the *Elections Act,* ruling six to three that unrestricted political advertisements could "manipulate or oppress the voter," in which case Parliament reasonably could limit the constitutional guarantee of freedom of expression (*Harper v. Canada,* [2004] S.C.C. 33).

4   Radio-Canada apart, which, on 18 January, had an item from a reporter in Saskatoon.

5   In its decision of 28 September 2001, the Supreme Court deemed race to be only one of the factors to be considered in determining the child's interests. It quashed the decision of the Court of Appeal and awarded custody to the mother.

6   Alain-Robert Nadeau, holder of a doctorate in constitutional law from the University of Ottawa, published a weekly column in *Le Devoir* from September 1999 to June 2001. He took a special interest in the power of judges and control over the constitutionality of laws. His columns discussed mainly the Supreme Court and its jurisprudence. They became semi-monthly in September 2001 and ended in June 2002.

7   Judge L'Heureux-Dubé was referring to the controversy that followed her criticism of a decision by Mr. Justice John McLung of Alberta in a sexual assault case.

## References

Alphonso, Caroline. 2001. Americans angry over blocked extradition. *Globe and Mail,* 17 February, p. A4.

Bailey, Sue (Presse canadienne). 2001a. La Cour suprême se prononcera jeudi. *Le Devoir,* 13-14 January, p. A5.

—. 2001b. High Court judgment protects Canadians and others facing death penalty. 15 February.

—. 2001c. Deux Canadiens recherchés pour meurtre aux États-Unis ne seront pas extradés s'ils risquent la peine de mort. *La Presse,* 16 February, p. A5.

Bell, Stewart. 2001. Court ruling could make Canada "haven" for terrorists, assassins.

*National Post,* 17 February, p. 1.

Bisson, Alain. 2000. Stockwell Day ne veut pas d'activistes à la Cour suprême. *Le Journal de Montréal,* 23 November, p. 8.

Boisvert, Yves. 2000. Suprême confusion. *La Presse,* 3 November, p. E1.

—. 2001. Requiem pour les bourreaux. *La Presse,* 19 February, p. A3.

—. 2004. E-mail correspondence. 14 January.

Boyd, David. 2001. There's a new kid on the environmental block. *Globe and Mail,* 3 July, p. A3.

Buzzetti, Hélène. 2001a. Robert Latimer connaîtra son sort aujourd'hui. *Le Devoir,* 18 January, p. A3.

—. 2001b. Pas de clémence pour Latimer. *Le Devoir,* 19 January, p. 1.

—. 2002. Interview by authors. Ottawa, 22 April.

Canadian Press. 2002. Supreme Court of Canada upholds law restricting election spending by third parties. *National Post,* 11 November, p. A8.

Chwialkowska, Luiza. 2000a. Supreme Court's caseload tends toward the technical. *National Post,* 5 September, p. A5.

—. 2000b. Unique judicial friendship, personal, professional. *National Post,* 28 September, p. A8.

—. 2001a. High court year 2000, revamped bench big on unanimity. *National Post,* 22 January, p. A8.

—. 2001b. Supreme Court rules this week on child porn ban. *National Post,* 23 January, p. A4.

—. 2001c. Freedom of expression not absolute: Three judges. *National Post,* 27 January, p. A8.

Corcoran, Terence. 2001. The corporate road to precaution hell. *National Post,* Editorial, 26 July, p. C15.

Cornellier, Manon. 2001. La peine de mort est "injuste," estime la Cour suprême. *Le Devoir,* 16 February, p. 1.

—. 2003. Interview by authors. Ottawa, 21 March.

Coyne, Andrew. 2000. Some freedom for some speech. *National Post,* 18 December, p. A15.

—. 2001. Free speech and the kiddie porn case. *National Post,* 5 February, p. A13.

des Rivières, Paule. 2001. La protection des enfants avant tout. *Le Devoir,* Editorial, 27-28 January, p. A12.

Dunn, Mark. 2001. Alliance would turf any accused. *Toronto Sun,* 16 February, p. 10.

Francoeur, Louis-Gilles. 2001. Les municipalités peuvent limiter l'utilisation des pesticides. *Le Devoir,* 29 June, p. A1.

Gatehouse, Jonathon. 2001. Protection could be extended to foreign nationals. *National Post,* 16 February, p. A10.

*Globe and Mail.* 2001a. The sentencing of Robert Latimer. Editorial, 19 January, p. A12.

——. 2001b. What a judge may say. Editorial, 20 March, p. A14.

——. 2001c. The tools to keep pesticides in check. Editorial, 29 June, p. A12.

Godfrey, Tom. 2001. Criminal haven. *Toronto Sun,* 20 February, p. 2.

Gravel, Pierre. 2001. Un bon début. *La Presse,* Editorial, 16 August, p. A11.

Greenaway, Norma. 2001. Lamer attack out of bounds: Alliance. *National Post,* 17 April, p. A6.

Gruda, Agnès. 2001. Pour l'amour des enfants. *La Presse,* Editorial, 27 January, p. A18.

Guillemard, Sylvette, and Maxime Saint-Hilaire. 2002. *Vingt ans de grands arrêts de la Cour suprême du Canada.* Montreal: Wilson et Lafleur.

Jack, Ian. 2000. Cities wait to see if pesticide ban survives: Challenge into court. *National Post,* 7 December, p. A7.

Klinkhammer, Ruth, and David Taras. 2001. Mercy or murder? Media coverage of the Robert Latimer Supreme Court decision. *Saskatchewan Law Review* 64: 573-90.

*La Presse.* 2001. L'affaire Sharpe: Un jugement vendredi. En bref, 23 January, p. A7.

*Latimer, R. v.,* [2001] 1 S.C.R. 3.

*Little Sisters Book and Art Emporium v. Canada (Minister of Justice),* [2001] 2 S.C.R. 1120.

Lortie, Marie-Claude. 2001. Dans la presse anglophone. *La Presse,* 25 February, p. A14.

Makin, Kirk. 2000a. Supreme Court blasted for incoherence. *Globe and Mail,* 29 September, p. A13.

——. 2000b. Supreme power surge. *Globe and Mail,* 16 September, p. A15.

——. 2001a. Top court rules 9-0: Child porn law stays. *Globe and Mail,* 17 January, p. A1.

——. 2001b. Latimer gets no mercy. *Globe and Mail,* 19 January, p. 1.

——. 2001c. Next up for court: Refugees who face torture. *Globe and Mail,* 17 February, p. A4.

——. 2001d. Court approves judge's removal. *Globe and Mail,* 8 June, p. A3.

——. 2001e. Municipalities can ban pesticides. *Globe and Mail,* 29 June, p. A3.

——. 2001f. Judge decries "savage attacks" in news media. *Globe and Mail,* 15 August, p. A7.

Makin, Kirk, and Robert Matas. 2001. Top court to rule on child porn. *Globe and Mail,* 23 January, p. A3.

Mickelburgh, Rod, and Colin Freeze. 2001. Both sides claim victory. *Globe and Mail,* 27 January, p. A4.

Miljan, Lydia, and Barry Cooper. 2003. *Hidden agendas: How journalists influence the news.* Vancouver: UBC Press.

Mofina, Rick. 2001. Complaint dismissed against high court judge. *National Post,* 17 March, p. A4.

Morton, F.L. 2000. Rulings for the many by the few. *National Post,* 2 September, p. B3.

Nadeau, Alain-Robert. 2000a. La rentrée de la Cour suprême. *Le Devoir,* 13 September, p. A7.

——. 2000b. Droit et convergences. *Le Devoir,* 4 October, p. A9.

*National Post.* 2000. Tolerant Canada, intolerant customs. Editorial, 16 December, p. A21.

—. 2001a. The right decision. Editorial, 19 January, p. A15.

—. 2001b. Sharpe ruling. Editorial, 27 January, p. A17.

Parent, Rollande (Presse canadienne). 2001a. La Cour suprême examine le cas des franco-protestants du Québec. *Le Devoir*, 20 August, p. A2.

—. 2001b. La Cour suprême examine le dossier des franco-protestants du Québec. *La Presse*, 20 August, p. A4.

Pratte, André. 2001a. Des juges de glace? *La Presse*, Editorial, 19 January, p. A8.

—. 2001b. Le gazon de la Cour. *La Presse*, 5 July, p. A11.

Presse canadienne. 2001a. La Cour suprême a eu une année bien remplie. *Le Journal de Montréal*, 3 January, p. 18.

—. 2001b. Robert Latimer connaîtra son sort jeudi. *La Presse*, 13 January, p. A27.

—. 2001c. Pas d'extradition s'il y a risque de peine de mort. *Le Journal de Montréal*, 16 February, p. 9.

—. 2001d. L'ex-juge en chef Antonio Lamer fustige les "jappements" de l'Alliance. *La Presse*, 15 April, p. A4; *Le Journal de Montréal*, 15 April, p. 10.

—. 2001e. Louise Arbour encourage les jeunes à chérir la démocratie. *Le Journal de Montréal*, 12 May, p. 26.

—. 2001f. Guy Bertrand veut maintenir les écoles protestantes. *Le Journal de Montréal*, 26 July, p. 10.

Richer, Jules (Presse canadienne). 2001a. La Cour suprême rend un jugement attendu vendredi. *Le Devoir*, 23 January, p. A12.

—. 2001b. Pornographie juvénile: La Cour suprême rend son jugement vendredi. *Le Journal de Montréal*, 23 January, p. 19.

—. 2003. Interview by authors. Montreal, 6 March.

Robitaille, Antoine. 2001. La peine capitale assassinée. *Le Devoir*, 17-18 February, p. A10.

Rocher, Guy. 1990. L'emprise du droit. In *La société québécoise après trente ans de changements*, ed. Fernand Dumont, 99-116. Quebec: IQRC.

Rodrigue, Isabelle. 2001. Pas de sursis pour les élèves des écoles franco-protestantes. *La Presse*, 31 August, p. A7.

Rubec, Stephanie. 2001a. Decade in jail for killer dad. *Toronto Sun*, 19 January, p. 5.

—. 2001b. Top court may kill kid porn law. *Toronto Sun*, 25 January, p. 23.

—. 2001c. Porn law solid: Top court. *Toronto Sun*, 27 January, p. 4.

Rubin, Sandra. 2001. Lawyers say judges not above media criticism. *National Post*, 16 August, p. A8.

Schmitz, Cristin. 2001a. Supreme Court goes "too far": Judge. *National Post*, 13 January, p. 1.

—. 2001b. Settle Native issues with talks: Judge. *National Post*, 15 January, p. A4.

Seeman, Neil. 2001. Who do you think you are? *Globe and Mail*, 20 February, p. A17.

*Sharpe, R. v.*, [2001] 1 S.C.R. 45.

Simpson, Jeffrey. 2001. Yes Victoria, there is a limit to free speech. *Globe and Mail,* 29 January, p. A13.

*Therrien (Re),* [2001] 2 S.C.R. 3.

Tibbetts, Janice. 2001a. Lamer attacks Alliance "yelping." *National Post,* 14 April, p. 1.

—. 2001b. Supreme Court: Focus will be on social issues, not criminal. *National Post,* 27 August, p. A6.

*Toronto Sun.* 2001a. Mercy. Editorial, 19 January, p. 14.

—. 2001b. For the children. Editorial, 27 January, p. 14.

*Trinity Western University v. British Columbia College of Teachers,* [2001] 1 S.C.R. 772.

Tuchman, Gaye. 1978. *Making news: A study in the construction of reality.* New York: The Free Press.

*United States v. Burns,* [2001] 1 S.C.R. 283.

*Van de Perre v. Edwards,* [2001] 2 S.C.R. 1014, 2001 S.C.C. 60.

Venne, Michel. 2001. Un meurtre. *Le Devoir,* Editorial, 19 January, p. A6.

# ——2——

# Equal in Alberta: The *Vriend* Case

KING'S UNIVERSITY COLLEGE in Edmonton, Alberta, describes itself as a Christian university "rooted in the historic Christian faith." Teachers and students at the college are expected to "fulfill their calling to develop the earth and to serve God and their neighbour in education" (King's College 2003). Delwin Vriend was employed as a computer-lab instructor at King's from 1987 to 1991. There was no question that Vriend was professionally competent. Rather, there was concern on the part of his employer that Vriend was gay; this disquiet was exacerbated by Vriend wearing a pink triangle pin (a symbol of the modern gay rights movement) to work one day. When confronted by the college president about his sexual orientation in February 1990, Vriend confessed he was in a sexual relationship with a same-sex partner. One year later, the college terminated his employment.

Vriend attempted to file a complaint of discrimination against King's College with the Alberta Human Rights Commission, but he could gain no access to that process. The commission turned Vriend away, under ministerial order not to accept jurisdiction to hear the complaint (Fraser 1994) – sexual orientation was not a prohibited ground of discrimination in Alberta. Vriend, together with a group of local Edmonton gay and lesbian organizations, challenged the conformity of the Alberta statute with the equality rights section of the *Canadian Charter of Rights and Freedoms* (section 15).

What might be considered, from one angle, a simple wrongful dismissal claim against a private religious college was also, from another angle, an explosive case that challenged the authority of the legislature of Alberta to choose not to prohibit discrimination against gays and lesbians. The Supreme Court of Canada was asked to either defer to the fully deliberated choices of the legislature or discipline the province for failing to comply with Charter norms.

As we discuss below, what is startling about this case is the way in which the debate over sexual orientation simply melts away in the media coverage. The media focus instead turned on portrayals of the Alberta legislature. This, in some ways, is not surprising. Most provinces already had prohibitions in place outlawing discrimination against gays and lesbians; Alberta simply was one of the last holdouts. The issue of whether sexual orientation was a prohibited ground of discrimination under the Charter had also been settled by the Supreme Court a few years earlier. In *Egan v. Canada,* the court declared that sexual orientation, though not expressly included among the enumerated grounds of discrimination listed in section 15, was analogous to the enumerated grounds. As the set of prohibited grounds was not closed (section 15 prohibits discrimination generally and in particular on the basis of certain grounds), sexual orientation was, like the grounds listed, "a deeply personal characteristic" that could give rise to invidious discrimination. This finding, though not controversial for the court in the *Egan* case, was complicated by the fact that the Attorney General of Canada conceded this very point (Hogg 1998, 980).

What made the case cut so close to the bone of legislative sovereignty was that the Alberta legislature had refused on at least five occasions to amend the *Individual Rights Protection Act* (Alberta's human rights act) to include sexual orientation as a prohibited ground of discrimination (McGovern 1994). This was despite the best advice of a succession of human rights commissioners (in 1984 and 1992) and a special Alberta Human Rights Review Panel (in 1994). On each occasion, the ministers responsible resisted (*Vriend* 1998, Factum, paras. 20-27). The *Vriend* case placed the issue of the supremacy of Charter over provincial rights squarely on the table. The Supreme Court of Canada would not shy away from this opportunity and, in the process, shone the spotlight squarely on the Alberta legislature.

## Actors and Arguments

Once the Alberta Human Rights Commission turned him away, Vriend joined with a variety of local groups in his legal action against the Government of Alberta – the Gay and Lesbian Awareness Society of Edmonton, the Gay and Lesbian Community Centre of Edmonton Society, and Dignity Canada Dignité, an organization for gay Catholics and supporters. As the case rose on appeal, Vriend and his coapplicants were joined by a number of interveners representing the interests of women (Alberta Federation of Women and Women's Legal Education and Action Fund), civil liberties, lawyers, and human rights (Alberta Civil Liberties Association, Canadian Bar Association – Alberta Branch, Canadian Human Rights Commission, Canadian Association of Statutory Human Rights Agencies), religious denominations (Alberta and Northwest Conference of the United Church of Canada and the Canadian Jewish Congress), the labour movement (Canadian Labour Congress), and gays and lesbians (Equality for Gays and Lesbians Everywhere, Foundation for Equal Families, and Canadian AIDS Society).

If Delwin Vriend appeared to be the main protagonist in this story, the premier of Alberta, Ralph Klein, claimed centre stage. The irascible Premier Klein had a finely tuned sense of public opinion in Alberta – no contemporary political leader in Canada could equal his skills as a populist. The Klein government resisted granting any form of "special treatment" to gays and lesbians in the province, fighting the *Vriend* case "tooth and nail" at every step (*Edmonton Journal* 1998d). Allied with Klein as the case proceeded to the Alberta Court of Appeal and then to the Supreme Court of Canada were the Evangelical Fellowship of Canada, the Focus on the Family Association, the Alberta Federation of Women United for Families, and the Christian Legal Fellowship. Significantly, though the case was pitched by Alberta as one concerning provincial rights, only the Province of Ontario intervened before the Supreme Court of Canada in support of the Province of Alberta.

Alberta's argument was centred on the idea of legislative silence. As the government had chosen not to include sexual orientation as a prohibited ground, the Alberta legislature had maintained a "neutral silence" on the issue. This silence did not amount to government action to which the Charter could apply – there could be no discrimination as a result of a legislative omission. "This is a social policy choice," the Attorney General of Alberta wrote in his submission to the Supreme Court, "and when a legislature makes decisions within the scope of legitimate social policy," there can be no denial of Charter equality rights (*Vriend* 1998, Factum, para. 56). Even if the Charter applied, the legislation created no distinction that could give rise to discrimination – both heterosexuals and homosexuals were treated the same. As sexual orientation received no mention in the act, there could be no denial of equality rights (ibid., para. 28).

At trial in 1994, Justice Anne Russell of the Alberta Court of Queen's Bench resisted the province's interpretation and found for Vriend. Other disadvantaged groups had a legal remedy available to them that was denied to Vriend as a member of a similarly disadvantaged group. By failing to include sexual orientation as a prohibited ground, the province had reinforced "negative stereotyping and prejudice thereby perpetuating and implicitly condoning its occurrence" (*Vriend* 1994, para. 53). This amounted to a denial of equality rights under the Charter. The province did not even attempt to justify the discrimination (under section 1 of the Charter) – there was no evidence tendered that the purpose of the legislative omission was a "pressing and substantial objective" or that it impaired rights as little as possible. Justice Russell could not be convinced that this omission was reasonable. By way of remedy, Justice Russell read in the words "sexual orientation" to the list of prohibited grounds. Though the omission by the legislature was no oversight, this was considered "less intrusive" than striking down the law. "It is safe to assume that the Legislature would have preferred an Act with sexual orientation included than no Act at all," she wrote (*Vriend* 1994, paras. 76, 79).

The response to Justice Russell's judgment was predictable: in a province where public opinion on this issue is polarized, opinions swung both ways (Feschuk 1994). Gays and lesbians, the human rights community, and civil libertarians – mostly urban based – applauded the ruling. Rural public opinion, represented by the ruling Conservative majority and its unofficial organ, *Alberta Report,* railed against it. "Who is this woman anyhow?" asked publisher Ted Byfield (1994). Labour Minister Stockwell Day wondered whether the province could do without the human rights commission (McGovern 1994). Premier Klein was of the view that an amendment to the human rights code was unnecessary, "since all people are protected" by the Charter – a misleading assessment since, on the Government of Alberta's view, the Charter did not apply to private actors in employment situations but only to governments (Gold 1996).

The Queen's Bench ruling was reversed in 1996 in spectacular fashion by the Alberta Court of Appeal. In a two-to-one decision, Justice John "Buzz" McClung defied judicial decorum and issued a tirade against the "rights-euphoric, cost-scuffing left" and "constitutionally hyper-active judges" (*Vriend* 1996, paras. 24, 25). Justice McClung, with Justice O'Leary concurring, accepted the government's position that, by remaining silent about the issue of sexual orientation, it had remained neutral. "When they choose silence, provincial legislatures need not march to the Charter drum," wrote McClung (para. 20). Even if the Charter applied, there was no distinction giving rise to discrimination. Full protection, on prohibited grounds such as race, ethnicity, and sex, was available to all, regardless of one's sexual orientation. Nothing in Alberta's *Individual's Rights Protection Act* condoned discrimination and, if any ensued, it was for "private, not government, resolution" (para. 14). In the alternative, if he was wrong about not finding a denial of Charter equality rights, the appropriate remedy in this case would be to declare the whole act constitutionally invalid and suspend the declaration of invalidity for one year rather than "read in," as Justice Russell had done (this was "pure legislation" wrote McClung [para. 52]). This would give the Alberta legislature sufficient time to choose how to respond, perhaps by repealing the legislation altogether. According to political scientist Ted Morton (1996), the Charter "counter-revolution" had begun with McClung's decision.

Justice Connie Hunt, in dissent, agreed with the lower court that legislative silence can result in a distinction that gives rise to discrimination. As did Justice Russell, Justice Hunt concluded that the limitation could not be reasonably justified. The appropriate remedy in this case, however, was not to read in sexual orientation but to declare the employment sections in the act constitutionally invalid and to suspend the declaration of invalidity for one year.

## Methodology and Preliminary Findings

We collected 163 television and newspaper stories about the *Vriend* case at the Supreme Court of Canada. Our collection period included a six-day period around the Supreme Court hearing in November 1997 and a ten-day period around the decision, released in April 1998. Television data were collected from four evening newscasts: CBC and CTV in the English language and TVA and Radio-Canada in the French language.[1] Newspaper data were collected in the English language from the *Globe and Mail,* the *Sun* chain tabloids in Alberta (the *Calgary Sun* and *Edmonton Sun*) and in Ontario (the *Toronto Sun*), the Southam broadsheets (the *Calgary Herald* and the *Edmonton Journal*), and the magazine *Alberta Report.* Of the French-language newspapers, we examined the broadsheets *La Presse* and *Le Devoir* and the tabloid *Le Journal de Montréal.*

References to the court were tabulated along a number of indicators, including the tone of stories as they relate to the court, its decision, Delwin Vriend, and the federal government. Tone was interpreted not merely on the basis of a positive or negative reference in a story but on the basis of an overall impression after reading an article or viewing a story. There had to be a preponderance of positive or negative references in a story in order for it to be considered not merely neutral in tone. In the case of *Vriend,* most references to the Supreme Court as an institution were neutral in tone; however, almost a third of the print media stories were negative in tone, the preponderance from Alberta media (see Table 2.1).

As regards the *Vriend* decision, again a majority of stories were neutral, with the preponderance of negative stories appearing in Alberta media (see Table 2.2).

**Table 2.1: Tone of reference to the Supreme Court as an institution**

| Newspaper | Positive | Negative | Neutral | Total |
|---|---|---|---|---|
| *Globe and Mail* | | 1 | 3 | 4 |
| *Calgary Sun* | 1 | 2 | 3 | 6 |
| *Edmonton Sun* | | 5 | 3 | 8 |
| *Toronto Sun* | | 1 | | 1 |
| *Calgary Herald* | 1 | 5 | 13 | 19 |
| *Edmonton Journal* | 1 | 4 | 19 | 24 |
| *Alberta Report* | | 4 | | 4 |
| *La Presse* | | 1 | 3 | 4 |
| *Le Devoir* | | | 2 | 2 |
| *Le Journal de Montréal* | | | 2 | 2 |
| **Total** | **3** | **23** | **48** | **74** |

Table 2.2: Tone of reference to the Supreme Court *Vriend* decision

| Newspaper | Positive | Negative | Neutral | Total |
|---|---|---|---|---|
| *Globe and Mail* | 1 | 1 | 9 | 11 |
| *Calgary Sun* | | 4 | 12 | 16 |
| *Edmonton Sun* | | 5 | 12 | 17 |
| *Toronto Sun* | | 1 | 3 | 4 |
| *Calgary Herald* | 3 | 6 | 19 | 28 |
| *Edmonton Journal* | 4 | 7 | 24 | 35 |
| *Alberta Report* | | 5 | 3 | 8 |
| *La Presse* | | 1 | 3 | 4 |
| *Le Devoir* | | | 2 | 2 |
| *Le Journal de Montréal* | | | 2 | 2 |
| **Total** | **8** | **30** | **89** | **127** |

A small minority of reports had a negative tone toward gays and lesbians (*Alberta Report,* not surprisingly, carrying the higher percentage of these), with Calgary newspapers being more negative than Edmonton ones. Of the few television stories, most were neutral in tone.

The greatest number of stories was found in the Alberta press (principally, the *Edmonton Journal* and *Calgary Herald*). Only eight print stories were found in three francophone newspapers and one television news report on Radio-Canada was broadcast at the time of ruling. There simply was no interest on the part of the Quebec press in this story. One reason might be that this issue – the protection of gays and lesbians against discrimination – had been long settled in Quebec. The Parti québécois government was the first in Canada to include sexual orientation as a prohibited ground in the Quebec Charter of Human Rights and Freedoms. If the story failed to garner interest in Quebec, this suggests that the Alberta government also failed, at least outside the province, to generate interest in its argument (embraced by Justice McClung at the Court of Appeal) that courts operating under the Charter were a threat to provincial sovereignty. This signals that the Vriend story was only a regional one, of not great interest to the rest of the country, other than perhaps as a curiosity. This is borne out by the ways in which the story was framed in the media accounts.

We found that a plurality of the stories (hard news, as well as editorial and op-ed) adopted what we call a strategic frame (see Table 2.3). By this we mean stories that highlight conflict between the parties, often invoking sports, battle, or war metaphors. Winners and losers are the focus of stories with a strategic frame. This is in contrast to issue frames, which focus on particular legal questions at issue (see Appendix B). These kinds of stories provide the background to or

**Table 2.3: Dominant frame by genre**

| Frame | Hard news | Editorials | Columns/ Opinion | Other | Total |
|---|---|---|---|---|---|
| Strategic | 57 | 3 | 21 | 1 | 82 |
| Issue | 34 | 5 | 23 | 9 | 71 |
| Human interest | 5 | | 1 | 1 | 7 |
| Moral order | | | 4 | | 4 |
| **Total** | **96** | **8** | **49** | **11** | **164** |

detailed examination of the legal decision, from both supportive and critical points of view.

Of the hard news stories, almost 60 percent adopted a strategic frame, in contrast to 35.4 percent adopting an issue frame. Interestingly, 62.5 percent of editorials adopted an issue frame, in contrast to a 37.5 percent strategic frame. This is best exemplified by the *Globe and Mail* editorial of 3 April 1998, which explains how the court came to its decision, including an important discussion, otherwise lacking in almost all news accounts, of the distinction between reading in and striking down legislation (*Globe and Mail* 1998b; Miljan and Cooper 2003, 163). This was supplemented by reprinted edited versions of the Supreme Court's joint opinion and the dissenting reasons on the remedy issue by Justice Major (*Globe and Mail* 1998a). The *Edmonton Journal* (1998a) also reprinted significant portions from the majority decision.

Although the majority of articles were considered to be hard news stories, a significant percentage of them were columns, opinion pieces, and guest commentaries (34 percent). Negative evaluations of the major actors – the Supreme Court, provincial politicians, and gays and lesbians – are most frequently found in this genre. Among columns, opinion pieces, and commentary, there was a roughly even split between the strategic and issue frames (see Table 2.4). This speaks well of the ability of columnists and others to engage readers not only with polemics but with detailed discussion of the court's ruling and techniques of Charter interpretation. Andrew Coyne (1998) in the *Calgary Herald* and Jeffrey Simpson (1998) in the *Globe* best exemplified this adeptness.

It also is apparent that this was not, for the most part, a good TV story. Aside from the very staged moment at Vriend's press conference following the ruling and the rally in support of Vriend on the steps of the Alberta legislature, there were few good visuals amid the behind-closed-door proceedings at the court and, subsequently, in the Alberta cabinet.

When we separate out those stories that adopt a strategic frame, we find two

**Table 2.4: Comparison of story genres in newspapers**

| Newspaper | Hard news | Editorials | Columns/ Opinion | Other | Total |
|---|---|---|---|---|---|
| *Globe and Mail* | 11 | 2 | | 1 | 14 |
| *Calgary Sun* | 6 | 2 | 9 | | 17 |
| *Edmonton Sun* | 12 | 1 | 5 | | 18 |
| *Toronto Sun* | 2 | | 2 | | 4 |
| *Calgary Herald* | 19 | 1 | 15 | 3 | 38 |
| *Edmonton Journal* | 28 | 2 | 13 | 4 | 47 |
| *Alberta Report* | 4 | | 4 | 1 | 9 |
| *La Presse* | 2 | | 1 | 1 | 4 |
| *Le Devoir* | 2 | | | | 2 |
| *Le Journal de Montréal* | 1 | | | 1 | 2 |
| **Total** | **87** | **8** | **49** | **11** | **155** |

predominant narratives. The first might be called a provincial rights story. Here, the Government of Alberta is portrayed as doing battle with an activist judiciary imposing social norms, such as nondiscrimination rights for gays and lesbians, over the objections of the democratically elected Alberta legislature. The second story might be described as an "Alberta as deviant" one, in which the province is portrayed as an outlier in the realm of human rights. Alberta was one of the only jurisdictions in Canada to fail to protect gays and lesbians from discrimination. According to this account, it was appropriate to impose well-accepted human rights norms on resistant provincial legislators. It is notable that, in either strategic frame, the substantive question of whether to include protection against discrimination against gays and lesbians in provincial human rights codes largely is elided. These findings are discussed in more detail below.

### The Hearing: Alberta's "Rough Ride"

By the time of the Supreme Court hearing, it was pretty clear where the court would go with this case. As mentioned, the court had already declared in *Egan* that gays and lesbians were a historically disadvantaged group analogous to the groups enumerated in section 15. For the purposes of equality rights analysis, sexual orientation was an analogous ground. Also, after the Alberta Court of Appeal ruling but before the Supreme Court hearing, the court had issued reasons in *Eldridge v. British Columbia (Attorney General)*. There the court ruled that underinclusive legislation – denying funding for sign translation to the hearing impaired when accessing medical services – could constitute discrimination under the Charter. It was predictable, then, that the Charter would apply and that the exclusion of a vulnerable group from a critical protective scheme could give rise to discrimination. One outstanding issue concerned the kind of remedy the court would prefer and how the members of the court would respond to the challenge levelled by Justice McClung and his supporters.

Not surprisingly, numerous stories published during the hearing focused on Vriend – on his uphill struggle, fighting the province seemingly against all odds (Arnold 1997a, 1997b; Ovenden 1997a). Senator Ron Ghitter, a former Alberta MLA and sponsor of the *Individual's Rights Protection Act* in the Alberta legislative assembly, characterized the hearing as a "day of shame" for Albertans. The Government of Alberta, and the numerous interveners in support of the province, stuck to the message that "democracy was at stake in Alberta" (Laghi 1997). For Vriend supporters, the issue was Alberta's legislative disdain for gays; for government supporters, the issue was the ability of Alberta to write its own laws (Arnold 1997b).

It was expected that the court would not welcome entirely the Government of Alberta's submissions. It was not expected, however, that the court would give so hard a time to Alberta's legal counsel, John McCarthy. This was headline news the day after the hearing. "High Court gives Alberta legislation rough ride" read the *Edmonton Journal* headline (Ovenden 1997c); "Alberta hammered on gay rights issue" read the *Calgary Herald* headline (Ovenden 1997b) (both published the same report by Norm Ovenden). Alberta's counsel was described as "beleaguered" under questioning by members of the court. "Every one of the nine justices had critical questions" for Mr. McCarthy, reported Ovenden (1997c). *Alberta Report* similarly described McCarthy as "facing intense criticism from all nine judges," calling it an "unusual display of overt prejudice on the bench" (Torrance 1997). Justice Frank Iacobucci prompted laughter in the courtroom when he described Alberta's position as the "McCarthy doctrine" (ibid.). The Vriend side suffered no such sarcasm, bristled Kelley Torrance for *Alberta Report* (ibid.). Audio excerpts from exchanges between McCarthy and the court, together with courtroom laughter, were later broadcast nationally on CBC Radio.

## Interregnum: Faulty Radar

It must have been clear to all parties where, on the substance of the case, the court was going. The political response still was largely unforeseeable – that is, until events in the Alberta legislative assembly one month before the release of the Supreme Court decision. These events are critical to understanding subsequent political developments; they also represent well Premier Klein's political dexterity.

In March 1998, five months after the Supreme Court hearing, Alberta justice minister John Havelock tabled in the legislature a bill to provide compensation for the victims of forced sterilization in Alberta (Bill 26). The province had, since 1928, authorized the forced sterilization of mentally disabled persons – a commonly followed but misguided eugenicist policy – until the repeal of Alberta's *Sexual Sterilization Act* in 1972. Some 2,700 people had been sterilized under the auspices of the act. The proposed *Institutional Confinement and Sexual Sterilization Compensation Act* limited financial redress for sterilization to $150,000. Having concerns that a cap on damages might run afoul of the Charter, the minister invoked the Charter's notwithstanding clause (section 33) in the bill. According to the minister's speaking notes, the clause was inserted "because the Government believes it is important that these historical claims be settled expeditiously without requiring a prolonged constitutional debate over the legislation, with the associated time and expense" (Havelock 1998).

In a hailstorm of public criticism from sterilization victims, the Liberal opposition, and the media, the premier reversed government policy in less than twenty-four hours. Premier Klein admitted his political radar failed him on this issue and that the use of the notwithstanding clause had been presented as a mere technicality (a "technical tool"). It became abundantly clear to Klein that "to individuals in this country the Charter of Rights and Freedoms is paramount and the use of any tool ... to undermine the Charter ... is something that should be used only in very, very rare circumstances" (Jeffs 1998). The premier would not, however, rule out use of the override clause in the *Vriend* case, a ruling that was expected soon. The government did promise, though, that before any attempted use of the clause, Albertans would be consulted (Jeffs 1998; Arnold 1998; Bray 1998). To this end, and days before the release of the *Vriend* decision, Premier Klein struck a small cabinet committee – including Justice Minister Havelock and provincial treasurer Stockwell Day – to examine legal options available to the province in the wake of the ruling (Johnsrude 1998).

## The Decision: Unsafe Assumptions?

In a decision written jointly by justices Cory and Iacobucci, the Supreme Court of Canada unanimously found for Vriend and read in the words "sexual orientation" to the Alberta human rights code. Justice Cory characterized the legislation as "underinclusive" – the legislature chose not to include a class of individuals from its protective scheme for human rights, which then rendered it susceptible to Charter review (*Vriend* 1998, para. 61). This underinclusion gave rise to a distinction, first, between gays and lesbians and other disadvantaged groups that secured protection under the scheme and, second, between homosexuals and heterosexuals. The exclusion had a far greater impact on the former group, the subject of stereotyping and discrimination, than on the latter. The distinction thus gave rise to discrimination: gays and lesbians were deemed less worthy of protection than members of other disadvantaged groups. It signalled to Albertans that discriminatory treatment of gays in the province was to be condoned.

Justice Iacobucci delivered reasons for the majority of the court on two further questions: first, was the denial of equality a reasonable limit on Charter rights and, if so, what was the appropriate remedy? The first issue was easily resolved. The exclusion of gays and lesbians from the protective scheme did not further a pressing and substantial objective, was not rationally connected to the furtherance of human rights, nor did it impair equality rights as little as possible. Turning to the appropriate remedy, Justice Iacobucci "pause[d] to reflect more broadly on the general issue of the relationship between legislatures and courts in the age of the Charter" (para. 129). Hardly "a day goes by," he wrote, "without some comment or criticism to the effect that under the Charter courts are wrongfully usurping the role of the legislatures" (para. 130). In a constitutional democracy, wrote Justice Iacobucci, the judiciary are bound to uphold constitutional rights as the trustees of Canada's constitutional order even over the objections of elected politicians. Here he introduced the metaphor of dialogue as better representing the relationship between courts and legislatures – courts "speak to the legislative and executive branches," and legislatures then respond to the courts (para. 138). This was a dialogue that enhanced democracy rather than undermined it. In these circumstances, the most appropriate remedy and the one most consistent with the Charter and the *Individual's Rights Protection Act*'s legislative objectives was to read in sexual orientation to the list of prohibited grounds. The legislature could always respond by passing new legislation or shielding the existing law under section 33, the ultimate parliamentary safeguard (para. 178).

Significantly, Justice Major, considered the Alberta appointee on the court, dissented on the remedy issue. He preferred not to read in but, rather, to suspend a declaration of invalidity for one year, leaving the matter for the Alberta legislature. According to Justice Major, reading in is appropriate when it is safe to conclude that the legislature would have done the same. This was not a safe assumption here (para. 195). "Given the persistent refusal" to protect gays and lesbians from discrimination (para. 198), Alberta may prefer to have a different human rights framework. This was a matter for Albertans, not the court, to decide.

## The Coverage: Provincial Rights/Deviant Provinces

As we have mentioned, the majority of news reports adopted a strategic frame, in which conflict and the metaphors of battle and war are emphasized. It might be expected that the principal conflict portrayed in the press would mirror the legal contest: that is, the conflict between gays and lesbians and the provincial government. What we found, instead, was that there were two other dominant angles to the Vriend story within the strategic frame. The first is a provincial rights story. This narrative mirrors the Alberta government's submissions to the court: the case concerned the capacity of provinces to choose whether to legislate on a matter of social policy. A judicial finding requiring that Alberta add protection for gays and lesbians would be characterized as judicial overreach, even judicial activism. The legal conflict, from this perspective, is seen as between the province and the court.

The second angle is an Alberta-as-deviant story. From this perspective, the province resisted legal reforms that had been adopted by a majority of seven other provinces. The province, as Vriend put it, "kicked and screamed and whined for the last seven years" before being forced by the Supreme Court to prevent discrimination under the human rights code (Makin 1998b). The conflict, from this angle, is usually personified as a battle between Vriend and Klein. "Ha ha, I win," Vriend taunted the premier at a post-ruling press conference (Chase 1998).

What is notable is that the provincial rights story predominates within the province, while the Alberta-as-deviant story is predominant in national media outlets. It is not that the Alberta government entirely does not succeed in getting its provincial rights story out; rather, it is to say that national media were far more interested in framing the province as a moral failure. We turn first to national media stories that adopted the provincial rights frame.

### Provincial Rights: National Media

The provincial rights frame was most prevalent at the time of the hearing. Kelly Crowe of CBC's *The National* quoted Alberta lawyers arguing that the case is "not about gay rights – it's about the right of the government to decide what's covered under its own legislation" (CBC 1997). Alberta lawyers were getting their message out to a national audience. Interveners also took up the government's cause. Elizabeth Chu on *CTV News* talked about how the province now was being "forced to protect gays from discrimination." Chu described Reverend Roy Beyers's position (of the Canada Family Action Coalition) that "Alberta should write its own laws, not have them imposed by Supreme Court appointees" (CTV 1998).

The *Globe and Mail* headline the day of the ruling described the case as one that "pits court against politicians (Makin 1998a). The day after the ruling, the *Globe* reported that the "ruling affirms the right of judges to step in and undo unfair governmental action" (Makin 1998b). Justice reporter Kirk Makin suggested in this piece that, though the ruling was about gay rights, the ruling's "subtext was the very right of judges to step in and undo the constitutional blunders of elected politicians." Rarely, he writes, "has the role of the judiciary been under such sustained attack."

Although Alberta was "on message" at the time of the hearing and upon release of the ruling, the national media reporting quickly turned to the province-as-deviant story. This might be explained by the focus of the story turning away from the court ruling to the reaction of the premier and the provincial government over the threatened use of the notwithstanding clause. Only a few days before the ruling, Klein had not ruled out use of the notwithstanding clause (Johnsrude 1998). On the day the decision was released, however, the premier definitively ruled it out. This political angle was, of course, a newsworthy aspect of the case and dominated news coverage throughout the rest of the week.

Ironically, the premier's strategy of ruling out the use of section 33 may have been precisely to fend off characterizations that Alberta was a deviant. The *Globe and Mail* headlined the premier's promise, as did the television news. Reg Sherren on CBC national news underlined that a premier who "had been talking tough about his options, suddenly had little to say." A chastened Premier Klein was shown saying, "It's pretty hard to go against that kind of judgement and that kind of consideration which was given about five months by the Supreme Court of Canada, the highest Court in the land" (CBC 1998a). On *CTV News,* the government is described by Elizabeth Chu as moving "quickly to accept the decision" (CTV 1998). This aspect of the story fits the provincial rights strategic frame, with the province backing down in the face of a nearly unanimous Supreme Court decision. The reaction of the conservative caucus, the religious and moral conservative lobby, together with the apparent waffling of the premier himself, gave the political angle of the story legs throughout the week, which provided space for the province-as-deviant picture to predominate.

### Province as Deviant: National Media

This aspect of the story was highlighted in television news coverage of the hearing. Kelly Crowe on CBC national news described Senator Ron Ghitter as being embarrassed by the position adopted by the Government of Alberta in this case: it was, to him, "disgraceful" (CBC 1997). Brian Laghi (1998a) filed a report for the *Globe and Mail,* in anticipation of the decision, that moral conservatives "have for many years held sway with a provincial government that has refused time and again to extend protection from discrimination to gays." The day after the ruling, the *Globe and Mail* headlined that, in Alberta, "phone-in talk shows reflect [a] full spectrum" of opinion, with "strong emotions colour[ing] most responses" (Mitchell 1998). Days later, Albertans were still "wrestl[ing] with the gay rights ruling" (Kenny 1998), opponents "bombarding Klein with phone calls" (*Globe and Mail* 1998c), at which point "Alberta's gay-rights fight turn[ed] ugly" (Laghi 1998b).

Although Premier Klein initially refused to consider use of the override, he began to waffle, explaining to the provincial media that this was a decision that appropriately would be made by caucus. Thus, all attention turned to the conservative caucus meeting scheduled to be held 9 April, one week after the court ruling. In the meantime, the premier drew his "line in the sand." "It is morally wrong to discriminate," Klein maintained, and he would push caucus to vote to reject use of

According to CBC's *The National,* "thousands of brochures" like this one were being distributed across the province of Alberta, protesting the Supreme Court decision in *Vriend.* The image underscored both the provincial rights theme and, in the context of the broadcast, the province's deviant nature. *Courtesy of CBC*

the override (Laghi 1998b). The mountain of phone calls and faxes in support of the use of section 33 had sickened the premier: "We have people writing letters that quite frankly make your stomach turn" (*Globe and Mail* 1998c). Both CBC and CTV national news devoted several nights to this story, highlighting some of the vitriolic opposition generated by the *Vriend* decision. On the eve of the caucus meeting, CBC anchor Peter Mansbridge reported where the premier stood, and after the meeting, reporter Kelly Crowe described a "clearly exhausted" Klein. "We have done the right thing relative to the Supreme Court decision," Klein says. "For this government it was a giant step" (CBC 1998b).

Local media reports indicate that Albertans were not pleased by this sort of attention. Peter Menzies (1998), editorial page editor of the *Calgary Herald*, wrote that this was intended to embarrass Albertans, but "you do not do things because of what Ontario thinks; you do them because they are right." Columnist Paul Stanway (1998a, 1998b), writing in the *Calgary Sun* and *Edmonton Sun*, complained that the high court "exposes us as a bunch of gay-hating bigots ... Alberta bad, gays good. End of story." Don Braid (1998) in the *Calgary Sun* quoted one national TV commentator as asking, "What is it about Albertans and sex?"

### Provincial Rights: Local Media

Klein's media strategy appears to have been to deflect this stereotyping of Albertans, first by declining to use the notwithstanding clause and, second, by characterizing the opposition at home as being about judicial activism and not about gay bashing. Among Alberta media, the premier was quite successful. The provincial rights story, in other words, took much better in Alberta than elsewhere. What was at stake in the decision, Rainer Knopff was quoted as saying, "is the government's right to govern" (Ketcham 1998).

Upon release of the decision, media reports reflected the fact that a well-orchestrated campaign to use the notwithstanding clause was under way. Columnists such as Lorne Gunter, Ted Byfield, and David Frum, together with guest columnists such as Ted Morton and Dave Rutherford, emphasized that "Alberta has the power to reverse [the] Vriend ruling" (Gunter 1998). Gunter described a temptation to "charge at the gallop into the SCC and lance its members for being remote, unelected, unaccountable and perverse." Gunter reminded readers of the Supreme Court's "atrocious" behaviour last fall at the *Vriend* hearing, "laughing at the arguments of the Alberta government, likening them to McCarthyism." According to Gunter, Alberta could do without a "formal" human rights code and so could reverse the decision simply by repealing the law to which the Charter applied (ibid.). This also was the argument taken up by Frum and Byfield. Alternatively, a plebiscite on the use of section 33 could be added to an upcoming municipal vote.

Editorial writers for the *Sun* chain called for use of the notwithstanding clause, not to encourage discrimination against gays (for which evidence, they argued, was nonexistent) but to send a clear signal to the court that it cannot rewrite Alberta law. The signed editorial in the *Edmonton Sun* spoke of an "arrogant" and "appalling" court, "unelected, unaccountable ha[ving] no business overriding the wishes of a duly elected and constituted legislature" (Jenkinson 1998). The *Calgary Sun* editorial declared that it was now "our turn to tell our appointed judges where to go" and that "Legislative power is the central issue in the case of Delwin Vriend case" (*Calgary Sun* 1998). Even the *Calgary Herald* editorial embraced this characterization of the case. Although the *Herald* "welcomed" the ruling, "the details of the ruling set a new and alarming standard in judicial activism" (*Calgary Herald* 1998). Other critiques concerned claims about the definition of family and the right to freedom of association – "employers have rights" too, wrote Linda Slobodian in the *Calgary Sun* (Slobodian 1998).

According to *Edmonton Sun* reporters David Bray and Alan Findlay (1998), wild rose residents were angry "not so much at the ruling, but reading in the ruling." Premier Klein adopted precisely this analysis in the period between the afternoon of the decision and his "drawing a line in the sand" (Laghi 1998b) – advising MNAs to accept the ruling – on the eve of the caucus meeting. Klein fuelled the provincial rights case by characterizing public opinion as being opposed not to the ruling but to the fact that the Supreme Court can "read their ruling into our legislation" (Waugh 1998). In the *Globe and Mail,* Klein is quoted as saying in the legislature that "the public needs to discuss the power of the courts ... What concerns the people and where my sense of anger is – and we've received well over 1,000 calls in my office – is with the issue of judicial activism" (Kenny 1998).

Although this message may have taken well in parts of the province, the failure to get this message out beyond the province is represented by the fact that the story was of no interest in Quebec. One might expect the rhetoric around provincial rights to have had some resonance there. Denis-Martin Chabot of Radio-Canada acknowledged that, in theory, the decision touched all the provinces but noted that, in reality, Alberta was one of the last provinces not to protect gays and lesbians from discrimination (Radio-Canada 1998). So the story was barely noticed in Quebec media – only a single opinion piece and not one editorial or guest commentary was devoted to the issue.

### Province as Deviant: Local Media

The provincial rights characterization, as we mentioned above, did not take everywhere. As in the national media, both perspectives were represented in regional media accounts. Columnists Catherine Ford and Don Martin in the *Calgary Herald* and Mark Lisac and David Staples in the *Edmonton Journal* resisted the characterization of the *Vriend* case as concerning judicial activism. Rather, as Ford put it (1998), the Klein government "humiliated themselves and the people of Alberta." More controversially, Staples (1998) likened Alberta's opposition to gay rights to Nazi Germany, fuelled further by an editorial cartoon depicting opponents of the ruling wearing the hood of the Ku Klux Klan.

Only the *Edmonton Journal* editorial page resisted the provincial rights aspect of the case. "The Vriend case is about bigotry," blared the editorial headline. The *Edmonton Journal* (1998b) criticized the premier's lack of commitment on this issue over the years, trying for years to "dress up their desire to institutionalize intolerance." In another editorial published five days later, the *Edmonton Journal* (1998c) emphasized that it was not so-called judicial activism that required Alberta to move on this issue but the Charter itself. It was the Charter that governments in Canada enacted and which they asked judges to enforce. On this point, the *Journal* had the support of Southam columnist Andrew Coyne, writing in the *Calgary Herald*. "The people of Canada gave judges the authority" to interpret the Charter, he wrote; "the Court merely was applying the law. Somebody had to" (Coyne 1998).

## Conclusion

What is striking about much of this coverage is that what we might call the moral question – whether gays and lesbians are deserving of equal protection and consideration under provincial law – largely disappears. This is an observation also made by Miljan and Cooper (2003, 165) based on a much smaller sample. This disappearing act is facilitated by the two dominant strategic frames we have identified. With the province-as-deviant story, there is no question that the province is wrong to exclude gays and lesbians from human rights protections. This fits well with national public opinion on this issue measured some time after the *Vriend* ruling. Legislatures "that had refused to protect gay rights through human rights legislation," Fletcher and Howe (2001, 275) write, "were clearly out of line with public attitudes." Alberta's provincial rights strategy also was compatible with this submerging of the moral question. Actors on the provincial side consistently got their message out that the case was about democracy, not morality. As a consequence, Delwin Vriend and the gay and lesbian equality rights movement virtually disappear from media accounts the day after the ruling, and Alberta (personified in Premier Klein) becomes the focus of the coverage.

The controversy over the court also vanishes. The debate on the use of the notwithstanding clause is the focus of analysis, not why the court ruled the way that it did. In some ways, the notwithstanding clause served precisely the purpose its framers intended. It shifted pressure away from the judiciary to elected politicians, who then have the opportunity of choosing whether to disregard a judicial pronouncement over rights. Also, as the framers of section 33 might have predicted, this was no easy thing for the premier of Alberta to undertake (though Alberta later would invoke section 33 to shield its *Marriage Act* from Charter review). Though the court embraced the metaphor of dialogue to explain its relationship with Parliament and legislatures, this metaphor did not capture well events immediately following the *Vriend* ruling. The court ruling simply fades away, its reputation intact, and politics takes over.

## Notes

1  Miljan and Cooper (2003, 163) identify only three CBC and two CTV national news stories after the *Vriend* decision was released. We collected four CBC and three CTV stories in addition to the French-language television stories.

## References

Arnold, Tom. 1997a. Albertan faces Supreme Court fight. *Calgary Herald,* 3 November, p. 11.

—. 1997b. Six years later, Vriend's fight enters the final round. *Edmonton Journal,* 3 November, p. A1.

—. 1998. Klein won't rule out use of clause in Vriend case. *Edmonton Journal,* 12 March, p. A5.

Braid, Don. 1998. Albertans can't hide from sex. *Calgary Sun,* 3 April, p. 4.

Bray, David. 1998. Klein keeping options open on Vriend case. *Edmonton Sun,* 1 April, p. 16.

Bray, David, and Alan Findlay. 1998. Protest over Vriend court decision: Albertans supremely frustrated. *Edmonton Sun,* 7 April, p. 4.

Byfield, Ted. 1994. An unelected ruler whose views we are not entitled to know. *Alberta Report,* 9 May, p. 52.

*Calgary Herald.* 1998. Sexual history: Judges and homosexuals flex their muscles. Editorial, 3 April, p. A22.

*Calgary Sun.* 1998. Slippery slope. Editorial, 3 April, p. 14.

CBC. 1997. Kelly Crowe (reporter). Alberta deliberately discriminating against homosexuals. *The National,* 4 November.

—. 1998a. Reg Sherren (reporter). Finally gay rights in Alberta. *The National,* 2 April.

—. 1998b. Kelly Crowe (reporter). Klein's decision: Protecting gays from discrimination. *The National,* 9 April.

Chase, Steve. 1998. Klein won't fight ruling on gays. *Calgary Herald,* 3 April, p. A1.

Coyne, Andrew. 1998. The court has the authority to interpret law. *Calgary Herald,* 8 April, p. A15.

CTV. 1998. Elizabeth Chu (reporter). Alberta's gays claim a major victory. *CTV News,* 2 April.

*Edmonton Journal.* 1998a. Supreme Court speaks on Vriend case. Editorial, 3 April, p. A18.

—. 1998b. The Vriend case is about bigotry: Government may undermine ruling. Editorial, 3 April, p. A16.

—. 1998c. Albertans value Charter of Rights: Klein uses courts for political ends. Editorial, 8 April, p. A14.

—. 1998d. An ugly week finally concludes: Why the long fight against Vriend? Editorial, 10 April, p. A14.

*Egan v. Canada,* [1995] 2 S.C.R. 513.

*Eldridge v. British Columbia (Attorney General),* [1997] 3 S.C.R. 624.

Feschuk, Scott. 1994. Alberta Tories in a bind over gay-rights decision. *Globe and Mail,* 14 April, p. A4.

Fletcher, Joseph F., and Paul Howe. 2001. Public opinion and Canada's courts. In *Judicial power and Canadian democracy,* ed. Paul Howe and Peter Russell, 255-96. Montreal and Kingston: McGill-Queen's University Press.

Ford, Catherine. 1998. Klein government skewed the true meaning of rights protection. *Calgary Herald,* 3 April, p. A23.

Fraser, Fil. 1994. It's up to Premier Klein to protect gays against discrimination. *Edmonton Journal,* 15 April, p. A14.

*Globe and Mail.* 1998a. Supreme Court: Alberta's law must include gays. 3 April, p. A17.

—. 1998b. The Supreme Court, equal to the task. Editorial, 3 April, p. A16.

—. 1998c. Foes of gay ruling bombard Klein. 8 April, p. A4.

Gold, Marta. 1996. Homosexuality a "lifestyle" – Klein. *Edmonton Journal,* 20 March, p. A3.

Gunter, Lorne. 1998. Alberta has the power to reverse Vriend ruling. *Edmonton Journal,* 5 April, p. F8.

Havelock, Jon. 1998. Speaking notes for the Honourable Jon Havelock (unpublished).

Hogg, Peter W. 1998. *Constitutional law of Canada.* Toronto: Carswell.

Jeffs, Allyson. 1998. About face. *Edmonton Journal,* 12 March, pp. A1, A5.

Jenkinson, Mike. 1998. It's time to opt out. *Edmonton Sun,* 3 April, p. 10.

Johnsrude, Larry. 1998. Tories gear up for court ruling. *Edmonton Journal,* 30 March, p. A1.

Kenny, Eoin. 1998. Albertans wrestling with gay-rights ruling. *Globe and Mail,* 7 April, p. A8.

Ketcham, Brock. 1998. Both sides in debate see court decision as milestone. *Calgary Herald,* 2 April, p. A2.

King's College. 2003. http://www.kingsu.ab.ca (accessed 3 May 2003).

Laghi, Brian. 1997. Gay seeks rights – Code protections case of Alberta teacher fired for sexual orientation goes before Supreme Court. *Globe and Mail,* 4 November, p. A4.

—. 1998a. Debate on gay rights polarizes Albertans. *Globe and Mail,* 2 April, p. A12.

—. 1998b. Alberta's gay-rights fight turns ugly. *Globe and Mail,* 9 April, p. A1.

Makin, Kirk. 1998a. How far should judges go? Ruling today in gay-rights case pits court against politicians. *Globe and Mail,* 2 April, p. A1.

—. 1998b. Court defends activist role in judgment. *Globe and Mail,* 3 April, p. A4.

McGovern, Celeste. 1994. One ruling too far. *Western Report,* 2 May, p. 6.

Menzies, Peter. 1998. Legislatures write laws. Let's keep it that way. *Calgary Herald,* 8 April, p. A14.

Miljan, Lydia, and Barry Cooper. 2003. *Hidden agendas: How journalists influence the news.* Vancouver: UBC Press.

Mitchell, Alanna. 1998. Phone-in talk show reflects full spectrum. *Globe and Mail,* 3 April, p. A4.

Morton, Ted. 1996. Power to the people, not the judges. *Western Report,* 11 March, p. 21.

Ovenden, Norm. 1997a. Gays in Alberta face bias on daily basis, Vriend says. *Edmonton Journal,* 4 November, p. A3.

—. 1997b. Alberta hammered on gay rights issue: Justices criticize province. *Calgary Herald,* 5 November, p. A3.

—. 1997c. High court gives Albert legislation rough ride. *Edmonton Journal,* 5 November, p. A1.

Radio-Canada. 1998. Denis Chabot (reporter). *Le Téléjournal,* 2 April.

Simpson, Jeffrey. 1998. Is Supreme Court bound to interpret Charter and laws as passed? *Globe and Mail,* 8 April, p. A14.

Slobodian, Linda. 1998. Ruling denies employers' rights. *Calgary Sun,* 3 April, p. 7.

Stanway, Paul. 1998a. Highest court supremely out of touch. *Edmonton Sun,* 3 April, p. 11.

—. 1998b. Like all of us, gays are already protected by a battery of laws: Rights decision absolute crock. *Calgary Sun,* 3 April, p. 15.

Staples, David. 1998. The Nazis weren't in favour of gay rights, either. *Edmonton Journal,* 5 April, p. A7.

Torrance, Kelley. 1997. A supreme display of judicial prejudice. *Alberta Report,* 17 November, p. 30.

*Vriend v. Alberta,* [1994] 6 W.W.R. 414.

*Vriend v. Alberta* (1996), 132 D.L.R. (4th) 595.

*Vriend v. Alberta,* [1998] 1 S.C.R. 493.

*Vriend v. Alberta,* [1998] 1 S.C.R. 493 (Factum of the Respondents).

Waugh, Neil. 1998. Right-wing Albertans are not happy. *Edmonton Sun,* 7 April, p. 11.

—3—

# Court and Spin Country:
# The *Quebec Secession Reference*

SEEING AS THE court's decision in the *Quebec Secession Reference* concerned the proposed division of one country into two, it was "among the most closely watched [cases] in the Supreme Court's history" (Millard 1999). In the hours after the court's ruling there were 22,000 hits to the complete text of the decision posted on the court's website (Poulin 1998). Not surprisingly, Canadian media invested immense resources in covering the *Secession Reference*. In terms of the numbers of stories alone, coverage of the hearing and decision dwarfed all the other cases we have examined for this study. Beyond the numbers, the stories contained greater depth and insight. There was more background information, which provided a context for both the reference questions and the court's role in the federation. Experts beyond number were interviewed; columnists penned innumerable opinion pieces. The resulting coverage admittedly was impressive. The justices of the Supreme Court of Canada could not have failed to take notice. Former Justice Frank Iacobucci echoed the opinion of many other Supreme Court justices we interviewed when he said, "I think that the media, both electronic and print, did a superb job on the reference to secession. I mean a superb job, not just a good job. First class. Why? Because everybody was interested. I think that the court did more than its share in summarizing what it was [we were doing]. We summarized at the end; we summarized at the beginning. We tried to anticipate as much as we could any kind of editorializing, any kind of spin doctoring as much as you can on these things" (Iacobucci 2001).

Despite the numbers of stories and the depth of coverage, our close study of articles, headlines, and broadcasts reveals a number of interesting trends. Our analysis of frames demonstrates that well over half of the articles were written in a strategic frame rather than an issue frame. This means that much of the coverage focused on words of war and conflict between federalists and sovereignists, rather than on the cool and detached discourse of law. The case pitted, in stark terms, Quebec versus the rest of Canada. This kind of coverage might have heightened tensions in readers because it played on the conflict angle, setting speakers against each other often at the expense of thoughtful, reasoned debate. Conflict coverage is often negative in nature, and our results demonstrate that the federal government was the target of much negative criticism. But the court, too, was the subject of some condemnation – most of it during the hearing, when suspicions and recriminations were running high in the face of uncertainty.

The release of the court's carefully crafted decision – which both affirmed the federal government's claims and legitimated the sovereignist project by outlining a new constitutional duty to negotiate – defused tensions and won praise from actors on all sides. While the positions and political posturings of federal and Quebec politicians were well examined during both the hearing and the decision stage, there was less coverage of the legal arguments and reasons. Although there was much coverage, and much excellent coverage, an analysis of the entire body of work shows that politics often supplanted legal reasoning – that the dispute between federalists and sovereignists overshadowed the court and its discourse.

The preponderance of reporting through the strategic frame reflected the ongoing competition for authority between the federal government led by Jean Chrétien and the Quebec nationalist movement led by Quebec premier Lucien Bouchard. The two sides faced off in the pages of newspapers and on television, seeking to place their stamp on the hearing and on the resulting decision. It was a "critical battle for public opinion" (CBC 1998e), an "unprecedented contest of spin and counter spin" (CTV 1998k). Each aimed to place an interpretive stamp on the reference that worked to their strategic advantage. Throughout, federalists sought to characterize the case as being one about the powerful idea of the rule of law. A Supreme Court opinion, federalists believed, would vanquish the illegal sovereignist project. For federalists, cool and detached legal reasoning would prevail over emotion (*Le Journal de Montréal* 1998a; CBC 1998a). (In this way, the federalist strategy resembled the province-as-deviant narrative embraced by national media in their coverage of the *Vriend* case.) Sovereignists sought to portray the reference as an usurpation of the will of the Quebec people and a manipulation of Supreme Court jurisdiction (and so resembled the failed provincial rights strategy adopted by the Alberta government in *Vriend*). As the case proceeded from the hearing to the decision stage, however, sovereignists changed their tack and characterized the court's decision as an affirmation of their movement and, in this sense, offered welcome "clarity" to the process by which Quebec might achieve sovereignty. For sovereignists, politics, not legality, would determine the future of Quebec. To the extent that the court decision moved beyond the strictly legal and into the terrain of the political, as we discuss below, it reinforced the sovereignist message. Media reporting similarly followed suit, reinforcing the sovereignist spin that the case largely was about politics and not law.

## Actors and Arguments: Getting the Message Out

The *Quebec Secession Reference* raised an issue rarely addressed to courts: whether a federal constitution permits subnational units unilaterally to secede. Quebec's status in the federation has been in the foreground of Canadian politics since at least the 1960s. The question of Quebec's capacity to secede has been considered mostly a political one. And yet the legal mechanism for the transition to secession is not readily transparent. Does the constitution of Canada entitle a province to secede and, if so, what level of consensus is called for? Political leaders in the rest of Canada have almost always been content to leave these questions for another day. In this case, however, a number of key events precipitated their movement to the front burner.[1]

In September 1995, the Parti québécois-led government of Quebec tabled Bill 1, *An Act Respecting the Future of Quebec*.[2] The bill outlined a process by which the government, one year after making an offer of political and economic partnership with the rest of Canada, could unilaterally declare the sovereignty of Quebec. The people of Quebec first would be asked to approve the process laid out in the bill in a referendum scheduled for October 1995. Sovereignist-turned-federalist and Quebec City lawyer Guy Bertrand (later sovereignist again) aimed to halt the Government of Quebec's referendum by seeking an order from the Superior Court of Quebec. The Attorney General of Quebec sought unsuccessfully to dismiss Bertrand's application. In protest, the Government of Quebec withdrew from the proceedings, as no Canadian court, it maintained, could stand in the way of the democratic will of Quebecers. On 8 September 1995, Justice Lesage denied Me. Bertrand his injunction but did issue a declaratory order, which would not interfere with the pending referendum. The declaration acknowledged that some of the provisions of Bill 1 were inconsistent with the constitution's amending formula and amounted to a "serious threat" to Bertrand's constitutionally guaranteed rights and freedoms (*Bertrand* 1995).

On 30 October 1995, a slim majority of Quebecers voted "no" to the question asked by the government (50.58 versus 49.42 percent). Bill 1 now was a dead letter. Me. Bertrand returned to the courts, however, and sought a definitive ruling on Quebec's ability to withdraw unilaterally from the federation. The Attorney General of Quebec again sought dismissal of the case. It was difficult for the Government of Canada to resist being drawn into this legal debate and so intervened in this second *Bertrand* hearing to advance arguments about the relevance of the constitution and the jurisdiction of Canadian courts on the question of Quebec secession. Justice Pidgeon of the Quebec Superior Court rejected the Quebec Attorney General's motion to dismiss, concluding that the issues raised were sufficiently serious, and not merely hypothetical, that they deserved a hearing on their merits. Justice Pidgeon identified a number of constitutional questions worthy of further investigation, including whether Quebec had the right unilaterally to secede from Canada and whether domestic law had precedence over international law (*Bertrand* 1996, 507-8). The Government of Quebec again removed itself from the *Bertrand* legal proceedings. Rather than continuing to sit simply on the sidelines as the case proceeded, the federal government chose to put three questions to the Supreme Court of Canada. These formed the basis of the reference.[3] The questions, simply put, were: (1) Under the constitution of Canada, can Quebec effect secession from Canada unilaterally? (2) Is there a right to self-determination under international law that would give Quebec the right to secede unilaterally? and (3) In the event of a conflict between domestic and international law, which would take precedence?

Why this sudden aggressive stance of the Canadian federal government? Formerly, federalists feared that framing the issue as a legal question could be seen, rightly or wrongly, as legitimating the secessionist project in political and constitutional terms. For sovereignists, on the other hand, formulating the issue in terms of legality was deeply problematic, as it would situate the debate in a context not of their own choosing but one determined by the rules laid down in Canada's 1982 constitution. The startlingly close referendum result shook the federal government to its foundations, resulting in this federalist turn to legality. Prime Minister Jean Chrétien appeared weak and beleaguered, resorting to a last-minute televised act of desperation recognizing Quebec as a "distinct society" and pledging not to initiate constitutional reform without Quebec's consent. In a teary-eyed confessional moment with his Liberal caucus behind closed doors, the prime minister admitted he almost lost the country to the sovereignists. This was in stark contrast to the confident and hard-line stance adopted by the Reform Party leader, Preston Manning. Manning would have been willing to negotiate with separatists, but only on terms favourable to the rest of Canada. The federal Liberal Party chose to pull a leaf from the Reform Party playbook. The Liberals would continue to pursue the traditional track of renewed federalism – the so-called Plan A. The 1997 Calgary Declaration, for instance, had nine premiers and the federal government in agreement on a program for constitutional renewal organized around seven principles. There would now be a second additional track – Plan B – which would pit federalists against sovereignists on the field of constitutional law. Here, the federalist cause would have a distinct advantage, for there is nothing in the constitution that would condone a threat of the unilateral secession of Quebec from Canada – a threat Quebec premier Jacques Parizeau had issued in the last referendum campaign. Though the 1995 referendum now was behind them, the federal Liberals were of the view that a legal ruling from the Supreme Court could be held in reserve until the next time Quebecers were asked to choose Quebec over Canada. A ruling from the court that secession outside of the Canadian constitution was "illegal," "unconstitutional," and contrary to the "rule of law" could be conscripted swiftly and effectively into any future referendum campaign, swaying the so-called soft sovereignist vote over to the federalist side.

The three questions were drafted in such a way as to ensure this federal victory. The right to secession does not appear anywhere in the Canadian constitution, the Attorney General of Canada argued (Canada 1997). The constitution's amending formula contemplated unilateral amendment only in section 45, and this provision did not concern secession but the "constitution of the province" – those operational rules of government that are not entrenched in the constitution (para. 101).[4] Though Canada's domestic constitutional order is "capable of accommodating any alteration of the federation," including the secession of a province, secession could not be accomplished unilaterally (paras. 85, 112).[5] The principle of self-determination in international law, the Attorney General also argued, did not condone a right to unilateral secession from a federation where the government "represents its people on the basis of equality" (para. 186). The third question left no doubt that the questions were intended to ensure a federalist victory. It was well established that in the case of conflict between the constitution of Canada and international law, domestic constitutional law will prevail.

There is no question that the federal government has authority to refer constitutional questions to the highest court. References, strictly speaking, are not about assigning rights and responsibilities between opposing parties. Rather, the reference power entitles the government to seek consideration by the court of "important questions of law or fact." Though the court usually is hesitant to issue rulings based on hypothetical situations in the ordinary course of constitutional litigation, it usually will do so in the context of a reference from government.[6] The court retains some control over the process, however. For one thing, the court can formulate orders and directives that supplement the Rules of Practice, which govern the roles of parties before the court. In this case, the court was confronted with the novel situation where the Attorney General of Canada, representing the federal government, would take a lead role in the reference but where, from the outset, the Government of Quebec refused to participate in that process. A large majority of Quebecers, according to public opinion polling data, viewed as illegitimate the Supreme Court of Canada answering questions that belonged only to the citizens of Quebec to answer (*Le Journal de Montréal* 1998a). Numerous other governments, organizations, and individuals were eager, however, to intervene in the case. Interveners included the Attorneys General of Manitoba and Saskatchewan, the ministers of justice of the Northwest Territories and the Yukon, Guy Bertrand, Roopnarine Singh (who also launched litigation in Quebec courts following the 1995 referendum), and Yves Michaud. Michaud was a well-known former journalist and Liberal MNA, and now a militant in the Parti québécois. Intervener status also was granted to First Nations and associated organizations, including the Grand Council of the Crees, the Kitigan Zibi Anishinabeg First Nation, the Makivik Corporation, the Chiefs of Ontario, and to other organizations such as the Minority Advocacy and Rights Council, the Ad Hoc Committee of Canadian Women on the Constitution, and the leader of the Libertarian Party of Canada, Vincent Pouliot. There was no one appearing before the court other than Michaud (who subsequently withdrew from the case), who would articulate the position of the Government of Quebec. The court, however, holds in reserve a power to appoint lawyers to argue in favour of the rights and interests of those not otherwise represented in the proceedings. The job of the amicus curiae is to help a court examine the other side of the argument submitted by the parties that are represented. And so the court, on 14 July 1997, appointed André Joli-Coeur, a Quebec sovereignist, to act as amicus curiae and to make arguments that would have been made by the Government of Quebec if it had chosen to intervene in the case.

Me. Joli-Coeur responded to the federal government's three questions by filing a variety of expert opinions and legal briefs. His first strategy, law professor Bruce Ryder notes, was to ask the court not to answer the questions (Ryder 1999, 78; *Quebec Secession* 1998, Factum). The amicus curiae argued that the court had no constitutional authority to answer questions by way of reference; alternatively, that the court had no authority to answer questions concerning international law; and, lastly, that the questions were too political and too hypothetical to be deserving of legal answer. The second strategy, Ryder (1999, 78) adds, was not to answer the domestic legal question directly and, instead, to seek firmer ground on international law. Though international law did not give Quebec the right unilaterally to secede, international law would condone secession if Quebec could effectively gain control of its territory following a declaration of sovereignty. The domestic legal order, the amicus curiae argued, would have to follow suit and acknowledge this principle of "effectivity" (Joli-Coeur 1997, para. 135). Montreal *Gazette* columnist Paul Wells rightly described Joli-Coeur's position as "tightly argued" and "relentlessly imaginative" (Wells 1998c).

The court was in a precarious situation. It was being asked to issue a ruling on highly contentious matters – its impartial authority being enlisted for a predominantly political purpose (*Globe and Mail* 1998a). Particularly in view of Quebec public opinion, this was a hazardous situation for the court. As we have noted in the Introduction, the Supreme Court's impartiality has been brought into doubt in years past. Quebec elites have accused the court of doing the bidding of the federal government in controversies over the division of legislative powers between the federal and provincial governments. Though Quebec elites, for the most part, have not cast doubt on the ability of the courts to rule in Charter of Rights cases (Morissette 1999), the suspicion that the court leans in favour of the federal government continues to linger. It was this suspicion that sovereignists would seek to exploit during the reference. Moreover, political leadership in Quebec – sovereignists and federalists alike, including the leader of the Progressive Conservative Party, Jean Charest – appeared to be unified in condemning the federal government's reference to the court. In contrast, the reference would be expected to play well in English Canada. After all, this hardball strategy was endorsed by the western-based Reform Party of Canada. Paradoxically, it precisely was this constituency which had been raising doubts about the court's legitimacy in Charter of Rights and Aboriginal cases. Now, both the future of the country and the future legitimacy of the court hung in the balance.

## Methodology and Preliminary Findings

The coverage that we have analyzed spans an eight-day period surrounding the hearing (two days before and two days after their completion) and a ten-day window around the release of the court's opinion (two days before the decision and seven days after). The number of articles and reports collected indicates that a high level of interest in the *Quebec Secession Reference* was present in both French- and English-language television and newspapers. A total of 445 articles were collected from the French- and English-language print media, including Montreal-based broadsheets the *Gazette, La Presse, Le Devoir,* Ottawa-based *Le Droit,* and Toronto-based *Globe and Mail,* together with the tabloids *Le Journal de Montréal* and the *Toronto Sun.* Sixty-seven television news stories were collected from the main evening broadcasts on Radio-Canada, TVA, CBC, and CTV during the same two periods. Coverage of the hearing was especially significant. It is rare for a Supreme Court hearing to garner even one story, but in this instance 215 stories, or 42 percent of the total number of television and newspaper articles collected, were run or published during the period when legal arguments were being made. That the hearing before the court (16-19 February 1998) took four days to complete helps explain this result, as does the highly contentious nature of the reference process itself. Table 3.1 and Table 3.2 show that although some media gave more coverage to the reference than others, overall each outlet surveyed gave both the hearing and the decision a great deal of space. Even the *Toronto Sun* published fifteen articles on the hearing – an unusual finding given the tabloid's propensity for the trivial and sensational.

In addition to the volume of material, a second exceptional feature of this case is its political nature. Often, media coverage of legal issues focuses on the conflict between personalities (what we have called the strategic frame).

**Table 3.1: Newspaper articles on secession hearing and decision**

| Newspaper | Hearing | Decision | Total |
|---|---|---|---|
| *Gazette* | 44 | 49 | 93 |
| *La Presse* | 35 | 41 | 76 |
| *Le Devoir* | 29 | 37 | 66 |
| *Le Droit* | 20 | 36 | 56 |
| *Le Journal de Montréal* | 18 | 31 | 49 |
| *Globe and Mail* | 26 | 40 | 66 |
| *Toronto Sun* | 15 | 24 | 39 |
| **Total** | **187** | **258** | **445** |

**Table 3.2: Television reports on secession hearing and decision**

| Network | Hearing | Decision | Total |
|---|---|---|---|
| Radio-Canada | 7 | 10 | 17 |
| TVA | 5 | 10 | 15 |
| CBC | 8 | 9 | 17 |
| CTV | 8 | 10 | 18 |
| **Total** | **28** | **39** | **67** |

Questions concerning the future of Quebec do not lend themselves to this kind of personality-driven coverage, as the question concerns abstract concepts, values, and competing visions of the country. Nevertheless, the eminently political nature of the conflict makes it natural to seek out the points of view of the relevant political actors. These actors' positions are then portrayed from a tactical point of view, emphasizing a conflict between opposing views on the future of the country. These protagonists' statements about the case are then situated in the framework of their political objectives.

Given the political nature of the conflict and the protagonists' struggle to capture public opinion, it comes as no surprise that the media treated it as if it were a political debate, leaving little room for the strictly legal aspects of the case. Most often, then, media reports took a strategic frame based on an adversarial approach. The aim of these reports was to identify who was the winner and who was the loser. Sports metaphors often appeared – references to battles, strategies, winner and losers were common. The *Toronto Sun* even referred to the case as "political wrestlemania" (Harris 1998). Table 3.3 and Table 3.4 show that use of the

**Table 3.3: Newspaper frames: Hearing and decision**

| Frame | Issue | | Strategic | | Other | | Total |
|---|---|---|---|---|---|---|---|
| | Hearing | Decision | Hearing | Decision | Hearing | Decision | |
| *Gazette* | 17 (18.3%) | 15 (16.1%) | 25 (26.9%) | 30 (32.3%) | 2 (2.2%) | 4 (4.3%) | 93 |
| *La Presse* | 11 (14.5%) | 8 (10.5%) | 24 (31.6%) | 33 (43%) | - | - | 76 |
| *Le Devoir* | 5 (7.6%) | 3 (4.5%) | 24 (36.4%) | 34 (51.5%) | - | - | 66 |
| *Le Droit* | 8 (14.3%) | 7 (12.5%) | 12 (21.4%) | 26 (46.4%) | - | 3 (5.4%) | 56 |
| *Le Journal de Montréal* | 5 (10.2%) | 3 (6.1%) | 13 (26.5%) | 26 (53.1%) | - | 2 (4.1%) | 49 |
| *Globe and Mail* | 9 (13.6%) | 16 (24.2%) | 10 (15.2%) | 21 (31.8%) | 7 (10.6%) | 3 (4.5%) | 66 |
| *Toronto Sun* | 7 (17.9%) | 10 (25.6%) | 8 (20.5%) | 14 (35.9%) | - | - | 39 |
| **Total** | 62 | 62 | 116 | 184 | 9 | 12 | |

**Table 3.4: Television frames: Hearing and decision**

| Frame | Issue | | Strategic | | Total |
|---|---|---|---|---|---|
| | Hearing | Decision | Hearing | Decision | |
| Radio-Canada | 3 | 3 | 4 | 7 | 17 |
| TVA | 3 | 2 | 2 | 8 | 15 |
| CBC | 4 | 4 | 4 | 5 | 17 |
| CTV | 1 | 2 | 7 | 8 | 18 |
| Total | 11 | 11 | 17 | 28 | |

strategic frame differs slightly from the hearing stage to the decision stage. During the hearing, 34 percent of the frames found in stories were issue frames (concerning primarily the legal issues and arguments) and 62 percent were strategic frames. The percentage of strategic frames found in decision coverage was slightly higher, with 71 percent being coded as strategic frames and 24 percent as issue.[7] These figures seem to indicate that after the court delivered its opinion, coverage leaned even more heavily toward the posturing of politicians. During the hearing phase, in contrast, there was slightly more attention paid to the patterns of legal argumentation.

If the coverage focused on the conflict between actors rather than on their legal arguments, most of the articles portrayed Quebec and Canada as adversaries. The dualistic nature of the conflict was underscored at every opportunity. The *Secession Reference*, however, was much more than a struggle between anglophones and francophones over the future of Quebec. It was a conflict between Quebec, which condemned the Supreme Court's interference, and the rest of Canada, which was seeking a legal solution to the threat of secession. It is not surprising, therefore, that most of the articles concentrated on the strategic aspects of the case. The accent was on the debates and quarrels between the protagonists, scenario playing, and predictions about who would win and who would lose. Legal aspects of the case rarely were in focus.

To the extent that the ensuing debate was portrayed in tactical rather than legal terms, this might be understood as a victory for sovereignists. So long as the case was characterized as primarily about politics and not about law, this underscored the sovereignist interpretation of the case. For the federalist side, an emphasis on the legal dimension of the case, rather than politics, underscored the message of illegality with which they sought to brand the Quebec sovereignty movement. Yet, even this message had to be delivered in ways the media would understand, namely, in terms of political conflict. One explanation for this result, then, is that the media resorted to the strategic frame as a reflex action. They simply focused

**Table 3.5: Main focus of headlines**

|  | Hearing | Decision | Total |
| --- | --- | --- | --- |
| Alliances/Strategies | 47 | 66 | 113 |
| Issue | 5 | 72 | 77 |
| Secession/Separatism | 19 | 39 | 58 |
| Hearing arguments | 46 | 1 | 47 |
| Court or justices | 28 | 14 | 42 |
| Winners and losers | 1 | 25 | 26 |
| All others | 41 | 40 | 81 |

on the obvious tactical elements and left in the shadow complex legal arguments that were seen as too abstract for public consumption. Contributing to this phenomenon was the preponderance of journalists covering the case who ordinarily would cover the political and not the legal beat. Of the newspaper journalists reporting on the case, only 2.3 percent were identified as legal reporters, while over 25 percent were identified as parliamentary or Ottawa bureau reporters.

The strategic approach was even more prevalent in the French-language than in the English-language media. As shown in Table 3.3, French-language newspapers were more likely to take a strategic approach to the decision as compared to their English-language counterparts. This again signals a tilt in favour of the sovereignist side in framing the reference as a political and not a legal dispute. Among newspapers, the highest percentage of articles with strategic frames (88 percent) was found in *Le Devoir*. In *Le Journal de Montréal,* 80 percent of the articles were in a strategic frame and in *La Presse* 75 percent. In English-language newspapers, the percentage of strategic articles was lower, with 47 percent in the *Globe and Mail* and 56 percent in the *Toronto Sun.* Even the Montreal *Gazette,* which serves a Quebec-based, mainly anglophone population, had just 59 percent strategic articles. Yet a strategic frame was not only prominent in francophone media reports. As shown in Table 3.4, among television networks, the largest percentage of strategic reports was on the anglophone CTV network (83 percent). Conflict-based, or strategic, frames accounted for 53 percent of coverage on CBC, 65 percent of coverage on Radio-Canada, and 67 percent of coverage on TVA.

Headlines, too, emphasized the conflict-oriented nature of coverage, with many focusing on political dimensions of the case. The majority of the headlines in newspapers were about strategies being employed by politicians or the alliances that were occurring between the main protagonists (see Table 3.5). These headlines highlighted the strategic actions being taken by political actors as they vied for public support. The legal dimension of the case became centre stage only in the immediate aftermath of the decision, when it was the focal point of the title in

Table 3.6: Main topic of story in English- and French-language newspapers and television

| Topic | English | French |
|---|---|---|
| Details of decision | 55 | 97 |
| Strategies employed by politicians | 38 | 48 |
| Speculation on secession procedures | 34 | 15 |
| Details of hearing | 33 | 41 |
| Background or history of case | 16 | 5 |
| Clear majority on clear question means negotiation | 12 | 19 |
| Court should not hear case | 11 | 6 |
| Issue is for Quebec to decide | 7 | 21 |
| Actions or demonstrations by separatists | 5 | 9 |
| Direct quote from decision or hearing | 5 | 5 |
| Economic factors | 5 | 2 |
| Other | 5 | 2 |
| Judicial activism | 3 | 1 |
| Canadian unity | 3 | 0 |
| Supreme Court or justices | 1 | 8 |
| **Total** | **233** | **279** |

72 of the 444 newspaper stories that had headlines.[8] Winners and losers were the angle in twenty-six headlines, predominantly falling, again, in the days after the decision was released.[9]

A large percentage of headlines focused on the comments or actions of politicians. Thirty-two percent of all headlines focused on politicians from both federal and provincial parties. These include all federal politicians, Parti québécois representatives, and members of parties from all other provinces. The headlines of 36 percent of the sample highlighted no specific protagonist. Instead, they described a situation or idea without referring to any protagonist. The court was mentioned as the primary protagonist only in 13 percent of the headlines. Of the 189 headlines that mentioned the Supreme Court or the individual justices, the tone of 70 percent was neutral, 15 percent were negative, and 15 percent were positive.

English- and French-language media covered similar main topics equally.[10] However, more than 15 percent of the English-language print media focused on the theme of secession as the main topic, whereas it accounted for just 5 percent of the French-language media (see Table 3.6). This might be explained by the fact that the advantages and disadvantages of secession have been debated in Quebec for a long time. There also was a discernible difference in the amount of coverage of whether the decision to secede belonged to the citizens of Quebec. This theme ran through 7.5 percent of the French media news stories, but was the main topic in only 3 percent of those in the English media sample. These results suggest a difference in degree between French- and English-language media in their views of the legitimacy of the secessionist project.

The third exceptional feature of the case is the seeming unanimity after the release of the court's decision. Once the ruling was issued, reports were not merely neutral: French- and English-language media were virtually in agreement that the decision adopted a common sense and pragmatic approach to the threat of unilateral secession. The decision had the effect of defusing a potentially explosive situation and delegitimating extremists on both sides of the question. We discuss this finding in more detail below. As a preliminary matter, it should be emphasized that, once the justices of the court successfully extracted themselves from this awkward situation, it allowed the media to return immediately to the political stakes involved and the strategic nature of the *Secession Reference*.

## The Hearing: "In the Field of Law"

In the lead-up to the hearing, media outlets invested significant resources to describing the reference and its context in plain language. Many devoted space to the three "crucial" questions the federal government submitted to the court; some of the central concepts relevant to court proceedings also were explained. In newspapers such as *La Presse* and the Montreal *Gazette,* articles were devoted to helping readers "disentangle the situation a little" (Boisvert 1998a) or, like the *Gazette,* provided "everything you need to know" guides.[11]

The media understood that there were high stakes involved. The *Secession Reference* made front-page news in all the papers under study. It was billed as "the case of the century" (Hébert 1998a; Chambers 1998), and the case that would go down in history (Tibbetts 1998; *Toronto Sun* 1998). Chief Justice Lamer was quoted as saying that the reference was "the most important case" in his eighteen years on the bench (*Le Journal de Montréal* 1998b), and that for the justices, it would be "the task of their lives" (Fraser 1998h). The justices of the court even arranged to have a photograph taken of the group on the eve of this momentous hearing.

Some reports equipped readers and viewers with more critical tools of analysis. TVA, for instance, on the eve of the hearing, interviewed Professor Alain Pellet, chairman of the UN International Law Commission, who had been retained to issue an expert opinion at the request of the amicus curiae (TVA 1998a; Auger 1998a). The pipe-smoking Pellet was reportedly shocked by the three questions, saying they imposed negative answers. The questions were so biased, he added, that if they were submitted to the International Court of Justice, there would be talk of manipulation of jurisdiction. The incendiary interview even made its way into the anglophone press (Séguin 1998e; Thompson 1998b).

Although the preponderance of reporting was balanced, if a tone was discernible, it was one that was decidedly negative toward the court during the hearing period. It might be expected that columnists and editorialists were more likely to reflect this tone, as they critically evaluated the event. Our data reveal, however, that there was no statistically significant relationship between negative or positive tone and opinion and editorial writing. One was just as likely to find an overall negative or positive tone in a hard news story as in an opinion piece.

The negative tone toward the court in the hearing period can be explained in part by the portrayal of Quebec elite and public opinion as unanimously condemning the reference. The media reported comments by public figures from all the political parties in Quebec, including Liberals Claude Ryan and Daniel Johnson; members of the Parti québécois, such as Lucien Bouchard and Bernard Landry; leader of the Action démocratique du Québec Mario Dumont (Thompson 1998a);

and the leader of Pro-Démocratie, Professor André Tremblay (TVA 1998b). Even Progressive Conservative leader Jean Charest (1998) opposed the reference to the court. A heated exchange in the House of Commons between Charest and Prime Minister Chrétien the day the hearing began was described on CBC's *The National* as "tense," "charged," and "personal" (CBC 1998c). Political leadership from Quebec condemned Ottawa for asking the Supreme Court to resolve an issue that only the people of Quebec were able to clarify – the identity of a society and nation is a political issue and certainly cannot be resolved using legal principles. Even Cardinal Jean-Claude Turcotte had condemned the reference the previous Christmas. According to a number of Quebec leaders, the secession issue was "inadmissible," and the Supreme Court should refuse to answer Ottawa's claims and "find a way to put it off" (*Globe and Mail* 1998a). Quebec minister of intergovernmental affairs Jacques Brassard said that Canada was "discrediting itself" (Girard 1998a) and "tarnishing its international reputation" (Delisle 1998c). The head of the Bloc Québécois, Gilles Duceppe, claimed that Chrétien was "seriously discrediting the Supreme Court" (Myles 1998a; Séguin 1998a) because the debate was political not legal. Separatists are "steaming," reported Jim Munson on CTV's national news the eve of the decision (CTV 1998a). Quebec's political class, Montreal *Gazette* columnist Don Macpherson (1998a) observed, was "as close to unanimous as it will ever get." If dominant Quebec public opinion was unified, the federalists were divided and isolated (Auger 1998a). Only former Quebec minister of intergovernmental affairs Gil Rémillard came forward to endorse the reference. That Rémillard's views were reported only in the *Gazette* raised suspicions in English Canada that this presumed unity in Quebec was a false front (Greenspon 1998a). Nevertheless, "separatists are having a field day with the split in federalist ranks," declared Jim Munson in his *CTV News* report (CTV 1998a).

In addition to questioning the Supreme Court's competence to hear the reference, a number of Quebec stakeholders wondered aloud about the court's impartiality. It was asked how "nine justices of the highest federal court, appointed unilaterally by the federal government, and mandated by that very federal government to answer three questions formulated by the federal government" could render a decision contrary to the interests of the federal government (Nuovo 1998). This was a suspicion that had been nurtured over the years by former Quebec premiers Maurice Duplessis, Daniel Johnson Sr., and René Lévesque. They had compared the Supreme Court of Canada to the leaning tower of Pisa, as it always leaned one way, namely, in the federalist direction. The image of the leaning tower

---

◄ "Official photograph of the Supreme Court justices." *Le Devoir*'s editorial cartoonist plays on the nationalist suggestion that the justices of the Supreme Court of Canada lean like the tower of Pisa, in the same direction as the federal government (17 February 1998). *Courtesy of Le Devoir*

was appropriated by sovereignist forces in print media – advertisements were taken out in the French-language press – and picked up in electronic media reports. Editorial cartoonists also exploited the Pisa image. On 17 February, *Le Devoir* published an editorial cartoon of the nine Supreme Court justices all leaning to one side with the caption "Official photograph of the Supreme Court justices" (*Le Devoir* 1998b).

The image of Quebec unity opposed to the fragmented federalists was underscored by various reports, including those about the so-called pilgrimage to Ottawa made by Bloc Québécois MPs and led by Gilles Duceppe on the first day of the hearing. The march ended in a rally on the steps of the Supreme Court Building with some five hundred supporters drawn from the "four corners" of Quebec (*Le Journal de Montréal* 1998c) – from Abitibi to Montreal (TVA 1998c and TVA 1998d). The crowd condemned, reported numerous newspapers, what it saw as the "misuse of the Supreme Court" by the federal government and laid siege to the Supreme Court, waving fleur-de-lys flags and chanting "Democracy: for Quebeckers to decide!"[12] On the second day, a number of Quebec artists associated the Supreme Court reference with an assault on freedom (Brosseau 1998a), adding their signatures to a petition condemning the reference. Some reports even wondered where Chief Justice Lamer and Justice L'Heureux-Dubé, who are of French Canadian origin, would sit on this question – this was a "special challenge" for them, according to the *Globe and Mail* (Fine 1998a). Would they dare to favour their origins and render a decision that was not in the interest of the government that had appointed them?

The antagonistic tone was underscored by an "us versus them" dichotomy (Greenspon 1998a): "Their rule of law, under their constitution, with their judges," declared Bloc leader Duceppe (CBC 1998c). This was mixed with outright anger: "We don't care at all about it. We don't believe in that court and all that fucking thing," an unidentified man declared on the *CTV News* on the eve of the hearing. The image of large crowds of sovereignists, chanting and waving flags, was a recurring one in the electronic media. On *CTV News*, viewers were reminded that Quebec premier Bouchard could stir up "passion" on such an issue (CTV 1998a). In print media, the *Toronto Sun* referred to "demonstrations, chants, and ritualistic lies" – an "auto-hypnotic frenzy" (Gamble 1998b). There were no complementary federalist rallies, however, to report in support of the reference. There was only, according to a *Toronto Sun* editorial, the decorum and calm of judicial proceedings (*Toronto Sun* 1998b). The week-long series of demonstrations – eventually these would peter out – culminated in a Parti québécois rally at the Palais des congrès de Montréal. The possibility of early elections looming on the horizon contributed to the heated atmosphere. For Quebec premier Lucien Bouchard, the court proceedings would be a "weapon" in the Parti québécois's election "armour" (Authier

1998a). It even could provide a catalyst for the "winning conditions" necessary for holding a third referendum on sovereignty. The result was the impression of Quebec opinion, loudly and unanimously opposed to the reference, pitted against the rest of Canada with no other resources than its resort to the quietude of the courtroom and the rule of law.

Opposition to the reference was reinforced by reports that focused on those conspicuously absent from the legal proceedings. That the Province of Ontario had not intervened was a focus of attention and surprised many (Fraser 1998d; Gratton 1998). The withdrawal by Yves Michaud from the proceedings on the eve of the hearing, the sole sovereignist to appear, attracted some attention.[13] It was front-page news in Le Devoir. Michaud said that he had no choice but to withdraw because the court had placed him in a "ridiculous situation" and offended him by its "petty" attitude. Michaud also authored an op-ed for Le Devoir, in which he presented the arguments that he would have submitted to the court, including his opposition to the "judicialization of politics" (quoting Mandel 1994). He asked the court not to play "Russian roulette with the future of the people of Québec" (Michaud 1998). With Michaud's withdrawal and the Government of Quebec's boycott of the hearing, this left the amicus curiae, Me. André Joli-Coeur, alone to respond to the federal government and those who shared its views.

Although the Government of Quebec was not a party to the proceedings, the media looked to government spokespersons for their reactions. The spokespersons' message was that the reference was all about politics, not law. Ultimately, Quebec alone had the power to decide its future. According to Jacques Brassard, Quebec had and would continue to have the last word (Delisle 1998d). The issue was more or less resolved by the fact that Quebec has a right to self-determination, which could justify a unilateral declaration of independence if its population so desired. The federal government did not need to ask for the court's opinion on this point or, rather, the Supreme Court should not have to, as André Picard (1998) put it, "wash Ottawa's dirty linen." Mario Dumont, leader of Quebec's Action Démocratique Party, in an article entitled "Hello Earth" (Allô la terre!), maintained that "Québec is today and will always be a distinct society, free and able to control its own destiny and development" (Dumont 1998). Former Quebec premier Jacques Parizeau was reported to have saluted the "Québec coalition" opposed to the reference (Le Droit 1998d). That this was a political question was the unanimous reaction of all the political parties in Quebec.

This required that the media depart from reporting on the strictly legal aspects of the case. Nevertheless, once the proceedings were under way, media reports focused more on the arguments presented before the court. In a marked departure from standard appellate practice, the justices of the Supreme Court would not ask any questions from the bench until toward the end of the hearing. "If we remain silent," said Chief Justice Lamer, "it is not because your remarks do not suggest questions, but because we are waiting until the end" (*Globe and Mail* 1998b). The media consequently were denied an important news resource. In remaining silent, the court could underline its appearance of impartiality, orderliness, and rationality while avoiding having the questions of individual justices broadcast on the evening news. Probing questions by the justices could have been interpreted by a lay audience as signalling prejudgment, heightening the already present tension and controversy. As Craig Oliver observed on *CTV News,* this was "just to cool the whole debate" (CTV 1998b). It also resulted in often very boring, gavel-to-gavel coverage all week long on CBC *Newsworld,* Réseau de l'information (RDI), and CPAC, the Canadian Parliamentary Affairs Channel (on tape delay). News outlets referred to the justices "sitting stone-faced" (Wells 1998a) and to the "nine clams on the Supreme Court" (Hébert 1998c).

The federal government's argument, presented on the first day of the hearing, maintained that the questions put to the court belonged "in the legal domain" and were "above all legal and merited responses from the justices" (Cornellier 1998a). Making the argument on behalf of the Attorney General of Canada was Yves Fortier, a prominent Montreal lawyer and former Canadian ambassador to the United Nations under Prime Minister Brian Mulroney. Fortier insisted that the Canadian Constitution was a barrier to a unilateral declaration of independence. Thus, lawyers for the federal government argued that this was a question for the Supreme Court to decide and that "it should rule on the legality of unilateral secession to put an end to political uncertainty" (*Le Journal de Montréal* 1998d; Young 1998a). Fortier claimed to be challenging the sovereignist approach, not its legitimacy, and reassured Quebecers by repeating that the government would not force them to stay in Canada if they felt the need to separate. It was important, however, that the court "stick to the questions and reinforce Canada's constitutional order, as the "rule of law was at stake," according to the 17 February *Globe and Mail* headline.

This precisely was the federal government's hoped-for result in the reference: that the court would condemn the illegality of unilateral secession and thereby undermine any future sovereignty referendum. The reference was not about staking out a middle ground; rather, it was about outlawing the threat of unilateralism once and for all. Although, as CTV's Craig Oliver stated, this was considered risky and divisive, it was worth it. The *Toronto Sun* echoed these sentiments: "But we believe it's worth that risk to let all Canadians know where they stand. If the court's answers are clear and unflinching, if Quebecers are finally given an honest referendum question, and, then, after all that, they still vote to secede, the Constitution won't matter. The glorious idea that is Canada will then be dead" (*Toronto Sun* 1998b).

Media reports the following day turned to the interveners, particularly to representatives of Aboriginal groups (the James Bay Cree, represented by Grand Chief Matthew Coon Come and counsel Claude-Armand Sheppard) and of minority groups. According to the Cree, a unilateral declaration of Quebec's independence would be a "power grab" (Young 1998b) and violate their constitutional rights, which the federal government constitutionally had a duty to honour and protect. Of particular interest was the argument that if Canada was divisible, then so was Quebec (Fraser 1998c). Were Quebec to secede unilaterally, so were the Cree entitled to secede from the newly created country and remain under Canada's constitutional order (Thompson 1998c). In the lobby of the Supreme Court Building, Grand Chief Matthew Coon Come raised the stakes by referring to the revolutionary program of the Péquistes as precipitating the "use of force to ensure that you have control over the territories that you're claiming to protect" (CTV 1998c). Among the rest of the interveners, the anglophone press particularly liked what the *Globe and Mail* described as the "impassioned argument" (Fraser 1998c) of John Whyte, Saskatchewan deputy minister of justice and former professor of constitutional law, on behalf of the Government of Saskatchewan. Whyte, drawing inspiration from the words of Georges-Étienne Cartier in 1867, spoke about Canada as a nation: "The threads of a thousand acts of accommodation are the fabric of a nation," said Whyte, and that nation could not be torn asunder unilaterally and extra-constitutionally (Fraser 1998c). Paul Wells (1998b) in the *Gazette* described Whyte as "reading quietly from a few pages of scribbled notes" and advancing the "radical theory that Canada is a nation that works." His "eloquent" remarks were the basis of an op-ed by Andrew Coyne in the *Gazette* (Coyne 1998c) and were published verbatim in the op-ed pages of the *Globe and Mail* the following day (Whyte 1998).

The appearance the next day of the "flamboyant federalist" (Ha 1998), Guy Bertrand, was greeted positively in the English-language media. Speaking without notes for about eighty minutes, Bertrand made fiery arguments on the "revolutionary project" to secede, "a revolution" that would "destroy the country" and "violate rights" (Radio-Canada 1998b). He rejected the sovereignists' claims to the effect that the debate was strictly political and not legal and concerned neither the federal government nor the Supreme Court (Fraser 1998e; Auger 1998b). On the *CTV News,* 18 February, Bertrand was reported to have likened "unilateral secession to a time bomb the judges must defuse." The *Globe and Mail*'s Graham Fraser (1998f) described Bertrand's argument as "eccentric" but a "bravura performance." Osgoode Hall Law School professor Patrick Monahan, who appeared alongside Bertrand at the hearing, was reported as having said to his children that this was "the man who is going to save Canada" (Ha 1998). This was a sentiment shared by William Johnson writing in both the *Toronto Sun* and Montreal *Gazette*. Bertrand's oral argument was a "tour de force," a "masterpiece of eloquence" (Johnson 1998b) and Bertrand was a "man of vision" (Johnson 1998a). Johnson likened his oral arguments to other great works in political theory, such as James Madison, Alexander Hamilton, and John Jay's *The Federalist Papers* (ibid.). A *Toronto Sun* columnist even described Bertrand as the Paul Revere of Canada (Harris 1998). By contrast, in some of the French-language media, Me. Bertrand (who had abandoned separatism at one point in his career, and later would embrace it again) did not fare so well. The hyperbolic and violent undertones of his oral argument – with references to "revolution," "bombs," and "destruction" – were excerpted for television viewers on TVA and Radio-Canada. The editorial cartoon in *Le Devoir* (1998a) depicted Guy Bertrand holding flowers, looking at himself in a mirror, and saying, "Je vais te faire la Cour ... suprême" (I am going to court you ... Supreme Court you). This was inspired by the hearing beginning on 16 February 1998, only a couple of days after Valentine's Day.

The day after the hearing began, an explosive development occurred outside of the court proceedings, though it would have repercussions within. Then minister of justice Anne McLellan was reported to have told the *Toronto Star* that if Quebecers voted in favour of separation, "one would be dealing with an extraordinary set of circumstances not comprehended, in our opinion, within the existing constitutional framework" (Hébert 1998b; Séguin 1998b). This misstep, suggesting that the questions before the court were not legal questions, carried some weight, as McLellan was both the lead minister instructing counsel appearing on behalf of the federal government and a former professor of constitutional law at the University of Alberta. She, therefore, "wouldn't be prone to make a legal mistake" (CBC 1998d). More significantly, the statement contradicted her own government's argument before the court that the constitution rendered illegal any unilateral secession. "In order to be legal, secession can be accomplished only in compliance with the present amending formula," argued her counsel Me. Fortier (Cornellier 1998e). Premier Lucien Bouchard "gleefully pounced" on the minister's statement (Wells 1998b) and called for a mistrial based on a "procedural error" (Cloutier and Myles 1998). McLellan's "smashing statement" proved (Séguin 1998b), sovereignists argued, that the reference was useless. Reporters had a field day with the contradictory statements: *La Presse* entitled Chantal Hébert's article "McLellan versus McLellan" (Hébert 1998b), Michel C. Auger (1998b) of *Le Journal de Montréal* spoke of a "Suprême court-circuit," and Michel David (1998a) in the *Gazette* wrote that "McLellan hit a home run for Premier Lucien Bouchard." Jason Moscovitz of CBC's *The National* suggested, over the course of two evening broadcasts, that McLellan's statement raised the ominous prospects of an emergency declaration, "and when it comes to Quebec, that conjures up a lot of memories" (CBC 1998d, 1998e). A CBC reporter even confronted the justice minister with a similar question asked of Prime Minister Trudeau on the eve of the 1970 *War Measures Act* declaration: "How far is the government willing to go, in terms of imposing, making sure that the rule of law is imposed?" While Trudeau famously shot back, "Just watch me," Minister McLellan declined to make any comment. McLellan's intervention underscored the confusion and fragmentation of the federalist forces.

The amicus curiae, Me. Joli-Coeur, was the last to appear before the court. He asked the Supreme Court to discontinue the proceedings and "not [to] answer the questions asked by Ottawa," which essentially were "hypothetical" and "political" (Boisvert 1998c). The hearing was a "useless waste of time" (CBC 1998e). According to Me. Joli-Coeur, secession is based on the democratic will of the people. Chaos and disorder would result not from secession but from a Supreme Court decision requiring the consent of the rest of Canada should Quebecers wish to found a sovereign state (*Le Journal de Montréal* 1998e; Gamble 1998b). He downplayed the significance of the threat of unilateral secession, as Quebec "had always extended a hand to Canada." The justice minister's faux pas did not go unnoticed. She was contradicting her own government's position when she stated to the *Toronto Star* that the amending formula would not apply in the case of unilateral secession. "It is unthinkable," Me. Joli-Coeur submitted, "that the will of the Quebec people should be subordinate to the demands of the amending formula that was, itself, imposed on Quebec" (Fraser 1998e; Radio-Canada 1998a). The amicus curiae's arguments were well captured in an editorial cartoon in *Le Droit* (1998c). Inspired by the Olympic Games being held in Nagano concurrent with the Supreme Court hearing, Me. Joli-Coeur was drawn doing an arabesque and saying, "I hope that will persuade the justices."

The justices, as we mentioned, remained silent until all the oral arguments had been made. They began the final day of the hearing by calling only on the federal government and amicus curiae to answer their queries. By now, much less attention was being paid to the proceedings – as columnists L. Ian MacDonald and Paul Wells insisted, Canadians were watching the Olympics, not the Supreme Court (L. MacDonald 1998; Wells 1998d). Nevertheless, columnist Don Macpherson of the *Gazette* maintained, the hearing was "getting plenty of attention, and Quebecers are hearing about it" (Macpherson 1998b), including "some hard questions for the sovereignist side as well" (Coyne 1998b). The justices, who had been "inscrutable all week," transformed from carps into "sharks," asking "embarrassing" questions concerning the "greatest uncertainties" (Boisvert 1998d) – such matters as the consequences of the breakdown in post-referendum negotiations, whether a simple majority was sufficient to effect secession, and the status of Aboriginal persons in and the borders of a sovereign Quebec (Fraser 1998g). Government counsel Fortier was described as "flustered" (Radio-Canada 1998b; Fraser 1998g) and engaging in "incomprehensible babble" (Wells 1998d) when the chief justice, in a "highly unusual reference to the media," confronted counsel with the McLellan quote (Fraser 1998h). This was said to have crippled Ottawa's lawyers (*Le Journal de Montréal* 1998f). Fortier's impromptu response went even further than McLellan's. Should good faith negotiations with Quebec prove intractable, he stated, "a way would be found in order to deal with and implement a clearly expressed wish on the part of Quebeckers to secede" (CTV 1998e; Fraser 1998g). Fortier even suggested that the federal government might have recourse to the doctrine of necessity in order to preserve the existing constitutional order. This suggested to the justices that they had no legal question to answer. Radio-Canada (1998b) televised clips of Fortier on his cellphone over the lunch break, presumably seeking instructions from his client. By the afternoon, Fortier had "retreated," submitting that the existing constitutional framework could accommodate every foreseeable scenario, including the secession of Quebec (Fraser 1998g; Fraser 1998h). "Stick to the questions," Fortier reiterated, as they would provide a guide for the country to follow in the event of separation (Fraser 1998g).

The amicus curiae deferred answering questions to the afternoon, and it was on this occasion that the hearing finally gave rise to some compelling television coverage. Of particular interest was an exchange between Chief Justice Lamer and Me. Joli-Coeur over the existence of a Canadian "people." The exchange, in French, was paraphrased for CBC viewers by reporter Jason Moscovitz: If there is a Quebec people, Lamer C.J. asked, "is there a Canadian people too?" Me. Joli-Coeur responded, "I have no opinion as [to] the existence or non-existence of the Canadian people, I am not a sociologist." The chief justice replied that he was "shaken by the fact" that the amicus curiae did not know if there was a Canadian people. Chief Justice Lamer's disgust with the amicus curiae's seeming impertinence is amplified by his nonverbal response of hands raised with palms up (CBC 1998f) – an image omitted in the Radio-Canada version (1998b). The exchange emphasized a matter of some sensitivity to English-speaking Canada: the fragility of its national identity. It recalled Lucien Bouchard's declaration during the 1995 Quebec referendum campaign that Canada is not a real country. The justices' questions also indicated that they were resisting being locked in the trap laid by the government's reference. They now were addressing secessionist scenarios not at all contemplated by the federal government's questions. But by moving beyond the terms of the reference, the questions also reinforced the sovereignist message that the reference concerned political and not strictly legal matters. According to Jason Moscovitz, "As much as the federal government wanted to concentrate on legal matters, the strategy appears to have fallen victim to more than thirty years of national unity politics. Courtrooms are places where legal precedents play such an important role, but when it comes to talk of Quebec secession, all the precedents are political" (CBC 1998f).

The general impression was that things had spiralled out of control for the federal government. Arguments before the court illustrated the extent to which the "federal government has lost control of the debate" (Cornellier 1998d). Craig Oliver on *CTV News* observed that the sovereignist side is "winning in the court of public opinion" (CTV 1998c). Newspaper headlines declared that "the federal strategy has failed" (Young 1998c).

The week culminated in a Parti québécois rally at the Palais des Congrès de Montréal, with some two thousand supporters inside and similar numbers outside – the "biggest sovereignist rally since 1995" announced the *Globe and Mail* (Séguin 1998c). Premier Bouchard, on a "post-Supreme Court bounce" (CTV 1998f), compared the federal government to the *Titanic*, which was supposed to be unsinkable but had hit an iceberg of democracy and was taking on water everywhere – "The federalist *Titanic* sank ... may it rest in peace" (CBC 1998g). Former premier Jacques Parizeau proclaimed the "end of a colonial regime" (Authier 1998c). So ended the federalist's "week from hell" (Hébert 1998d). These setbacks, however, did not puncture the confidence of the federal government about the impending result (Young 1998d; Morris 1998).

In what direction would the court take the case? As we have noted, the court was in an awkward position, being handed reference questions with scripted answers, while its very legitimacy in Quebec was at stake. Some journalists predicted where the court might go. *La Presse* columnist Lysiane Gagnon (1998a, 1998b) wrote that she would expect a "moderate decision, such as those that the court has rendered many times in the past on similarly sensitive issues." A prescient editorial appeared in the *Globe and Mail* on the eve of the hearing: "The Supreme Court itself may deliver an opinion that is ambiguous in its content and tone – as it did in the famous 1981 reference on patriation ... The Supreme Court has shown a tendency to look for middle ground in major disputes involving Quebec and the Constitution. Any proclivity for middle ground in this case would constitute a clear defeat for the federal government" (*Globe and Mail* 1998a).

L. Ian MacDonald (1998) observed, "The Supreme Court doesn't like being dragged into political controversies, and has a history of dodging or nuancing the issues." Though the unprecedented judicial hearing in the *Quebec Secession Reference* would keep many observers guessing, the court's ruling would prove some of these commentators correct.

## The Decision: "No, But"

Andrée Lajoie (1997, 207) has observed that "The judge ... gives meaning to a text the normative nature of which forces him or her to take the effect of interpretation into account." Courts, in other words, often – even if unconsciously – take into account the effects of their decision on various audiences, including the general public. Perelman and Foriers (1978) claim that judges have two distinct audiences in mind when they render a ruling: a universal audience consisting of the parties and their lawyers, the media, and the general public who are more concerned with the equitable resolution of legal conflict; and a particular audience consisting of other jurists, law professors, legislators, and other specialists concerned with coherence and integrity in judicial decision making (see also Lajoie 1997, 54, 72). Although all our case studies reflect this two-audience theory, perhaps nowhere is it more clearly operative than in the case of the *Quebec Secession Reference*.

The court was in the sticky situation of having to reply to the federal government's carefully scripted questions designed precisely to ensure a federalist victory over sovereignist forces. The court thereby was being conscripted into a political fight over the future of the country. It would carefully have to find a way of remaining impartial. Second, the court's reasons would be scrutinized by lawyers, academics, and the national media. The court, as Justice Major later admitted, would therefore craft a judgment that could be read and understood by a broad segment of society, reproduced in newspapers, and taught in universities (Fine 1998b). Here, we turn to a summary of the court's lengthy reasons.

The court first had to dispense with the amicus curiae's plea that the court refrain from answering the reference questions. The referral, the court concluded, was constitutionally sound and authorized by legislation (*Quebec Secession Reference*, paras. 8, 15). It gave rise to questions of law appropriate for judicial proceedings (paras. 18, 28). There was somewhat more difficulty with the court answering the second question, on the status of international law. The Supreme Court of Canada, after all, was a national court of appeal, not a court of international law. Nevertheless, the justices insisted, it was appropriate for the court to take stock of international law in the course of interpreting Quebec's constitutional ability to unilaterally secede; indeed, it was unavoidable (para. 23).

In order to answer the first question, the court refused to restrict itself to a literal reading of the constitution. Instead, it insisted on identifying a number of intangible principles that are an implicit part of the constitution. The court explained that the constitution was not limited to the written text but included a whole set of rules and principles governing the exercise of power. These underlying principles were identified as federalism, democracy, constitutionalism and the rule of law, and respect for minorities. These principles, the court maintained, were not entirely explicit in the text of the constitution but nevertheless were its lifeblood (para. 51).

Applying these principles to the secession context, the court, as predicted, held that the secession of a province from Canada required a constitutional amendment. It could not be achieved unilaterally and also be consistent with the constitution (para. 97). Other partners in the Canadian federation would have to consent to a constitutional amendment designed to effect the secession of Quebec. Although different amending formulae could apply – one requiring the consent of seven out of ten provinces representing more than 50 percent of the population, together with the federal government, another requiring the unanimous consent of all governments – the court refused to identify the degree of consent required for such an amendment to come into effect (para. 105).[14]

The court also answered the second question as the Attorney General had requested. The principle of self-determination in international law did not condone secession from an existing state unless a people were under colonial rule, subject to foreign occupation, or denied meaningful access to self-government. Quebecers simply did not qualify under these standards (para. 138). The court gave short shrift to the amicus curiae's argument about the principle of effectivity: the principle could not operate retroactively so as to create a right of secession where it otherwise was illegal to do so (para. 146). Lastly, as there was no conflict between domestic and international law, there was no need to answer the third question (para. 147).

If the court had stopped there, it would have given the federal government everything it had asked for. Instead, the court gave the government more than it probably wanted. Referring to the unwritten constitutional principles (most every one of which have origins in the written text), the court declared that should the citizens of Quebec by a "clear majority on a clear question" decide to secede from the federation (para. 93), the rest of Canada would be obliged constitutionally to "acknowledge and respect that expression of democratic will by entering into negotiations" (para. 88). As negotiations would precede any possible amendment to the constitution, they would have to be conducted in accordance with the unwritten constitutional principles. This new constitutional duty to negotiate was not a legally enforceable one, however (paras. 98, 99). Here, the court admitted, it was entering a realm that "defies legal analysis," namely, the realm of politics (para. 101). The court would not police whether negotiations were conducted consistent with the constitutional principles. Nor did the court lend any clarity to what was a clear majority or a clear question that would give rise to the constitutional duty to negotiate, only that the question had to "be free of ambiguity" and that the majority had to be clear according to a "qualitative evaluation" (para. 87). A clear expression of will in response to a clear question would suffice to trigger a corresponding obligation to negotiate a constitutional amendment "to respond to that desire" (para. 88). All the parties would therefore have to come to the table (paras. 88, 92). In such a case, the negotiations would not involve the eleven heads of government but, according to the court, representatives of two legitimate majorities (para. 93).[15] Negotiations, the court continued, would concern various issues, often complex and difficult, with the very real possibility that they would end in deadlock (para. 97). The parties' conduct would then be important because it would be the basis on which the legitimacy of any act of unilateral secession would be judged under international law.

The members of the court clearly resisted being locked into the federal government's framework. Their analysis went beyond the letter of constitutional text, presenting a discerning vision of relevant legal principles while taking care to indicate what remained to be determined politically. The court's ruling was presented by the media as a decision in which there was something for everyone. Nevertheless, the media continued to portray the decision in an adversarial manner. This was because the media relied on competing interpretations of the court ruling as advanced by the leading protagonists. Federalists insisted that the decision vindicated their rule of law approach to secession. Sovereignists, by contrast, emphasized the new constitutional duty to negotiate. To the extent the court departed from strictly legal dimensions and entered the terrain of the political – indeed, the court admitted that it was straddling that divide in its ruling – sovereignists could claim victory. An emphasis on the traditional legal aspects of the ruling, on the other hand, would favour federalists. It was this interpretive struggle that would play itself out in coverage of the decision. To the extent that media reports focused not on the legal subtleties of the decision but on comments and interpretation by political figures, it might be said that, though the federalists legally were victorious, they did not win the public relations battle.

## The Coverage

### The Day of Decision: A Big But

On 20 August, decision day, Andrew Duffy (1998) reported on the calm before the storm in the Supreme Court Building: There was "no pomp, no ceremony, and the judges themselves are nowhere to be seen." Instead, the lobby of the building was "charged with anticipation," with television anchor desks, and about one hundred observers, including the "tanned and supremely confident" Guy Bertrand. Other reporters were stationed in Quebec, waiting for comments from key players.

At 9:45 a.m., the decision was released and journalists and experts alike scrambled to decipher the decision. Live reports described the answers to the three questions as "no," "no," and "moot." At bottom, the court declared unanimously that there is no unilateral right to secession. So that was a clear no ... but, should Quebecers choose to secede by a clear majority on a clear question, then there was a constitutional duty on the part of the federal government and the provinces to negotiate. Nothing could be less clear. On TVA's evening news, it was announced that the court had made "independence illegal but negotiable" (TVA 1998e). Josh Freed (1998) in the *Gazette* described the frustration of the live television coverage experienced by many viewers: "for the next two hours, our anchors and commentators hunch studiously over sheaves of paper, leafing through them on LIVE TV, then one suddenly exclaims: 'Look Rob — it says here that the non-justiciability of political issues that lack a legal component does NOT deprive the surrounding constitutional framework of its binding status' … zzz."

Newspaper headlines reflected well this ambiguity. According to *La Presse* (Boisvert 1998e), "Quebec cannot legally separate without negotiating"; for *Le Devoir* (1998d), "The division of Canada must be negotiated"; and for *Le Droit,* "A secession [has] to be negotiated" (Young 1998e). In the English-language press, the *Gazette* declared that "Court says NO to unilateral declaration of independence, YES to negotiated split" (Thompson 1998d); the *Toronto Sun,* that "Both sides claim victory" (Gamble 1998d); and, the *Globe and Mail* wrote: "The Quebec ruling: Canada must negotiate after YES vote" (Fraser 1998i). Only *Le Journal de Montréal* kept things simple: "Québec cannot secede unilaterally" (Fortier 1998b).

For the federal government, there were reasons to be "very satisfied," said Minister of Intergovernmental Affairs Stéphane Dion (Fraser 1998i; Fife 1998a). It was "full of good sense" (*Le Droit* 1998e) because it required "Lucien Bouchard to renounce the independence of Québec" (Fortier 1998c). It was now obvious, Dion remarked at the National Press Gallery, that "50 percent plus one is not enough" (CBC 1998h). Described as the *bête noire* of the sovereignty movement, in a feature TVA interview, Dion insisted that the court had affirmed "precisely what the federal government had been saying" but refrained, in contrast to his affirmation earlier in the day, from stating whether 50 percent plus one was sufficient to trigger the duty to negotiate (TVA 1998e). A jubilant Me. Bertrand proclaimed, "We won." For Bertrand, he considered this not only a great victory for Canada but a personal victory. "We may sleep well tonight," he told a crowd of supporters on the steps of the Supreme Court Building (CTV 1998h). Editorial cartoonists in Quebec had their fun, once again. *Le Devoir* (1998c) portrayed him with the Supreme Court's decision in one hand and a handkerchief in the other, saying, "It's so beautiful … that I could have written it myself!" *Le Journal de Montréal* (1998g) portrayed Bertrand with a huge smile on his face, his teeth twinkling with stars in the shape of maple leaves.

Even though they had refused to participate in the process, sovereignists welcomed the new constitutional duty to negotiate. Quebec Intergovernmental Affairs Minister Jacques Brassard was described as "beaming" and "pleasantly surprised" (Authier 1998a). The court vindicated the claim that sovereignists always had made: that English Canada would sit down and negotiate secession if Quebecers were to choose sovereignty in any future referendum result, in which 50 percent plus one would be sufficient (TVA 1998e). Brassard said that Dion had become the "arroseur arrosé" (sprinkler sprinkled) (K. Gagnon 1998a; Cloutier 1998c).

FONDÉ EN 1910

# LE DEVOIR

nous sommes d'un peu de glaise / un moment d'inattention / de l'origine / peut-être Sylvain Campeau, «La pesanteur des âmes»

VOL. LXXXIX · N° 190 MONTRÉAL, LE VENDREDI 21 AOÛT 1998 87¢ + TAXES = 1$ / TORONTO 1$

## LA DÉCISION DE LA COUR SUPRÊME

*William Johnson: la fin de la «baguette magique» de Bouchard* • *Matthew Coon Come: désormais, les intérêts des autochtones devront être pris en compte* • *Jean Chrétien: la cour a bien servi les Canadiens* • *Jacques Brassard: le fédéral est «l'arroseur arrosé»*

PERSPECTIVES

## Une accalmie

**L'avis de la Cour suprême sur la sécession du Québec ne provoquera pas la tempête politique appréhendée. Le gouvernement Bouchard, qui cache mal sa satisfaction, n'y trouve aucun prétexte de déclencher des élections immédiatement. Et Ottawa pourrait être tenté de rengainer son plan B. Il reste toutefois quelques nuages à l'horizon; ils sont concentrés dans le camp fédéraliste.**

Hier, les marchés financiers autant que Jean Charest appréhendaient la réaction du Québec à cet avis du plus haut tribunal au pays. M. Bouchard allait-il profiter de l'opinion des juges suprêmes pour déclencher des élections? Lui-même y avait déjà fait allusion dans des discours passés. Si la cour avait nié le droit du Québec de décider de son propre avenir, il aurait pu appeler le peuple aux urnes pour faire mentir les juges et affirmer le droit du Québec à l'autodétermination.

*Michel Venne*

Or l'opinion de la cour donne au contraire satisfaction au gouvernement Bouchard, qui n'y trouve aucun prétexte à déclencher des élections existentielles. Certes, certains péquistes pourraient le regretter. Une campagne électorale déclenchée dans un contexte aussi dramatique aurait pu faciliter la tâche au PQ en faisant glisser au second rang des préoccupations le bilan du gouvernement.

Mais l'argument électoral perdu est compensé par le fait que l'avis de la Cour suprême donne aux souverainistes des arguments plus forts et plus précieux à utiliser lors d'un éventuel débat référendaire.

Le ministre Brassard a lui-même mis en lumière hier le fait que ce jugement rend légitime le combat souverainiste au sein du Canada tout en obligeant le Canada à négocier avec le Québec si une majorité claire, répondant à une question claire, vote en faveur de la sécession. Aux yeux des souverainistes, cette obligation créée par la cour aura, la prochaine fois, un effet rassurant sur plusieurs électeurs qui, craignant le désordre au lendemain d'un référendum gagné, préféraient voter NON.

Rasséréné par la cour, le gouvernement Bouchard ne semble voir aucune raison de raviver le débat sur la souveraineté, ni au sein de la population ni au sein du parti. Le PQ semble satisfait de son programme actuel. Il trouve que la question posée en 1995 était claire et que la majorité absolue est assez claire pour répondre aux critères de la Cour suprême.

Québec va donc s'en tenir à un programme prévisible d'ici aux élections: une tournée régionale pour expliquer les réformes contestées et écouter la population; procéder à un remaniement ministériel; adopter les correctifs nécessaires aux réformes; présenter le budget du déficit zéro assorti de quelques engagements; aller aux urnes.

De son côté, Ottawa ne semble plus très chaud à l'idée de poursuivre ouvertement son plan B. Le ministre Dion disait hier qu'il n'y avait pas lieu, d'ici aux prochaines élections québécoises, de mettre en branle un processus visant à définir les conditions et les règles de la sécession. Il semble avoir écarté, du moins pour l'instant, l'idée qui était la sienne d'adopter une loi fédérale pour dicter la marche à suivre en prévision d'un futur référendum. Ottawa voudra probablement éviter de faire des vagues à ce sujet, ne serait-ce que pour ne pas nuire à Jean Charest.

Car si quelques nuages apparaissent dans le ciel politique au lendemain de cet avis de la Cour suprême, c'est dans le camp fédéraliste qu'ils surgiront. Déjà, puisque la cour a abordé la question de la majorité requise pour une sécession, le chef libéral Jean Charest a été forcé de réitérer une position traditionnelle de son parti et du Québec voulant que la majorité de 50 % plus un vote soit suffisante. En soi, cette prise de position ne peut que déplaire à plusieurs fédéralistes irréductibles qui, comme Stéphane Dion et Jean Chrétien, continuent de croire nécessaire d'établir un seuil plus élevé. La mésentente entre les leaders fédéralistes est déjà apparente. Ce désaccord va se répercuter chez les militants avec Dieu sait quel effet.

En outre, déjà, le chef réformiste Preston Manning presse Jean Chrétien de clarifier les règles du jeu alors que le gouvernement semble au contraire ne voir aucune urgence à cette démarche. Jean Chrétien invitait hier les Québécois à mettre de côté la question nationale. Enfin, lorsque, dans le reste du Canada, on va s'apercevoir des effets positifs de cet avis de la Cour suprême pour le mouvement souverainiste du Québec, c'est toute la stratégie fédérale qui sera remise en cause par ses alliés partout au Canada, ce qui risque d'affaiblir encore davantage le leadership du gouvernement libéral à Ottawa et susciter la prudence de sa part plutôt que l'initiative.

# La division du Canada doit être négociée

L'AVIS DES JUGES

## Le projet du PQ est légitime

MANON CORNELLIER
DE NOTRE BUREAU D'OTTAWA

Le Canada est divisible. Les Québécois ont le droit de décider de leur avenir. Mais pour respecter la Constitution, une sécession ne peut pas se faire de façon unilatérale. Elle doit faire l'objet de négociations auxquelles le reste du pays ne peut se soustraire advenant une «majorité claire» à une «question claire», ont conclu à l'unanimité hier les neuf juges de la Cour suprême du Canada.

*«La sécession d'une province du Canada doit être considérée, en termes juridiques, comme requérant une modification de la Constitution, qui exige forcément une négociation»*, écrit la cour dans sa réponse aux trois questions que le gouvernement fédéral lui a soumises en septembre 1996.

La cour estime illégale, tant en droit canadien qu'international, toute déclaration unilatérale d'indépendance. Mais elle rejette tout autant la possibilité d'une fin de non-recevoir du Canada anglais à une démarche souverainiste légitime. *«Les droits des autres provinces et du gouvernement fédéral ne peuvent retirer au gouvernement du Québec le droit de chercher à réaliser la sécession, si une majorité claire de la population du Québec choisissait cette voie, tant et aussi longtemps que, dans cette poursuite, le Québec respecte les droits des autres.»*

Les juges sont toutefois catégoriques. *«Il reviendra aux acteurs politiques de déterminer en quoi consiste "une majorité claire en réponse à une*

VOIR PAGE A 12: PROJET

REUTERS

Le chef du Bloc québécois, Gilles Duceppe, a été le seul chef d'un parti fédéral à avoir pu être photographié hier aux abords de la Cour suprême du Canada. La réponse historique des juges au renvoi fédéral contient des points favorables aux souverainistes, estime-t-il.

À QUÉBEC

## Péquistes et libéraux satisfaits

MARIO CLOUTIER
DE NOTRE BUREAU DE QUÉBEC

Le gouvernement péquiste et l'opposition libérale accueillent sur le même ton et plutôt positivement l'avis de la Cour suprême sur le renvoi du gouvernement fédéral quant à une éventuelle déclaration unilatérale d'indépendance du Québec. Soulignant les mêmes éléments de l'avis juridique, les deux principaux partis à l'Assemblée nationale ont de nouveau dénoncé hier la stratégie d'Ottawa.

Le ministre des Affaires intergouvernementales canadiennes, Jacques Brassard, a qualifié le gouvernement fédéral *«d'arroseur arrosé»* et a indiqué que la position du Québec demeurait *«claire et inchangée»*; tandis que le chef libéral Jean Charest pense qu'il s'agit de la *«fin du plan B»* et d'un *«retour à la case départ»*.

Les deux principales formations politiques québécoises sont d'accord pour lire dans l'avis de la Cour suprême que le droit du Québec de décider de son avenir est confirmé et qu'il doit être débattu dans l'arène politique. Bref, personne ne s'est dit surpris hier. Tout le monde, semble-t-il, avait prévu le coup et y a trouvé son compte, à l'exception de munitions pour la future campagne électorale.

*«Je ne pense pas que ça puisse devenir un enjeu unique»*, a dit M. Brassard. *Une élection, ça comporte bien des enjeux puis c'est tout à fait normal. Il y a une reddition de comptes qui est essentielle à l'occasion d'une élection.»*

VOIR PAGE A 12: PÉQUISTES

À OTTAWA

## La balle se retrouve dans le camp de Québec, croit Stéphane Dion

MANON CORNELLIER
DE NOTRE BUREAU D'OTTAWA

Même s'il juge avoir eu gain de cause devant la Cour suprême du Canada, le gouvernement fédéral n'entend pas faire connaître avant les élections québécoises ce qu'il considère comme des majorité et question claires pouvant conduire à des négociations constitutionnelles sur la sécession. En fait, Ottawa estime que la balle est maintenant dans le camp de Québec.

*«Ce ne serait pas convenable aujourd'hui d'ajouter quoi que ce soit à ce que la cour a présenté parce que c'est déjà un apport important qu'il faut relire, méditer et étudier plus à fond. D'ici la prochaine élection provinciale au Québec, il n'y aura pas de démarche en vue de faire une sécession. Après l'élection, il n'y en aura probablement pas non plus. Le seul gouvernement qui est vraiment interpellé par l'avis de la cour, c'est le gouvernement actuel du Québec, qui est le seul à envisager de faire une sécession unilatérale. C'est à ce gouvernement et à ce parti politique d'ajuster leur projet en fonction du droit. Il faut leur laisser le temps»*, a déclaré en conférence de presse, hier, le ministre fédéral des Affaires intergouvernementales, Stéphane Dion.

S'ils ne le font pas, dit-il, cela équivaudra à dire aux Québécois qu'ils les invitent à endosser un projet politique irréalisable et dénué de bases juridiques, ce qui donnerait une raison de plus aux citoyens pour le rejeter.

VOIR PAGE A 12: DION

### LA DÉCISION DE LA COUR SUPRÊME


- Anglophones et autochtones applaudissent, page A 2
- Un jugement équitable, considère Claude Ryan, page A 2
- Le Québec a eu le dessus, estiment des constitutionnalistes, page A 3
- La SSJB reste de glace, page A 4
- Guy Bertrand jubile, page A 4
- L'éditorial de Bernard Descôteaux: B comme dans boomerang, page A 10
- Le texte intégral de la déclaration des juges: *www.ledevoir.com*
- Écrivez-nous vos réactions: *coursupreme@ledevoir.com*


## Les Américains frappent des sites terroristes

AGENCE FRANCE-PRESSE

Washington — Les États-Unis ont mené hier des frappes militaires contre des sites terroristes au Soudan et en Afghanistan liés aux réseaux du milliardaire Oussama ben Laden, accusé d'être responsable des récents attentats anti-américains en Tanzanie et au Kenya, a annoncé le président Bill Clinton. Ces opérations militaires ont été approuvées par la Grande-Bretagne, l'Espagne, le Canada et Israël mais condamnées par la Libye, l'Irak, le Soudan et le Hamas palestinien.

*«Nos services de renseignements sont en possession d'informations probantes selon lesquelles le réseau terroriste de ben Laden était responsable de ces attentats»*, a déclaré M. Clinton au cours d'une allocution télévisée depuis le Bureau ovale de la Maison-Blanche.

*«Ayant reçu des preuves indubitables que les groupes des membres du réseau ben Laden étaient en train de préparer d'autres attaques contre les Américains et d'autres peuples épris de liberté, j'ai décidé que l'Amérique devait agir»*, a indiqué M. Clinton, qui a précipitamment interrompu ses vacances à Martha's Vineyard (Massachusetts).

*«Notre cible était la terreur. Notre mission était claire: frapper le réseau de groupes extrémistes affiliés à et financés par Oussama ben Laden, qui est peut-être aujourd'hui l'organisateur et le financier du terrorisme international le plus important au monde»*, a souligné M. Clinton.

Au cours de sa brève intervention, il a également rendu M. ben Laden responsable d'une série de récents attentats en Somalie ou en Égypte. Selon lui, ses réseaux ont également préparé des attentats contre le président égyptien Hosni Moubarak et le pape Jean-Paul II, ainsi que contre des avions civils américains.

Menés par des missiles de croisière lancés depuis des bateaux de l'US Navy croisant dans la mer Rouge et le golfe Arabo-Persique, les raids de représailles américains ont frappé six sites afghans et une usine pharmaceutique de Khartoum (Soudan), soupçonnée d'abriter la fabrication d'armes chimiques, ont indiqué des responsables militaires américains.

Au Pentagone, le chef d'état-major interarmes américain, le général Henry Shelton, a précisé que les opérations s'étaient déroulées respectivement à 19h30 locales au Soudan et à 22h locales en Afghanistan. Il s'est refusé à donner plus de précisions sur ces frappes.

Selon un haut responsable des services de renseignements américains, l'usine de al-Chifaa, à Khartoum, faisait partie du complexe militaro-industriel soudanais, financé en partie par Oussama ben Laden, et produisait notamment un composant de base dit «précurseur» nécessaire à la fabrication du gaz neurotoxique VX.

VOIR PAGE A 12: AMÉRICAINS

Autres informations en page A 5

MÉTÉO

| Montréal | Québec |
| --- | --- |
| Dégagement le matin. Passages nuageux | Averses en matinée. Dégagement |
| Max: 23 Min: 12 | Max: 22 Min: 12 |
| | Détails, page A 6 |

INDEX


| | | | |
| --- | --- | --- | --- |
| Agenda | B 9 | Le monde | B 6 |
| Annonces | A 6 | Les sports | B 8 |
| Avis publics | B 7 | Mots croisés | B 7 |
| Culture | B 11 | Politique | A 2 |
| Économie | A 8 | Télévision | B 10 |
| Éditorial | A 10 | Tourisme | B 4 |


www.ledevoir.com

Gilles Duceppe was described as being delighted with the decision since it made things more difficult for the government of Jean Chrétien (Fortier 1998a; Wills 1998b). In the lobby of the Supreme Court building, Duceppe insisted that the questions were clear both times (in 1980 and again in 1995) and that a clear majority is 50 percent plus one. Bernard Landry saw positive features in the court's decision (TVA 1998e; *Le Journal de Montréal* 1998h): "[It was] good news for us" (CBC 1998j) and "could change the atmosphere in Canada" (Marissal 1998). As the *Le Devoir* editorial proclaimed, the "B" in the federalist Plan B was the "B as in Boomerang" (Descôteaux 1998). Tom Kennedy of CBC news delivered to an English-Canadian audience the preferred sovereignist interpretive spin: "If they ever win a referendum, the court has told Canada it must negotiate the break up [of Canada]" (CBC 1998j). This, of course, is not what the court had decided; only that there was a constitutional duty to undertake good faith negotiations which could very well end in deadlock.

Other political leaders seemed pleased as well. Mario Dumont said he was happy with the court's opinion (*Le Journal de Montréal* 1998j). Jean Charest was satisfied that the decision had defused tensions and put the ball back in the politicians' court, where it belonged (Little 1998a; *Globe and Mail* 1998d). Even Claude Ryan, who had criticized and condemned the reference from the beginning, spoke of a "balanced judgment" (O'Neill 1998). Provincial premiers were polled for their reactions, and they too were pleased – "it probably was as good a ruling as they could get" (Gray 1998a). Former premier of Alberta Peter Lougheed called it a "significant, positive step" (ibid.).

Curiously, Aboriginal leadership applauded the decision. According to Grand Chief of the Cree Matthew Coon Come, the decision affirmed the right of self-determination (Cobb 1998). Yet, as some of the media reports correctly pointed out, the court refrained from ruling on the claim advanced by Aboriginal interveners – there was almost nothing in the ruling about Aboriginal peoples (TVA 1998a). Grand Chief Coon Come maintained, however, that the ruling would assist in their obtaining a seat at the table in any future negotiations (Toupin 1998a; Buzzetti 1998a; Cobb 1998).

Although media would have to wait until the following day to get reactions from Chrétien and Bouchard, newspapers almost unanimously portrayed the decision in the most positive terms possible. *La Presse* (1998c) spoke of a "Solomon's judgment," and *Le Devoir* added that "the PQ's goal is legitimate" (Cornellier 1998g). The *Gazette* spoke of a "masterful" ruling (Bronskill 1998). It was noted that "anglophones are happy" (M. Ducas 1998). This meant that the "PQ and Liberals [were]

---

◄ That "the division of Canada is negotiable" is the principal lesson *Le Devoir* draws from the court's ruling in the *Quebec Secession Reference* (21 August 1998). *Courtesy of Le Devoir*

**Table 3.7: Tone of references to Supreme Court as institution in newspapers**

| Case status | Press | Positive | Negative | Neutral | Total |
|---|---|---|---|---|---|
| The hearing | Anglophone | 2 (2.4%) | 3 (3.6%) | 79 (94%) | 84 |
| | Francophone | 3 (3%) | 18 (17.8%) | 80 (79.2%) | 101 |
| | **Total** | **5** | **21** | **159** | **185** |
| The decision | Anglophone | 4 (5.5%) | 3 (4.1%) | 66 (90.4%) | 73 |
| | Francophone | 19 (13.4%) | 5 (3.5%) | 118 (83.1%) | 142 |
| | **Total** | **23** | **8** | **184** | **215** |

both satisfied" (Cloutier 1998c) and, as the *Globe and Mail* put it, "The federalists win but the sovereigntists don't lose" (Greenspon, Ha, and Peritz 1998). Even the dollar was stimulated by the decision, with a small upsurge on decision day. The White House, speaking through an unnamed State Department official, also was reported to have been pleased by the ruling (*Globe and Mail* 1998e; Martin 1998). As the justices anticipated, some newspapers, including *Le Devoir, Le Droit,* and the *Gazette,* published complete excerpts of the original opinion. Some papers, such as *Le Devoir, Le Droit,* and the *Globe and Mail,* also presented the highlights.

What is striking about all these news reports in the immediate aftermath of the release of the decision is the positive portrayal of the court and its ruling in both the English- and French-language print media.[16] As shown in Table 3.7, content analysis reveals that, at the hearing stage, almost 18 percent of the articles in the French-language press portrayed the Supreme Court as an institution in a negative light.[17] The results virtually were reversed in the decision period, when 13.4 percent of the French-language stories placed the court in a positive light.[18]

In the decision period, 22 percent of the francophone press portrayed the court's decision in a positive light[19] – exceedingly positive portrayals of the Supreme Court as an institution – while almost 18 percent in the English-language

**Table 3.8: Tone of references to Supreme Court decision in newspapers**

| Case status | Press | Positive | Negative | Neutral | Total |
|---|---|---|---|---|---|
| The decision | Anglophone | 16 (17.8%) | 5 (5.6%) | 69 (76.7%) | 90 |
| | Francophone | 31 (22%) | 8 (5.7%) | 102 (73.2%) | 141 |
| | **Total** | **47** | **13** | **171** | **23** |

press spoke positively about the decision (see Table 3.8).[20] A small number of articles in both languages portrayed the decision negatively.

Where articles were not neutral, the "balanced" and "common sense" approach adopted by the court – giving something to both sides of the political debate – was portrayed positively in media accounts. In the immediate aftermath of the ruling, there was applause all around. Who would win the war of spin between the federalists and sovereignists? The two main protagonists were poised to weigh in on the debate.

## Getting the Message Out

The opposing positions of Chrétien and Bouchard on the judgment's meaning were featured in all media outlets the couple of days following the judgment. The interpretive meaning to be attributed to the decision was still up for grabs – was it a win for federalists or sovereignists or both? As the "heavyweights of Canada's unity debate" (CBC 1998k) "squared off" in the media (Greenspon and McIlroy 1998), readers reasonably would continue to be confused by the opposing interpretations placed on the case by both sides.

The image of battling political titans was reinforced by opposing front-page photographs published in many of the newspapers in our sample. Though *La Presse* reported that both Chrétien and Bouchard were "happy with the judgment" (K. Gagnon 1998b; Toupin 1998b), each politician emphasized different aspects of the ruling. Bouchard is reported to have "embraced" the judgment (Greenspon and McIlroy 1998). According to Bouchard, "the federal strategy has been shaken" (*Le Journal de Montréal* 1998i) and "sovereignty strengthened" (Cloutier 1998b) because the court had legitimated the goal of sovereignty. Moreover, as the press was keen to report, the Supreme Court had just created a "winning condition" for the next referendum (see K. Gagnon 1998b; Greenspon and McIlroy 1998; Thompson 1998e; CBC 1998k), though there were indications that the pending election campaign would now be postponed (CTV 1998h). At his press conference, Premier Bouchard described Minister Dion as "the Einstein of politics." This ruling was "the product of their [Dion's and Chrétien's] inventive minds" (Séguin 1998e; Fife 1998c).

Chrétien, "obviously irritated by Mr. Bouchard claiming victory" (Séguin 1998e) – a point emphasized in CTV's television news coverage that evening – shot back, focusing on the clear question and clear majority requirement and on the issue of borders. A simple majority would not constitute a clear one, according to the ruling – "You know everybody knows that," insisted Chrétien (CBC 1998k) – nor could earlier referendum questions have been characterized as clear. According to the prime minister, the question now would have to be about separation and not partnership or association (Séguin 1998e), putting an end to sovereignists'

# La Presse

**ÉDITION DU SAMEDI**
Montréal, samedi 22 août 1998
114e année No 298
134 pages, 8 cahiers

Le dollar aujourd'hui
**64,86** cents US

Arts et spectacles
Grande première de Céline à Boston
page D14

Tennis
Les favorites tiennent bon
pages F1 et F2

---

## Avec les Expos pour cinq ans

# Bouchard et Chrétien heureux du jugement

*Une « condition gagnante » pour un prochain référendum*

*Une barrière que les séparatistes devront franchir*

KATIA GAGNON
du bureau de La Presse, QUÉBEC

Le projet souverainiste se trouve « singulièrement renforcé » par le jugement de la Cour suprême, estime le premier ministre Lucien Bouchard, puisque les Québécois sauront désormais qu'un éventuel OUI « forcera le Canada à négocier ».

GILLES TOUPIN
du bureau de La Presse, OTTAWA

Le premier ministre Jean Chrétien a réagi formellement hier à l'avis de la Cour suprême sur la sécession du Québec en déclarant que le jugement a enterré les principaux mythes que les partisans de la séparation ont tenté de créer au fil des ans.

Lucien Bouchard

Jean Chrétien

*Voir RÉFÉRENDUM en A2*

*Voir BARRIÈRE en A2*

Autres textes sur l'avis de la Cour suprême en pages A10, A11 et A12

Vladimir Guerrero, qui est sur le point de fracasser quelques records des Expos, se sent de plus en plus à l'aise à Montréal, où il vient de le rejoindre son frère Wilton (à gauche).

## Vladimir Guerrero sur le point de signer un contrat à long terme

RONALD KING

La direction des Expos et l'agent de Vladimir Guerrero, Jim Bronner, en sont venus au cours des derniers jours à une entente verbale qui lierait les deux clans pour les cinq prochaines saisons.

---

## Menaces de représailles

Selon Washington, l'opération de jeudi, riposte aux attentats du 7 août contre les deux ambassades américaines, a causé des dégâts relativement importants. Les sondages indiquent que de 66 à 80% des Américains soutiennent les frappes militaires. Mais les régions visées le condamnent et font craindre des contre-représailles.

Pages A20, A21 et A22

---

**497** JOURS AVANT L'AN 2000

**INDEX**

MÉTÉO
Généralement ensoleillé
page F14

---

tricks (Chrétien 1998; Fortier 1998d). Nor would an independent Quebec's borders necessarily remain intact (Wills 1998c; Fife 1998e). Negotiations, in other words, would not be easy – this was "a major obstacle for the separatists," Chrétien explained (Toupin 1998b; Greenspon and McIlroy 1998). He was persuaded, moreover, that the rest of Canada would never agree to Quebec's secession (CBC 1998k), notwithstanding that the Supreme Court called for good-faith negotiations on all sides.

Published reports were not entirely positive. Josée Legault (1998a, 1998b), a freelance sovereignist commentator, writing in the *Globe and Mail,* described the ruling as an "outrageous imposition" on Quebec's self-determination. "Colonialist federalism is at the heart of the court's opinion," she wrote. Labour leader Lorraine Pagé insisted at a rally that the court continued to lean in the same federalist direction (Heinrich 1998), eschewing the Parti québécois's new talking points on this matter. In the Montreal *Gazette,* law professor Rob Martin (1998) called the decision pure judicial invention and "arrogant and mischievous." There was much consternation about the decision in the pages of the *Toronto Sun.* Reporter Robert Fife (1998d) claimed that the ruling provided a "legal foundation" for separatist plots and that the federal government had "misfired and breathed new life into the sovereignist ranks." Political scientist Ted Morton (1998) described the decision as "useless at best and dangerous at worst," with a "newly minted right to negotiated secession." David Frum (1998) called on journalists not to be complicit in covering up what he called the federal government's humiliating failure.

That the sovereignist reading of the *Secession Reference* was triumphing over the federalist emphasis on legality was underscored by Minister Dion, at week's end, firing off a letter to Premier Bouchard claiming that he was selectively reading the court's decision. His "harshly worded letter," wrote Anne McIlroy (1998b) in the *Globe and Mail,* "is a clear sign he fears the Quebec Premier is winning the public relations battle." "There's a growing concern," Dave Rinn of *CTV News* reported on 26 August, that the federalist message "didn't get through." As the *Gazette*'s editorial page put it, Dion was "anxious to dispel the myth that Mr. Bouchard was the winner" (Martin 1998). According to *Toronto Sun* columnist Hartley Steward (1998), there was little doubt that Bouchard had won the war of public relations. "In what is surely one of the most successful spin-doctoring exercises in Canadian history," he wrote, "Bouchard turned what appeared to be almost defeat into what appeared to be a total victory ... It was BS baffling brains on a scale seldom seen even in Canadian politics. I, for one, am sort of awed by it."

---

◄ Bouchard and Chrétien "happy with judgment" announces *La Presse* on its front page, underscoring the ambivalent nature of the decision in the *Quebec Secession Reference* (22 August 1998). *Courtesy of La Presse*

As the struggle for interpretive authority was being played out in national and local media, the court quietly slipped away into the background. What talk there was about the court mostly was unerringly positive. Once the court's decision was rendered, the media focused on the interpretations of the protagonists rather than on the opinion of the court. Yet, most of the justices we interviewed characterized the reporting on this decision among the best they had seen. That the justices' reasons so quickly faded from public debate does not fit well with the impression that media reporting is a means of informing the public about their constitutional rights and the corresponding obligation of governments to respect them. We should question, then, why it is that the justices of the court so liked the reporting in this case. We can only presume that this satisfaction flows from the acceptance of the justices' reasons by both sides to the dispute. By constructing a new constitutional duty to negotiate, the court revealed that it had an instinctive sense of where Quebec and English Canada stood on such questions: that Bouchard's "wall of Quebec public opinion" (CBC 1998g) opposed to the reference was a false front and that many in English Canada would prefer good-faith negotiations over acrimony. The court, thereby, escaped unscathed from the politically charged atmosphere into which it had been thrust. It successfully emerged with its legitimacy intact.

## Conclusion

Justice Louis LeBel, appointed to the court after the *Secession Reference,* said that, "in some ways, the highest court in the land rehabilitated itself in the eyes of Quebecers when it gave its opinion on the Chrétien government's reference on the secession of Quebec. Federalists and sovereigntists both cried victory. Quebecers were able to see the justices' open-mindedness, and their concern to develop solutions able to take into account the interests of all groups" (Samson 2003).

Paradoxically, to the extent that the court had rehabilitated itself, it had to have recourse to new constitutional principles and duties far removed from the strictly legal questions the federal government had placed before it. At the same time, the closer to the edge of the political the court proceeded, the more the decision reinforced the sovereignist argument that the reference really was about political choices that were to be made by Quebecers only. The media focus on the political aspects of the case rather than on the strictly legal questions and their answers, at both the hearing and decision stages, helped to underscore the sovereignist reading of the *Secession Reference.* This struggle really was a battle to win hearts and not just minds. Having exhausted our period of data collection, we might score the contest: "Advantage Bouchard" (Radio-Canada 1998a). But this would not put an end to the war of spin.

Having failed to place their interpretive stamp on the *Secession Reference,* federalist forces regrouped and sought to reinforce their interpretation by introducing into Parliament the *Clarity Act* (SC 2000, chap. 26). The act purported to lay down the conditions under which the Government of Canada would negotiate the sovereignty of Quebec. The House of Commons would be entitled to authorize negotiations only where the House determined that many of the conditions laid down by the Supreme Court of Canada in the *Secession Reference* were satisfied. These included such matters as the question asked, the size of the majority obtained, and the positions of various constituent actors in the federation, including the Senate and Aboriginal peoples. If referendum processes failed to meet these criteria, as determined by the House, no constitutional duty to negotiate would arise – the federal government then could ignore any referendum result. The passage of the *Clarity Act* infuriated the Quebec government, which retaliated with its own legislation issuing from the National Assembly. The *Fundamental Rights Act* (SQ 2000, chap. 46) recites that Quebecers alone would determine when and in what circumstances secession can be pursued. The "winning option," the act states, "is the option that obtains the majority of the valid votes cast, namely, fifty per cent of the valid votes cast plus one" (section 4). The spinning continues.

## Notes

1  We have drawn, in part, from Schneiderman (1999a). See also the helpful discussion in Newman (1999).

2  Replacing the draft bill, *An Act Respecting the Sovereignty of Quebec,* tabled in the Quebec National Assembly 6 December 1994.

3  By Order-in-Council dated 30 September 1996 (PC 1996-1497).

4  Citing *OPSEU v. Ontario,* [1987] 2 S.C.R. 2 at 40.

5  See discussion generally in Leclair (1999, 73).

6  See *Reference re Canada Assistance Plan (BC),* [1991] 2 S.C.R. 525 at 545 where the court ruled that it could decline to answer a reference where the question would take the court beyond "its proper role within the constitutional framework of our democratic form of government." In the *Reference re Same-Sex Marriage* 2004 SCC 79, the court agreed to answer three of four questions referred to it. Of the last question (asking whether heterosexual marriage offended the Charter), the court wrote that it was not appropriate to answer a reference question where it would serve no legal purpose, upset vested rights, and cause confusion (paras. 62-70).

7  Percentages in Table 3.3 do not add up to 100 because of the Other category.

8  One story did not have a headline, so the total number of headlines (444) does not equal the total number of newspaper articles (445).

9  It should be noted that the Winners and losers category and the Alliances/Strategies category can both be regarded as conflict-based since they deal with power struggles between actors.

10  By "main topic," we have asked what is the story about? Information provided in a story

usually results in one central idea or topic, and this is coded as the main topic. Where there is more than one topic, the story was coded as NA and then coded for subtopics.

11 Unless otherwise indicated, this chapter contains our translations of French-language headlines and comments.

12 For more on the crowd's reaction, see Duceppe 1998; *La Presse* 1998b; Thompson, Wills, and Authier 1998; and Wills 1998a.

13 For more on the reaction to Yves Michaud's withdrawal from the proceedings, see Cornellier 1998b; Pineau 1998; and *Le Droit* 1998a.

14 "In accordance with the usual rule of prudence in constitutional cases, we refrain from pronouncing on the applicability of any particular constitutional procedure to effect secession unless and until sufficiently clear facts exist to squarely raise an issue for judicial determination" (para. 105).

15 Perhaps this was recognition on the part of the court of the purported sociological fact that Me. Joli-Coeur would not admit: that Quebec and Canada each constitute a people.

16 There were too few television stories on this score to be noteworthy.

17 Of eighteen articles, eight were in *Le Devoir* and four in *Le Journal de Montréal*.

18 Of nineteen articles, ten were in *Le Devoir* and five in *La Presse*.

19 Of thirty-one articles, twelve were in *La Presse*, ten in *Le Devoir*, and four in *Le Journal de Montréal*.

20 Of sixteen articles, seven were in the Montreal *Gazette*, five in the *Globe and Mail*, and four in the *Toronto Sun*.

## References

Auger, Michel C. 1998a. Ratés juridiques. *Le Journal de Montréal*, 16 February, p. 26.

—. 1998b. Suprême court-circuit. *Le Journal de Montréal*, 17 February, p. 11.

Authier, Philip. 1998a. Ottawa UDI strategy a failure. Montreal *Gazette*, 14 February, p. A18.

—. 1998b. Don't fall for federal intimidation: Brassard. Montreal *Gazette*, 17 February, p. A8.

—. 1998c. Bouchard: Tide is against federalists: Likens Supreme Court case to sinking ship. Montreal *Gazette*, 21 February, p. A12.

Authier, Philip, and Terrance Wills. 1998. Declare mistrial: Bouchard. Montreal *Gazette*, 18 February, p. A8.

Bantey, Ed. 1998. Doing Ottawa's dirty work: Supreme Court has been asked to formalize Quebec's status as a colony of Canada. Montreal *Gazette*, 15 February, p. A9.

Bauch, Hubert. 1998. After the storm, the tempest. Montreal *Gazette*, 21 February, p. B1.

Beauchemin, Yves, et al. 1998. C'est à nous de décider de notre avenir! *La Presse*, 18 February, p. B2.

Bellavance, Joël-Denis. 1998. La décision de la Cour suprême: Non, mais. *Le Soleil,* 21 August, p. A1.

Bergeron, Viateur. 1998. La Cour suprême apportera les meilleures réponses possible. *Le Droit,* 19 February, p. 19.

*Bertrand v. Québec (A.G.)* (1996), 138 D.L.R. (4th) 481 (Que. S.C.).

*Bertrand v. Québec (Procureur Général)* (1995), 127 D.L.R. (4th) 408 (Que. S.C.).

Bindman, Stephen. 1998. The justices. Montreal *Gazette,* 21 August, p. A9.

Boisvert, Yves. 1998a. Au sujet du "renvoi" sur la sécession du Québec. *La Presse,* 14 February, p. B9.

—. 1998b. Ottawa conteste la démarche souverainiste, pas sa légitimité. *La Presse,* 17 February, p. B1.

—. 1998c. Des questions "théoriques" et "politiques." *La Presse,* 19 February, p. B1.

—. 1998d. La Cour suprême soulève plusieurs questions difficiles. *La Presse,* 20 February, p. A15.

—. 1998e. Le Québec ne peut se séparer légalement sans négocier. *La Presse,* 21 August, p. B1.

Bronskill, Jim. 1998. Legal experts praise "masterful" ruling. Montreal *Gazette,* 21 August, p. A9.

Brosseau, Daniel. 1998a. Claude Ryan y trouve un heureux équilibre. *Le Journal de Montréal,* 21 August, p. 12.

Bryden, Joan. 1998. Get set for landmark case on legality of UDI. Montreal *Gazette,* 14 February, p. B1.

Buzzetti, Hélène. 1998a. Les autochtones applaudissent. *Le Devoir,* 21 August, p. A2.

—. 1998b. Guy Bertrand jubile. *Le Devoir,* 21 August, p. A4.

Canada. 1997. Factum of the Attorney General of Canada (No. 25506).

CBC. 1998a. Saša Petricic (reporter). In the Commons. *The National,* 16 February.

—. 1998b. Tom Kennedy (reporter). On the streets. *The National,* 16 February.

—. 1998c. Jason Moscovitz (reporter). The Supreme Court hears arguments. *The National,* 16 February.

—. 1998d. Jason Moscovitz (reporter). McLellan misstep. *The National,* 17 February.

—. 1998e. Jason Moscovitz (reporter). Arguments ended in Supreme Court. *The National,* 18 February.

—. 1998f. Jason Moscovitz (reporter). Last day in the Supreme Court. *The National,* 19 February.

—. 1998g. Tom Kennedy (reporter). PQ solidarity. *The National,* 20 February.

—. 1998h. Jason Moscovitz (reporter). Quebec can't separate. *The National,* 20 August.

—. 1998i. Susan Harada (reporter). Reaction to court's ruling on Quebec. *The National,* 20 August.

—. 1998j. Tom Kennedy (reporter). What sovereignists say. *The National,* 20 August.

—. 1998k. Tom Kennedy (reporter). The day after the decision. *The National,* 21 August.

—. 1998l. Tom Kennedy (reporter). Quebec separation. *The National,* 26 August.

Chambers, Gretta. 1998. Covering the case of the century. Montreal *Gazette,* 20 February, p. B3.

Chaput-Rolland, Solange. 1998. Cour suprême: Claude Ryan a bien raison. *La Presse,* 14 February, p. B3.

Charest, Jean. 1998. For Canada, it's a lose-lose situation: Separation is a political question. Montreal *Gazette,* 14 February, p. B2.

Chrétien, Jean. 1998. Fini les astuces! *Le Devoir,* 22 August, p. A9.

Cloutier, Mario. 1998a. Brassard fait son propre "renvoi" au fédéral. *Le Devoir,* 21 February, p. A8.

—. 1998b. La souveraineté est renforcée, croit Bouchard. *Le Devoir,* 21 August, p. A5.

—. 1998c. Péquistes et libéraux satisfaits. *Le Devoir,* 21 August, p. A1.

Cloutier, Mario, and Brian Myles. 1998. Bouchard plaide le vice de procédure. *Le Devoir,* 18 February, p. A5.

Cobb, Chris. 1998. Court affirmed our right to self-determination: Indians. Montreal *Gazette,* 21 August, p. A9.

Cornellier, Manon. 1998a. Trois questions cruciales. *Le Devoir,* 14-15 February, p. A1.

—. 1998b. Le seul souverainiste à comparaître devant la Cour suprême se désiste. *Le Devoir,* 16 February, p. A1.

—. 1998c. Sur le seul terrain du droit. *Le Devoir,* 17 February, p. A1.

—. 1998d. Ottawa perd le contrôle du débat. *Le Devoir,* 18 February, p. A1.

—. 1998e. L'avocat du fédéral désavoue la ministre de la Justice. *Le Devoir,* 20 February, p. A1.

—. 1998f. La balle se retrouve dans le camp de Québec, croit Stéphane Dion. *Le Devoir,* 21 August, p. A1.

—. 1998g. Le projet du PQ est légitime. *Le Devoir,* 21 August, p. A1.

Coyne, Andrew. 1998a. The law is a barrier – so be it. Montreal *Gazette,* 16 February, p. B3.

—. 1998b. What right to secede? Montreal *Gazette,* 17 February, p. B3.

—. 1998c. Canada has right to say no to secession. Montreal *Gazette,* 19 February, p. B3.

CTV. 1998a. Jim Munson (reporter). The Supreme Court gets set to decide Canada's future. *CTV News,* 15 February.

—. 1998b. Craig Oliver (reporter). The Supreme Court began hearing arguments on rules for breaking up Canada. *CTV News,* 16 February.

—. 1998c. Craig Oliver (reporter). Quebec's Cree Indians present their case on the unity issue to the Supreme Court. *CTV News,* 17 February.

—. 1998d. Roger Smith (reporter). Historic legal arguments wrapped up at the Supreme Court's hearings into Quebec's right to separate. *CTV News,* 18 February.

—. 1998e. Roger Smith (reporter). The Supreme Court answers questions about secession. *CTV News,* 19 February.

—. 1998f. Scott Laurie (reporter). Premier Lucien Bouchard and the PQ party gave the rest of Canada their verdict on the Supreme Court hearings into separation. *CTV News,* 20 February.

—. 1998g. Rosemary Thompson (reporter). Will a Supreme Court ruling allow Quebec to split from Canada? *CTV News,* 19 August.

—. 1998h. Roger Smith (reporter). The Supreme Court says no separation without negotiation. *CTV News,* 20 August.

—. 1998i. Roger Smith (reporter). The federalists view of the Supreme Court ruling on separation. *CTV News,* 21 August.

—. 1998j. Rosemary Thompson (reporter). The separatists spin on the Supreme Court ruling on separation. *CTV News,* 21 August.

—. 1998k. Dave Rinn (reporter). Intergovernmental affairs minister Stéphane Dion has gone on the offensive in the debate over national unity. *CTV News,* 26 August.

David, Michel. 1998a. Court reference muddies the waters. Montreal *Gazette,* 20 February, p. B3.

—. 1998b. L'os dans le poulet. *Le Droit,* 21 August, p. 5.

Delisle, Norman (Press canadienne). 1998a. Dumont blâme Ottawa. *Le Droit,* 14 February, p. 24.

—. 1998b. Dumont rappelle Chrétien et Dion à l'ordre. *La Presse,* 14 February, p. B12.

—. 1998c. Le Canada ternit son image internationale, selon Brassard. *Le Devoir,* 17 February, p. A4.

—. 1998d. Le dernier mot appartient au peuple du Québec. *Le Droit,* 21 February, p. 23.

—. 1998e. Le dernier mot continuera d'appartenir au peuple du Québec – Jacques Brassard. *Le Journal de Montréal,* 21 February, p. 38.

Derriennic, Jean-Pierre. 1998. Court's thinking best revealed now: Supreme Court intervention is inevitable. Montreal *Gazette,* 14 February, p. B2.

Descôteaux, Bernard. 1998. B comme dans boomerang. *Le Devoir,* Editorial, 21 August, p. A10.

Ditchburn, Jennifer. 1998. "Clear" as mud. Montreal *Gazette,* 22 August, p. A9.

Dubuc, Alain. 1998. Les limites du droit. *La Presse,* Editorial, 17 February, p. B2.

Ducas, Isabelle. 1998. L'avis embêtera les purs et durs des deux camps. *Le Droit,* 21 August, p. 5.

Ducas, Marie-Claude. 1998. Les anglophones sont contents. *Le Devoir,* 21 August, p. A2.

Duceppe, Gilles. 1998. Une utilisation perverse de la Cour suprême. *Le Devoir,* 18 February, p. A9.

Duffy, Andrew. 1998. No pomp, judges as unity returns to front burner. Montreal *Gazette,* 21 August, p. A7.

Dumont, Mario. 1998. Allô la terre! *La Presse,* 17 February, p. B3; *Le Devoir,* 17 February, p. A7.

Evenson, Brad. 1998. Voters in rest of Canada give ruling mixed reviews. Montreal *Gazette,* 21 August, p. A9.

Ferretti, Lucia. 1998. L'Église a son mot à dire dans le débat constitutionnel. *Le Devoir,* 21-22 February, p. A13.

Fife, Robert. 1998a. Table new deal, PM urged. *Toronto Sun,* 21 August, p. 2.

—. 1998b. The key questions. *Toronto Sun,* 21 August, p. 3.

—. 1998c. Court backs us: PQ; PM "Einstein of politics," Bouchard sneers. *Toronto Sun,* 22 August, p. 2.

—. 1998d. PM rolled the dice – and lost. *Toronto Sun,* 22 August, p. 17.

—. 1998e. A split decision: PM warns Quebec it could be chopped up, too. *Toronto Sun,* 24 August, p. 2.

Fine, Sean. 1998a. The Supreme Court reference: Case puts spotlight on Dubé, Lamer: Long-time judges French-Canadian. *Globe and Mail,* 16 February, p. A1.

—. 1998b. Behind the scenes as history was made. *Globe and Mail,* 21 August, p. A1.

Fortier, Marco. 1998a. Duceppe se réjouit de la décision. *Le Journal de Montréal,* 21 August, p. 11.

—. 1998b. Le Québec ne peut faire sécession unilatéralement. *Le Journal de Montréal,* 21 August, p. 10.

—. 1998c. Stéphane Dion somme Lucien Bouchard de renoncer à l'indépendance du Québec. *Le Journal de Montréal,* 21 August, p. 11.

—. 1998d. Jean Chrétien y voit la "fin des astuces." *Le Journal de Montréal,* 22 August, p. 9.

Francis, Diane. 1998. No more trick questions. *Toronto Sun,* 22 August, p. 15.

Fraser, Graham. 1998a. The Supreme Court reference: Top court faces Quebec issue. *Globe and Mail,* 16 February, p. A1.

—. 1998b. The Supreme Court reference: Rule of law at stake. *Globe and Mail,* 17 February, p. A1.

—. 1998c. The Supreme Court Reference: Crees demand right to stay in Canada. *Globe and Mail,* 18 February, p. A1.

—. 1998d. L'Ontario, la grande absente. *Le Devoir,* 19 February, p. A8.

—. 1998e. The Supreme Court reference: Federal case moot, court told. *Globe and Mail,* 19 February, p. A1.

—. 1998f. Flamboyant federalist has his day in court. *Globe and Mail,* 19 February, p. A4.

—. 1998g. Supreme Court asked to stick to basic issues. *Globe and Mail,* 20 February, p. A4.

—. 1998h. Justices face hard questions on legality of secession. *Globe and Mail,* 21 February, p. A4.

—. 1998i. The Quebec ruling: Canada must negotiate after yes vote. *Globe and Mail,* 21 August, p. A1.

Freed, Josh. 1998. Tale of two soaps. Montreal *Gazette,* 22 August, p. A2.

Frum, David. 1998. Lambs to the slaughter. *Toronto Sun,* 25 August, p. 15.

Gagnon, Katia. 1998a. Dion devient "l'arroseur arrosé," dit Brassard. *La Presse,* 21 August, p. B1.

—. 1998b. Bouchard et Chrétien heureux du jugement: Une "condition gagnante" pour un prochain référendum. *La Presse,* 22 August, p. A1.

Gagnon, Lysiane. 1998a. L'écran de fumée. *La Presse,* 17 February, p. B3.

—. 1998b. Un vase clos bien perméable. *La Presse,* 19 February, p. B3.

Gamble, David. 1998a. Butt out, high court told: Foes united on separation issue. *Toronto Sun,* 16 February, p. 4.

—. 1998b. "Disorder" if court quashes secession. *Toronto Sun,* 19 February, p. 18.

—. 1998c. Dion praises court efforts, wishes he had argued fed case against UDI. *Toronto Sun,* 21 February, p. 4.

—. 1998d. Both sides claim a victory: Quebec can't leave unilaterally. *Toronto Sun,* 21 August, p. 2.

*Gazette* (Montreal). 1998a. Everything you need to know. 14 February, p. B2.

—. 1998b. Momentous questions go to the heart of the system. 21 August, pp. A10-11.

—. 1998c. What the players said. 21 August, p. A1.

—. 1998d. Ottawa has say on question: Dion. 26 August, p. A14.

—. 1998e. Heed the court's ruling. Editorial, 27 August, p. B2.

Girard, Normand. 1998a. Le Canada se discrédite, dit Jacques Brassard. *Le Journal de Montréal,* 17 February, p. 14.

—. 1998b. La cause en Cour suprême compromise par la ministre fédérale Anne McLellan. *Le Journal de Montréal,* 18 February, p. 14.

—. 1998c. Le "vaisseau amiral" prend eau de toutes parts, selon Bouchard. *Le Journal de Montréal,* 21 February, p. 14.

*Globe and Mail.* 1998a. Canada, Quebec and the Supreme Court. Editorial, 16 February, p. A18.

—. 1998b. The Supreme Court reference: What was said (part 1). 17 February, p. A4.

—. 1998c. The Supreme Court reference: What was said (part 2). 18 February, p. A4.

—. 1998d. Day of decision: The Supreme Court answers. 21 August, p. A7.

—. 1998e. White House lauds ruling. 27 August, p. A6.

Gratton, Denis. 1998. L'ACFO trop occupée pour le Canada. *Le Droit,* 17 February, p. 6.

Gray, John. 1998a. Premier cautious but hopeful that nation can be made to work. *Globe and Mail,* 21 August, p. A7.

Greenspon, Edward. 1998a. The Supreme Court reference: Federal strategists dread us-versus-them scenario. *Globe and Mail,* 17 February, p. A4.

—. 1998b. The Supreme Court reference: Liberals target Charest for views on Supreme Court reference. *Globe and Mail,* 18 February, p. A4.

Greenspon, Edward, and Anne McIlroy. 1998. Bouchard and PM square off. *Globe and Mail,* 22 August, p. A1.

Greenspon, Edward, Tu Thanh Ha, and Ingrid Peritz. 1998. A verdict guaranteed to dampen the flame. *Globe and Mail,* 21 August, p. A1.

Ha, Tu Thanh. 1998. The Supreme Court reference: Separatists survived "close call." *Globe and Mail,* 19 February, p. A4.

Harris, Michael. 1998. Quebec case ignores Natives. *Toronto Sun,* 19 February, p. 19.

Hébert, Chantal. 1998a. La cause du siècle. *La Presse,* 16 February, p. A1.

—. 1998b. McLellan contre McLellan. *La Presse,* 17 February, p. B1.

—. 1998c. Les neuf carpes de la Cour suprême! *La Presse,* 18 February, p. A1.

—. 1998d. Une semaine infernale. *La Presse,* 20 February, p. B1.

Heinrich, Jeff. 1998. Ruling elicits reactions that are poles apart. Montreal *Gazette,* 21 August, p. A7.

Iacobucci, Justice Frank. 2001. Interview by authors. Ottawa, 26 October.

Johnson, William. 1998a. Federalist hopes lie no longer with politicians. Montreal *Gazette,* 20 February, p. B3.

—. 1998b. Who'll speak up for Canada? *Toronto Sun,* 20 February, p. 15.

Joli-Coeur, André. 1997. Mémoire de l'amicus curiae (No. 25506).

Lajoie, Andrée. 1997. *Jugements de valeurs: Le discours judiciaire et le droit.* Coll. Les voies du droit. Paris: PUF.

*La Presse.* 1998a. Les députés bloquistes en pèlerinage. 14 February, p. B9.

—. 1998b. Les souverainistes manifestent. 17 February, p. B1.

—. 1998c. Un jugement à la Salomon. 21 August, p. A1.

Larocque, Hubert. 1998. Stéphane Dion et la Cour suprême. *Le Droit,* 14 February, p. 21.

Leclair, Jean. 1999. The attorney general's vision. In Schneiderman 1999b, 71-76.

Legault, Josée. 1998a. How to deny Quebec's right to self-determination. *Globe and Mail,* 21 August, p. A19.

—. 1998b. Comme si le Québec vivait une seconde conquête. *Le Devoir,* 25 August, p. A7.

*Le Devoir.* 1998a. Editorial Cartoon, 14-15 February, p. A8.

—. 1998b. Editorial Cartoon, 17 February, p. A6.

—. 1998c. Editorial Cartoon, 21 August, p. A10.

—. 1998d. La division du Canada doit être negociée. 21 August, p. A1.

—. 1998e. L'avis de la Cour suprême. 21 August, p. A11.

—. 1998f. Les points saillants. 21 August, p. A2.

*Le Droit.* 1998a. Michaud ne camparaîtra pas. 16 February, p. 2.

—. 1998b. Un millier de souverainistes manifestent à Ottawa. 17 February, p. 22.

—. 1998c. Editorial Cartoon, 18 February, p. 18.

—. 1998d. Parizeau salue la "coalition" du Québec. 19 February, p. 25.

—. 1998e. Ottawa est "très" satisfait. 21 August, p. 5.

*Le Journal de Montréal.* 1998a. À la Cour suprême de définer le droit à la sécession unilatérale. 16 February, p. 26.

—. 1998b. La cause "la plus importante," selon le juge Antonio Lamer. 16 February, p. 26.

—. 1998c. 1000 personnes manifestent devant la Cour suprême. 17 February, p. 10.

—. 1998d. Ottawa rejette les prétentions des souverainistes. 17 February, p. 11.

—. 1998e. Bertrand et Joli-Coeur aux antipodes quant au droit de la cour de se prononcer. 19 February, p. 16.

—. 1998f. Les avocats d'Ottawa désemparés par les juges. 20 February, p. 2.

—. 1998g. Cartoon, 21 August, p. 12.

—. 1998h. Landry y voit de bons aspects. 21 August, p. 11.

—. 1998i. La stratégie fédéraliste est ébranlée, selon Bouchard. 22 August, p. 9.

—. 1998j. Mario Dumont trouve dans l'avis deux bons motifs de se réjouir. 22 August, p. 8.

Little, Bruce. 1998a. Quebec jitters drive dollar to low. *Globe and Mail,* 20 August, p. B1.

—. 1998b. Supreme Court ruling gives dollar small lift. *Globe and Mail,* 21 August, p. B3.

MacDonald, L. Ian. 1998. The provinces: Quebec: The court's political hot potato. *Globe and Mail,* 17 February, p. A19.

MacDonald, Michael. 1998. UDI ruling boosts loony. Montreal *Gazette,* 21 August, p. F2.

McIlroy, Anne. 1998a. Day of decision: Supreme Court leaves hard questions to politicians. *Globe and Mail,* 21 August, p. A8.

—. 1998b. Dion shifts strategy in PR battle over court decision. *Globe and Mail,* 27 August, p. A6.

Mackie, Richard. 1998. Day of decision: Premiers cautious but hopeful that nation can be made to work. *Globe and Mail,* 21 August, p. A7.

Macpherson, Don. 1998a. Hard to make political hay out of constitution. Montreal *Gazette,* 17 February, p. B3.

—. 1998b. Court case shines light on federal arguments. Montreal *Gazette,* 18 February, p. B3.

Maltais, Murray. 1998. Le guêpier. *Le Droit,* Editorial, 18 February, p. 18.

Mandel, Michael. 1994. *The Charter of Rights and the legalization of politics in Canada.* Toronto: Thomson Educational Publishing.

Marissal, Vincent. 1998. "Ça peut changer l'atmosphère au Canada," croit Landry. *La Presse,* 21 August, p. B4.

Martin, Robert. 1998. Making it up as they go along. Montreal *Gazette,* 26 August, p. B3.

Michaud, Yves. 1998. Ne jouez pas à la roulette russe avec le destin du peuple québécois. *Le Devoir,* 16 February, p. A7.

Millard, Gregory. 1999. The Secession Reference and national reconciliation: A critical note. *Canadian Journal of Law and Society* 14 (2): 1-19.

Morris, Jim. 1998. No contradictions in federal case, Dion insists. Montreal *Gazette,* 21 February, p. A14.

Morrissette, Yves-Marie. 1999. Le juge canadien et le rapport entre la légalité, la constitutionnalité et la légitimité. In *The judiciary as third branch of government: Manifestations and challenges to legitimacy,* ed. Mary Jane Mossman and Ghislain Otis, 29-65. Montreal: Canadian Institute for the Administration of Justice and Les Éditions Thémis.

Morton, Ted. 1998. Pucker up for more neverendum. *Toronto Sun,* 23 August, p. C7.

Myles, Brian. 1998a. Chrétien "discrédite gravement" la Cour suprême, estime le Bloc. *Le Devoir,* 17 February, p. A1.

—. 1998b. La colonie artistique se mobilise. *Le Devoir,* 18 February, p. A5.

—. 1998c. Un millier de souverainistes assiègent la Cour suprême. *Le Devoir,* 17 February, p. A4.

Newman, Warren J. 1999. *The Quebec Secession Reference: The rule of law and the position of the Attorney General of Canada.* Toronto: York University.

Nuovo, Franco. 1998. Quoi de neuf? *Le Journal de Montréal,* 21 August, p. 6.

O'Neill, Pierre. 1998. Un jugement équilibré, dit Ryan. *Le Devoir,* 21 August, p. A2.

Patry, André. 1998. Une question irrecevable. *Le Devoir,* 14-15 February, p. A9.

Perelman, Chaim, with Paul Foriers. 1978. *La motivation des décisions de justice.* Brussells: Établissement Émile Bruylant.

Picard, André. 1998. Québécois voices: The court should not "wash Ottawa's dirty linen." *Globe and Mail,* 19 February, p. A25.

Pineau, Yann. 1998. Se disant dans une "situation ridicule," Yves Michaud préfère se désister. *La Presse,* 16 February, p. A6.

Poulin, Daniel. 1998. Le monde canadien de l'information juridique: Du recueil au Web in Association pour le développement de l'informatique juridique, *Actes du Congrès international. L'information juridique: Contenu, accessibilité et circulation,* 22-23 October, Paris: Maison des avocats.

*Quebec Secession Reference,* [1998] 2 S.C.R. 217, available online at http://www.canlii.org/ca/cas/scc/1998/1998scc63.html.

*Quebec Secession Reference,* [1998] 2 S.C.R. 217 (Factum of the Respondents).

Radio-Canada. 1998a. Christine St-Pierre (reporter). *Le Téléjournal,* February 18.

—. 1998b. Christine St-Pierre (reporter). *Le Téléjournal,* February 19.

—. 1998c. Michel Cormier (reporter). *Le Téléjournal,* August 21.

Richer, Jules. 1998. Une victoire personnelle pour l'avocat Guy Bertrand. *La Presse,* 21 August, p. B4.

Ryder, Bruce. 1999. The Argument of the *amicus curiae.* In Schneiderman 1999b, 77-82.

Samson, J.-Jacques. 2003. Visite de la Tour de Pise (2). *Le Soleil,* 27 May, p. A16.

Schneiderman, David. 1999a. Introduction in Schneiderman 1999b, 1-13.

—, ed. 1999b. *The Quebec decision: Perspectives on the Supreme Court ruling on secession.* Toronto: Lorimer, 1999.

Séguin, Rhéal. 1998a. The Supreme Court reference: Separatists flying high at top court: PQ, Bloc relish condemnations. *Globe and Mail,* 17 February, p. A1.

—. 1998b. The Supreme Court reference: Bouchard calls for declaration of mistrial. *Globe and Mail,* 18 February, p. A4.

—. 1998c. Ottawa like the *Titanic. Globe and Mail,* 21 February, p. A1.

—. 1998d. Day of decision: Ruling legitimizes sovereignty drive, PQ leaders say. *Globe and Mail,* 21 August, p. A7.

—. 1998e. Federalist cause poisoned by ruling, Bouchard says. *Globe and Mail,* 22 August, p. A3.

Steward, Hartley. 1998. Snatching defeat from the jaws of victory. *Toronto Sun,* 16 August, p. 16.

Thompson, Elizabeth. 1998a. Dumont joins critics of UDI reference. Montreal *Gazette,* 14 February, p. A18.

—. 1998b. Secession case tries a federalist's faith. Montreal *Gazette,* 17 February, p. A8.

—. 1998c. We'll stay in Canada, Crees vow. Montreal *Gazette,* 18 February, p. A1.

—. 1998d. Court says no to UDI, yes to negotiated split. Montreal *Gazette,* 21 August, p. A1.

—. 1998e. We win, both claim. Montreal *Gazette,* 22 August, p. A1.

Thompson, Elizabeth, Terrance Wills, and Philip Authier. 1998. Top court's hearing on UDI opens: 1,000 separatists march to protest against case. Montreal *Gazette,* 17 February, p. A1.

Tibbetts, Janice (Presse canadienne). 1998. Vu l'importance de la cause, la cour posera pour l'Histoire. *Le Devoir,* 16 February, p. A4.

Tison, Marie. 1998. Bouchard prédit une crise politique. *Le Droit,* 14 February, p. 22.

*Toronto Sun.* 1998a. Judges pose for historic picture. 16 February, p. 4.

—. 1998b. Order in the court. Editorial, 17 February, p. 14.

Toupin, Gilles. 1998a. Pour les autochtones, une porte ouverte à l'autodétermination. *La Presse,* 21 August, p. B5.

—. 1998b. Bouchard et Chrétien heureux du jugement: Une barrière que les séparatistes devront franchir. *La Presse,* 22 August, p. A1.

TVA. 1998a. Paul Larocque (reporter). *Le TVA, Édition réseau,* February 15.

—. 1998b. Monique Grégoire (reporter). *Le TVA, Édition réseau,* February 16.

—. 1998c. Monique Grégoire (reporter). *Le TVA, Édition réseau,* February 18.

—. 1998d. Paul Larocque (reporter). *Le TVA, Édition réseau,* August 20.

—. 1998e. Bernard Plante (reporter). *Le TVA, Édition réseau,* August 26.

Venne, Michel. Une accalmie. *Le Devoir,* 21 August 1998, p. A1.

Wells, Paul. 1998a. Full speed ahead for Lamer. Montreal *Gazette,* 17 February, p. A8.

—. 1998b. Democracy – in action and words. Montreal *Gazette,* 18 February, p. A8.

—. 1998c. Joli-Coeur's hat running out of rabbits. Montreal *Gazette,* 19 February, p. A10.

—. 1998d. Court case offers little to sneer at: Bad week for some separatists. Montreal *Gazette,* 21 February, p. A1.

Whyte, John D. 1998. If Quebec leaves, it must leave by the rules. *Globe and Mail,* 19 February, p. A25.

Wills, Terrance. 1998a. Charest, PM trade barbs: Bloc leads 1,000 in protest on court's steps. Montreal *Gazette,* 17 February, p. A8.

—. 1998b. Secession rules can wait: Feds. Montreal *Gazette,* 21 August, p. A8.

—. 1998c. PM to Bouchard: Get real. Montreal *Gazette,* 22 August, p. A9.

Winsor, Hugh. 1998. The Supreme Court of Canada: The power game: Charest wise to trust his instincts. *Globe and Mail,* 19 February, p. A4.

Young, Huguette. 1998a. La Cour suprême doit trancher. *Le Droit,* 17 February, p. 1.

—. 1998b. L'indépendence du Québec représenterait pour les Cris un "coup de force." *Le Droit,* 18 February, p. 21.

—. 1998c. La stratégie fédérale connaît des ratés. *Le Journal de Montréal,* 21 February, p. 38.

—. 1998d. Dion reste confiant. *Le Devoir,* 22 February, p. A8.

—. 1998e. Une sécession à négocier. *Le Droit,* 21 August, p. 1.

# —4—

# "Sea of Confusion": *R. v. Marshall*

ALTHOUGH THE SUPREME Court of Canada came under increasing criticism in the 1990s, it is probably accurate to say that it faced unprecedented anger when it released its 17 September 1999 decision in the Donald Marshall fishing rights case. The decision stemmed from charges laid against Donald Marshall Jr., the same Mi'kmaq Aboriginal who spent eleven years in prison after being wrongfully convicted of murder. In 1993, Marshall was accused of fishing and selling 210 kilograms of eels without a licence in a closed season. He claimed that as a Mi'kmaq he had a right to fish based on the LaHave treaties of 1760-61.

When the Supreme Court acquitted Marshall on all charges and found that the 1760 treaty did give him a limited commercial right to fish, reaction within the Maritimes was largely split along Aboriginal/non-Aboriginal lines. Aboriginal communities, particularly those engaged in fishing activities, hailed the decision as a major victory and began to exercise their newly recognized rights by setting traps for lobster despite the season being closed. Conversely, non-Aboriginal fishers condemned the decision, saying it placed their livelihoods in jeopardy. They were also furious that Aboriginal fishers were taking lobster out of season.

As data from our study of a year in the life of the court show, Supreme Court rulings rarely hold the media's attention for more than a day, and this ruling might have followed that same pattern had it not been for the violence being threatened on Maritime docks. As tensions between Mi'kmaq and non-Aboriginal fishers increased, so too did media interest. The story took on the momentum of a runaway train. Soon political columnists, academics, and Aboriginal rights advocates were jumping into the spotlight. Strangely, the group that could have stopped or at least eased the tension – the federal government – remained silent.

It is standard practice that courts speak only through their decisions. Once a ruling is handed down, the court remains silent, leaving it to the media, through the voices of columnists, academics, and politicians, to interpret decisions for the public. The *Marshall* case marks a stunning departure from that convention, as the court took the opportunity to comment on its initial decision. On 17 November, two months to the day after the release of the first *Marshall* decision (hereinafter referred to as *Marshall 1*), the court responded to a motion for a rehearing and stay made by the West Nova Fishermen's Coalition with a thirty-two-page ruling (hereinafter referred to as *Marshall 2*). The ruling not only addressed the concerns of the coalition but revisited the court's position on the treaty rights it had found and discussed issues that had not been brought before the court by the parties in *Marshall 1* (Wildsmith 2001; Saunders 2000; Barsh and Henderson 1999). The move shocked the legal community, was condemned by the Mi'kmaq, and was applauded by non-Aboriginal fishers and their supporters. More than one commentator suggested the court had bowed to public pressure. Russell Barsh (2000, 739) pointed out that in *Marshall 2,* the court took the "unprecedented step of rephrasing its rulings and reasoning and addressing issues relating to the scope of federal regulatory authority that had not previously been raised or argued by the parties." There were also people critical of the *Marshall 2* ruling. Bruce Wildsmith (2001, 235), the lawyer who defended Donald Marshall, wrote that in penning *Marshall 2,* "the Court bowed to the intense controversy that resulted from its decision, to the confrontations between natives and non-natives, and to the public criticism that was directed to the Court."

## A Region in Turmoil

One of the reasons *Marshall 1* raised the level of anxiety among non-Aboriginal fishers is the precarious state of the Atlantic fisheries. Traditionally, the economy of Atlantic Canada has relied heavily on fishing and on the cod fishery in particular. When cod stocks plummeted in the early 1990s and the federal government declared a moratorium on cod fishing, the region plunged into an economic crisis. Not only did Ottawa have to step in with more economic aid for out-of-work cod fishers but pressure increased on other fisheries, such as lobster. Although these fisheries provided some economic relief, they could not compensate for the loss of the cod fishery. When the Supreme Court's *Marshall 1* was incorrectly interpreted by journalists and Aboriginal fishers as giving the Mi'kmaq an unfettered right to fish, non-Aboriginal fishers saw it as yet another threat to an already extended resource. As Don Cunningham, spokesman for the West Nova Fishermen's Coalition put it, "We're dealing with a finite resource here and there's no way to add more entrants to the resource without harming it" (Underhill 1999a). The worry gnawing at fishers was probably compounded by uncertainty over what the ruling actually meant.

But if non-Aboriginal fishers were uncertain about the meaning of the decision, the Mi'kmaq weren't. Within four days of the ruling, Mi'kmaq were exercising what they saw as their newly recognized rights by taking to the water in search of lobster. As one Mi'kmaq fisher put it, "This means so much to us. It's just like Christmas and we want to thank the Santa Claus that gave it to us – the Supreme Court of Canada" (Cox 1999b). Given the history of the Mi'kmaq under colonial and then Canadian rule, it is no surprise they would rush to take advantage of any decision that provided them with some type of economic gain. As journalist Geoffrey York (1990) points out, the story of the Mi'kmaq is one of poverty brought on to some extent by the federal government's repeated and bungled attempts at resettling the Mi'kmaq in different locations.

The Mi'kmaq of Nova Scotia have also spent years battling the provincial and federal governments over the interpretation of treaties (Wildsmith 2001). One of the more important of these, *R. v. Simon,* has a familiar ring to it. In 1985, the Supreme Court found that the Treaty of 1752 gave James Matthew Simon, a member of the Shubenacadie Indian Brook band, the right to hunt. The court refused to rule on whether the treaty had been terminated by subsequent hostilities between the Mi'kmaq and the British, writing that it was up to the Crown to provide evidence to that effect. In the wake of the decision, Nova Scotia officials continued to press charges against band members for hunting off season and the federal government refused to say whether it believed that the treaty had been terminated (Wildsmith 2001). It was only during pretrial arguments in the *Marshall* case that the Crown revealed it was going to argue that the Treaty of 1752 was invalid. This foot-dragging over the interpretation of a decision is apparent in, and one of the reasons for, the conflict over *Marshall 1.* If the federal government had been more timely in its interpretation of *Marshall 1,* some of the strife in the Maritimes might have been avoided.

Two other factors contributed to the confusion and chaos in the Maritimes: the wording of the ruling, and media reporting that was incomplete or, at its worst, inaccurate. Journalistic accounts of *Marshall 1* demonstrate the problems that can arise when Supreme Court rulings are reported by journalists unfamiliar with Supreme Court jurisprudence. Through an analysis of the *Marshall* decisions and newspaper and television accounts of the ruling, we will argue in this chapter that poor understanding by journalists of a complex and sometimes ambiguous decision may have contributed to the mayhem in the Atlantic fisheries in the fall of 1999.

## Legal Background

According to traditional dogma, decisions do not spring like inventions from the minds of judges. They are steeped in tradition and precedent, in legal principles and case law. This process provides an element of stability to the law. While no one can be exactly sure what a judge will decide in any given case, seasoned court observers do know that the decision will fall within a range of possible actions. Aboriginal and treaty rights have been slowly evolving, and the ruling that Marshall did have a treaty right to limited commercial fishing was not wholly unpredictable.

*Marshall* was the first case in which the court analyzed treaty rights using section 35 of the *Constitution Act, 1982*. Treaty rights cases have appeared before the court since 1982 but they have involved provincial legislation and the court's reasoning relied on section 88 of the *Indian Act,* which imposes restrictions on the application of provincial regulations to Aboriginal people. In *Marshall,* charges stemmed from Marshall's violation of federal fisheries regulations. Therefore, the court had to decide whether or not Marshall had a treaty right to fish within the meaning of section 35 and, if a right was found, whether federal regulations prohibiting fishing infringed that right.

The court did find a treaty right, and it used both *R. v. Sparrow* and *R. v. Badger* to discuss steps the Crown must take to justify infringing Aboriginal and treaty rights. In *Sparrow,* a member of the Musqueam band was charged with fishing with a drift net longer than permitted by the band's food-fishing licence. The appellant claimed an Aboriginal right to fish and said the net restriction was inconsistent with section 35(1) of the *Constitution Act, 1982*. In finding for the appellant, the court laid down steps appellants and the Crown must take to first prove there is a right and then justify its infringement. In the first section of the test, the appellant must establish that a right exists, that it has not been extinguished, and that it has been infringed. In the second part of the test, the Crown must demonstrate that the regulation or legislation infringing the right fulfills a valid objective, such as resource conservation. In addition, the Crown must show that Aboriginal rights were given a priority, that care was taken so that there was as little infringement as possible, and, where appropriate, that compensation was offered. In *Badger,* a decision the court repeatedly referred to in *Marshall 1* and *2,* the court said that the justificatory standards established in *Sparrow*, an Aboriginal rights case, also applied to treaty rights cases. Although in *Marshall* the court did not engage in an extensive dialogue of the steps laid down in *Sparrow,* people familiar with Aboriginal and treaty rights jurisprudence would have understood exactly what the court meant when it said the right could be regulated as per *Badger* and *Sparrow*.

Although *Marshall* represents the first time the court found that a treaty affords a limited commercial right to fish, previous Aboriginal rights decisions make it appear that the court was taking small but incremental steps toward this end. In the 1996 *R. v. Van der Peet* case, the appellant Dorothy Van der Peet, a member of the Sto:lo Nation, argued that the regulations prohibiting her from selling fish for sustenance (but not commercial) purposes infringed on an Aboriginal right and were, therefore, invalid under the terms of section 35. In this instance, the majority found the Sto:lo did not have an Aboriginal right to exchange fish for money or goods because the band could not demonstrate that trading fish for goods was an integral, distinctive part of Sto:lo culture before contact with Europeans. In separate dissents both Justice L'Heureux-Dubé and Justice McLachlin found that the First Nation had the right to exchange fish for money.

In *R. v. Gladstone*, two members of the Heiltsuk band were charged with attempting to sell herring spawn on kelp. Unlike the appellant in *Van der Peet*, the Gladstones were arguing for an Aboriginal right to trade on a commercial level. The court found that the band did have a commercial right to fish because the "commercial trade in herring spawn on kelp was an integral part of the distinctive culture of the Heiltsuk prior to contact and was not incidental to social or ceremonial activities." It wrote that the Crown had not produced sufficient evidence to demonstrate that federal regulations infringing on the Aboriginal right were justified, and it sent the case back to trial. Clearly, *Marshall 1* should not have come as a complete surprise to governments and the media because it was based on slowly unfolding precedent.

## The Case

It was not mere happenstance that Donald Marshall was charged with illegal fishing in 1993. Marshall knew he was flouting the law because on one of his forays onto the water he had been issued a warning by Department of Fisheries and Oceans officials. He called Membertou Reserve chief Terence Paul to ask for advice. Chief Paul told Marshall to "keep fishing" (Cox 1999a). The next day, fisheries officials seized some of Marshall's gear. Again Chief Paul advised Marshall to continue to fish. Another day, another confrontation. This time, Marshall told the chief that officials had seized all his gear. "I told him to get a pole and keep fishing. I felt strongly that he had a right to be there and gain a livelihood," said Chief Paul to reporters after the release of *Marshall 1* (Cox 1999a). It wasn't until Marshall sold 210 kilograms of eels that officials charged him with illegally fishing and selling eels.

Marshall admitted to fishing, but claimed he had a right to fish stemming from the Treaty of 1752, which states, "The said Tribe of Indians shall not be hindered from, but shall have free liberty of Hunting and Fishing as usual" (*Marshall 1*, para. 15). Although the fishing right is clearly stated in this treaty, reliance on it was dropped during trial proceedings for two reasons: (1) the Crown was allowed to lead evidence that this treaty had been terminated because of hostilities that occurred after it had been signed; and (2) under cross-examination one of the Crown's experts, Dr. Stephen Patterson, expressed the opinion that the British would have known that the Mi'kmaq lived by hunting and gathering, that these activities would provide them with goods to trade, and that the Mi'kmaq, therefore, had the right to trade those goods (Wildsmith 2001, 218). Patterson also testified that all Mi'kmaq followed the Treaties of 1760-1761 and that these treaties were still valid and operative. After Marshall's attorneys heard Patterson's testimony, they felt more secure using the LaHave treaties of 1760-61, whose truckhouse clause reads: "And I do further engage that we will not traffick, barter or Exchange any Commodities in any manner but with such persons or the managers of such Truck houses as shall be appointed or Established by His Majesty's Governor at Lunenburg or Elsewhere in Nova Scotia or Acadia" (*Marshall 1*, para. 5).

While this clause is not as strong as the right defined in the Treaty of 1752, Wildsmith, Marshall's lawyer, believed it contained the right to fish and trade the fish. The Crown argued that the truckhouse clause was a negative covenant. Instead of granting a right, in this instance the right to trade, it prevented the Mi'kmaq from trading with anyone other than the British. At trial, Judge Embree agreed that the truckhouse clause gave the Mi'kmaq a positive right to trade the products of their hunting and fishing. He refused to acquit Marshall because, in his opinion, the treaty right had been extinguished when the truckhouse system was abandoned.

At the Nova Scotia Court of Appeal, Justices Roscoe and Bateman (Justice Flinn concurring) confirmed the lower court's decision that there was no existing treaty right to catch and sell fish. In addition, the court found that the truckhouse clause did not grant a positive right to trade. In fact, the Appeal Court wrote that the primary purpose of the truckhouse clause had less to do with trade than with encouraging ongoing peaceful relations between the British and the Mi'kmaq. The British never intended to convey trading rights. Instead, the clause represented a negative covenant that prohibited the Mi'kmaq from trading anywhere other than with the truckhouses. When the truckhouse system ended, so did the prohibition.

The Supreme Court found that both courts erred when they concluded that the text of the treaty contained all the obligations agreed to by the British and the Mi'kmaq. Writing for the majority, Justice Binnie found that the trial judge was mistaken in finding a positive right to trade in the truckhouse clause. Clearly, the clause imposes a negative covenant on the Mi'kmaq. The court found that the trial judge relied too heavily on the text of the treaty, which was weighted in favour of the British. The Mi'kmaq would not have agreed to such a restrictive clause. Instead, the trial judge should have given more weight to the perspectives of the Aboriginal people. The Supreme Court found that the truckhouse clause would not have advanced the British desire to achieve peace or the Mi'kmaq objective of obtaining British goods unless there was an explicit or implicit understanding between the two parties that access to wildlife would continue.

Key to the court's decision was its willingness to rely on extrinsic evidence. Justice Binnie wrote that, "Even in the context of a treaty document that purports to contain all the terms, this Court has made clear in recent cases that extrinsic evidence of the historical and cultural context of a treaty may be received even absent any ambiguity on the fact of the treaty" (*Marshall 1*, para. 11). Then, drawing heavily on the historical, political, and economic contexts in which the treaty was written, Binnie found that the treaty did contain a right to trade fish. And more importantly, that within the right to trade was an implicit right to catch fish because the right would not have any meaning if the right holder could not exercise it. He rejected the Crown's argument that the truckhouse system was a temporary measure and that the right to trade fish disappeared with truckhouses. He wrote, "where a right has been granted, there must be more than a mere disappearance of the mechanism created to facilitate the exercise of the right to warrant the conclusion that the right itself is spent or extinguished" (*Marshall 1,* para. 54).

Of particular relevance in terms of subsequent media coverage was the majority's stress that these treaty rights could be regulated. In more than one place, Binnie stressed that the right is one that can be regulated, and he pointed to the justificatory steps in *Badger* (para. 56). Reasons for regulation can include conservation and issues of public safety. In both *Marshall 1* and 2 the court stressed that the Crown had the option of justifying its regulations but chose not to, presumably because it could not rationalize regulating the eel fishery for conservation purposes. The court also stated that government was able to regulate the fishery for reasons other than conservation. *Marshall 2* went so far as to say that government authority "extends to other compelling and substantial public objectives which may include economic and regional fairness" (para. 41). In other words, the historic reliance of non-Aboriginal fishers on a resource could be factored into any government decision to impose limits on treaty fishing rights.

The court in *Marshall 1* also made it clear that government could limit the Mi'kmaq catch despite the fact that a treaty right to fish for trading purposes had been found. The decision states, at paragraph 57, that "the ultimate fear is that the appellant, who in this case fished for eels from a small boat using a fyke net, could level the treaty right into a factory trawler in Pomquet Harbour gathering the available harvest in preference to all non-aboriginal commercial or recreation fishermen ... This fear (or hope) is based on a misunderstanding of the narrow ambit and extent of the treaty right."

Binnie wrote that the Mi'kmaq in 1760 would have understood that the right to fish and trade would provide them with nothing more than a sustenance lifestyle. That view, he said, continues to govern the right. Therefore, "catch limits that could reasonably be expected to produce a moderate livelihood for individual Mi'kmaq families at present-day standards can be established by regulation and enforced without violating the treaty right" (para. 61).

The text of this ruling, which granted the Mi'kmaq a limited right to trade, and the references to decisions such as *Badger* and *Gladstone,* made it clear that governments did have wide latitude in controlling Mi'kmaq fishing. Not only could rights be regulated for conservation purposes (as per *Badger*), they could also be curtailed to protect regional economic interests in the fishery (as per *Gladstone*).

Non-Aboriginal concerns that the resource was going to be decimated could have been quickly addressed instead of being allowed to spiral out of control. As University of Windsor law professor Leonard Rotman (2000, 640) writes: "Images of Aboriginal fishers driving Rolls-Royces and living in sprawling mansions ... are no more realistic than the notion that the *Marshall* case signals the destruction of the fishery."

While *Marshall 1* and *2* were clear that the treaty right to fish could be regulated, the decisions were murky when it came to defining the scope of the right. This led to public confusion over what could and could not be harvested. Were the Mi'kmaq allowed to take lobster? Were they allowed to harvest timber? What about oil and gas rights? Academic Phillip Saunders (2000, 76) notes that "the majority in *Marshall* #1 defined the scope of resources and activities covered by the treaty right in different words at different points, but focused fairly consistently on the rights to obtain and trade in the produce of hunting, fishing and 'gathering' activities, as reflected in their modern evolutions." Despite mentioning repeatedly that the treaty right was the right to hunt and fish, the court also noted that the regulations against selling eels without a licence infringed on the appellant's treaty rights. In *Marshall 2*, the court made an attempt to clarify the limits of the resources by saying the decision found a community treaty right that allowed the appellant to participate in the eel fishery. But the court also said, a number of times in different ways, it was "only hunting and fishing resources to which access was affirmed" (*Marshall 2*, para. 38). Given the dual messages in both rulings, it is no wonder that journalists, the Mi'kmaq, and non-Aboriginal fishers were confused over the scope of the right.

A dissent in *Marshall 1* written by Justice McLachlin, with Justice Gonthier concurring, added to the morass because it could be argued that even the Supreme Court could not agree on the existence of a right. Justice McLachlin agreed with the lower court findings that the Treaties of 1760-1761 created a limited right to bring goods to trade, as long as the truckhouse system was in existence. When that system died, so did the right to trade and the incidental right to bring goods to trade.

## Methodology and Preliminary Findings

Because the *Marshall* decisions followed so closely on the heels of one another, they provided a unique opportunity to study extended coverage of a decision. Stories about *Marshall 1* did not stop after a few days; instead, they continued for two months. Data collection began on 15 September 1999 and continued through to 24 November. Newspaper data were collected from the *Globe and Mail, National Post, Le Devoir, La Presse*, Halifax *Chronicle Herald, L'Acadie Nouvelle* (a French-language daily published in Caraquet, New Brunswick), and from the tabloids *Le Journal de Montréal* and the *Toronto Sun*. We also monitored stories in the *Mi'kmaq-Maliseet Na-*

## Table 4.1: Frequency of articles in newspapers

| Newspaper | MARSHALL 1 | | MARSHALL 2 | Total |
| --- | --- | --- | --- | --- |
| | 15-24 Sept. | 25 Sept.-14 Nov. | 15-24 Nov. | |
| Globe and Mail | 4 | 20 | 9 | 33 |
| National Post | 4 | 26 | 4 | 34 |
| Chronicle Herald | 9 | 33 | 7 | 49 |
| Toronto Sun | 1 | 7 | 1 | 9 |
| Mi'kmaq-Maliseet Nations News | 0 | 4 | 1 | 5 |
| La Presse | 2 | 17 | 1 | 20 |
| Le Devoir | 2 | 18 | 3 | 23 |
| Le Journal de Montréal | 0 | 9 | 0 | 9 |
| L'Acadie Nouvelle | 5 | 25 | 8 | 38 |
| **Total** | **27** | **159** | **34** | **220** |

*tions News,* a monthly tabloid published in Truro, Nova Scotia. As Table 4.1 shows, a total of 220 articles were collected over this two-month period. The Maritime newspapers ran the greatest number of stories the week following the decision, while the fewest number were in Quebec newspapers. As the table shows, initially there was little interest in the *Marshall* decision.

Data were also collected from three television newscasts: CTV's national news, *CTV News*; CBC's *The National*; and Radio-Canada's *Le Téléjournal*.[1] In these television newscasts there was even less coverage than in the newspapers sampled (see Table 4.2). *CTV News, The National,* and *Le Téléjournal* each ran one story the day of the decision and then, with the exception of the CBC, which ran one more story on 24 September, aired nothing else for close to two weeks.

This lack of interest in the decision is reflected in the fact that none of the media organizations in our sample covered the 1998 hearing. Federal Court justice James O'Reilly, the court's executive legal officer at the time, recalls there was low attendance at the briefing that preceded the decision: "There were only three or four people in the room for *Marshall*. There was only one person that actually knew what that case was about ... The other people in the room came over because they saw Donald Marshall's name on something and they wanted to know what it was about. They had no idea what the case was about. And you know, when I said it was a case about catching eels, I think they turned around and left the room" (O'Reilly 2002).

Our data show that there was heightened interest in the story a full week after *Marshall 1* was released. In most instances, coverage of Supreme Court decisions ends after a day or two. Coverage of the *Marshall* decision mirrored the escalation of violence between Aboriginal and non-Aboriginal people on the docks at Burnt

Table 4.2: Frequency of reports on television networks

| Television network | MARSHALL 1 15-24 Sept. | 25 Sept.-14 Nov. | MARSHALL 2 15-24 Nov. | Total |
|---|---|---|---|---|
| CBC | 2 | 12 | 1 | 15 |
| CTV | 1 | 7 | 1 | 9 |
| Radio-Canada | 1 | 7 | 1 | 9 |
| **Total** | **4** | **26** | **3** | **33** |

Church, New Brunswick. As tension in the Maritimes grew, so too did media interest in the ruling.

## Marshall 1 Coverage – The Case of the Missing Court

Editors decide where to place stories in newspapers based on a combination of factors, including story importance and public interest. For example, the most important story of the day is always placed at the top of the front page. For newspapers, the first opportunity to run decision coverage was the day after the decision – 18 September. When this day's coverage and story placement are analyzed, it appears there was little interest in this decision in Quebec. Only *Le Devoir* carried a story about the decision, and it was published on page 4. *La Presse* and *Le Journal de Montréal* did not run stories until 23 September and 4 October, respectively, and these too were on inside pages. Even in the Maritimes, where the decision would have the greatest impact, the French-language *L'Acadie Nouvelle* did not cover the decision until 20 September and the article was buried on page 13. Although the *Globe and Mail* and *National Post* both gave the *Marshall* decision front-page coverage, their stories were placed below the fold. In fact, the *Post* ran less than three inches on the front and continued the remainder of the story inside. The Halifax *Chronicle Herald* devoted the top half of its front to coverage of the decision and the monthly *Mi'kmaq-Maliseet Nations News* gave the entire front page of its October issue (its first opportunity to cover the decision) to a story and photo, running two additional articles inside.

Much of the coverage the day after the decision focused on Donald Marshall. Looking camera shy but relaxed at a media conference in Halifax, Marshall confessed he had been trying to live a normal life. When this treaty issue surfaced, he felt he had to take up the gauntlet for the good of his people: "This time I went to the Supreme Court for fishing. I wasn't there for myself. I was there for my people" (Cox 1999a). Marshall was cast in the archetypical role of hero – he was portrayed as someone who had faced and overcome great adversity not once, but twice (Lule 2001). On the day of the decision, a Radio-Canada story focused on

Marshall, portraying him as someone who was accustomed to fighting injustice. The story contained a clip from the made-for-TV movie, which depicted Marshall's fight against his wrongful murder conviction. The voice-over to the film clip is representative of the media's attitude toward Marshall: "As the film reminds us, he's a man accustomed to fighting injustice. He spent 11 years of his life in prison for a murder he didn't commit."[2] But journalists did not focus on Marshall for long. Our statistics show that Marshall or his lawyer were quoted in just 7.3 percent of the 253 newspaper and television stories collected for analysis. In addition, Marshall was quoted as a first source in just 9 stories and as a second source in 6 stories. And, he was the main focus in just 3 of 220 newspaper heads. These statistics show that the man who generated the decision faded quickly from the media spotlight. This was partly because of Marshall's aversion to centre stage and partly because of growing tensions on Maritime docks, which drew the media's attention like moths to a flame.

For an analysis of the decision, journalists turned to Marshall's lawyer, Bruce Wildsmith, and, more interestingly, to Aboriginal lawyers and Mi'kmaq chiefs. Our data show that in television and newspaper pieces in which someone was quoted, Aboriginal sources appeared first more often than any other source. In newspapers they were quoted first 48 times compared with the majority court's 41 times, the Liberal government's 44 times, and the non-Aboriginal fishers' 20 times. The paper that used Aboriginal people as a first source most often was the Halifax *Daily Chronicle,* with 17 articles quoting Mi'kmaq people first. *Le Devoir* and *La Presse* used Aboriginal spokespeople first more often than the *National Post* and the *Globe and Mail.* The television networks also used Aboriginal sources first more often than other sources. The two tabloids, *Le Journal de Montréal* and the *Toronto Sun,* used them least often. The *Mi'kmaq-Maliseet Nations News* used only Aboriginal sources in all its stories.

Initially, this finding would appear to be a positive one for Aboriginal people because the position of first speaker in a news story is one of prominence. The first speaker's statements set the agenda against which other speakers react. However, in this case, the speakers, who represented Mi'kmaq leaders and fishers, were not shown in a positive light because they were represented as a threat to the established order. Previous research on the portrayal of Aboriginal people in the news demonstrates that First Nations are most often shown in positions of conflict with non-Aboriginal society. In his examination of Montreal *Gazette* coverage of the 1990 Oka crisis, Marc Grenier (1992, 274) wrote that Aboriginal people "tend to be portrayed by mass media as strange, as unpredictable threats to social order, and as heavily engaged in emotive and largely deviant forms of conflict." Grenier's research shows that media interest in the Oka crisis intensified after the prospect of armed physical violence at the Oka-Mohawk blockade site grew. Benjamin

Singer's survey of five years of coverage of Aboriginal people in Ontario demonstrated that most news items about Aboriginal people were focused on conflict (1982). Singer concluded that "The image of the Indian based on the news items is apt to be that of an individual whose relationships to Canadian Society are essentially mediated by dependence on government and presumably aggressive land claims. The second major image component presented is that of conflict-deviance" (357). In other words, Aboriginal people were shown as deviants and as "threats" to the established order.

In her analysis of coverage of a public inquiry into relations between Aboriginal people and the RCMP in northern British Columbia, Elizabeth Furniss (2001) found that coverage supported the local non-Aboriginal hierarchy and reinforced negative stereotypes of Aboriginal people. Further, she wrote that when economic resources were the issue, "there is a tendency for news reporting to protect established economic/political interests by rejecting Aboriginal claims" (29). Our research shows that all these findings are relevant to coverage of the *Marshall* decisions. Not only did news about the decision increase after violence occurred but Mi'kmaq fishers were accused of destroying a resource and a way of life for non-Aboriginal fishers. What is extremely interesting about this accusation is that its basis in fact was never questioned. Charges by non-Aboriginal fishers that the Mi'kmaq were decimating the lobster fishery were printed without question. But the estimated 6,000 traps set by approximately 100 Mi'kmaq was a small number when compared with regular season figures. For instance, in the 1997-98 season, 1.5 million traps were set by more than 6,000 fishers in the Maritime region (Coates 2000).

While coverage of Aboriginal people was primarily neutral, the proportion of stories, editorials, and opinion pieces that placed them in a negative light was higher than it was for non-Aboriginal people. Our data show that 9.7 percent of the newspaper stories that referred to Aboriginal people were negative in nature. For non-Aboriginal fishers that figure is 3.9 percent. We also found that two-thirds of these negative references (fourteen out of twenty-one) were found in the French-language newspapers we surveyed. There were no negative references to Mi'kmaq people or non-Aboriginal fishers on the television networks, but there were visuals of violent confrontations between the two groups which, as shall be discussed shortly, did not favour the Mi'kmaq. Some of the negative references in newspapers blamed the Mi'kmaq for the violence that followed the decision. For instance, in *Le Devoir* Alain-Robert Nadeau (1999) wrote that the people really responsible for the crisis were the Mi'kmaq. By throwing their lobster cages into the water before the ink was dry on the decision, the Mi'kmaq broke the delicate peace between themselves and their non-Aboriginal neighbours. In another *Le Devoir* piece, Laval University professor Ghislain Otis said the Mi'kmaq demonstrated a lack of understanding of the fragility of the situation (Myles 1999).

In the two or three days after the ruling, there were a few stories in which Aboriginal people were shown celebrating their right to fish. Mi'kmaq leaders spoke about the benefits that the ruling would have both for their people and for the rest of society. Nova Scotia chiefs pointed out that the ruling would allow First Nations to become less dependent on government support, and Peter Bernard, a spokesman for the Lennox Island fisheries group, said that "for those that are on welfare, this is going to give them a half-decent living" (Legge 1999b; Cox 1999a). Burnt Church chief Wilbur Dedam said, "A lot of little businesses are going to boom, people who are out there (fishing) are shopping" (Cox 1999b). But these positive portrayals of an excited, hopeful people were juxtaposed against the words of angry, frightened non-Aboriginal fishers who worried their own livelihoods were being threatened. In effect, these duelling realities flipped the Mi'kmaq people from their stereotypical role of white men's victim into that of the oppressor. This message was particularly poignant in the television news stories that used visuals of Mi'kmaq fishers hauling in lobster and non-Aboriginal fishers posing in front of empty lobster cages.

Even more damning were portraits of Aboriginals as a defiant people determined to exercise their rights no matter what the cost to others. Mi'kmaq leaders warned that there were going to be major changes in the industry. Millbrook chief Lawrence Paul said, "The non-Indians don't want to share ... But due to the Supreme Court decision, the rules of the game have changed and they'll have to share, whether they like it or not" (Morris 1999). Bruce Clarke, the lawyer representing the Native Council of Canada, was quoted as saying commercial resource industries in the Maritimes were going to have to "make some room for the aboriginal commercial harvest of timber, perhaps minerals, certainly fish" (Mofina 1999a). Journalists also made note of this attitude. In *Le Journal de Montréal,* author Franco Nuovo wrote that "The Native, now sanctioned by the country's highest court, doesn't give a damn about the fishing season rules" (1999a). This angry "us against them" attitude expressed by Aboriginal fishers and noted by writers put the Mi'kmaq in a position of defiance against non-Aboriginal fishers and, by extension, Canadian society.

In these early days, the decision was reported as an overwhelming victory for the Mi'kmaq. Bruce Clarke's contention that the decision applied to more than eels was expressed in a number of media reports – either overtly through direct reference to hunting and fishing or covertly by not asking whether the ruling had, in fact, given Mi'kmaq the right to fish for lobster. Without exception, all journalists and columnists who covered the decision assumed the court had given the Mi'kmaq a treaty right to hunt and fish for more than eels. Headlines declared "Donald Marshall wins again," "Mi'kmaq rights upheld," and "Marshall scores new court win" (Makin 1999a; Underhill 1999a; Dunn 1999). The lead in *Globe and*

*Mail* justice reporter Kirk Makin's story (1999b) described the decision as "a major legal victory." Makin was one of the few reporters who correctly cited the decision as it related to restrictions and limits. He wrote (1999a) that the court stated that government could "legitimately create catch limits that allow Micmac families to achieve a 'moderate livelihood,' but no more."

Although readers and viewers were told that the Mi'kmaq could not set up large-scale commercial fishing enterprises, stories often ignored the court's assurances that the right could be regulated. In the Halifax *Chronicle Herald* the stress was on the First Nation's right to fish year round without being subject to federal regulations, including licensing requirements. When restrictions were mentioned, it was in connection to the court's finding that commercial fishing could be used only to earn a moderate living as opposed to turning a huge profit (Underhill 1999a). Radio-Canada's *Le Téléjournal* told audiences that "natives have the right to sell the fish they catch because fishing laws do not apply to them" (Miller 1999).[3] In the *Mi'kmaq-Maliseet Nations News* readers were told that the treaty right could be regulated, but again it was discussed in the context of the open-ended accumulation of wealth. Regulation as a conservation measure was not mentioned (Googoo 1999). Articles such as these left the impression that the Mi'kmaq could fish for whatever they wanted whenever they wanted.

Non-Aboriginal fishers were immediately concerned about their own livelihoods. Fishers predicted the demise of the industry and angrily asked why another group should receive preferential treatment. Don Cunningham, a spokesperson for the West Nova Fishermen's Association, said First Nations fishers had been given an unfair advantage, and he compared the situation to "Ontario losing its automobile industry" (Mofina 1999a). Non-Aboriginal fishers were brimming with questions. Which First Nations did the ruling apply to? How many Mi'kmaq would be allowed to fish? What was the definition of "moderate livelihood"? Eyes turned to Ottawa for answers.

Ottawa had been caught napping and was slow to wake up. As the *National Post* (1999b) would later write, "In Ottawa, the entire Chrétien government, including Herb Dhaliwal, the Fisheries Minister, was caught off guard." In fact, our data show that as a topic, the call for government to take action and/or criticism of government action was one of the top three subjects. Of the 253 news stories we analyzed, there were 47 stories about conflict and violence, 40 stories about the decision, and 40 on the action, or inaction, of government leaders. Many of these stories on government inaction were critical of politicians who apparently had not considered the possibility that the court might find in Marshall's favour. For instance, in a 4 October television news story, CTV journalist Tom Walters said, "But caught off guard, the Fisheries Department has no management plans and in the vacuum, chaos" (CTV 1999c). Politicians were angry as well. A Conservative MP from Newfoundland was quoted as saying, "The government ... knew the case was before the Supreme Court. They knew they would likely lose, and yet they are completely out of touch with the situation" (Hamilton 1999f).

There were also angry calls for action from non-Aboriginal fishers. In late September, fishers in Yarmouth, Nova Scotia, threatened to pull Aboriginal lobster traps out of the water unless the federal government came to a quick decision on Mi'kmaq fishing (Mofina 1999b). During this period, ten stories fell in our "government is inept" category; they were, of course, critical of the federal government. In fact, our results show that 44 of the 222 stories that referred to the federal government were negative in tone, compared with 30 negative references to the decision and 21 negative references to Aboriginal people.

While government was dragging its heels, officials at the provincial level were moving quickly. On 17 September, Nova Scotia's fisheries minister Ernie Fage contacted federal fisheries officials to seek advice on the meaning of the ruling (Underhill 1999a). He came away with no answers. At the same time, Department of Indian and Northern Affairs officials were consulting with Ministry of Justice staff to determine the ruling's implications.

By Monday, 20 September, Mi'kmaq fishers were setting lobster traps, and the frustration of non-Aboriginal fishers was increasing from a simmer to the boiling point. Mike Belliveau, executive secretary of the Maritime Fishermen's Union, called for immediate action from Ottawa: "I don't want a battery of lawyers up in Ottawa going over every fine line, making this interpretation and that interpretation ... You need reasonable interpretations right now" (Hamilton 1999a). On 22 September, the federal government finally decided to speak; however, federal fisheries minister Herb Dhaliwal chose to communicate to the media through a written statement instead of in person at a media conference. He called for "patience and restraint" while officials reviewed the ruling (Hamilton 1999a). To add insult to injury, the department's director of communications told the media that officials weren't sure how long the review would take.

In the weeks following the decision, tensions continued to mount and the possibility of violent confrontation was raised by non-Aboriginal fishers. On 23 September, less than a week after the ruling, Harold Theriault, president of the Bay of Fundy Inshore Fishermen's Association, said federal inaction was dangerous, and he warned that unless control was brought back to the oceans, "somebody's going to get killed" (Hamilton 1999b). His views were echoed by other non-Aboriginal fishers. The immediate concern was the lobster fishery. For at least three years, the Department of Fisheries and Oceans had been imposing more restrictions on the fishery and, at the time of the decision, fishers were facing a new federal proposal to

A Mi'kmaq man, framed by a broken window, waves the Warrior Society flag in this *National Post* photograph by John Lehmann. During the violence that followed the Supreme Court's *Marshall 1* decision, Aboriginal people were prominently featured in TV and newspaper images. *Courtesy of the National Post*

limit the size of lobsters taken (Legge 1999a). To add fuel to the fire, the Mi'kmaq were taking lobster out of season and at a time when the lobster were vulnerable because they had come inshore to moult, lay eggs, and feed. As one fisher put it, "At the end of June, if I set 325 traps I might catch 100 pounds of lobster. Now if I could set 325 traps, I'd get closer to 1000 pounds" (MacGregor 1999a).

There were voices of reason. Donald Marshall, who had not been heard from since the day of the decision, called for calm and asked Mi'kmaq fishers to pull their nets while negotiations took place. His remarks were actually disparaged by one Mi'kmaq fisher, who commented, "That's Donald's opinion ... he opened the door for us – and we're going through" (MacGregor 1999a). But other Aboriginal and non-Aboriginal fishers said they believed both sides could work together to come to an agreement. Mi'kmaq fishers repeatedly stated that they were follow-ing conservation procedures and were throwing back small lobster and females with berries. One of the dominant messages from Aboriginal fishers was that conservation had always been a priority for First Nations people. Mi'kmaq fish-ers also stressed that the decision had given them a way to get off welfare. CBC's *The National* offered an especially poignant portrayal of a people struggling to gain economic independence in the form of footage of a young Mi'kmaq family carry-ing a lobster trap to the water (CBC 1999a). This was not the stuff of big business. Rather, the clip and accompanying interview with the young mother made it ap-parent who the real beneficiaries of the treaty rights would be.

Given the furor created by the court's decision, it could be considered unusual that so little attention was paid to the institution itself. Finally, on 30 September, the media cast its gaze toward the court. In a scathing column, the *Globe*'s Jeffrey Simpson (1999a) unleashed a barrage of criticism against the court. The reader's first cue that this was not going to be a cakewalk for the court was the headline "In the fishery verdict, a win for chaos." Simpson argued that the justices were overly generous in their interpretation of the 1760 treaty. He accused the court of being out of touch with the real world and said, "A truck can be driven through its at-tempt to define the Micmac's right to a 'moderate livelihood' for the purposes of 'day to day needs.'" That same day the *National Post* (1999a) took the court to task in an editorial that was flawed in its interpretation of the court's decision. Although *Marshall 1* repeatedly and clearly stated the right to fish could be regulated, the editorial criticized the court for finding the Mi'kmaq had the right to fish for profit "without need of a licence or other restrictions." In a *Le Devoir* column, Louis-Gilles Francoeur (1999) said the court's decision broke well-established conserva-tion practices, and he predicted there could be a backlash against what people perceived as the development of two sets of laws for the people of Canada.[4]

Government continued to fumble its way through the controversy. Herb Dhali-wal finally called a media conference for 30 September, only to cancel and re-schedule it for the next day. In the meantime, Atlantic chiefs and fisheries officials were given a Department of Fisheries and Oceans (DFO) memo which stated that although the Mi'kmaq could continue to fish, they would be "subject to regulation and will be licensed by DFO" (Jackson and Maich 1999). When Minister Dhaliwal finally spoke to the media, he announced his intention to negotiate temporary re-strictions and said he could not order the Mi'kmaq off the water. He explained, "The rights affirmed by the highest court of the country apply now." He was also firm in his resolve that fishing "be conducted in an orderly and regulated manner" (Hamilton 1999c).

His response satisfied no one. Non-Aboriginal fishers had been hoping for an immediate moratorium on fishing and were infuriated that the Mi'kmaq could continue to fish. The Mi'kmaq felt that their rights were once again being usurped. Bernd Christmas, a Mi'kmaq lawyer who had been meeting with a group of Atlantic chiefs, said, "It was clear on their face, their disappointment. They said it was like, I guess, the days haven't changed. It's just the way it was before where people would tell us this is what you're going to do, this is what you're not going to do" (CBC 1999b). Adding to their upset were remarks by Nova Scotia premier John Hamm, who called for a stay of the decision while its impact was clarified. An angry Chief Lawrence Paul responded bluntly that Hamm's remarks "make me want to puke" (Jackson and Maich 1999). The chief asked why Hamm had not brought his concerns directly to Mi'kmaq leaders; "instead he tried to torpedo us through the back door."

## The Court under Fire

What happened during the following week in terms of media coverage provides a strong testament to the theory that media are attracted to controversy and violence. There were just twenty-six newspaper and television stories the week after the decision was released (see Figure 4.1). Three of these were television stories that ran on 17 September, seven were newspaper stories that ran on 18 September. The remainder of the newspaper stories were scattered throughout the week. There was a slight climb in numbers the second week after the decision, as an unusually high number of stories – ten – ran on 30 September. In week three, which begins 1 October, coverage spikes sharply. When the data are examined in detail they show that on 5 October (day five of week three), twenty newspaper articles were published. This is the largest number of articles published or aired on any day during the two-month collection period.[5] On 6 and 7 October, eleven articles ran each day, the third highest number of articles to run on any given day. From 5 to 7 October, the *Globe and Mail* ran seven pieces, which were either editorials or columns, and on 7 October, it devoted close to two full pages to coverage.

A survey of the week's events offers an explanation for this renewed interest in the case. Tensions were running high and the federal government's one foot in, one foot out posture was only inflaming emotions. Violence was threatened, protest meetings and rallies were held, and finally, clashes between the two sides occurred. On 3 October, fishers in Burnt Church, New Brunswick, destroyed an estimated 3,500 Mi'kmaq lobster traps in Miramichi Bay and vandalized three fish plants suspected of processing lobster caught by Mi'kmaq fishers (Hamilton 1999e). Wilbur Dedam, chief of the Burnt Church reserve, declared, "It'll be an eye for an eye," and later that evening fire was set to two trucks belonging to non-Aboriginals

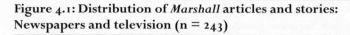

**Figure 4.1: Distribution of *Marshall* articles and stories: Newspapers and television (n = 243)**

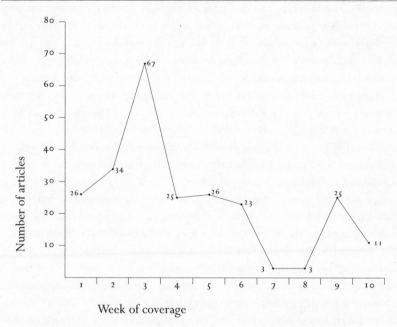

(Hamilton 1999d). Violence escalated throughout the night, leaving homes and vehicles damaged and at least one Mi'kmaq man in the hospital with injuries.

It is hardly surprising that after this mayhem, media attention intensified. Headlines such as "Fish war of words" and "Ottawa gropes for response to fish battle" are examples of the conflict and battle metaphors that dominated coverage of the confrontations (Durkan 1999; Leblanc 1999). But the photos spoke more loudly than the headlines or the text. Both the *Chronicle Herald* and the *Toronto Sun* carried photos of Mi'kmaq men on the bed of a pickup truck dressed in army fatigues.[6] The *Globe and Mail* and the *National Post* carried photographs of the Mi'kmaq Warrior Society flag. The *National Post* also carried a photo of a burning truck which, according to the caption, the Mi'kmaq had set on fire in retaliation for vandalized lobster traps.[7] All these pictures recalled the violence that occurred nine years earlier at Oka, Quebec, when images of Mohawk warriors wearing army camouflage gear were splashed across the country's newspapers. And although neither the headlines nor the stories blamed one side or the other for the violence, the photos clearly depicted the Mi'kmaq as aggressive if not aggressors.

Television, with its heavy reliance on visuals, was drawn to the violence. In fact, 75 percent (eighteen) of the English-language television frames and 66.7 percent (six) of the French-language television frames were strategic as opposed to issue frames. These conflict-based stories showed and commented on acts of provocation and resistance by both communities. There was film footage of Mi'kmaq warriors in camouflage gear, of Aboriginal and non-Aboriginal fishers charging each other with boats and, most spectacularly, of burning buildings and vehicles. There were also numerous shots of pushing and shoving matches between antagonists. The destruction of equipment and other acts of vandalism took front and centre stage. For instance, on 3 October, *CTV News* anchor Wei Chen opened the Burnt Church story with: "After simmering for weeks, the east coast fishing dispute exploded today as non-natives wrecked a native fishery pulling up and destroying hundreds of lobster traps." Her introduction was followed by journalist Alison Vuchnich, who said, "It finally came to this. Where the rule of law collided with outlaw justice in the waters" (CTV 1999a). This language, with its powerful war metaphors, continued through the remainder of the news story and was augmented with scenes of angry Aboriginal and non-Aboriginal fishers. In this and other similar stories, text and image combined to present a tense portrayal of the situation in the Maritimes.

A Radio-Canada news item with the image of a car burning on the dock at Burnt Church along with an agitated crowd had an ugly feel to it. In a voice-over to this scene, journalist Solveig Miller flagged the event as "the native community's revenge"[8] (Radio-Canada 1999a). Although much of the violence was perpetrated by non-Aboriginals who were angry that the Mi'kmaq were fishing for lobster, in French-language television coverage, Aboriginal people stood out as belligerent. One Mi'kmaq was quoted as saying, "It's an eye for an eye this time,"[9] while another "scoffs" that he won't have to work all winter like the "whites" because he had already made his money (Radio-Canada 1999a).[10] When interpreting Mi'kmaq quotes from English to French, Radio-Canada journalists sometimes made the quotes more hostile than likely intended by the speaker. Robert Levi, chief of the Big Cove Reserve in New Brunswick said, "We're not doing anything wrong, we're out there trying to earn moderate livelihoods." This was translated by journalist Ginette Lebreton as "'We're not doing anything illegal,' says Chief Robert Levi, and the natives won't give up anything" (Radio-Canada 1999c). Lebreton presented the Aboriginal community as if it would make no concessions.

On English-language television Aboriginal fishers were also depicted as angry and defiant. A CTV story opened with a shot of Mi'kmaq warriors as they occupied the docks at Burnt Church and voice-over by anchor Lloyd Robertson, who commented, "It is a very un-Canadian way of settling disputes but tonight Native warriors escalated a bitter Maritime battle over fishing rights. They have taken over a government wharf vowing to do whatever it takes to protect Native property" (CTV 1999b). This statement separated Aboriginal people from the rest of Canadian society by characterizing their actions as un-Canadian. CBC showed an outraged Mi'kmaq fisher yelling, "We have the fucking right to be out there" and "They're our fucking traps" (CBC 1999c). In another CBC story, an Aboriginal fisher defiantly said he was going home to get more traps: "I have 30 out there, there are going to be 150 now" (CBC 1999d). Both CBC and Radio-Canada captured and aired a shoving match between an angry Mi'kmaq and a non-Aboriginal fisher (CBC 1999c; Radio-Canada 1999b). The violence was accompanied by angry words uttered by the Mi'kmaq: "It does not give you the right to fucking cut my traps. Does it! Does it! No, it doesn't!"

That the majority of television news stories were strategic frame reflects the distinctive style of television reporting. In newspapers, issue frames dominated English-language coverage, while the strategic frame was more prevalent in French-language newspapers. Indeed, 74.4 percent of all articles, columns, and editorials in French-language newspapers were written in a strategic frame (see Table 4.3). For the English-language papers, this figure was only 27.9 percent. A closer analysis of the data reveals that when the French-language media covered the clarification, they switched to using an issue-based frame. In fact, just 25 percent of the stories about *Marshall 2* were in strategic frames compared with 66.7 percent of the stories about *Marshall 1* and 84 percent of the stories that ran in the period between the two decisions. In the English-language papers, 28 percent of the stories in the *Marshall 1* collection period, 30 percent of the stories in the interim, and 18 percent of stories on the clarification were in strategic frames. Although it seems intuitive that stories published when violence was occurring in Burnt Church would be in strategic frames, the difference between French- and English-language newspapers suggests that francophone journalists viewed the situation using a more combative frame. It is also important to remember that we discarded stories that were primarily about the fishing dispute – articles had to focus on the Supreme Court or the decision.

With events spinning out of control, the media shifted into overdrive. Politicians were scrummed, academics were interviewed, and columnists stepped up to bat. Prime Minister Jean Chrétien mused that the federal government might ask the Supreme Court for a stay. His staff, on the other hand, told the media that a negotiated settlement was the preferred solution. Later that same afternoon, Herb Dhaliwal said a stay would not be sought, and he threatened to close the fishery if Mi'kmaq chiefs did not agree to conservation measures. New Brunswick premier Bernard Lord appealed for calm. The Atlantic premiers issued a statement that called on Ottawa to quickly provide an interim plan (Leblanc 1999). The Reform Party waded in with leader Preston Manning blaming the federal government for being caught off guard. Reform also called on the government to ask for a stay and said a new

**Table 4.3: Frames in English- and French-language newspapers**

| Media | Strategy | Issue | Other | Total |
|---|---|---|---|---|
| Anglophone | 36 (28%) | 83 (64%) | 11 (8%) | 130 |
| Francophone | 67 (75%) | 22 (24%) | 1 (1%) | 90 |
| **Total** | **103 (47%)** | **105 (48%)** | **12 (5%)** | **220** |

settlement should be reached that provided one set of laws for everyone.

The court and its decision were placed under a magnifying glass. For the first time since the decision was issued, newspapers ran excerpts of the ruling (*Chronicle Herald* 1999b; *Globe and Mail* 1999a). The *Globe* published its first editorial on 5 October and its second a day later. A flurry of columns appeared. Most commentary was critical of the court. Table 4.4 and Table 4.5 show the distribution of negative articles that discussed the court or the justices (without mentioning details of the decision) and articles that were about the decision and its impact but did not discuss the court as an institution or the justices. The highest percentage of negative articles, including editorials and columns, was in the *National Post,* followed by the *Globe and Mail*. Given Quebec's recent history of conflict with the Mohawk people, the low number of critical comments in French-language newspapers could be regarded as surprising. Television data show that there were no negative references to the court or the decision on any network. Most negative references to the court were located in editorials, columns, comments, and opinion pieces printed at least one week after the decision was released. In fact, between 24 September and 14 November, half of the editorials about the decision and the court and close to half of the columns and opinion pieces were negative.

One-third of the headlines about the court were negative and tore into the institution with phrases such as "Supreme Court ignites the fire" (*Le Journal de Montréal* 1999),[11] "Supreme anarchy" (*L'Acadie Nouvelle* 1999),[12] "The Supreme Court as battering ram" (Simpson 1999b), "Supreme blindness" (Leishman 1999) and "Supreme Court, supreme arrogance" (Cummins 1999). What's worse is that they were an accurate reflection of the articles' content. One theme that ran through these criticisms was that the court was removed from the reality of everyday life. In the *Toronto Sun,* Peter Worthington (1999) wrote: "In the sterile sanctity of the Supreme Court, decisions are made that imperil livelihoods, jobs, resources, with little apparent concern for reality." A *Globe and Mail* (1999b) editorial chastised the court for not anticipating the chaos its decision would cause: it "foolishly" did not suspend the ruling so federal legislation could be amended. *National Post* columnist Andrew Coyne (1999) suggested it was time for the court and the federal govern-

Table 4.4: Tone of references to the decision

| Newspaper | Positive | Negative | Neutral | No. of stories |
|---|---|---|---|---|
| *Globe and Mail* | 0 | 7 | 25 | 32 |
| *National Post* | 0 | 8 | 26 | 34 |
| *Chronicle Herald* | 0 | 4 | 44 | 48 |
| *Toronto Sun* | 0 | 4 | 5 | 9 |
| *Mi'kmaq-Maliseet Nations News* | 1 | 0 | 4 | 5 |
| *La Presse* | 0 | 1 | 19 | 20 |
| *Le Devoir* | 0 | 1 | 22 | 23 |
| *Le Journal de Montréal* | 0 | 1 | 8 | 9 |
| *L'Acadie Nouvelle* | 0 | 4 | 34 | 38 |
| **Total references** | **1** | **30** | **187** | **218** |

ment to move out of the past. He wrote: "My point here is not to quibble with the court's reasoning, but rather to suggest that decisions about fisheries management in 1990s Canada ought not to be guided by the geopolitical calculations of the 1760s." Another columnist hinted the court was out of touch with the reality faced by people impacted by its decisions (MacGregor 1999b). Halifax *Chronicle Herald* columnist Ralph Surette (1999) put it succinctly: "Hello, Supreme Court: If you're going to be making laws, think of the consequences."

Politicians, too, expressed frustration with the court. Newfoundland premier Brian Tobin said, "The court has a responsibility to make themselves aware of how the fishery works. And if there is anarchy today ... the Supreme Court of Canada has to take responsibility for that" (Leishman 1999). The implication of all these remarks was that the justices were emotionally, physically, and intellectually removed from mainstream society.

Several commentators were critical of the undemocratic nature of the court and accused it of usurping Parliament's power. Richard Gwyn (1999) wrote that the justices "are accountable only to history. This powerlessness of the public, which doesn't elect the judges, and equally that of the government, which appoints the judges but has no right to discipline them thereafter, contrasts with the extraordinary power of the Supreme Court judges." Jeffrey Simpson (1999b) wrote that the court had taken on a "battering ram" role in finding and foisting Aboriginal rights on governments and other courts. Freelance journalist Rory Leishman (1999) accused the court of usurping "the law-making powers of Parliament by changing the law." In Quebec, *Le Journal de Montréal* columnist Franco Nuovo (1999a) criticized the court for validating an ancient treaty and giving special rights to a few people. This seemed to be a favourite theme for Nuovo, because the next day he

**Table 4.5: Tone of references to the court**

| Newspaper | Negative | Neutral | No. of stories |
|---|---|---|---|
| Globe and Mail | 6 | 23 | 29 |
| National Post | 10 | 13 | 23 |
| Chronicle Herald | 3 | 22 | 25 |
| Toronto Sun | 1 | 3 | 4 |
| Mi'kmaq-Maliseet Nations News | 0 | 4 | 4 |
| La Presse | 1 | 19 | 20 |
| Le Devoir | 3 | 20 | 23 |
| Le Journal de Montréal | 3 | 6 | 9 |
| L'Acadie Nouvelle | 2 | 36 | 38 |
| **Total** | **29** | **146** | **175** |

again asked why the court found it necessary to dig up old stories and parchments (1999b).

Commentators also used Justice McLachlin's dissent to demonstrate the unreasonableness of the majority decision. A *Globe* editorial pointed out that McLachlin, in discussing treaty interpretation, wrote that while treaty language should be generously construed, it should not be stretched beyond what the language makes possible or realistic (*Globe and Mail* 1999c). On the other hand, continued the editorial, Binnie used an "increasingly elastic series of logical links" to find a right to fish. In the *Post,* Rory Leishman (1999) praised McLachlin for siding with the lower courts. One columnist commended her for being a "strong advocate of judicial activism, but in a conservative way" (Gwyn 1999) and William Thorsell (1999) was so enamoured of McLachlin's dissent he called for her elevation to the position of chief justice on the retirement of Chief Justice Lamer. Thorsell also suggested that Parliament rein in the court's power by making the appointment process more consultative, by writing laws with a statement of intent leaving no room for judicial misinterpretation, and by establishing a standing justice committee to review all judgments that affect legislation.

Coverage was not completely lopsided. With the exception of the *National Post,* newspapers devoted space to alternative viewpoints. Daniel N. Paul, a human rights activist who was also a member of the Mi'kmaq Nation, blamed successive federal and provincial governments for the mess. He pointed out that if the Mi'kmaq had been allowed an equitable share of natural resources in the first place, the treaty issue would not have been before the court (Paul 1999). Both Theresa McClenaghan, counsel to the Canadian Environmental Law Association, and Terry Glavin, an author and member of the federal Pacific Fisheries Resources

Conservation Council, stressed that the treaty right was subject to regulation – both to restrict catches to "moderate livelihoods" and for purposes of conservation and public safety (McClenaghan 1999; Glavin 1999). McClenaghan asked that the Mi'kmaq be trusted to exercise their rights in a responsible manner because conservation had always been part of their approach to the land. And the *Globe* ran an excerpt of a speech given by Phil Fontaine, national chief of the Assembly of First Nations, in which he said that Ottawa's suggestion that the decision be set aside was unreasonable (Fontaine 1999). Canada had refused to honour its fiduciary obligations to First Nations, thereby forcing them to seek remedy in the courts. On those occasions when the courts find for Aboriginal people, government still hedges on incorporating those rights. That, said Fontaine, is unacceptable.

After this avalanche of news in the wake of the violence of 3 October, coverage stabilized for two weeks and then faded until the release of *Marshall 2* in November. But events continued to unfold. On 14 October, Bob Nault, the minister of Indian and Northern Affairs, announced that treaty rights talks with Aboriginal leaders would begin soon. A day later, Dhaliwal appointed James MacKenzie, a lawyer and land claims negotiator, as an arbitrator. Both announcements were greeted with cynicism by Mi'kmaq chiefs: "The chiefs have a different view. This is the treaty rights of Mi'kmaq people, and it's the Mi'kmaq people who will decide how they will integrate their rights into the greater milieu" (Scoffield and MacKinnon 1999). On 18 October, the West Nova Fishermen's Coalition, which was an intervener at the first hearing, applied to the court for a stay and rehearing on the Department of Fisheries' ability to regulate the fishery. Criticism of the court continued, but at a much reduced pace.

In an unusual move, Dr. Stephen Patterson, a New Brunswick historian whose testimony for the Crown at trial was cited by the majority court, accused Justice Binnie of "seriously distorting" his evidence (Fife 1999a). In the decision, Patterson is quoted as saying that implicit in the Treaties of 1760-1761 is a right to continue to live in traditional ways, which implied the British accepted that the Mi'kmaq would continue to hunt and gather. But Patterson told the *National Post*'s Robert Fife that at trial he had also testified that the treaties made it clear the Mi'kmaq would be subject to the same laws as other subjects. In Patterson's view, Justice Binnie had "simply ignored all aspects of my testimony that established the context within which my remarks were given and comes to a conclusion that when I said they had rights, it was a section 35(1) privileged right ... I said these treaties made native people subjects of the British Crown and as subjects of the British Crown, they have rights ... but it is the same right as anyone else's rights" (Fife 1999a). Another historian who testified for the defence agreed with the court's finding and said it was logical that when a right to trade was granted, the right to hunt and fish was also assured (Makin 1999b).

## Marshall 2 – Damage Control

While *Marshall 1* arrived to relatively little fanfare, the same cannot be said of *Marshall 2*. On 17 November, the *National Post, Globe and Mail,* and *Chronicle Herald* all ran brief stories announcing that the rehearing decision was forthcoming. The day after the ruling, the *Globe* devoted front-page coverage, an editorial, and a full page of stories to the issue. While the *Post* did not devote as much space to the decision, it did give it extensive coverage. Headlines such as "Judges rule Natives not immune to fishing laws," "Marshall ruling clarified: Trees, minerals, gas not covered," and "Natives enraged by Supreme Court interpretation" all implied the Mi'kmaq had lost ground.

Kirk Makin wrote that the court's decision reflected the anger of the justices. He said the court had issued "an unprecedented rebuke" making it clear that its decision had been either misread or simply not read (Makin 1999c). The court "sardonically" said it had not ruled Marshall could gather everything and anything and "scornfully rejected the coalition's argument that a non-aboriginal fisherman should never be displaced by a treaty right" (Makin 1999c). The *Post's* main story, on the other hand, used a winner-loser frame and stressed Mi'kmaq losses. The Supreme Court, it said, had made it clear that Aboriginal people did not have "access to forestry, mineral and oil resources on Crown lands" (Fife 1999b). Aboriginal fishers were subject to federal regulations, including a closed fishery. This winner-loser frame was also used by the *Chronicle Herald*.

Aboriginal people were critical of the court and the clarifying ruling. Leaders felt "betrayed" and said the court had caved in to "mob and vigilante rule" (Fife 1999b). Not only would the decision cause the Mi'kmaq to distrust the justice system but the court had set a dangerous precedent by backing down in the face of public opinion. Chief Paul said the court had damaged its credibility "not just in the eyes of Canada but also in the eyes of the world" (Cox 1999c). There were a few upbeat reactions. One Aboriginal chief said he believed logging was still included in the treaty (Cox 1999a) and Bruce Wildsmith, Marshall's counsel, said "the idea that the Marshall case applied only to eels was quashed. Clearly, the case applies to other species" (Underhill 1999b).

Politicians on both sides of the political fence were jubilant – albeit for different reasons. Opposition politicians took the opportunity to attack ministers Nault and Dhaliwal, demanding their resignations. Reform MP John Cummins, a former fisher who had fished illegally in 1986 to protest Musqueam fishing rights, praised the ruling as a "huge victory" and said treaty rights "can justifiably be infringed upon and that's the issue that the court makes very clear here: that treaty rights are not absolute" (Cox 1999c). Bloc leader Gilles Duceppe said the court had stressed that treaty rights applied only to fishing, and not, as Minister Nault claimed, to hunting, natural resources, and forestry (ibid.). Nault denied saying that the rights awarded

in *Marshall 1* extended to gas deposits and logging but stood by his contention that
Native treaty rights did extend to natural resources (Underhill 1999b). Dhaliwal
said the ruling only confirmed what he had been asserting all along – the right to
fish was regulated (ibid.).

The court's lengthy reprise was greeted with surprise by academic and legal
communities. General consensus held that the court was trying to smooth the water by providing clarification of *Marshall 1*. As one observer said, "I think they feel
that they've stepped in a bit of a cow patty here and are trying as delicately as they
can to get their foot out of it" (Hamilton 1999g). Wayne MacKay, then a professor
of constitutional law at Dalhousie University, said fishers were not the only ones
who didn't fully understand the initial ruling – "I've read it carefully and taught
that decision. It's certainly open to interpretation" (Hamilton 1999g). Of course
the *Post*, which had been unfailingly critical of the court, took another opportunity
to kick the cat. "Have no doubt," wrote the editorial board, "the Supreme Court
of Canada blinked" (*National Post* 1999c). The *Post* lambasted the court for crossing
into political territory belonging to democratically elected governments and also
criticized the judges for penning complex and convoluted decisions that defied
logic. It compared the court's behaviour to that of a political party sending up a
trial balloon, only to change its policy in the face of negative public opinion. But,
as previously mentioned, the *National Post* displayed a lack of knowledge of the law
in an editorial (*National Post* 1999c) that condemned *Marshall 2* for inventing the
concept of a regulated right. Despite that the concept of regulated rights has been
ingrained in constitutional law under the Charter for close to twenty years (in section 1(1) of the *Constitution Act, 1982*) and that the court found that the right could
be regulated in *Gladstone,* the editorial stated: "This clumsy invention probably
emerged because the court was not prepared to withdraw its original judgement."

Others were more sympathetic toward the court. Patrick Monahan, a York
University law professor, called the decision "a welcome intervention" because it
helped clarify the "false and misleading interpretations given the original judgement" (*Globe and Mail* 1999d). He added that the controversy over the decision
was "absurd" and a moral should be drawn from the experience – that "inflamed
rhetoric is no substitute for careful reading of a court judgement." As the *Chronicle
Herald* (1999a) put it, "Sometimes a case about catching eels is a case about catching eels. And a judgment says what it says." The significance of the unanimity of
the justices in *Marshall 2* was also discussed. Jeffrey Simpson (1999c), apparently
forgetting that *Marshall 1* set a precedent, wondered how Justices McLachlin and
Gonthier could join the majority in a ruling which, at its base, endorsed the judgment against which they had originally dissented. Others believed that handing
down *Marshall 2* had been a wise and strategic move on the part of the court; it
was warning Canadians to read judgments more attentively.

Although reporting dwindled over the following weeks, the decision's ramifications continue to reverberate in the Maritimes. In the wake of *Marshall 2*, the
federal government began to negotiate agreements with First Nations communities to provide start-up assistance, gear, and vessels and assist with so-called capacity building. By 2002, agreement had been reached with thirty-one of thirty-four
communities impacted by the decision, including Burnt Church. Negotiations for
longer-term agreements are under way. Despite the settlements, the fishing crisis
has continued to escalate in the Maritimes. In 2003 the cod fishery was closed in
some areas, and in May 2003 crab fishers rioted in Shippagan, New Brunswick, to
protest quota reductions and the allocation of crab licences to Aboriginal people
and fishers from the cod and lobster fishery (Cox 2003). Among the fishing plants
and boats damaged were a vessel owned by the Big Cove band and a processing
plant that handled crabs caught by the Mi'kmaq. In a comment sounding reminiscent of 1999, Big Cove band chief Robert Levi said, "There is a lot of confusion and
a lot of anger" (Cox 2003). Although they had just 10 percent of the crab licences
in the Maritimes, Aboriginal fishers were, apparently, still reviled for holding what
some regarded as special privileges.

## Conclusion

Although it appears the court survived its *Marshall* crisis with its reputation relatively intact, there are signs that the fallout from both decisions left cracks in the
institution's facade. Numerous criticisms were written in academic journals about
the differences between the two decisions and on the reasons the court issued *Marshall 2*. In one of the most convincing of these, Bruce Wildsmith (2001) argues that
the court yielded to public pressure: "To my mind the judges had been watching
the television coverage, listening to the radio, and reading the newspapers ... It is
evident from the discussion of 'gathering' in *Marshall (No. 2)* that they knew about
the logging trials and the Sable natural gas pipeline issues."

There are also indications that the decision and ensuing coverage created tension among the justices. In a news conference ten days before *Marshall 2* was
handed down, Chief Justice McLachlin declared that the judiciary should not
operate in a vacuum. McLachlin, who had just been named to the chief justice
position, said, "I think the idea that there's some law out there that has nothing
to do with consequences and how it plays out in the real world is an abstract and
inaccurate representation of what the law is. You cannot have a rule that ignores
consequences" (Tibbetts 1999). A full year later, Justice Bastarache, who had not
sat on *Marshall 1* or *2*, said that he had not agreed with the majority in *Marshall 1*.
He told *LawyersWeekly* journalist Cristin Schmitz (2001) that Aboriginal rights cases
were extremely difficult to adjudicate because they dealt with rights that were "ill-
defined" and "historical." Bastarache said he was very concerned by public reaction

to the decision and he blamed the media and the parties involved for misinterpreting *Marshall 1*. Alluding to the plight of non-Aboriginal fishers, he said the court must always be aware of the circumstances of all the parties coming before it. His statements caused further furor: the Atlantic Policy Congress of First Nations Chiefs and Ontario's Criminal Lawyers' Association filed complaints to the Canadian Judicial Council, which, after an investigation, found no breach of conduct.

The comments of McLachlin and Bastarache did more than provide court watchers with entertaining reading. They drew back the curtains, if only for a moment, on the cloistered world of the justices. Although it is impossible to say with certainty, it appears that in *Marshall 2* the justices were, to some extent, responding to political pressure. Patrick Monahan, of Osgoode Hall Law School, commented that the court was lucky that the opportunity to clarify *Marshall 1* appeared in the guise of the West Nova Fishermen's Coalition's application for rehearing (*Globe and Mail* 1999d). Perhaps. The court's lengthy clarification made it appear that it was playing to public opinion; that it was, in some respects, just like other institutions – concerned about its image. The irony is that one of the reasons the court maintains its respect is precisely because it is seen as being above the rough and tumble of politics. While *Marshall 2* might have helped bureaucrats sort out the mess in the Maritimes (although even that is debatable), it might have done the court more harm than good over the longer term.

Other schisms were highlighted by media coverage of the *Marshall* decisions. Tensions between Aboriginal and non-Aboriginal people in the Maritimes were underscored through coverage of sparring on the Burnt Church docks. The repeated footage of Aboriginal people fishing while non-Aboriginal people sat by empty traps served only to enhance the stereotype of Aboriginal people as a threat to the survival of Maritime fishers. Both sides were actively engaged in negotiations to find solutions. But backroom talks make for poor film footage and the media's eye was naturally drawn to conflict and confrontation on the docks. This gave Canadians the false impression that the court had left governments and fishers with no options.

Another disturbing finding is the differences between French-language and English-language portrayals of Aboriginal people. Not only were there more negative references to Aboriginal people in the French-language dailies but stories were placed in conflict frames more often. Francophone readers and viewers found out even less about the reasons for the court's decisions than people in the rest of Canada. This finding warrants more study to see whether this was an isolated incident or a long-term pattern of coverage. Chronic negative coverage of an ethnic group will reinforce the idea that the group exists outside the mainstream of society.

On the other hand, coverage in the English media, while not as conflict based, had its shortcomings. Most articles did not state that the fishing right granted to the Mi'kmaq could be regulated for reasons of conservation. And it appears that little effort was put into understanding the background that gave rise to the court's decision. Although the court was roundly criticized for being out of touch with the reality of life in the Maritimes, the same could be said for sources and some journalists about constitutional law and Supreme Court jurisprudence. The majority of journalists we interviewed for this project said they did not think that reporters covering the courts needed any kind of legal training. Instead, it was more important that reporters have the ability to recognize a story and the skills to tell it to the public in a comprehensible way. According to journalists, the danger in having legally trained correspondents is that they might not be able to write simply enough for the general public. The errors and omissions made by journalists covering this case would seem to indicate that journalists covering the Supreme Court need more background in constitutional law. At the very least, when covering decisions they need time to dig into the history of the case in order to piece together the complicated roadmaps that make up Supreme Court jurisprudence.

## Notes

1  The television data set is not complete because we were unable to get video copies of some days. For instance, we could not locate tape of *The National*'s 17 September coverage of the first decision. In addition, we were not able to obtain any video clips or transcripts from TVA.

2  From the French: "Comme le rappelle ce film, c'est un homme habitué à lutter contre l'injustice. Il a passé onze ans de sa vie en prison pour un meurtre qu'il n'avait pas commis." Unless otherwise noted, all translations are our own.

3  In French: "Le plus haut tribunal du pays reconnaît qu'en vertu des vieux traités, les autochtones ont le droit de vendre des poissons qu'ils pêchent puisque les lois sur la pêche ne s'appliquent pas à eux."

4  From the French: "La Cour suprême rompt l'un des plus importants consensus établis en Amérique en matière de faune ... L'arrêt Marshall bouleverse cette sage allocation. Ce chambardement dévastateur pour les règles et les ententes de partage déjà négociées par plusieurs provinces pourrait amorcer un ressac contre ce que plusieurs perçoivent désormais comme une société de droit à deux vitesses, suscitée par la plus haute cour d'un pays qui n'arrive pourtant pas à se concevoir dans un fédéralisme minimalement asymétrique!"

5  The second highest number of articles to run was eighteen, on 18 November, the day after the second Marshall decision. By comparison, on 18 September, the day after *Marshall 1* was handed down, only seven articles were published or broadcast.

6  See photos page 7, *Toronto Sun,* 5 October 1999, and page A1, *Chronicle Herald,* 5 October 1999.

7  The photo appeared on page A1 of the 4 October 1999 paper.

8  In French: "Vengeance de la communauté autochotone."

9  In French: "'Oeil pour oeil, dent pour dent,' lance ce pêcheur autochtone."

10 In French: "Narguant les pêcheurs commerciaux, cet autre Mi'kmaq soutient qu'il a déjà fait son argent et qu'il n'a pas l'intention d'aller en mer comme le feront les Blancs pour leur saison d'hiver qui commence à la fin du mois de novembre."

11 In French: "La cour suprême allume la mèche."

12 In French: "L'anarchie suprême."

## References

*Badger, R. v.,* [1996] 1 S.C.R. 771.

Barsh, Russell. 2000. Constitutional powers and treaty rights. *Saskatchewan Law Review* 63: 719-49.

Barsh, Russell, and James (Sákéj) Youngblood Henderson. 1999. Marshalling the rule of law in Canada: Of eels and honour. *Constitutional Forum* 11 (1): 1-18.

CBC. 1999a. Laurie Graham (reporter). Native fishing rights. *The National,* 24 September.

—. 1999b. Laurie Graham (reporter). Maritimes tension. *The National,* 30 September.

—. 1999c. Laurie Graham (reporter). Native fishing rights dispute. *Sunday Report,* 3 October.

—. 1999d. Laurie Graham (reporter). An uneasy peace on Burnt Church wharf in the wake of the violence yesterday. *The National,* 4 October.

*Chronicle Herald* (Halifax). 1999a. A mess of eels. Editorial, 20 September, p. C3.

—. 1999b. R. v. Marshall. Editorial, 10 October, p. B5.

Coates, Ken. 2000. *The Marshall decision and native rights.* Montreal: McGill-Queen's University Press.

Cox, Kevin. 1999a. Marshall eager to leave spotlight after court win. *Globe and Mail,* 18 September, p. A3.

—. 1999b. Ruling on fishing "just like Christmas." *Globe and Mail,* 2 October, p. A3.

—. 1999c. Natives enraged by Supreme Court interpretation. *Globe and Mail,* 19 November, p. A3.

—. 2003. Defaced flags signal fishermen's anger. *Globe and Mail,* 6 May, p. A1.

Coyne, Andrew. 1999. A lobster trap set in 1760. *National Post,* 1 October, p. A19.

CTV. 1999a. Alison Vuchnich (reporter). The lobster war explodes on the Maritimes. *CTV News,* 3 October.

—. 1999b. Alison Vuchnich (reporter). Stand off at Burnt Church wharf over Native fishing rights. *CTV News,* 4 October.

—. 1999c. Tom Waters (reporter). The Chrétien government is considering all possible options to contain the Native fishing crisis. *CTV News,* 4 October.

Cummins, John. 1999. Supreme Court, supreme arrogance. *National Post,* 11 October, p. A14.

Dunn, Mark. 1999. Marshall scores new court win. *Toronto Sun,* 18 September, p. 25.

Durkan, Sean. 1999. Fish war of words. *Toronto Sun,* 6 October, p. 7.

Fife, Robert. 1999a. High court accused of "distorting" history. *National Post,* 28 October, p. A1.

—. 1999b. Judges rule Natives not immune to fishing laws. *National Post,* 18 November, p. A1.

Fontaine, Phil. 1999. We need a return to treaties, not a downgrading of them. *Globe and Mail,* 13 October, p. A19.

Francoeur, Louis-Gilles. 1999. Le méchant Indien. *Le Devoir,* 30 September, p. A8.

Furniss, Elizabeth. 2001. Aboriginal justice, the media, and the symbolic management of Aboriginal/Euro-Canadian relations. *American Indian Culture and Research Journal* 25 (2): 1-36.

*Gladstone, R. v.,* [1996] 2 S.C.R. 723.

Glavin, Terry. 1999. The politics of fishing and flouting the law. *Globe and Mail,* 8 October, p. A15.

*Globe and Mail.* 1999a. Aboriginal fishing rights: Where the Supreme Court judges disagree. 5 October, p. A15.

—. 1999b. The Supreme Court all at sea. Editorial, 5 October, p. A14.

—. 1999c. The burden of language in the Mi'kmaq case. Editorial, 6 October, p. A14.

—. 1999d. In support of the court. 18 November, p. A3.

Googoo, Maureen. 1999. Canada's highest court upholds treaty rights of Mi'kmaq, Maliseet and Passamaquoddy. *Mi'kmaq-Maliseet Nations News* 10 (10): 1.

Grenier, Marc. 1992. The centrality of conflict in Native-peoples coverage by the Montreal *Gazette:* War-zoning the Oka incident. In *Critical studies of Canadian mass media,* ed. Marc Grenier, 271-99. Toronto: Butterworths.

Gwyn, Richard. 1999. The Supreme Court: Power without responsibility. Halifax *Chronicle Herald,* 10 October, p. B1.

Hamilton, Graeme. 1999a. Maritimes Mi'kmaq setting lobster traps out of season. *National Post,* 22 September, p. A8.

—. 1999b. N.S. lobster fishermen ready to trap illegally. *National Post,* 23 September, p. A9.

—. 1999c. Vow of interim rules for Native fishery fails to satisfy. *National Post,* 23 September, p. A4.

—. 1999d. Violence erupts in N.B. as Natives' lobster traps cut. *National Post,* 4 October, p. A1.

—. 1999e. Dhaliwal threatens to close fishery. *National Post,* 5 October, p. A1.

—. 1999f. U.S. tribe plans to fish in Canadian waters. *National Post,* 6 October, p. A1.

—. 1999g. Supreme Court's lengthy clarification a rare move, experts say. *National Post,* 18 November, p. A13.

Jackson, David, and Steve Maich. 1999. Hamm eyes suspending native ruling. Halifax *Chronicle Herald,* 1 October, pp. A1-2.

*L'Acadie Nouvelle.* 1999. L'anarchie suprême. Editorial, 18 October, p. 12.

Leblanc, Daniel. 1999. Ottawa gropes for response to fish battle. *Globe and Mail,* 5 October, p. A1.

Legge, Lois. 1999a. Mi'kmaq rights upheld: Marshall celebrates landmark victory. Halifax *Chronicle Herald,* 18 September, p. A1.

—. 1999b. Fish ruling spawning fear, hope. Halifax *Chronicle Herald,* 19 September, p. A3.

Leishman, Rory. 1999. Supreme blindness. *National Post,* 6 October, p. A18.

*Le Journal de Montréal.* 1999. La Cour suprême allume la mèche. 5 October, p. 30.

Lule, Jack. 2001. *Daily news, eternal stories: The mythological role of journalism.* New York: Guilford Press.

Makin, Kirk. 1999a. Donald Marshall wins again. *Globe and Mail,* 18 September, p. A1.

—. 1999b. Taking on Marshall a mistake: Historians. *Globe and Mail,* 19 November, p. A27.

—. 1999c. Top court issues rebuke in fish furor. *Globe and Mail,* 19 November, p. A1.

*Marshall, R. v.,* [1999] 3 S.C.R. 456 *[Marshall 1].*

*Marshall, R. v.,* [1999] 3 S.C.R. 533 *[Marshall 2].*

McClenaghan, Theresa. 1999. Give the Micmacs a chance. *Globe and Mail,* 5 October, p. A15.

MacGregor, Roy. 1999a. We're not going to rape the land. *National Post,* 30 September, p. A5.

—. 1999b. Justice takes a fall in N.B. *National Post,* 5 October, p. A19.

Mofina, Rick. 1999a. 1760 treaty gives Mi'kmaq right to fish: High court. *National Post,* 18 September, p. A1.

—. 1999b. Cabinet may suspend ruling giving Natives year-round fishing rights. *National Post,* 28 September, p. A5.

Morris, Chris. 1999. Non-Indians will "have to share" – Paul. Halifax *Chronicle Herald,* 23 September, p. A3.

Myles, Brian. 1999. Confusion à Ottawa. *Le Devoir,* 5 October, pp. A1-A8.

Nadeau, Alain-Robert. 1999. Totem et tabou. *Le Devoir,* 6 October, p. A11.

*National Post.* 1999a. Lobster boil. Editorial, 30 September, p. A19.

—. 1999b. How do we calm the waters? 7 October, p. A8.

—. 1999c. Supreme retreat. Editorial, 18 November, p. A15.

Nuovo, Franco. 1999a. L'Indien et le homard. *Le Journal de Montréal,* 5 October, p. 6.

—. 1999b. Moi l'autochtone. *Le Journal de Montréal,* 6 October, p. 6.

O'Reilly, James. 2002. Interview by authors. Ottawa, 6 November.

Paul, Daniel. 1999. Recognition of Aboriginal rights poetic justice. Halifax *Chronicle Herald,* 15 October, B2.

Radio-Canada. 1999a. Solveig Miller (reporter). *Le Téléjournal,* 3 October.

—. 1999b. Solveig Miller (reporter). *Le Téléjournal,* 4 October.

—. 1999c. Ginette Lebreton (reporter). *Le Téléjournal,* 6 November.

Rotman, Leonard. 2000. My hovercraft is full of eels: Smoking out the message in *R. v. Marshall. Saskatchewan Law Review* 63: 617-44.

Saunders, Phillip. 2000. Getting their feet wet: The Supreme Court and practical imple-
mentation of treaty rights in the *Marshall* case. *Dalhousie Law Journal* 23 (1): 48-101.

Schmitz, Cristin. 2001. SCC wrong forum for Native land claims: Bastarache. *Lawyers
Weekly* (19 January): p. 20.

Scoffield, Heather, and Mark MacKinnon. 1999. Dhaliwal appoints arbitrator to resolve
Native fishing issue. *Globe and Mail,* 16 October, p. A4.

*Simon, R. v.,* [1985] 2 S.C.R. 387.

Simpson, Jeffrey. 1999a. In the fishery verdict, a win for chaos. *Globe and Mail,* 30 September, p. A16.

—. 1999b. The Supreme Court as battering ram. *Globe and Mail,* 6 October, p. A14.

—. 1999c. Mi'kmaq patty whack. *Globe and Mail,* 19 November, A19.

Singer, Benjamin. 1982. Minorities and the media: A content analysis of Native Canadians
in the daily press. *Canadian Review of Sociology and Anthropology* 19 (3): 348-59.

*Sparrow, R. v.,* [1990] 1 S.C.R. 1075.

Surette, Ralph. 1999. Treaty rights: Directions not included. Halifax *Chronicle Herald,* 25
September, p. C3.

Thorsell, William. 1999. How to keep the Supreme Court from fishing off Parliament's
dock. *Globe and Mail,* 16 October, p. A25.

Tibbetts, Janice. 1999. Rulings must consider consequences: McLachlin. *National Post,* 6
November, p. A6.

Underhill, Brian. 1999a. Mi'kmaq rights upheld: High court decides Natives exempt from
fishing rules. Halifax *Chronicle Herald,* 18 September, p. A1.

—. 1999b. Marshall ruling clarified. *National Post,* 18 November, p. A1.

*Van der Peet, R. v.,* [1996] 2 S.C.R. 507 (S.C.C. 1996).

Wildsmith, Bruce. 2001. Vindicating Mi'kmaq rights: The struggle before, during and after
*Marshall. Windsor Yearbook of Access to Justice* 19: 203-40.

Worthington, Peter. 1999. The New Brunswick lobster boil. *Toronto Sun,* 7 October, p. 16.

York, Geoffrey. 1990. *The dispossessed: Life and death in Native Canada.* Toronto: Little, Brown
and Company.

# ——5——

# "Parents Can Sleep Soundly": The Queen v. John Robin Sharpe

AFTER THE MEDIA sting following the *Marshall* decisions, Supreme Court of Canada proceedings were, once again, front-page news. The stakes were as high as could be. In *R. v. Sharpe* the court was confronted with an overbroad criminal prohibition on the possession of child pornography. Though this was material usually with no redeeming features, the law still was vulnerable to constitutional attack. The court had few options before it. The court could strike down the prohibition, as had lower courts in British Columbia, which had "unleashed sustained" (*Province* 2001a) "nationwide outrage" (Skelton 2000). Parliament then would be under pressure to invoke the Charter's notwithstanding clause, preserving the law from declarations ofconstitutional invalidity. The court, alternatively, could contrive some way to uphold the law and so manage to avoid the rebuke of Parliamentarians, police, children's advocates, and media pundits.

A significant contextual factor was the recent installation of Beverley McLachlin as chief justice, succeeding Antonio Lamer. Formerly a legal academic at the University of British Columbia, McLachlin was appointed a trial judge of the British Columbia Supreme Court at a relatively young age and quickly moved up through the ranks to become the first female chief justice of Canada. McLachlin is considered a hard-nosed judge. She issued important dissents in cases such as *R. v. Keegstra* (1990), where she ruled that the Criminal Code prohibition on the promotion of racial hatred was too broad to withstand Charter scrutiny, and in *Marshall,* where she read the "truck-house" clause so as to rule out a treaty right to fish. Her appointment was lauded almost universally, if cautiously. The *Sharpe* case would provide her with an important early occasion to place her mark on the chief justiceship of the Supreme Court.

As we described it in our "Judgment Day: A Vignette" and Chapter 1, "A Year in the Life of the Supreme Court," the case was framed as a contest between vulnerable children and the freedom of expression rights of the accused, John Robin Sharpe. Though there was a great deal of interest in the case, there was not much interest in what the court specifically had to say. Once the court issued its ruling, salvaging the overbroad law, the media quickly declared vulnerable children the winners. Lost in the translation was the subtle constitutional analysis of the court, and the defences that the court elucidated and from which Sharpe, himself, later would benefit. The court avoided the torrents of outrage that would have accompanied striking down the law, but without finding the law constitutionally invalid. The often sensationalized nature of the reporting in the case ensured that these legal manoeuvres largely were lost on citizens at the expense of the short-sighted objective of declaring winners and losers.

## Actors and Arguments: High Anxieties

The origins of the case lie in the dying days of the Progressive Conservative government led by Prime Minister Kim Campbell. Rushed through Parliament in June 1993, months before a fall election which would see the Tories go down in flames, an all-party consensus ensured that Criminal Code amendments concerning child pornography would be enacted quickly (Persky and Dixon 2001). Under Brian Mulroney, the Tories had several times attempted to amend Canada's obscenity law without success (Borovoy 1988, 59-60). On this occasion, there would be no opportunity for disagreement. About to embark on an election campaign, political parties did not want to be seen as soft on pedophilia. As the Tory justice minister noted in testimony before a Senate committee, opinion polls showed that 94 percent of Canadians supported a law against child pornography (Chwialkowska 2000). There would be little time to debate the merits of the proposed new law or to weigh the impact of the law on the constitutional guarantee of freedom of expression. Moreover, the Supreme Court had sent clear signals, in its earlier ruling in *R. v. Butler* (1992) concerning Canada's obscenity provisions (covering both adult and child pornography), that it would more easily find such prohibitions to be reasonable limits on the Charter's guarantee of freedom of expression. It would have been fair to surmise that the court would treat gingerly any law aimed at proscribing expressive materials that exploited children.

The law, however, went far beyond a mere prohibition of materials that exploit children. The law prohibits possession of child pornography, which is defined to include (1) any visual representation of persons depicted as being under eighteen years of age and engaged in "explicit sexual activity" or (2) depicting the sexual organ or anal region of a person under eighteen the "dominant characteristic" of which is for a "sexual purpose." It also is an offence to possess (3) any written material or visual representation that "advocates or counsels sexual activity" with

a person under eighteen that is a criminal offence (section 163.1). This is a reference to other provisions of the Criminal Code that make it an offence to engage
in sexual activity with a person under the age of fourteen. For persons in a position of trust or authority, it also is an offence to engage in sexual activity with a
young person under their care who is under eighteen years of age (sections 150.1,
153). There are some defences available. No one can be found guilty of the offence
of child pornography if the written material or visual representation has "artistic
merit or an educational, scientific or medical purpose" (section 163.1) or is in the
service of the public good (section 163(3)).

The scope of the new prohibition was tested early on in the prosecution of
Toronto artist Eli Langer. Langer's controversial pen-and-ink drawings depicted
young boys engaged in explicit sexual activity. The display of these drawings in a
Toronto gallery led to charges of child pornography, forfeiture of the drawings, a
criminal trial, and ultimate acquittal. The material, an Ontario trial judge ruled,
had "artistic merit" and so did not qualify as child pornography (Blatchford 2000).

John Robin Sharpe was a different sort of accused. He was charged in 1995
with two counts of possession of child pornography and two counts of possession
for the purpose of distribution. Returning by bus from the United States, en route
from Asia and Holland, Sharpe was found by Canada Customs in the possession
of undeveloped film and photographs of nude boys in sexually provocative positions. He also had in his possession computer diskettes containing a collection of
his self-authored "Boyabuse" stories – among them, "The Spanking" and "Suck It: A
Devotee's Lament" – many of which were violent and sexually explicit. Thirteen
months later (see Bohn 2001), police seized from Sharpe's apartment a collection
of four hundred photographs of boys displaying their genital organs or anal regions
or engaged in explicit sexual activity (*Sharpe* 1999, para. 5).

The media focus throughout much of the legal proceedings was trained, not
surprisingly, on the accused. A sixty-seven-year-old retired municipal worker
from Vancouver, Sharpe was unrepentant. He insisted that government had no
business meddling in his choice of sexual preference and that, in any event, his self-
authored material had literary merit (*Toronto Sun* 2001). The constitutional challenge focused solely on the criminal *possession* of this self-authored material. Whatever the outcome of that challenge, Sharpe would continue to face other charges
relating to possession of child pornography for the purpose of distribution.

Taking Sharpe's side in the case were the Criminal Lawyer's Association and two
civil liberties organizations, the BC Civil Liberties Association and the Canadian
Civil Liberties Association. Together with Sharpe's counsel, they argued the law
was too vague and overbroad to withstand constitutional scrutiny. No author or
artist could reasonably know whether their work transgressed the Criminal Code
prohibitions, they argued. What was called for, instead, was a prohibition on visual

materials in which children actually were used in their production. No exclusively written materials should be caught by the prohibition. Sharpe himself nicely summarized the argument in a clip TVA broadcast on 18 January 2000, the first day of the hearing: "Nothing written should be illegal," he declared.[1]

Allied with the federal government defending the law in the Supreme Court were six provinces, police associations, religious and family groups, and children's rights advocates. As Brian Myles (2000) of *Le Devoir* remarked, in a rare instance of unanimity, the Attorney General of Canada was allied with six provincial Attorneys General to defend the law. Even the minister of justice for Ontario, Jim Flaherty, took the unusual step of appearing before the court in the hearing of the case (Dunn 2000a). The stakes were high not only for the government then in power; the Reform Party also had a vested interest in the outcome of the legal contest. The child porn law initially was a federal Tory initiative, part of a larger law and order agenda (including proposed bills on stalking, sexual assault, and proceeds of crime). The federal Liberals, on the eve of the election campaign, responded with their own twenty-seven-point program (Chwialkowska 2000). The Reform Party, nevertheless, was intent on making the issue its own.

Reformers quickly seized the initiative after the release of Justice Duncan Shaw's trial level decision on 13 January 1999. Justice Shaw ruled that the Criminal Code prohibitions on child pornography unreasonably limited Sharpe's freedom of expression. Child pornography, Shaw admitted, may reinforce the cognitive distortions of pedophiles and may aid in the "grooming" of children to participate in sexual acts. The objectives served by the criminalization of simple possession, however, could not outweigh the profoundly detrimental effects on freedom of expression and personal privacy (*Sharpe* 1999, paras. 23, 49). Justice Shaw's decision elicited outrage from many quarters, much of it making its way into the media by way of columns and letters to the editor (Culbert 1999; MacGregor 1999; Martinuk 1999). Even a death threat resulted (Hall 1999). Sometime later, Justice Shaw (2003, 102) laid part of the blame for this vilification on unfair reporting in a national newspaper. Though he did not mention the *National Post* by name, Shaw likely had the paper in mind, as he was misquoted on the front page of the *Post*. There "is no evidence that demonstrates a significant increase in the danger to children caused by pornography," the paper quoted Shaw as saying (Dubé 1999). The sentence, however, should have read: "There is no evidence that demonstrates a significant increase in the danger to children *related to the confirmation of cognitive distortion* caused by pornography" (emphasis added), which is a more subtle and less explosive observation. Justice Mary Southin noted on appeal that Shaw's decision "generated a great deal of outrage in the media": "I infer that many of those who gave vent to their outrage knew nothing whatever of the text of s. 163.1. What, in their ignorance, they conjured up in their minds was the spectre of a judge giving judicial approval to sexual exploitation of the prepubescent, whether of the male or female sex, contrary to the will of Parliament" (*Sharpe* 2000, para. 5).

For Justice Southin, sitting on the British Columbia Court of Appeal, criminal possession of expressive material was inconsistent with Canadian "political ethic" and could never be a reasonable limit in a free and democratic society. "Such legislation bears the hallmark of tyranny," she wrote (*Sharpe* 2000, paras. 94, 95). Justice Anne Rowles also concluded that the law caught far more material than was necessary in order to achieve its objective. The prohibition was constitutionally overbroad as it caught within its net the privately held thoughts and expression of adolescent teenagers (*Sharpe* 2000, para. 193). A majority of the British Columbia Court of Appeal (with Chief Justice MacEachern dissenting) agreed with Justice Shaw and dismissed the government's appeal.

Ever since the release of Shaw's ruling in January 1999, the Reform Party had been calling on the federal Liberal government to invoke the notwithstanding clause to shield the Criminal Code provisions from further declarations of Charter invalidity. For Reform, the courts had proven unreliable guardians of children. By invoking the notwithstanding clause, parliamentarians could put an end to judicial meddling in this priority area. A Reform motion to this effect failed in Parliament (though it is reported that seventy Liberal MPs signed a petition in support of the initiative). The federal justice minister, Anne McLellan, expressed regret over these court rulings but maintained that the government would not consider using section 33 until all appeals had been exhausted. Only after the Supreme Court had done its work could such avenues be contemplated (Chwialkowska 1999).

## Methodology and Preliminary Findings

As all eyes were focused on the Supreme Court of Canada, the case attracted a fair amount of media attention. We collected ninety-three television and newspaper stories about the *Sharpe* case in the Supreme Court of Canada. Our collection period included a six-day period around the Supreme Court hearing on 18 January 2000 (from 16 to 21 January 2000) and a ten-day period around the decision, released on 26 January 2001 (24 January to 2 February 2001). Television data were collected from four evening newscasts: CTV and CBC in the English language and TVA and Radio-Canada in the French language. Newspaper data were collected from the English-language broadsheets the *Globe and Mail,* the *National Post,* and the *Vancouver Sun,* and from the French-language broadsheets *Le Devoir* and *La Presse.* We also examined the tabloids the Vancouver *Province* and the *Toronto Sun* in the English language, and *Le Journal de Montréal* in the French language.

The data, as shown in Table 5.1, reveal that television broadcasters were more interested in the Supreme Court hearing of *Sharpe* than in the decision itself (seven stories as compared with five), while newspapers printed almost double the number of stories at the time of the decision than at the time of the hearing. Given television's fixation on visuals, it is not surprising that more attention was focused on the hearing. Sharpe, a BC resident, attended the Supreme Court hearing, and his presence there attracted a lot of media attention. He was not in Ottawa for the release of the decision.

**Table 5.1: Frequency of television stories and newspapers articles**

|  | Hearing | Decision | Total |
|---|---|---|---|
| Television | 7 | 5 | 12 |
| Newspaper | 29 | 52 | 81 |
| **Total** | **36** | **57** | **93** |

A comparison between French- and English-language news stories, as shown in Table 5.2, reveals that the French-language press was not as interested in the *Sharpe* case as was the English-language press.

**Table 5.2: Frequency of newspaper articles**

| Newspaper | Frequency | Percent of total |
|---|---|---|
| *La Presse* | 6 | 7.4 |
| *Le Devoir* | 8 | 9.9 |
| *Le Journal de Montréal* | 5 | 6.2 |
| *Globe and Mail* | 16 | 19.8 |
| *National Post* | 14 | 17.3 |
| *Toronto Sun* | 12 | 14.8 |
| *Province* | 8 | 9.9 |
| *Vancouver Sun* | 12 | 14.8 |
| **Total** | **81** | **100** |

Although the case represented a high percentage of the year's stories about the court in the francophone press, it simply did not measure up to the anglophone interest. The frequency of English-language coverage was more than double the French-language coverage in both television and newspapers. Although Robin Sharpe was under the media lens in many of these stories – he was the most frequently quoted source – the French-language press was less likely to use Sharpe as the first source quoted in their stories. *Le Journal de Montréal, La Presse,* TVA, and Radio-Canada did not use Sharpe first in any of their stories. This is in contrast, for instance, to the *Toronto Sun,* which quoted Sharpe first the most number of times

**Table 5.3: First source quoted in television stories**

| First source | CTV | CBC | TVA | Radio-Canada | Total |
|---|---|---|---|---|---|
| Majority court | 1 | 1 | 1 | 1 | 4 |
| Robin Sharpe | 2 | 3 | | | 5 |
| Cheryl Tobias (lawyer) | 1 | | | 1 | 2 |
| Person on the street | | | 1 | | 1 |
| **Total** | **4** | **4** | **2** | **2** | **12** |

**Table 5.4: First source quoted in newspapers**

| | Sharpe | Majority court | Minority court | Federal government | Opposition | BC courts | Legal experts |
|---|---|---|---|---|---|---|---|
| *La Presse* | | 3 | | | | 2 | |
| *Le Devoir* | 2 | 2 | | 1 | | 1 | |
| *Le Journal de Montréal* | | 2 | | 1 | | 1 | |
| *Globe and Mail* | 4 | 1 | 1 | 1 | 1 | 2 | 1 |
| *National Post* | 2 | 3 | 1 | 2 | | | |
| *Toronto Sun* | 5 | 2 | | 2 | | | |
| *Province* | 2 | | 1 | | | | |
| *Vancouver Sun* | 3 | 1 | | | | | 3 |
| **Total** | **18** | **14** | **3** | **7** | **1** | **6** | **4** |

of any news organization. (See Table 5.3 and Table 5.4.) This might be explained by Sharpe's inability to speak French, but more likely is explained by Sharpe not being from Quebec. There simply was less interest in conducting a moral crusade against him in the francophone press. This is in contrast to the intensity of interest in Sharpe in the anglophone press – so much so that reporters camped outside his apartment door on decision day seeking an interview with this reviled but usually media-friendly personality.

## The Hearing

We argued in the previous chapter that the symbolic authority of the Supreme Court of Canada was threatened by the media response to *Marshall*. The court did not emerge unscathed after the release of its second "clarifying" ruling, though the response was more muted. Nor was the federal government unblemished by this episode – it did not have an appropriate plan of response after the first ruling and, as the court made clear in the second ruling, it had a broadened range of constitutional authority, which it had failed to exercise.

Both actors would have anticipated negative publicity associated with the hearing of the *Sharpe* case. For the newly installed chief justice, the case was a first opportunity to navigate along the rocky shore of public opinion massed against an unpopular respondent who had fared rather well before the courts to date, winning rulings both at trial and then on appeal. The hearing was described in the *National Post* by Janice Tibbetts (2000b) as an "explosive case ... the first and arguably the most significant in the Supreme Court's winter session." For the federal government, this was an opportunity to be seen to be at the ready with a range of legislative responses to any declaration of constitutional invalidity. It would not want to be seen to be dropping the ball as it did following the first *Marshall* ruling. No amount of preparation would have satisfied Reform Party stalwarts. For them, the federal government should have invoked the notwithstanding clause following the trial decision in *Sharpe*. For the *Globe and Mail* editorial board, however, this case did not pose a similar challenge to the court's authority as did *Marshall*. This case, the *Globe and Mail* (2000) opined, did not "raise the spectre of an activist Supreme Court unduly interfering in Parliament's prerogatives." The court here is not being asked to "add anything to an existing law"; "it is not being asked to flesh out the contents of a vague centuries-old aboriginal treaty"; rather, it "is being asked whether a particular law meets well-established tests of proportionality in limiting a citizen's liberty – a normal question." Should the law fail the test of proportionality (as outlined in the *R. v. Oakes* case of 1996), then the court would be called upon to strike down the law, rather than "make" law. The *Globe* was comfortable with the court playing this second-guessing role of parliamentary preferences particularly where, as here, Parliament clearly had overreached. "At its core," the editorial concludes, Parliament and not the court "is the body on trial" in this appeal.

The preponderance of reports during the hearing of the case before the court emphasized a strategic frame. This is true for both English- and French-language media. An accentuation on conflict is not surprising for a number of reasons. For one, as mentioned, Sharpe was in attendance throughout the hearing in Ottawa. The proverbial "dirty old man" (CTV 2000a) and "poster boy for perverts" (Bonokoski 2000) was at ease with the media – he provided quotable and visual focal points for the journalists. As Kirk Makin commented, Sharpe could speak "comfortably to a sizable media scrum," casting himself as "a hero both of free expression and to men who are aroused by the idea of having sex with children" (Makin 2000b). Most every newspaper featured images of Sharpe and his self-authored materials; most every newscast featured images of or interviews with Sharpe. Typical is the Radio-Canada television broadcast during the course of the *Sharpe* hearing. According to reporter Bernard Drainville, for some, Sharpe is a monster; for others, he is a victim of a law *abusive*. The visuals accompanying Drainville's report for Radio-Canada (2000) emphasize the monster side: Sharpe is shown responding to an interview, proceeding with his lawyers down the Vancouver courthouse steps, some of the photocopied material authored by Sharpe is displayed, and a "warning" poster with Sharpe's photograph is shown – the camera closes in on Sharpe's image. The poster – a photograph of Sharpe together with his home address – was circulated in Sharpe's Vancouver neighbourhood in the days following the trial decision (*Province* 1999).

Opposed in array against Sharpe were some fifty demonstrators waving placards outside the court building, together with a phalanx of approximately two dozen lawyers representing provinces and interveners (Tibbetts 2000a). Both the CTV and TVA 18 January newscasts opened with a shot of a group of protestors praying "against this man" (the CBC's Susan Harada mentioned the protestors in passing in her report on *The National* that evening). The theme of conflict was underscored by the retelling of the two sides to the legal argument, with accompanying footage from the Supreme Court of Canada hearing over the course of a day and a half, including submissions from legal counsel and questions from the bench. Much of the reporting during the hearing – both print and electronic – was devoted to a faithful recounting of the two sides of the legal conflict.

By the second day of the hearing, Sharpe had become incensed by media coverage focused on his sexual predilections. According to Makin, Sharpe was "distressed by the derision heaped upon him in some overnight media accounts as well as comments from some judges during the appeal." "He was especially annoyed," writes Makin (2000c), "by reporters who aggressively demanded he reveal details of his sexual tastes, his pornography collection, and how he intends to achieve sexual gratification if the court ends up prohibiting the possession of child pornography." Roger Smith of *CTV News*, likely one of those reporters annoying Sharpe, noted at the outset of his 19 January report that Sharpe "gets cagey when asked if he circulates his own racy stories about young boys." Sharpe, seemingly angered, is then shown saying: "I have friends, look, okay" (CTV 2000b). Lashing out at reporters the following day, Sharpe claimed he merely was "trying to be as candid" as he could be, but had come to the realization that "it's not the best way to deal with the media. It's hopeless" (Makin 2000c).

Although there understandably was a great deal of emphasis on Sharpe during this phase of the case, much of the reporting amounted to a summation of the legal arguments before the court. On the one side, it was claimed, were laws for the protection of children. This was well represented, for many media outlets, including CBC, TVA, and Radio-Canada, by federal government lawyer Cheryl Tobias's submission to the court that "we ought not to sacrifice children on the altar of the Charter" (Tibbetts 2000a; Dunn 2000b). On the other side were the rights of individuals to express their intimate thoughts in writing. For many of these same news outlets, this argument was encapsulated in the submission of Richard Peck, legal counsel for Sharpe, that the "legislation is thought control – we're there" (Tibbetts 2000a).

Some journalists, taking hints from the courts' questioning, surmised the direction the justices would take in their subsequent ruling. After the first day's hearing, CBC television news reporter Susan Harada suggested that the court might "throw out only part of the child pornography law" (CBC 2000). Taking note of the justices' questioning, the *Globe and Mail*'s Kirk Makin (2000a) reported that, "toward the end of the day, several judges hinted at the direction they may favour by questioning lawyers about severing small portions of the law without striking it down outright." While acknowledging that a judge's questioning is not an entirely reasonable gauge of what a particular judge will do, Makin (2000d) correctly predicted that at least three judges would favour retaining most or all of the law, while four others "gave the appearance of being open to striking down some or all of the possession law."

## The Court's Ruling: "A Proper Construction"

Although the federal government was preparing for any number of alternative scenarios (Laghi 2001a), including the introduction of new replacement legislation, it turned out that nothing further should have been required of legislators. The court unanimously upheld the Criminal Code prohibitions. Six of the nine justices, however, found that the law was insufficiently protective of freedom of expression regarding two "peripheral" forms of expressive activity: self-created expressive material that is privately held, and recordings of lawful sexual activity also privately held. The Criminal Code, henceforth, would be read down to exclude these two categories of material so that the law could survive the constitutional challenge intact.

The court, in other words, engaged in a salvage operation so as to avoid a declaration of constitutional invalidity. To this end, Justice McLachlin interpreted various provisions so as to "minimize the alleged overbreadth" (*Sharpe* 2001, para. 32). The requirement that visual representations portray "explicit sexual activity" was read down to include only "extreme" or "non-trivial" depictions of sex by those under age eighteen – images portraying nudity, for instance, or sexual organs. It was not intended, the court concluded, that the law should catch within its scope less extreme forms of "casual" sexual conduct, such as kissing, hugging, and fondling, as civil libertarians had feared (paras. 46-49). The "dominant characteristic" requirement (visual representations that had as their dominant characteristic the depiction of sexual organs or anal regions) was read down to exclude certain expressive material. According to the court, materials may depict the sexual organs of those under eighteen so long as this is not its dominant characteristic, in which case, family photos of children in the bath would not be caught. If those photos were accompanied by captions suggesting sexual stimulation as a dominant purpose, then they would be caught (para. 51). Similarly, the words "advocates or counsels" (in the prohibition on written or visual materials that advocates or counsels sexual activity with a person under eighteen that is otherwise a criminal offence) required "active" encouragement or inducement to commit the offence of child pornography. Mere description of sexual encounters with those under eighteen – as in Vladimir Nabokov's *Lolita* – were insufficient to rise to an offence (para. 56).

Statutory defences, moreover, had to be given a proper interpretation. The defence of artistic merit, the court ruled, was broad enough to include all expression "reasonably viewed as art," however "crude or immature" (para. 63). In the 1995 *Langer* case, the trial judge had ruled that in order to qualify for the artistic merit defence, the work must comport with "community standards." A judicial creation, this is the standard measure for determining obscenity under the Criminal Code. Justice McLachlin would not read in a community standards requirement, as this was not included in the amendments and, in any event, material with artistic merit would pose little risk of harm to children (para. 65). The community standards and "internal necessities" tests (that the sexual portrayal be internally necessary or essential for the artistic, scientific, or educational purpose of the work) – creatures of judge-made law – would not be imported into a statutory defence of artistic merit. These defences, then, would operate differently from the law of obscenity (para. 67). As we learn below, this finding concerning the defence of artistic merit turned out to be important in the subsequent acquittal of Sharpe for some of the possession charges. It also would trigger subsequent proposals to amend the Criminal Code.

Having laid down these foundations, the court then read in two exceptions for (1) privately held "self-created expressive materials" – written diaries, stories, and drawings – and (2) "private recordings of lawful sexual activity" – video recordings of sexual activity, for instance, between two teenagers of consenting age that are kept private. All this, Chief Justice McLachlin concluded, should be sufficient to pacify civil libertarian concerns. In the meanwhile, filmmakers, visual artists, and others could continue to be subject to criminal penalty for the public display of expressive materials that explore juvenile sexuality or that depict sexual activity that is otherwise lawful (by those between the ages of fourteen and eighteen). Similarly, writers and their books could be the subject of criminal prosecution should they be seen as counselling illegal sexual activity by adolescents – positive portrayals of sexual activity, presumably, can be seen as active encouragement. The same words if spoken rather than written will not be caught.

Three justices (Justices L'Heureux-Dubé, Gonthier, and Bastarache) upheld the legislation but also dissented in part. The Charter, they began, "must not be used to

... defeat measures intended to protect disadvantaged and comparatively power-less members of society," namely, children and adolescents (para. 133). In contrast to the majority, the dissenting justices questioned whether child pornography fell within the scope of the Charter's guarantee of freedom of expression, though this last point had already been conceded by the Crown. Given the "low value" of the expression at issue and that harm flowed from "the very existence of images and words which degrade and dehumanize children" (para. 217), Parliament is justified in prohibiting the possession of all visual and written material that reasonably falls within the definition of child pornography. This includes the possession of adoles-cent self-created visual material and self-authored privately held material, the two areas carved out of the Criminal Code by the majority.

## The Coverage: "Both Sides Claim Victory"

Increasingly, journalists anticipate important Supreme Court rulings with a pre-view, aided by the executive legal officer's briefing as described in our opening vignette, of the decision to come. The *National Post* story (Chwialkowska 2000a) prominently featuring a photograph of Sharpe, helpfully explained the lower court rulings in British Columbia and speculated on the firestorm that would follow a declaration of constitutional invalidity. The Reform Party, now reconstituted as the Canadian Alliance under the leadership of Stockwell Day, would seek to reclaim ownership of the issue. Alliance Solicitor General critic Randy White advised that the first order of business would be to invoke the notwithstanding clause. Justice Minister Anne McLellan maintained her position that she would await the court's ruling the next day. White characterized this position as "gambling with the social fabric of our country." The feds, however, would be at the ready with "various, undisclosed versions of a new law" in case the court struck down the legislation (Chwialkowska 2000a).

Kirk Makin (2001a) of the *Globe and Mail* anticipated a "winner" next Friday "in a mighty clash between the principle of free expression and the need to sup-press child pornography" and proceeded to review the lower court rulings. In an interview with Makin, Sharpe had grown pessimistic because of the long wait for the ruling (one year had passed since the hearing, an unusually long period to wait for a Supreme Court ruling), a recent Supreme Court ruling upholding the ability of customs officials to seize at the border gay and lesbian pornography – the *Little Sisters* case (2000) – and an inability to find work because of the publicity the case had attracted. Makin anticipated that, should the court strike down the legislation, it likely would delay any declaration of invalidity to give Parliament time to enact a new law. The court also was likely to suggest alternative measures in its ruling that would be less restrictive of free expression than the impugned scheme. A sepa-rate story the following day by *Globe and Mail* parliamentary reporter Brian Laghi

(2001a) explained that Ottawa would, if necessary, have replacement legislation in hand "as soon as possible" after the release of the decision. As Parliament would be reconvened the following week, court watchers anticipated that the court would be striking down the law, Laghi reported, allowing the House of Commons to "act with speed on the issue." In the days before the release, Alliance would keep the notwithstanding issue alive by releasing a letter from Alliance leader Stockwell Day to Prime Minister Chrétien. The letter called on the government to use the notwithstanding clause if the court "strikes down this law or sends it back to Parliament requesting changes." Makin had already noted that the court was unlikely to immediately declare the law invalid; rather, it would grant Parliament some time – usually six months – to respond with replacement legislation. Yet Day continued to insist that the notwithstanding clause be invoked "regardless of any arbitrary deadlines imposed by the courts" (Laghi 2001b).

On the morning of decision day, Canada's twenty-four-hour news stations got to work. After release of the decision, CBC *Newsworld*'s scrawl informed viewers that the court "upholds law on possession of child porn," while the text on CTV *Newsnet* read, "SCC upholds child porn law." Competing for space with a devastating earthquake in Pakistan, national newspaper headlines shouted: "High court upholds child porn ban" (Chwialkowska 2001b). Sharpe, however, was not to be seen that day. He was locked in his apartment on Vancouver's east side with journalists and cameramen camped outside his door. Sharpe would do no interviews other than via telephone – he would be seen only in archival photographs and video footage. Rumours were that he had changed his appearance to avoid the negative publicity associated with the child-porn charges (CBC 2001; Hall 2001a). For the "normally photo-ready" Sharpe (Mickelburgh and Freeze 2001), decision day would be unlike media coverage during the earlier hearings. There would be no scrums with Sharpe in the lobby of the Supreme Court Building, no visuals of protestors on the courthouse steps. In any event, it might have been difficult for Sharpe to be in Ottawa for the release of the decision. Ordinarily, the Supreme Court provides litigants with about one week's notice that a decision will be released. On this occasion, notice was given only four working days before release of the decision. Travel costs would have been high with that little notice, and Sharpe claimed he was financially broke as a result of the proceedings (Hall 2001b). Whatever the reason for the abridged notice period, the effect would be to dampen the media's interest in the case.

Sharpe, nevertheless, did interviews over the phone in which he seemed angered and at times incoherent. This was most evident in an interview with CBC *Newsworld*'s Don Newman, widely repeated in English- and French-language print media. Sharpe insisted that children were meant to have sex: "Do you think God made a mistake in the fact kids reach puberty about [age] 12? ... What is

**Table 5.5: Use of frames during hearing and decision**

| Frame | Hearing | Decision | Total |
|---|---|---|---|
| Strategic | 14 (38.9%) | 3 (5.3%) | 17 (18.3%) |
| Issue | 17 (47.2%) | 45 (78.9%) | 62 (66.7%) |
| Human interest | 4 (11.1%) | 6 (10.5%) | 10 (10.8%) |
| Moral | | 3 (5.3%) | 3 (3.2%) |
| Other | 1 (2.8%) | | 1 (1.1%) |
| **Total** | **36 (100%)** | **57 (100%)** | **93 (100%)** |

the purpose of that if not for kids to enjoy sex or have sex?" "Did God goof?" he asked (Bailey 2001; Myles 2001c). In interviews, Sharpe insisted that his work had literary merit and that he would continue to fight the charges against him (Mickelburgh and Freeze 2001; Hall 2001a; *Province* 2001b).

With Sharpe out of the picture, so to speak, the dominant media frame immediately following release of the decision was an issue one (see Table 5.5), with a focus on the reasons for judgment of Justice McLachlin for the majority of the court (there was far less interest in the three dissenting justices, who would not allow any exceptions, with virtually no mention on television).

The interests of both English- and French-language television, with little or no visuals and no lingering parliamentary story, did not last beyond decision day. For both the print and electronic media, stories most often were accompanied by a photograph of Sharpe, and sometimes also of the Supreme Court Building. Both CBC and CTV news ran images of Sharpe's green apartment door opening slightly then closing shut while old video stock of Sharpe outside the Vancouver courthouse or bounding up the Supreme Court steps was replayed. Perhaps an example of Quebec's distinctiveness when it comes to issues of sexuality, *Le Journal de Montréal* ran a photo of Sharpe together with a webpage photo promoting the "web's hottest teens." This included an image of what is, presumably, a teenage girl revealing one of her breasts – an image that would have run afoul of the law but qualified, perhaps, under the defence of "educational purpose." In the *National Post,* pictures of the justices figured prominently along with key excerpts from the ruling (Cudmore and Jack 2001). Excerpts also appeared in the *Globe and Mail* (Laghi 2001c), while illustrative examples of material caught and not caught by the law were printed in *Le Devoir* (Myles 2001a).

Reporting reflected the consensus of many parties to the dispute that the court had issued a well-reasoned judgment. "McLellan welcomes balanced ruling" read a *Globe and Mail* headline (Laghi 2001c); "Victory for children: Liberals" read a *National Post* headline (Cudmore and Jack 2001); "Decision walks fine line" read a *Vancouver Sun* headline (Culbert and Munro 2001). The court found a middle ground, according to CBC's *The National*, 26 January. The decision was declared a victory for children in the *Toronto Sun* ("Victory for children," Granatstein and Rubec 2001), as it was in *Le Journal de Montréal* ("Une belle victoire pour les enfants," Fortier 2001) and in *Le Devoir* ("Protection des enfants d'abord, liberté d'expression ensuite," Myles 2001b). As these headings suggest, the federal Liberal government was relieved by the ruling. Justice Minister Anne McLellan "welcomed" the ruling, as did police officers and children's advocates. The exceptions, according to police spokespersons, would not hamper their work, while Alliance leader Stockwell Day was "on board" (CBC 2001). "Parents can sleep more soundly," said Darrel Reid of Focus on the Family to the *Globe and Mail* (Makin 2001c). The ruling was reported even to have quieted "the worst fears of civil libertarians" (ibid.). CBC television reporter Susan Harada reported in the 19 January edition of *The National* that the BC Civil Liberties Association (BCCLA) considered the ruling "not bad." Craig Jones, BCCLA president, described the decision as "almost overwhelmingly a positive decision" (Culbert and Munro 2001; Bohn 2001). Bruce Ryder of Osgoode Hall Law School and one of the BCCLA counsel in the *Sharpe* case explained that the "court has rescued the law by shearing off the most problematic areas and saving the rest." The decision, in his view, "was a real achievement" (Mickelburgh and Freeze 2001). The *Globe and Mail* headline could reasonably proclaim that "both sides claim victory" (ibid.).

Columnists and editorialists also welcomed the ruling. It was described by Paule des Rivières of *Le Devoir* as "une grande clarté" for the population in general, politicians, and police (des Rivières 2001) and by Brian Myles (2001c) in the same paper as "une décision d'une extrême clarté." Alain-Robert Nadeau (2001) in his *Le Devoir* column went so far as to describe the merits of judicial review under the Charter as preferable to the experience of judicial review under the US Bill of Rights: the US instrument has no comparable provision to the Charter's "reasonable limits" clause in section 1, which allows for justifiable limitations on rights and freedoms where "demonstrably justified in a free and democratic society." Nadeau admitted that there was great merit in "la qualité de cette intervention chirurgicale," which circumscribed with precision the contours of the Criminal Code prohibition. In *La Presse*, Agnès Gruda (2001) described the decision as constitutionally correct: "la Cour a réussi à faire preuve d'équilibre et de grand sens commun dans une affaire hautement explosive."[2] The *Globe and Mail*'s Jeffrey Simpson (2001), a long-time critic of the court, hailed the court's ruling as balanced: only the "most expansive interpretation of the Charter's protection of free speech" could have led a court to strike down the law.

There were few exceptions to this trend. Television newscasts in both English and French gave space to the views of organizations devoted to defending the interests of children. They expressed dismay over the majority ruling and, in agreement with the three dissenting justices, opposed any exemptions for privately held self-created materials. A clip in a *CTV News* broadcast on 26 January showed Darrel Reid of Focus on the Family saying that "you could drive a truck through" these exemptions. Brian Clemenger of the Evangelical Fellowship of Canada described the exemptions as creating a "crack in the wall" against the prohibition on child pornography (Culbert and Munro 2001). A spokesperson for the organization Beyond Borders was in attendance at the Supreme Court the day the decision was released. In both French- and English-language television newscasts, Mr. Hecht brought attention to the international obligations to protect children undertaken by Canada and which were undermined by these exemptions. Christian broadcaster Lorna Dueck (2001), in a *Globe and Mail* opinion piece, critiqued the court for reading down the criminal law. She described a victim of child sexual abuse whom she knew was "disgusted with the exemptions allowed by the Supreme Court." The Vancouver *Province*'s Susan Martinuk (2000) was unceasingly critical of the case at both the hearing and decision stages: "It is almost shocking to think that a case of this nature should even rise to the highest level of our courts, let alone be on a 2-0 winning streak," she wrote on the eve of the hearing. Nor was the court's ruling very much welcomed, with exceptions "destined to bring out the creative side in pedophiles." She described the majority ruling variously as "naïve," "deluded," and one that "ultimately legitimizes" the thoughts and actions of "child porn addicts" (2001).

In contrast to the Martinuk columns, much of the reporting can be characterized as neutral. Much of it also reflected positively on the Supreme Court. Over 22 percent of print headlines can be read as positive (see Table 5.6). This is significant, as headlines purport to "define" the story, and the information imparted in a headline is the most likely to be recalled by readers (van Dijk 1991, 69, 50). Print news stories were replete with positive references (see Table 5.7): commentators were described as "relieved," "welcomed," "pleased," and "happy." The decision was "hailed" and "applauded" as a "real achievement," a "clear victory," and "balanced." In the francophone press, the ruling was described as a victory for children – "La protection des enfants avant tout" (Toupin 2001). A victory for children was a victory for the court in terms of preserving, even enhancing, its symbolic authority. There was also a great deal of interest in the French-language press in the nuanced reasoning of the court.

Most English-language editorial pages applauded the decision. The *Toronto Sun* (2001) called it a "sensible" and "reasonable" ruling. The *Vancouver Sun* (2001) described the "careful" ruling as a "sound compromise" and "wise decision." For the Vancouver *Province* (2001c), the ruling was "as deft an exercise in compromise as you'll ever see," though its editorial expressed concern that it was the court that

**Table 5.6: Tone of newspaper headlines that mention the decision**

|  | Positive | Negative | Neutral | Total |
|---|---|---|---|---|
| Hearing |  |  | 7 | 7 |
| Decision | 7 | 2 | 15 | 24 |
| **Total** | **7** | **2** | **22** | **31** |

**Table 5.7: Tone of reference to Sharpe decision in newspapers**

|  | Positive | Negative | Neutral | Total |
|---|---|---|---|---|
| *La Presse* |  |  | 3 | 3 |
| *Le Devoir* | 1 |  |  | 1 |
| *Le Journal de Montréal* | 1 |  | 2 | 3 |
| *Globe and Mail* | 2 | 1 | 4 | 7 |
| *National Post* |  |  | 8 | 8 |
| *Toronto Sun* |  |  | 4 | 4 |
| *Province* |  | 1 |  | 1 |
| *Vancouver Sun* | 3 |  | 1 | 4 |
| **Total** | **7** | **2** | **22** | **31** |

"added in exemptions" and not, more appropriately, Parliament. The *National Post* (2001) "welcome[d]" the ruling and characterized as scandalous the fact that, until now, possession of child pornography had been legal – "reasonable people have wondered whether the legal system has gone mad." The defects in the law were not so great as to justify striking down the law, as lower courts had done, nor did their excision mount to "impermissible redrafting." The *Post* instead aimed its artillery at political leaders who failed to remedy the law's defects. Questions of "morality and social policy should not be the preserve of a constitutional court, but should be debated and acted upon by those who represent us in Parliament. The justices deserve applause for meeting the challenge; our political leaders deserve opprobrium for sloughing it off."

There were exceptions to this reverie. Newspaper and television journalists gave space to the contrarian views of the Canadian Civil Liberties Association (CCLA): Patricia Jackson (special counsel for the CCLA) was quoted in the *Globe and Mail,* while A. Alan Borovoy (the organization's general counsel) appeared in a clip that evening on the CBC national news. The court, they said, failed to be attentive to the "chilling effect" of the law on artists and others: "Many people could be forgiven for not wanting to expose themselves" to charges of possession

Les juges de la Cour suprême ont tranché hier le débat sur la pornographie juvénile : protection des enfants et droit à la création artistique. Reste maintenant à John Robin Sharpe de subir son procès. C'est là qu'on connaîtra la nature de ses écrits.

# La protection des enfants avant tout

## Jugement de la Cour suprême sur la pornographie juvénile

**GILLES TOUPIN**

OTTAWA – La bataille entre le principe de la liberté d'expression et l'interdiction de la possession de pornographie juvénile a fait un vainqueur hier. La Cour suprême a résolument choisi la protection des enfants.

Elle a confirmé la constitutionnalité de la Loi sur la pornographie infantile, donc le caractère illégal de la possession de ce matériel (lié à l'exploitation sexuelle des enfants), tout en y apportant deux exceptions : les écrits et les enregistrements personnels d'activités sexuelles non illégales en autant qu'ils soient conservés pour des usages strictement personnels.

La voix du procureur de la Couronne, Cheryl Tobias, a été entendue. Ce dernier avait réitéré solennellement les traqués de la Cour suprême, le 18 janvier 2000, à « ne pas sacrifier le bien-être des enfants sur l'autel de la Charte » des droits et libertés.

Par contre, la voix de l'Association des policiers canadiens n'a pas, elle, été entendue en totalité par le plus haut tribunal au pays. Les policiers souhaitaient ardemment que la cour retienne la partie de la loi qui criminalise la possession d'œuvres d'imagination

qui, disaient-ils, « sont profondément troublantes et souvent sadiques, barbares, violentes, dégradantes et causent du mal ».

Mais la Cour suprême a jugé que la loi de 1993 était trop vague de sorte qu'elle donnait trop de pouvoirs aux policiers. Ces derniers pouvaient arrêter des gens pour des raisons aussi anodines que la tenue d'un journal personnel ou d'un cahier de création pour la création d'œuvres d'art, ce qui en soi ne constituait pas une menace au bien-être des enfants.

John Robin Sharpe, l'accusé dans cette histoire et qui fut à deux reprises acquitté par des tribunaux de la Colombie-Britannique, a fait valoir devant la Cour suprême que ses écrits personnels — même s'ils mettent en présence des adolescents engagés dans des activités sexuelles — reposent sur le droit fondamental de tout individu à la création artistique. Les interdire, c'est « adouber au » contrôle de la pensée », c'est donc violer la Charte canadienne des droits et libertés.

Il est vrai que les gouvernements conservateurs et libéraux qui se sont succédé à Ottawa depuis l'avènement de la Charte en 1981 ont toujours défendu la suprématie de cette dernière. Cependant, cette fois, Ottawa et ses alliés dans l'affaire Sharpe ont appuyé leur argumentation sur l'article un de la Charte qui affirme que les droits et libertés peuvent, dans certains cas, être restreints par une règle de droit « dans des limites dont les raisons raisonnables ».

La Cour suprême a tenté en quelque sorte de trouver un équilibre raisonnable entre cette liberté d'expression et la crainte qu'on puisse affirmer que les droits et libertés des deux exceptions contenues dans le jugement.

Donc, oui à la liberté d'expression, dit le tribunal, mais à l'intérieur de règles précises. Dans quel cas, par exemple, un livre ou un récit personnel serait considéré comme pornographie juvénile ? « Pour ce qui est des écrits, répond la juge en chef Beverley McLachlin dans son jugement, que les représentations qui préconisent ou conseillent une activité sexuelle avec une personne de moins de 18 ans, qui constituerait une infraction au Code criminel, l'exigence voulant que le matériel « préconise » ou « conseille » signifie que, pris objectivement, ce matériel doit être considéré comme encourageant activement la perpétration des infractions en cause avec des enfants. »

Est-ce que le roman Lolita de Nabokov fait partie des œuvres qui « préconisent » ou « conseillent » des actes illégaux ? Celui qui serait en sa possession devrait-il être condamné pour avoir violé la loi sur la pornographie juvénile ? Non, dit la Cour suprême. Ce roman fait partie des œuvres qui sont vouées à la description et à l'exploration de différents aspects de la vie qui, de manière incidente, font état d'actes illégaux accomplis avec des enfants. Il n'est donc pas visé par la loi canadienne sur la pornographie infantile.

« Même si Lolita de Nabokov, Baumerale Boccace et le Banquet de Platon représentent ou analysent des activités sexuelles avec des enfants, écrit la juge en chef, on ne saurait dire, objectivement, que ces œuvres préconisent ou conseillent un tel comportement au sens de l'encourager activement. »

Voilà pour la première exception qui fait désormais appliquer la Cour suprême, celle concernant le « matériel expressif créé par l'intéressé », c'est-à-dire les représentations créés par l'accusé seul et conservés par ce dernier exclusivement pour son usage personnel.

La deuxième exception qui respecte la Charte concerne la possession d'enregistrements privés d'une activité sexuelle légale. La cour parle de « tout enregistrement visuel créé par l'accusé ou dans lequel ce dernier figure, qui ne représente aucune personne de 18 ans ou qui représente une personne qui en a 18 mais dont l'activité sexuelle illégale et qui est conservé par l'accusé exclusivement pour son usage personnel ».

Cette exception irait jusqu'à protéger deux adolescents de 17 ans, par exemple, qui auraient enregistré leurs ébats amoureux, à la condition que l'enregistrement soit strictement conservé en privé et destiné au seul usage personnel du couple. L'exception protège les deux adolescents en autant que l'activité sexuelle enregistrée ne soit pas illégale, ce qui est le cas dans notre exemple où toutes les parties ont consenti.

Maintenant reste à savoir si les deux exceptions de la cour permettront à John Robin Sharpe de se tirer d'affaire. Son procès nous le dira, car on ne connaît pas encore très bien la nature précise de ses écrits.

En attendant, il ne faut peut-être pas oublier que l'homme de Vancouver a porté devant le plus haut tribunal du pays sa cause, ce qu'il y avait d'assurément peu fait dans la loi de 1993. Non seulement c'est toute la question de la liberté d'expression et du bien-être des enfants qui était en cause dans ce procès, mais c'est aussi la qualité d'une loi, adoptée peut-être un peu trop vite à l'époque à la veille du déclenchement des élections de 1993. C'est le Parlement du Canada aussi qui était jugé hier.

# Un discours du Trône sans surprise

**GILLES TOUPIN**

OTTAWA – Jean Chrétien n'a rien eu d'un dandy à la Pierre Trudeau. Il est certes impeccablement vêtu, portant en général des complets sombres assortis de chemises blanches et d'un jeu de cravates superbes que ceux qui le côtoient tous les jours connaissent par cœur. Mais il n'a aucune prétention s'épater la galerie avec de nouvelles parures vestimentaires spectaculaires.

Le discours du Trône que lira mardi prochain dans la chambre du Sénat la gouverneure générale, Mme Adrienne Clarkson, sera un peu à l'image de la garde-robe du premier ministre. On y retrouvera les mêmes habits que les lors du précédent Parlement, avec peut-être une ou deux cravates neuves. Mais rien de plus.

« Vous serez surpris si vous n'avez pas lu mon programme », a déclaré cette semaine le premier ministre. Et si vous avez lu mon programme, vous ne serez pas surpris. »

Son programme ? C'est le livre rouge intitulé L'avenir pour tous. Lancé en pleine campagne électorale et calqué sur le minibudget du 18 octobre 2000 – dont les grandes lignes avaient été dévoilées lors du budget de février 2000 –, ce catéchisme libéral rappelle principalement les engagements du gouvernement à réduire les impôts de 100 milliards sur une période de cinq ans, à accélérer le remboursement de la dette et à verser aux provinces sur cinq ans 23,4 milliards pour la santé et la petite enfance.

Pour le reste, les Canadiens entendront parler de nouvelle économie, des initiatives du gouvernement fédéral pour placer le Canada du 3e millénaire un meneur mondial dans les technologies de l'information, de la biotechnologie et de l'industrie aérospatiale. En somme, le discours sera celui qu'a tenu le premier ministre tout au cours de la campagne électorale du mois de novembre dernier.

Pour les surprises, il faudra s'adresser ailleurs.

## On repart à zéro

Il ne faut guère s'étonner dans ce contexte que Jean Chrétien n'ait pas procédé à un remaniement ministériel des postes clés et d'un jeu de chaises musicales dans ce jeu de chaises musicales du 27 novembre. Pour des raisons d'efficacité, il aura voulu conserver intacte sa vieille garde ministérielle afin que le programme législatif tout mijoté de la dernière session soit remis dans le collimateur de la Chambre des communes et mené à bon port. Une vingtaine de projets de loi ministériels sont morts au feuilleton lors de la dissolution du Parlement, dont au moins une dizaine que le Cabinet souhaite voir ressusciter.

Prenez seulement la réforme de la Loi sur l'assurance-emploi qui a valu aux libéraux de gros gains importants dans les Maritimes le 27 novembre : le premier ministre a fait de la réintroduction de cette réforme, qui vise principalement à éliminer les pénalités pour les utilisateurs fréquents du régime, l'une de ses priorités.

Mais c'est véritablement du côté de la justice que le discours du Trône remettra en plan les projets du précédent gouvernement. La ministre de la Justice, Anne McLellan, a déjà confirmé qu'elle peut avoir procéder avec fort bientôt un projet de loi omnibus qui reprendra quelques projets de loi majeurs du dernier cabinet, question d'éviter de soumettre séparément aux longueurs du processus parlementaire l'adoption de nouvelles mesures.

C'est lors du dépôt, dans la semaine du 5 février, de ce projet de loi omnibus que les Canadiens connaîtront enfin les détails des changements que le gouvernement apportera à la loi antigang de 1997. On y trouvera également une surcroisse de nouvelles dispositions pénales concernant la cruauté envers les animaux, le harcèlement des personnes et les crimes commis lors de l'invasion d'un domicile, sans compter des mesures pour venir en aide aux victimes d'erreurs judiciaires et pour accroître la protection des policiers. La ministre de la Justice a aussi précisé cette fois les modifications qu'elle souhaite apporter à la loi pour réprimer la conduite en état d'ébriété.

Côté environnement, le ministre Anderson reviendra à la charge pour que soit bien l'intention de le déposer à nouveau es urgences, et qui ne manqueraient pas de soulever l'ire du Bloc québécois, du gouvernement du Québec, du bureau du Québec et d'un nombre important d'intervenants québécois soucieux de préserver dans la province un système pénal pour les jeunes dont l'efficacité et le caractère avant-gardiste ont fait leurs preuves depuis longtemps.

Quant au projet de loi controversé sur les jeunes contrevenants, Ottawa a fort bien l'intention de le déposer à nouveau es urgences, et qui ne manqueraient pas de soulever l'ire du Bloc québécois, du gouvernement du Québec, du bureau du Québec et d'un nombre important d'intervenants québécois soucieux de préserver dans la province un système pénal pour les jeunes dont l'efficacité et le caractère avant-gardiste ont fait leurs preuves depuis longtemps.

Si surprises il y a dans le discours du mardi prochain, c'est fort probablement du côté des autochtones ainsi que le drame des limits de Davis Inlet. Le premier ministre Chrétien a promis qu'il ferait tout

pour mettre un terme à la misère de ces populations. En ce qui concerne les nouvelles techniques en biologie, le gouvernement canadien semble être sur le point de corriger une lacune de taille, celle de l'absence au pays de politique sur le clonage humain. Le ministre de la Santé Allan Rock serait en train de préparer une loi qui régira ce vaste champ d'activités et qui interdira le clonage humain.

Peut-on ? Peut-être pas. On se souvient que les nouveaux projets dans le minibudget représentaient seulement six milliards de nouvelles dépenses en quatre ans, le gros des surplus ayant été réservé aux baisses d'impôt. Ces nouvelles dépenses – si l'on se fie aux promesses du gouvernement – front à la création de trois nouveaux programmes. Les libéraux ont en effet promis dans le livre rouge III de créer un régime enregistré d'apprentissage personnel (REAP) qui coûterait 12,5 milliards sur quatre ans. Ce programme permettrait aux contribuables de mettre de côté jusqu'à 8000 $ par année déductibles d'impôt) pour payer des cours en institution publique ou privée. L'État viendrait ajouter à chaque année 1000 $, les revenus des participants, une aide supplémentaire qui pourrait aller jusqu'à un maximum de 2000 $. Ce programme toucherait un million de Canadiens.

Le livre rouge parle également de la création d'un programme de construction de logements sociaux doté d'un budget de 600 millions sur quatre ans. De plus, les libéraux fédéraux ont promis d'injecter 420 millions sur quatre ans dans une stratégie antidogue nationale dont un apprenda pour être reparti en quoi elle consiste dans ses grandes lignes.

Et si l'on compare le coût de ces nouveaux projets aux baisses d'impôt annoncées, on peut affirmer qu'elles sont à l'ensemble des dépenses de l'État ce que trois nouvelles cravates sont à la garde-robe du premier ministre.

## Table 5.8: A sampling of second sources on television and in newspapers

| Second source | Total |
|---|---|
| Robin Sharpe | 10 |
| Majority court | 6 |
| Minority court | 2 |
| Federal government | 7 |
| Opposition | 4 |
| Cheryl Tobias (lawyer) | 4 |
| BC courts | 7 |
| Free speech advocates | 4 |
| Child welfare advocates | 6 |
| Legal experts | 3 |

of child pornography, Jackson said (Makin 2001c). This view also was taken up by criminal lawyer Eddie Greenspan (a long-time CCLA board member) in a *National Post* op-ed. Greenspan was amused to see the *Post* applaud the ruling in its editorial. To salvage the scheme, Greenspan (2001) noted, "the Court had to engage in judicial activism," yet the *Post,* "in order to save the legislation, has never supported judicial activism."

That a variety of viewpoints were canvassed in the media reports is confirmed by the diversity of second sources consulted by media outlets. Our data show that free speech advocates were as likely to be consulted as child welfare advocates (see Table 5.8).

Yet readers of newspapers would have been left with the dominant impression that this case was about children and not about freedom of expression. An analysis of the eighty-one newspaper headlines reveals that a majority of them concerned child pornography and child protection (see Table 5.9).

When the court was mentioned in a headline, whether it was in English or French, it usually had a positive rather than negative tone. Overall, the Supreme Court garnered the largest number of positive references in either language; Robin Sharpe, not surprisingly, the fewest. The federal government also attracted a fair amount of criticism, either from the Reform Party critics on the one side or from Sharpe's lawyers and civil libertarians on the other (see Table 5.10).

Since the press has a long tradition of defending freedom of expression claims, we expected to find more concern expressed that freedom of expression remained

---

◄ "The protection of children above all" is the message *La Presse* draws from the court's decision in *Sharpe*. Note the Supreme Court edifice reflected in the windows of (presumably) a federal government building prominently flying a very large Canadian flag – an unusual image in Quebec newspapers – and the diminutive photograph of Sharpe in the far corner (27 January 2001). *Courtesy of La Presse*

**Table 5.9: Main focus of newspaper headlines**

| Headline focus | Hearing | Decision | Total |
|---|---|---|---|
| Decision/Ruling | | 15 | 15 |
| Robin Sharpe | 5 | 6 | 11 |
| Child pornography law | 5 | 13 | 18 |
| Freedom of speech | 2 | 4 | 6 |
| The hearing | 10 | | 10 |
| Case a challenge for the court | 3 | | 3 |
| Winners/Losers | 1 | 4 | 5 |
| Child protection | 2 | 5 | 7 |
| Supreme Court or justices of the court | | 4 | 4 |
| Other | 1 | 1 | 2 |
| **Total** | **29** | **52** | **81** |

under threat. Rather than an emphasis on child protection, we expected to find an emphasis on civil liberties, at least in the editorial pages of newspapers. The *Globe and Mail* was the only newspaper in our study, however, that critiqued the *Sharpe* ruling in its editorial pages. The editorial summarized the relevant portions of the Criminal Code and the exemptions the court carved out, which it described as "too cautious." The court should have gone as far as Sharpe and others had argued: it should have struck down the offence of possessing material that "advocates and counsels" illegal sexual activity with someone under the age of eighteen; "although the law makes certain defences available to the accused – artistic purpose, scientific or medical purpose, the public good – any attempt to criminalize speech should have to scale a much higher burden than this law sets" (*Globe and Mail* 2001).

We fairly can conclude that the court emerged unscathed from this challenge to its symbolic authority. It was no mistake for the Canadian public to look to the Supreme Court of Canada for the resolution of deeply divisive and difficult constitutional questions, the media reports signalled. The court could be viewed as a valuable national institution fully capable of sensibly balancing opposing interests, just as it had in the *Quebec Secession Reference*. Numerous other actors involved in

**Table 5.10: Frequency of tone of reference**

| Tone | Positive | Negative | Neutral | Total |
|---|---|---|---|---|
| Supreme Court | 8 | 1 | 70 | 79 |
| *Sharpe* decision | 15 | 3 | 28 | 46 |
| Robin Sharpe | 1 | 19 | 57 | 77 |
| Federal government | 2 | 9 | 51 | 62 |

the question emerged as winners: the federal government and provincial governments, police associations, and children's advocates. Civil libertarians even had something in the decision they could applaud. The Alliance position was vindicated by the court, though, since the law survived the constitutional challenge virtually intact, and there was little or nothing left for the Alliance Party to do with this issue. Even Sharpe, as we note below, would later emerge a partial winner.

Something may have been sacrificed in the result, according to some commentators: the court was exhibiting more timidity in its constitutional rulings. Accompanying the *Globe and Mail*'s report of the *Sharpe* ruling on page 1 was a lengthy piece authored by Kirk Makin addressing the question of whether the Supreme Court had taken a more deferential turn toward Parliament. "Activist days long gone for deferential court" read the front-page headline. Court watchers were unanimous in their verdict that the court was moving gingerly on constitutional rights so that the "once-bold Supreme Court of Canada is turning into a cautious court of deference" (Makin 2001b). "I think the novelty of being a mini-legislature wore-off," criminal law professor Alan Young of Osgoode Hall Law School is quoted as saying (Makin 2001b). This was not an unfortunate result according to Jeffrey Simpson. The court's success in this case, says Simpson, is attributable to the lesson learned in *Marshall*. Rather than being more timid, the court now "seems to be drifting toward a more balanced approach" in Aboriginal law and criminal justice matters. Whereas the court had been "pushing the law's envelope well beyond where Parliament or the people wanted to be," the court now had a "heightened sense of realism about the Court's role in relation to Parliament and in relation to public opinion." So rather than being overly deferential, the court was becoming more realist. This was precipitated by the "mess it created with the first Marshall decision about Aboriginal rights in the East Coast fishery. Had it overturned the Criminal Code provisions against child pornography, the outcry would have reverberated from one end of Canada to the other" (Simpson 2001).

Simpson and others failed to take notice of the lengths to which the court had gone to salvage the child pornography law from a declaration of constitutional invalidity. It should be recalled that the law was rushed into passage, with little concern for its free speech implications, and that both the BC Supreme Court and BC Court of Appeal found the law constitutionally unsound. According to most journalists, the court upheld the law and so there was not much further interest in what the court actually did in the case. However, Yves Boisvert, a columnist at *La Presse,* took notice of the court's manoeuvring (as did Greenspan [2001] in his *National Post* op-ed). In substance, Boisvert (2001) wrote, the court said pretty much the same thing as the lower courts but without striking down the law. Instead, the court used methods of interpretation so as to excise the offending portions of the law. The court discovered the merits "du scalpel, du fil et de l'aiguille à traiter les lois 'malades.' Bravo!" (of the scalpel, of the thread and needle to treat sickly laws. Bravo!). So Boisvert saw not a more timid but a more pragmatic court emerge, one that spoke in a clearer, more unified voice. For this, Boisvert wrote, the court should not be faulted.

## Conclusion: The Marquis de Sharpe

Sharpe's trial on child pornography charges took place before Justice Duncan Shaw shortly after the Supreme Court ruling. The trial concerned the possession and distribution of Sharpe's "Boyabuse" stories together with photographs of boys and teenagers displaying their genital and anal regions. Justice Shaw found that the photographs constituted child pornography and that they did not fall within the court's exception concerning self-created, privately held visual material. Sharpe's self-authored prose was another matter. This material, Justice Shaw concluded, though morally repugnant, did not counsel or advocate the commission of sexual crimes against children (*Sharpe* 2002, paras. 33, 107). If Justice Shaw was wrong about this, he was prepared to find, alternatively, that Sharpe's written material had artistic (or literary) merit. Sharpe's counsel had led expert evidence that the stories were in the manner of "transgressive literature" in the tradition of the Marquis de Sade (para. 64). The Victorian theme of fortitude was prominent, as was the use of irony, all of which displayed Sharpe's "skill as a writer." The Crown's expert witness disparaged Sharpe's writing as boring and disgusting (para. 86). Justice Shaw discounted this evidence as importing standards of morality – one of tolerance based on community standards – which were rendered impermissible according to Justice McLachlin in the *Sharpe* ruling. It will be recalled that the court would not require that, in order to qualify under the statutory defence of artistic, scientific, or educational purpose, materials satisfy a community standards test (a test of tolerance based on vague notions of a national community standard). This seemingly innocuous development – a part of the ruling that was not picked up in any of the media reports – turned out to be a key component in Sharpe's defence.

Justice Shaw found evidence of artistic merit based on his own reading of Sharpe – the stories were "reasonably well written," using "parody and allegory." Though characterizations were "thin," the plots show "some imagination and are fairly sometimes complex." Sharpe was "not devoid of literary skill" (para. 109). So if Justice Shaw was wrong that these stories did not qualify as child pornography – that the stories did not advocate and counsel illegal sexual activity with children – he found, in the alternative, that the stories qualified for the defence of artistic merit, as Sharpe had claimed all along. Sharpe was acquitted on charges related to his own writing but could not escape conviction on two counts of possession and possession for the purposes of distribution of photographs. Justice Shaw sentenced Sharpe to a four-month conditional sentence in light of his declining health and good behaviour over the course of six years of legal proceedings.

The acquittal moved the actors opposed to Sharpe once again into action. The federal justice minister in December 2002 tabled amendments to key child pornography provisions of the Criminal Code (Bill C-20) that would preempt a replay of the Sharpe acquittal. Specifically, the federal government proposed to expand the criminal law to include not only a prohibition on written material or visual representation that advocates or counsels illegal sexual activity, but a prohibition on "written material the dominant characteristic of which is the description, for a sexual purpose, of sexual activity with a person under the age of eighteen years of age that would be an offence under this Act." So written material that merely describes, rather than advocates and counsels, illegal sexual activity for a sexual purpose would now be caught. In addition, the defence to child porn charges of artistic merit or educational, scientific, or medical purpose, together with a public good defence, shrank to include only acts that "serve the public good" (section 7). The defence of artistic or literary merit would no longer be available under the proposed amendment. A new and improved version of the defence was tabled in the House of Commons in October 2004 (Bill C-2). No person can be convicted of a child pornography offence if he or she has "a legitimate purpose related to the administration of justice or to science, medicine, education or art" and does not "pose an undue risk of harm to persons under the age of eighteen years." The constitutional validity of the amendments precipitated by the Sharpe story remains an open question.

## Note

1  The *Vancouver Sun* took note of an interesting split between Sharpe and his legal counsel. Sharpe would have preferred that nothing in one's possession be considered illegal. His counsel, however, conceded that the most "extreme forms of child pornography," such as photos of young children engaged in sexual activity, should be criminalized (see Skelton 2000).

2  In French: "The court displayed balance and great common sense in a highly explosive case."

## References

Bailey, Ian. 2001. Children meant to have sex, accused says. *National Post,* 27 January, p. A9.

Blatchford, Christie. 2000. How to make the laudable proper. *National Post,* 19 January, p. 6.

Bohn, Glenn. 2001. B.C. court ruling gutted child porn law. *Vancouver Sun,* 27 January, p. A6.

Boisvert, Yves. 2001. Pornographie juvénile: Retour sur terre. *La Presse,* 29 January, p. E1.

Bonokoski, Mark. 2000. *Toronto Sun*, 20 January, p. 15.

Borovoy, A. Alan. 1988. *When freedoms collide: The case for our civil liberties.* Toronto: Lester and Orpen Dennys.

*Butler, R. v.,* [1992] 1 S.C.R. 452.

CBC. 2000. Susan Harada (reporter). Possessing child pornography. *The National,* 18 January.

—. 2001. Susan Harada (reporter). The Supreme Court ruled in child pornography case. *The National,* 26 January.

Chwialkowska, Luiza. 1999. Case inflames debate over judicial activism: Are courts going too far? *National Post,* 27 April, p. A8.

—. 2000. MPs admit child porn law was rushed: Supreme Court hears case. *National Post,* 18 January, p. A7.

—. 2001a. Supreme Court rules this week on child porn ban. *National Post.* 23 January, p. A4.

—. 2001b. High court upholds child porn ban. *National Post,* 27 January, p. A1.

CTV. 2000a. Roger Smith (reporter). A controversial case on child pornography goes before the Supreme Court tomorrow. *CTV News,* 17 January.

—. 2000b. Roger Smith (reporter). The Supreme Court of Canada wrapped up hearings into the law prohibiting possession of child pornography. *CTV News,* 19 January.

Cudmore, James, and Ian Jack. 2001. Victory for children: Liberals. *National Post,* 27 January, p. A8.

Culbert, Lori. 1999. Successful appeal of child porn ruling imminent, professor says. *National Post,* 18 January, p. A6.

Culbert, Lori, and Harold Munro. 2001. Decision walks fine line between privacy, harm. *Vancouver Sun,* 27 January, p. A7.

des Rivières, Paule. 2001. La protection des enfants avant tout. *Le Devoir,* 27-28 January, p. A12.

Dubé, Francine. 1999. Top B.C. court strikes down child-porn law. *National Post,* 16 January, p. A1.

Dueck, Lorna. 2001. The road not taken. *Globe and Mail,* 29 January, p. A13.

Dunn, Mark. 2000a. Supreme test for kid-porn rulings. *Toronto Sun,* 18 January, p. 26.

—. 2000b. "Don't sacrifice" kids. *Toronto Sun,* 19 January, p. 12.

Fortier, Marco. 2001. Anne McLellan y voit une belle victoire pour les enfants. *Le Journal de Montréal,* 27 January, p. 6.

*Globe and Mail.* 2000. Parliament and pornography. Editorial, 18 January, p. A20.

—. 2001. Bringing proportion to the child-porn law. Editorial, 27 January, p. A12.

Granatstein, Rob, and Stephanie Rubec. 2001. Victory for children. *Toronto Sun,* 27 January, p. 5.

Greenspan, Edward L. 2001. What, exactly, is child porn? *National Post,* 29 January, p. A14.

Gruda, Agnès. 2001. Pour l'amour des enfants. *La Presse,* 27 January, p. A18.

Hall, Neal. 1999. Child-porn case judge gets death threat. *Vancouver Sun,* 23 January, p. A1.

—. 2001a. Sharpe "at risk" if child porn decision goes in his favour. *Vancouver Sun,* 26 January, p. A6.

—. 2001b. "I could have murdered a dozen people and be seen more respectfully." *Vancouver Sun,* 27 January, p. A1.

*Keegstra, R. v.,* [1990] 3 S.C.R. 697.

Laghi, Brian. 2001a. Ottawa preparing new child-porn law. *Globe and Mail,* 24 January, p. A2.

—. 2001b. Day wants child porn exempt from Charter. *Globe and Mail,* 26 January, A4.

—. 2001c. McLellan welcomes balanced judgment. *Globe and Mail,* 27 January, p. A5.

*Little Sisters Book and Art Emporium v. Canada (Minister of Justice),* [2000] 2 S.C.R. 1120.

MacGregor, Roy. 1999. Madness in the courts. *National Post,* 19 January, p. A19.

Makin, Kirk. 2000a. Child-porn case spurs intense arguments. *Globe and Mail,* 19 January, p. A1.

—. 2000b. Sharpe at ease in role as self-styled hero. *Globe and Mail,* 19 January, p. A3.

—. 2000c. Man at centre of case lashes out at reporters. *Globe and Mail,* 20 January, p. A9.

—. 2000d. Top court finishes child-porn hearing. *Globe and Mail,* 20 January, p. A9.

—. 2001a. January 23. Top court to rule on child porn. *Globe and Mail,* p. A3.

—. 2001b. Activist days long gone for deferential court. *Globe and Mail,* 27 January, p. A1.

—. 2001c. Top court rules 9-0: Child porn law stays. *Globe and Mail,* 27 January, pp. A1, A5.

Martinuk, Susan. 1999. Justice Duncan Shaw: "What planet is he on, anyway?" Vancouver *Province,* 20 January, p. A24.

—. 2000. What's more important, safety of children or right to look at porn? Vancouver *Province,* 19 January, p. A16.

—. 2001. Exemptions in child-porn ruling ask us to trust pedophiles. Vancouver *Province,* 31 January, p. A20.

Mickelburgh, Rod, and Colin Freeze. 2001. Both sides claim victory. *Globe and Mail,* 27 January, p. A4.

Myles, Brian. 2000. La protection "des plus vulnérables" est invoquée en choeur. *Le Devoir,* 19 January, p. A5.

—. 2001a. Anne McLellan est satisfaite. *Le Devoir,* 27-28 January, p. A2.

—. 2001b. Protection des enfants d'abord, liberté d'expression ensuite. *Le Devoir,* 27-28 January, p. A1.

—. 2001c. La pédophilie sans loi. *Le Devoir,* 30 January, p. A1.

Nadeau, Alain-Robert. 2001. Le chas. *Le Devoir,* 31 January, p. A7.

*National Post.* 2001. Sharpe ruling. Editorial, 27 January, p. A17.

Persky, Stan, and John Dixon. 2001. *On kiddie porn: Sexual representation, free speech and the Robin Sharpe case.* Vancouver: New Star Books.

*Province* (Vancouver). 1999. Posters warn residents. 19 January, p. A3.

—. 2001a. Judgment day on child porn. 26 January, p. A26.

—. 2001b. Sharpe will be back in court. 28 January, p. A20.

—. 2001c. Rumours that court runs country are not exaggerated. Editorial, 28 January, p. A40.

Radio-Canada TV. 2000. Bernard Drainville (reporter). *Le Téléjournal,* 18 January.

*Sharpe, R. v.* (1999), 169 D.L.R. (4th) 536 (B.C.S.C.).

*Sharpe, R. v.,* [2000] 1 W.W.R. 241 (BCCA).

*Sharpe, R. v.,* [2001] 1 S.C.R. 45.

*Sharpe, R. v.* (2002), 91 C.C.R. (2d) 235 (B.C.S.C.).

Shaw, Duncan W. 2003. Child pornography and the media: *R. v. Sharpe.* In *Dialogues about justice: The public, legislators, courts, and the media,* ed. Patrick Molinari, 99-106. Montreal: Édition Thémis.

Simpson, Jeffrey. 2001. Yes Victoria, there is a limit to free speech. *Globe and Mail,* 29 January, p. A13.

Skelton, Chad. 2000. Sharpe, lawyers at odds as porn case opens in Supreme Court. *Vancouver Sun,* 18 January, p. A1.

Tibbetts, Janice. 2000a. Protesters demand court uphold ban on child porn. *Vancouver Sun,* 19 January, p. A1.

—. 2000b. Supreme Court task: Thought control or saving children? Porn hearing ends today. *National Post,* 19 January, p. A6.

*Toronto Sun.* 2001. For the children. Editorial, 27 January, p. 14.

Toupin, Gilles. 2001. La protection des enfants avant tout. *La Presse,* 27 January, p. B2.

van Dijk, T.A. 1991. *Racism and the press.* London: Routledge.

*Vancouver Sun.* 2001. Pornography decision a sound compromise. Editorial, 27 January, p. A22.

—6—

# Judges and Journalists

SUPREME COURT REPORTING is at least to some degree a distinct kind of journalism. Supreme Court justices sit at the top of a judicial, and some would argue political, pyramid that provides them with extraordinary power and accords them extraordinary deference, a deference that is largely absent from other institutions or professions. For some journalists, reporting from the Supreme Court seems more like covering a religious institution than covering a political body. There is circumspection and a dependence on the encyclicals that are handed down. Judges remain for the most part hidden from view and the inner workings and politics of the court are seldom reported. Ordinary journalistic routines such as cultivating and negotiating with sources, operating in packs, scooping others, and providing insider accounts of who's winning, who's losing, and who's gaining are largely absent from Supreme Court reporting. The court is also spared the sharp conflicts that often characterize the relationship between politicians and journalists. When journalists go to the Supreme Court, they enter a different world.

But court reporting also has to fit within the frames and routines of contemporary journalism. As we recounted at the beginning of the book, in covering the *Sharpe* decision, Christine St-Pierre had to work within the rules and expectations that apply to virtually every story. She had intractable deadlines. She relied on sources to provide a balance of views and perspectives. She needed compelling, eye-catching footage. She had to cram the story into a tight two-minute package. And senior producers decided where the story would be placed in the newscast using the usual journalistic criteria of human interest, conflict, and controversy, as well as the availability and quality of visuals.

The clash of cultures between judges and journalists is remarkable on several levels. Where journalists are driven by immediate deadlines, often have to make instant decisions, and see their stories vanish from public view almost as soon as they are reported, judges are not ruled by time to nearly the same degree. They will often spend months writing, debating, and refining their decisions, and these decisions can have an enduring quality. Their judgments can set the boundaries and standards for legal and societal behaviour for decades.

Moreover, decisions judges might consider important because they address critical issues in the law are often ignored by journalists because they lack the dramatic ingredients that journalists are looking for. Journalists almost instinctively recognize which cases make good news stories and which don't. Consequently, judges have found themselves beset by controversy and under attack over rulings that barely registered in their view of being important.

There is another glaring anomaly. Supreme Court judges are invariably at the pinnacle of their profession. They have years of experience and accomplishment, and they are usually in their fifties and sixties, if not older. A fifty-five-year-old justice is by the standards of the court a young justice. The reporters who cover the court are, on the other hand, sometimes young, inexperienced, and at the beginning of their careers. While there are many talented journalists covering the court and some of them are at mid-career and have achieved considerable stature, the great lions of Canadian journalism are generally not at the court. There is an odd imbalance.

This chapter will describe the relationship between these two different institutions: how judges and the court see and deal with the news media and how journalists interact with and cover the Supreme Court. The chapter is based on interviews conducted with justices and former justices and with journalists and media managers who have reported from or about the court. Most judges and journalists are satisfied with the relationship – it is for the most part one of distant cordiality and one in which there is a keen and increasing understanding of each other's needs. The executive legal officer (ELO) plays a unique role both as a symbol of the court and as an intermediary between the two worlds. To a large degree the ELO is the linchpin that holds the system together and much of the credit for sustaining the relationship and for creating respect and good feeling belongs to him or her. But there have been instances in which the differences between the two worlds – the routines, pressures, and objectives that drive each of them – have led to errors, resentments, and misunderstandings. There are a number of people in both institutions who believe that the public is not always well served by the current situation.

As described in the Introduction, the media-judicial system is at its core a contest for power and legitimacy, a struggle for authority. Such battles inevitably produce measures of both cooperation and conflict and, of course, frustration. The judges are well aware of the stakes in this crucial game. Justice Ian Binnie (2001) described the simple but harsh realities: "I certainly think that over the long run the legitimacy of the court is critical and the media role is important in maintaining that legitimacy or destroying it if destruction is warranted. They should therefore exercise their power of explanation with a sense of responsibility."

## The Most Open Court in the World

### Establishing Media Relations from Laskin to the ELOs

The justices often argue that in terms of media relations, the Supreme Court of Canada is the most open in the world (Lamer 1998, 358). Over the course of a generation, the court has gone from being a protected and cloistered institution that did not engage in media relations of any kind to one where it recognizes the power of the news media and the need to get its own messages out to the public. None of this happened overnight. The court did not leap suddenly into a new world. Policies were put into place in slow, incremental, and often hesitant steps. What is clear, however, is that the court has now created a system of institutions and relationships that constitute its public face. When reporters deal with the court, they encounter a process that has been put in place to both accommodate their needs and protect the interests of the judges.

According to former chief justice Antonio Lamer (2002), the first concerted effort to deal with media relations began with Bora Laskin, who served as chief justice from 1973 to 1984. Lamer remembers a particular incident that he feels was the turning point. Laskin was upset by a sensational headline that appeared on the front page of the *Globe and Mail*, which Lamer remembers as reading something like: "Supreme Court against beards and kitchens." The case was about the authority of a particular arbitrator who had ruled that a worker at a food processing company had to cut his beard. The decision was about the arbitrator's authority and not about the worker's beard. Laskin thought that the headline was outrageous and the article poorly written. He had already taken a number of initiatives to facilitate reporting from the court. By 1980, the court was sending notices to the press gallery one or two days before rulings were handed down and a weekly agenda was sent to the parliamentary press gallery and to Canadian Press. But none of these steps seemed to have had an appreciable effect, as was evident by the *Globe*'s headline. Laskin's solution was to establish a media relations committee. The committee, created in 1981, still operates today. Consisting of three justices, it meets five or six times a year. It also meets informally over dinner with representatives of the media once or twice a year. The committee is the place where complaints are aired, ideas floated, and details such as where cameras and microphones can be located or whether reporters can use particular shots or clips are first discussed.

By the standards of today, the Laskin court remained a closed world. When in 1975 the CBC requested permission to do a documentary on the court, Laskin refused (Sharpe and Roach 2003, 290-91). A request made in 1978 by then

*Maclean's* reporter Barbara Amiel to interview and then describe the backgrounds of the judges was also turned down (Sharpe and Roach 2003, 291). Laskin opposed the notion that there should be someone at the court who could assist reporters and tried to prevent law clerks from dealing with the press.

The boldest steps were taken by Chief Justice Brian Dickson, who served as chief justice from 1984 to 1990. The Charter had been the catalyst for a dramatic increase in coverage, and the court beat was no longer the preserve of a tiny and cozy nest of three or four reporters. Pressures to accommodate the larger number of news organizations that wanted access to the court could not be ignored. Dickson met with newspaper editors, released advance copies of his speeches, and granted interviews to journalists. In September 1985 Dickson allowed a documentary crew from CTV's *W5* into the court's inner sanctums: the corridors, judges' chambers, conference and dining rooms that had previously been off limits. The camera crew also captured the judges at home and at play: Dickson riding a horse, Justice Willard Estey playing tennis. Radio-Canada's *Le Point* did a similar documentary in 1986 (Sharpe and Roach 2003, 293).

Dickson also ensured that the court would hand down only a few judgments at one time so that reporters would not be overwhelmed. And, most critically, where the justices had once chastised lawyers for speaking to journalists before hearings, believing this violated the sanctity of the court, they now recognized that talking to reporters was a legitimate part of a lawyer's work.

These practices were consolidated and indeed extended during Antonio Lamer's tenure as chief justice from 1990 to 1999. Lamer spoke out publicly and often forcefully on issues facing the court. Indeed, some believe that Lamer relished the spotlight and enjoyed taking on and vanquishing the court's critics. In 1997, after much internal debate and several test runs, the court allowed gavel-to-gavel coverage of its hearings to be broadcast on CPAC, the public affairs cable channel. The court also allowed TV networks to take clips out of the broadcast provided that the entire hearing had been or would be aired. During the *Secession Reference*, network news anchors were allowed to broadcast from the lobby of the Supreme Court Building. Under Lamer the number of briefings that the court provided reporters was increased. He also, after years of complaints by journalists, agreed that judgments would be handed down at a specific time (usually 9:45 a.m.) and on a specific day (usually Thursdays) so that journalists could plan their coverage.

The most important move was undoubtedly the creation of the position of executive legal officer in 1985. Journalists had complained about being confused by the complex and abstract legal language that permeated factums and judgments. Many found the documents they had to work with impenetrable. At the very least, they needed someone who could act as an interpreter. In 1984, after years of mounting complaints by journalists, the first ELO, James MacPherson, was appointed. Justice Thomas Cromwell, who served as the ELO between 1992 and 1995, described the position as being the equivalent in status to an assistant deputy minister. The ELO acts to some degree as the executive assistant to the chief justice: helping the chief justice administer the court, ensuring that schedules are met and documents filed, working with the Canadian Judicial Council and other organizations, writing speeches for the chief justice, and, finally, acting as the liaison between the court and the news media. Media relations consume approximately one-quarter to one-third of the ELO's time.

The duties of the ELO with regard to the media have evolved over time. The first two ELOs, James MacPherson and Robert Sharpe, did not provide the press with regular briefings. Instead, they were available only to answer reporter's questions after decisions were released. Briefings were instituted in a piecemeal fashion. First, there were post-decision briefings. Pre-judgment day briefings, pre-session briefings, and pre-hearing briefings were added over time.

Daniel Jutras, the ELO at the time that this book was being written, notes that there is hardly a day when he doesn't receive at least one call from a journalist. On the day that a typical judgment is released he usually receives five or six phone calls and at least the same number of e-mails. When there is a significant judgment, the number of calls spikes to about twenty (Jutras 2003b). Many if not most of the calls are from journalists who couldn't attend briefings or who need follow-up information. But dealing with reporters is not the only aspect of public relations that the ELO handles. The ELO is often asked to advise the chief justice on which of many speaking requests to accept, and he prepares the first drafts of speeches that the chief justice will give. This is not a small task given that Chief Justice McLachlin gives twenty-five to thirty speeches per year, itself a testament to how much things have changed (Jutras 2003a).

ELOs are appointed for a term of no more than five years and are normally drawn from law faculties. Of the eight people who have served in the position since 1984, six have come from universities. That the ELOs are not permanent officials whose careers are linked to the court and are not professional public relations or media experts may be a key factor in explaining the relationship of trust that the ELOs have been able to establish with journalists.

Unlike the media relations officers who work for governments, political parties, or corporations and who are an integral part of the organizations they represent, the ELOs operate at a considerable distance from the justices. The key to their relationships — and the basis of much of the trust that they have garnered from reporters — is that the ELOs do not consult with the justices or receive instructions about what they can or cannot say. They are positioned as neutral and independent experts; they explain the law, describe the options the justices face, and point journalists to the key parts of decisions. They are not there to defend, editorialize, embellish, or spin what the justices have said. They are also careful to maintain an arm's-length relationship with reporters. Although some of the ELOs have had regular lunches with journalists, they usually avoid other kinds of socializing. There is little of the chumminess, alliance forming, and back-channel deal making that characterizes the political world.

Most of the journalists who were interviewed for this book view the ELO as a neutral figure, someone they can trust completely and who is beyond reproach. Jules Richer, the news editor for *Le Devoir,* for instance, contrasts his experience dealing with political parties and their spin doctors in Parliament to the cool and neutral professionalism of the ELOs (Richer 2003). Richer is particularly impressed by the fact that the ELOs will point out and explain the disagreements between the majority and minority opinions in a judgment and reasoning behind dissents. He believes that the ELOs he has dealt with have not tried to sell a position or push one perspective over another.

In an interview that we conducted with Radio-Canada's Daniel L'Heureux, Denis Ferland, and Daniel Lessard, the three journalists contrasted their experiences covering Parliament Hill with their experiences dealing with the ELO (L'Heureux 2001; Ferland 2001; Lessard 2001). Asked if the ELO engaged in public relations or political spin doctoring, they replied:

L'Heureux: "My God, no. He is really providing information in the noble sense of the term."
Ferland: "It's very different."
Lessard: "It's straight. It's not biased. They would not have anything to win, anyhow."
L'Heureux: "They want the court to be covered well, they want their decisions to be well understood."

Some observers believe, however, that the ELO is a subtle instrument of persuasion. The trust that most journalists place in the ELO gives the court enormous leverage. First, the executive legal officer reinforces the image of professional detachment that the court wishes to present to the public. Just as the court wishes to be seen as being above the rancour and partisanship of the political world, the ELO is above the blatant spin doctoring that is found elsewhere in Ottawa. Second, the ELO's main job is to point journalists to what the judges have written. The message that underlies all the ELO's briefings is that the "reasons" behind a judgment, the arguments and the logic of the judges, are the story.

Lastly, some would contend that by directing journalists to one part of a judgment and not another, the ELO has the capacity to set the media agenda. In some cases, an ELO's pronouncements and summaries of cases have appeared word for word in stories: used by journalists, in the words of former ELO Eugene Meehan (2002) "as if they were their own." When reporters phone after a decision has been announced to ask if what they have written is correct – to ask in effect if they have got the story right – the ELO's natural reflex presumably is to ensure that the court's interests are protected. As James O'Reilly, a former executive legal officer, has described the situation, "Indeed, in reality, the ELO can influence considerably the way some journalists report on the court's judgments. Some of them will actually ask for the ELO's reaction to a proposed lead. Others will ask for a description of the court's judgment or a characterization of its importance and then will write a story around the ELO's comments without attribution" (O'Reilly 2002).

Some journalists believe that some spin is inevitable and that journalists have to be careful not to rely too heavily on what the ELOs are telling them. Christopher Waddell, a former parliamentary bureau chief for CBC television news, expressed his concern this way: "The reliance on the ELO has come about because too many reporters assigned to cover SCOC decisions are not regular legal reporters and quickly latch on to someone who can explain things quickly and concisely and offer reporters the background reporters need to do their jobs in a high-pressure situation when a decision is released. My guess is no one considers it to be spin but in some cases it may be precisely that" (Waddell 2003).

The most recent development in the court's media relations system was its agreement in 2003 to a pilot project: there would be a one-hour lockup prior to the release of a major decision. This move followed years of complaints by journalists that they had little time to digest the meaning of a decision before they had to go on air or file stories. Now, journalists would be briefed on and allowed to read and digest the judgment before it is released. This can be seen as a historic step, the first time that any Supreme Court in the world has instituted a pre-judgment media lockup. Craig Oliver, CTV's long-serving Ottawa bureau chief, described the move as the "last frontier" in giving the media access to the court (Oliver 2001). Indeed, some would argue that the court has simply taken all the steps that it can possibly take; it has now gone as far as it can go to meet the needs of journalists.

It remains to be seen, however, whether the planned lockup will alter the frantic nature of TV reporting in particular. The principals in a case, and the groups and experts who are the main sources that journalists use for news stories, will not be invited into the lockup. Journalists will still be forced to make near-instant pronouncements about decisions. Others fear that the lockups will perpetuate the Ottawa reporter hegemony; news organizations will feel compelled to have reporters in the lockup and will forgo the more analytic pieces that supposedly can only be done at a distance from the turmoil and competitive fever at the court. They also worry that lockups will further enhance the power and authority of the ELO: the briefings will last longer and the ELO's explanations will carry more weight. It may also be the case that with TV's ever tightening deadlines, the lack of resources in newsrooms and the complexity of decisions little will change.

### The Judicial Lens: How Judges View Media Reporting

Unlike political leaders who are consumed by media coverage often to the point of obsession and devote hours out of their day to honing and delivering their messages, the justices spend very little time discussing media coverage or media relations. A clipping service provides judges with articles about the court and legal issues that have been published in newspapers across the country. Some judges briefly scan the articles, while others barely pay any attention to what has appeared in the papers that day. A number of justices read the *New York Times,* particularly the articles written by Linda Greenhouse, who covers the US Supreme Court for the *Times.* All in all, judges engage in little more than a general scanning of the media horizon.

According to Chief Justice Beverley McLachlin (2001), "If I counted the number of times media comes up in our discussion, they'd be very, very few. The only time it really comes up in our discussions is when there are some articles written either about cases or about judges, and we might say, you know that paper got it right or they really didn't pick up on this or that, or just as you would expect. Similarly if a particular judgment is attacked, obviously we'll talk about it amongst ourselves. We obviously feel badly when that happens." Although Justice John Major (2001) agrees that "there is not a lot of discussion," he also thinks that some of his colleagues are very sensitive about the media coverage the court receives. His contention is that the lack of discussion may stem more from frustration than lack of interest; not much can be done to alter the situation, so why bother discussing it? "If I thought that there was a serious interest in better informing the public about what the court does, I'd be interested," said Justice Major, "but I don't think there is. The premise for getting my interest doesn't exist and I never expect it's going to exist. Why should Conrad Black, or anybody else trying to sell newspapers, have much interest in what I think about how they should do their job?"

The degree of interest in media reporting is guided by a number of other considerations. The most important consideration is that in making decisions, judges must focus exclusively on legal arguments and on the ramifications of a particular decision. The justices claim that while they are not oblivious to the latest gusts of public or editorial opinion, they cannot let these winds sway their judgments. Justice Ian Binnie, for instance, has in his experience "never heard media coverage discussed in connection with the disposition of a pending case. It never has any influence. We never say, well, we're going to get skewered or we're going to get praised. We are aware of what is in the media, as everyone else is, but in my experience it has zero effect in that sense" (Binnie 2001). Interestingly, Justice Binnie also suspects that there is a tendency for justices to believe that the media are superficial in their criticism and that these criticisms can therefore be easily dismissed. As he put it, "The media essentially has very little effect within the court because people in the court hold to their own opinions about the correct legal solution. To the extent media criticism is thought to be off the mark, it is discounted – maybe excessively so" (Binnie 2001).

Some observers would dispute the claim that judges pay little attention to media reporting. Rainer Knopff, one of Canada's leading authorities on the Supreme Court, argues that the court is "watching the media as much as the media is watching the Court" (Knopff 2002). Indeed, part of the court's success has been its ability to gauge the political climate; moving cautiously when caution is warranted and taking bolder steps when bold steps would be accepted by the public. While there may be little discussion of press reporting on a day-to-day basis, one can argue that the court maintains an active surveillance at a general level. Moreover, there is little doubt that for crucial decisions, such as the reference on Quebec secession, the court tried to anticipate the needs and reactions of reporters by writing its decision in language that could be easily understood. We previously noted former justice Frank Iacobucci's (2001) comments indicating that he thought "the court did more than its share of summarizing. We summarized at the end. We summarized at the beginning. We spent a great deal of time to ensure we explained matters as fully and clearly as possible." These efforts seemed to pay off and the justices whom we interviewed thought that the media had done a superb job.

Some of the judges who were interviewed for this book believe that media coverage has been positive overall. They see the glass as being at least half full. They are pleased that the court is receiving more coverage, that Canadians are aware of the Charter and are conscious of their rights, and that the court is held in high regard. These are tangible victories. But there are other judges who see media reporting less positively. Almost all judges interviewed for this study could identify cases where they thought reporting had been especially poor. They could point to mistakes that journalists had made in reporting decisions, instances in which cases had been sensationalized out of all proportion, where reporters had missed the main points or had come to the wrong conclusions.

Perhaps the major complaint that judges have about media reporting is that the reasons behind a decision, the basis on which decisions are made, are rarely reported. For judges, the reasons supporting a decision or the reasons that lie behind a dissent are critical to public understanding. To retain legitimacy, the court must demonstrate that its decisions are supported by sound reasoning and are not made arbitrarily or driven by a political agenda. The reasons are the basis of their power. Whether the reasons are reported has become the gold standard for some of the judges. And by this standard, the media often fall short.

According to Chief Justice Beverley McLachlin (2001), all too often a story will "talk about the high points of a decision, attempting in one paragraph to say what the significance of it is. Then there will be a couple of quotes from the lawyers involved or a law professor. Now that does give the public an idea of what the court did and the general reaction, but it really doesn't give the public any idea about the legal reasoning involved or the doctrines involved or the basis of the decision." Frank Iacobucci (2001) expresses almost the same sentiments: "Often I don't think there is a genuine media interest in really getting into the guts of the decision as opposed to saying, well, the spokesman for the Aboriginal people said this; the spokesman for the government said this." Former justice Peter Cory (2001) claims that there are often instances where it is apparent that reporters have not even read the reasons behind a judgment, let alone reported on them.

Justice Ian Binnie's view is that the pro and con, for and against, format that is used in almost all news stories often leads to less understanding of the issues in a case. As Binnie (2001) describes much of media reporting, "They get someone who likes the decision and someone who doesn't like it. In that sense the story is usually fairly balanced because they're presenting two opposing reactions. You quite often don't get a collision of views. You get two opinions that pass each other and the viewer is often none the wiser as to what in fact the case was about."

Most of the justices that were interviewed believe that the problem lies with the brevity of news stories and the reporters' lack of expertise. The general impression is that with the exception perhaps of the *National Post,* the *Globe and Mail,* and *Le Devoir,* news organizations have little interest in covering anything but the most sensational cases or in providing background or in-depth analysis. Although this lack of interest is treated much like the weather (justices can't worry about what they can't control), some justices are perplexed, even bewildered, by the lack of attention to the court.

Although former justice Louise Arbour had sympathy for the situation that journalists find themselves in, she was surprised by the superficial nature of court reporting. She felt that the news media missed far too much of what is happening at the court:

I'm of the impression that the electronic press has little interest in what is happening here except in cases when decisions are eagerly awaited or when decisions are perceived as sensational. I know that reporters are worried about having to deal with something quite complex in such a passing, rapid way. From our perspective, we would prefer to see more attention to subtleties, more thorough analysis. They don't have much time. They don't have many interesting images to work with either. But in the end there isn't much interest in the workings of the court, and that's a bit surprising. There are cases here that would lend themselves very well to more in-depth studies in television documentaries and commentaries. But we see very little of that. (Arbour 2001)

Judges recognize that media reporting will change with circumstances, that journalism in effect has different seasons. There have also been times when the court has been widely praised for its wisdom, as was the case with the *Quebec Secession Reference* decision. On other occasions, such as after the *Marshall 1* decision, its judgments have provoked scathing criticism. In the early days of the *National Post,* during what was in effect the *Post*'s crusade against the court, the justices were exposed to a level of scrutiny and attack that some found deeply disturbing. While the *Post* still maintains a critical editorial stance, with a change of ownership, the fever has abated.

There is little doubt, however, that despite the changes in season, the temperature of media reporting, the level of scrutiny and criticism, has risen over time. Eugene Meehan, a former executive legal officer, in describing the new reality, notes that "being a Supreme Court judge is probably a little like being a soccer World Cup goal keeper where everybody is firing penalty shots at you and if you let one in, the crowd throws stuff at you, people in your end boo, and everyone says you're an idiot. You therefore have to develop a thick shell and a thick skin" (Meehan 2002). But not all the judges feel comfortable in the heat. Antonio Lamer made headlines when as chief justice he observed in 1998 that reporting has gone beyond "acceptable criticism" and that unless these criticisms were curtailed or countered in some way, they "threatened to undermine public confidence in the judicial system" (Stewart 1998).

Justice Ian Binnie, however, believes that the increased heat has been beneficial: "When the political lions and tigers aren't generating much interest, group sport may be had of the judicial giraffe. The bottom line in my view is if the price of bringing these rights and awareness and consciousness and empowerment to Canadians has been accomplished by the media then a little sport with the judicial giraffe is not too high a price to pay" (Rubin 2001).

## Journalists at the Court

### Beats and Sources

Although senior news managers recognize that the Supreme Court and particularly the Charter have dramatically changed Canadian society, budget cutbacks have meant that there are fewer and fewer specialized reporters. Indeed, there is not a single reporter in the country who reports from the court on a full-time basis. The majority of reporters who cover the court come from parliamentary bureaus, and the court is only a small and intermittent part of their job. Their principal task is to cover the prime minister and the opposition leaders, question period, political issues and controversies, and the twists and turns of party politics. Covering the court is an add-on; it is the something else that they do in addition to their main job. There is also a small coterie of justice reporters who cover the Supreme Court as part of a wider portfolio. Their beats include covering crime in all its dimensions – victims, police investigations, criminals, prisons, lower court cases, rulings by provincial superior courts, and sometimes related areas such as immigration or terrorism.

Of course, every news organization has its own culture and routines. At Radio-Canada, for instance, there is a deliberate policy of giving the story to the reporter in the region in which the case originates. The notion is that the reporter will be closer to the story and so coverage will be more human and less judicial. *La Presse* employs a tag-team strategy: an Ottawa reporter will write a "facts" piece that will be accompanied by a more analytical article written by columnist Yves Boisvert.

The journalistic culture that surrounds the court is the product of both tradition and circumstance. One of the key differences between the court and the political arena is that, unlike political leaders who are almost always available to go on camera or at least speak "on background," judges remain largely inaccessible. The negotiating, sharing, leaking, and cajoling that are the daily bread of parliamentary reporting simply does not exist at the court. Justices believe that "le devoir de réserve" – their duty to remain silent – is necessary to preserve the appearance of unity and impartiality and, indeed, the very sanctity of their decisions. Speaking out – justifying and embellishing arguments and responding to critics and perhaps other judges – would only diminish the court's authority.

Although the court prides itself on being the most open of any court in the world, when compared to other institutions in Ottawa it is remote and unapproachable. Even reporters who have covered the court for years have often had only sporadic contact with judges. For instance, Janice Tibbetts of the CanWest News Service recounts that although she has conducted interviews with Beverley McLachlin and with one or two of the justices, other requests for interviews have been refused, and repeated requests go unanswered. As a member of the Supreme Court-media liaison committee, she has had some contact with judges, but these discussions are off the record. As she notes, the relationship is such that if she saw a justice at a conference "she would just say 'hi.'" Tibbetts believes that cultivating relationships is hardly worth the effort because judges are limited in what they can discuss. From her perspective, it's better to "report something the way I think it should be reported without thinking about what they think" (Tibbetts 2001).

The late Michael Fitz-James, who covered the court for almost twenty years as editor of *Lawyers Weekly* and then as a writer for the *Law Times,* had only brief encounters with the justices. He used to have lunch with John Sopinka, who was apparently the only judge who would consistently reach out to journalists. Fitz-

James (2002) believes, however, that some judges play favourites, "picking their buddies if they want to give interviews." Kirk Makin of the *Globe and Mail* has had a good response rate in being granted interviews, although he admits that he has asked for such access only sparingly (Makin 2002b). Susan Harada, a former justice reporter for CBC television, "never actually called up a justice about a specific case or specifically for background," although she admitted that access to judges would have been "terrific" (Harada 2001).

Justice John Major probably spoke for most of the Supreme Court judges when he observed, "I'll talk to a reporter, but not about a case. If they want to know about something in general, I'd like to think that I'm pretty accessible. It's just that I don't pay much attention to them. I'd like to think that I pay as much attention to them as they pay to me. Neither of us know much about the other" (Major 2001).

What's important to note is that the relationship is largely a one-way street – reporters will sometimes try to interview judges, judges almost never try to gain access to reporters. Even when justices agree to answer reporters' questions or comment on larger issues, the timing and circumstances are of their choosing and not that of the reporters. The justices clearly believe that there is little to be gained by currying favour with journalists. Executive legal officer Daniel Jutras believes that it is important to understand that judges and politicians have completely different agendas. The simple fact is that while judges have little to gain by interacting with journalists, politicians cannot survive without the oxygen of media exposure. As Jutras (2003a) explains, "If you are a minister, it's very important to be seen. And I think that journalists understand that. The court speaks through its judgments because that is the nature of what it does, but it is not doing so with ulterior motives. It's this lack of further consequence or a further expectation of benefit, re-election for instance, that makes the court more credible than politicians in its relationship with the media."

The justices may also believe that the current regime of maintaining a dignified distance is succeeding and hence, there is little need to do things differently. The current formula seems to have reaped dividends – the court is seen as being above partisan politics because it doesn't indulge in the massaging and spinning that are found in virtually all other institutions. Interestingly enough, communications scholar Joshua Meyrowitz (1985) has written that authority is enhanced by "distant visibility" and weakened by "excess familiarity." Respect and reverence can only be maintained with distance. One can argue that much of the court's positive image with the Canadian public and with journalists, and its ability to exercise symbolic authority, have come from maintaining that certain distance.

The justices are also aware of the dangers of speaking to journalists. As mentioned previously, Justice Michel Bastarache gave an interview to *Lawyers Weekly* in January 2001 in which he criticized his colleagues for reasoning that was sometimes "subjective" and "inconsistent" and for making policy rather than simply applying the law in a rigorous manner (Schmitz 2001, 1). The interview stirred considerable controversy, and Bastarache has apparently since been reluctant to speak to reporters. In fact, he declined to be interviewed for this study.

There was also negative publicity when a biography of former justice Bertha Wilson revealed that some of her fellow justices often engaged in what she described as "repugnant" lobbying to ensure that there would be a majority on issues they considered important. She claimed that cliques were formed based on personality and that female justices were usually excluded from closed-door meetings (Anderson 2001). Antonio Lamer responded by publicly attacking Wilson for refusing to engage in the kind of "horse-trading that unites judges and results in strong common opinions." He thought that she was "stubborn as a mule" (Makin 2002a). The court's dirty linen was exposed for all to see.

More recently, a book on the life of Brian Dickson described the many frustrations he experienced attempting to iron out delicate compromises, dealing with judges who were paralyzed by indecision or by illness, including depression, and contending with the first onslaught of media criticism. The book quotes Justice William McIntyre as saying that the court acted "irresponsibly" in interpreting the Charter and that the country was "ill-served" by the court during the Charter's first ten years (Sharpe and Roach 2003).

Notably, both of these insider accounts came in scholarly biographies that described battles that had long since taken place. They were not written by journalists who had gained behind-the-scenes access to the manoeuvring and bargaining behind the court's recent decisions.

The relatively closed nature of the court may be one of the reasons why there are so few stories dealing with the internal politics of the court and the personalities and perspectives of individual judges. No Canadian reporter has been able to break through the court's high defensive walls in the way that Bob Woodward and Scott Armstrong did in their 1979 book about the US Supreme Court – *The brethren: Inside the Supreme Court*. Indeed, in the aftermath of *The brethren,* reporters and commentators in the United States have routinely gone behind the scenes, using justices and law clerks as sources, to describe the internal battles and the ideologies of particular judges. They cover the court much as they would the political arena. The focus of their stories is often on battles for supremacy and the politics behind decisions. In fact, American reporters almost never refer to individual justices without also naming the president who appointed them. Justices are thus viewed primarily as Republican or Democratic appointees.

Moreover, in the United States, judges are skewered with the same sharp knives and in the same merciless fashion as politicians. One of the most prominent American journalists, Maureen Dowd of the *New York Times,* has lampooned Justice

Antonin Scalia as being "Archie Bunker in a high-backed chair" and observed that, "Like Archie, Nino is the last one to realize that his intolerance is out-of-date" (Dowd 2003). In her columns Scalia is simply referred to as Nino. Although lacking Dowd's penchant for brutal characterization, Linda Greenhouse, also of the *Times,* picks apart decisions with scalpel-like precision, often highlighting and dwelling at length on the divisions between the judges. Ironically, a number of the Canadian justices interviewed for this study thought that Greenhouse's work set a standard to which Canadian journalist should aspire.

Clearly, some Canadian justices are horrified and deeply repelled by what they see happening in the United States and wish to ensure that the Canadian Supreme Court does not follow the American example. Former justice Peter Cory (2001) has particularly strong feelings on this issue: "I hope that the court that I used to belong to and am so proud of doesn't become an American court, where they say the most outrageous things about each other, as you know. This is an aberration. It sets back the law of the United States one hundred years. How do you go in the next day and work with your colleagues on leaves to appeal or something else? That's rough. I think that because we don't do that that perhaps we don't make it as exciting for journalists. But manners and courtesy are the lubrication of society."

On the few occasions that the veil has been lifted on their personal lives and political views, the judges have felt vulnerable and in some cases deeply hurt. Former Supreme Court justice Claire L'Heureux-Dubé was stung by articles in the *National Post* that discussed the circumstances in which her husband had committed suicide and that criticized her feminist views. According to L'Heureux-Dubé (2001), "They attacked me personally. They said that I was no good, that I wasn't a good person, they said that I was stupid. You don't come to the Supreme Court to get that kind of treatment. You do your homework. You do your best. We can all have our own way of seeing things. But to be publicly massacred, to be singled out – that is not acceptable." Former justice Louise Arbour (2001) worried that personal attacks could create an atmosphere of "intellectual terror" and that "intimidation should never be permitted"; in the end, "judges must live in an environment that allows them to think."

The reticence with which most justices approach the media was perhaps best expressed by Justice Louis LeBel. As LeBel (2001) put it, "It should not be that justices start to individually develop their own network of public relations. I think that you should be available and ready to answer a certain number of questions. Obviously, this should be within the bounds of prudence because you can get burned easily enough."

The reason that the politics of the court are rarely covered in Canada may not lie entirely with the closed nature of the court. Clearly, news organizations have to shoulder some of the responsibility. The lack of resources in newsrooms and of full-time legal reporters has had a crucial impact. The simple reality is that news organizations don't report on the judges because they don't have the resources to devote to covering the court on an ongoing basis. Arguably the lack of coverage may have a catch-22 effect – the dearth of such stories may in turn create little appetite for them among viewers and readers. The lack of reporting feeds on itself and becomes self-perpetuating, and may be particularly damaging when it comes to informing citizens about their rights.

The situation may have hit a low point in 2002 and 2003 when Marie Deschamps and Morris Fish were named to the court. Soon after Deschamps was appointed, a brief profile of the new justice appeared in the *Ottawa Citizen* as well as other CanWest papers. One observer noted that the picture of Deschamps's face that ran alongside the article was "about the size of Deschamps' real head." It was as if "the story was saying these people are very smart people. See how big their heads are? And that's all you really need to know."[1] Few papers ran profiles of the then forty-nine-year-old justice – someone who is likely to play a major role in Canadian life for at least the next twenty-five years. There was a similar lack of interest when Quebec Court of Appeal judge Morris Fish was appointed to the court in July 2003. According to some journalists, Fish had refused to give interviews.

This was not the case, however, when Paul Martin's Liberal government appointed Louise Charron and Rosalie Abella to the court in August 2004. A new and controversial procedure that allowed MPs to question Justice Minister Irwin Cotler about the appointments, the continuing controversy over same-sex marriages, and the liberal views of Justice Abella produced a one-day splash of coverage. The *Globe and Mail* published eight articles, including an editorial and two commentaries. The *National Post,* which focused its attention primarily on Justice Abella, had a two-page spread and six articles in its front section. The appointments were also a front-page story in *Le Devoir,* though only a page 3 story in *La Presse.*

The blunt reality is that on those few occasions when the justices have pried open their doors just enough to allow slivers of sunlight to shine in, the media have shown little interest. For instance, all the justices made themselves available for one-hour biographical interviews on CPAC, the public affairs cable channel. The justices gave the producers access to their spouses and family members and sat down for interviews that could not be edited. Admittedly, CPAC reaches a small, even tiny, boutique audience so there was little risk. But it's important to note that the major TV networks have not pursued similar opportunities in almost twenty years.

So a combination of declining resources in news bureaus that would allow reporters the time to write investigative pieces or in-depth stories, the high barriers erected by the court, and what is perceived to be little appetite on the part of the public ensure that the status quo remains in place – little access and little desire for stories about the politics of the judges and the court. As Luiza Chwialkowska, the former justice reporter for the *National Post,* has described the situation, "It's a bit like the Bank of Canada. It's kind of this black box where things go on and things come out but you don't know a lot about what's on the inside, so that puts a premium on information" (Chwialkowska 2001).

There are some journalists, however, who would like to see the cloak of distant and protected authority removed entirely. Members of the *National Post*'s editorial board during that paper's crusade against the court from 1998 to 2001 certainly took this view. According to former editorial board member Ezra Levant (2002), as we quoted earlier, the judges could not expect that their decisions would be treated as if they had been "handed down from Mount Sinai." The *Post*'s position was that judges needed to be treated not as unquestioned authorities but as people with their own political biases and agendas. Their viewpoints could not be ignored by journalists.

Although few of the journalists interviewed for this study shared Levant's zeal for treating judges like politicians, a number of journalists believe that greater openness and exposure are necessary if some thread of accountability is to be maintained. The late David Vienneau, former Ottawa bureau chief for Global News who covered the court for close to twenty years and was probably alone in having had close personal relationships with a number of justices, argued that "the public wants to know more about the type of person who is there. Demystifying the court is important because it allows the public to know who is making these decisions. And if they don't like the type of judge who is making these decisions, they can complain to their MPs. It's better to know who is doing you right and who is doing you wrong than to have no idea who these nine people are who were traditionally cloistered in a building and were afraid to be seen in public" (Vienneau 2001).

Stephen Bindman, a former reporter who now works for the Department of Justice, also believes that more reporting on the justices and their backgrounds would be beneficial. But he believes care must be taken. According to Bindman (2001), "There's been little attention paid to the personalities on the court. In fact, most reporters couldn't name all nine judges. But there's a difference between knowing about the judges and knowing what their expense account was last week, what they eat for breakfast, what their wife does, and what kind of house they live in. You do want to know about their backgrounds and leanings and where they stand on particular issues. So we need more about who they are, but it's not the same extent as, say with a prime minister."

Kirk Makin believes that the issue of accountability is not easily resolved. As Makin (2003) has argued,

What is "sufficient" accountability? To be sure, there ought to be a good look at their jurisprudence and standing in the legal/judicial community when they are appointed. If there are scandals and shortcomings, they are increasingly likely to be discovered (critics and denigrators call when they have something to say that is negative, trust me) and exposed. But should we engage in long-running attacks because Michel Bastarache was active on French-language issues prior to his appointment, because Louise Arbour lived outside marriage for many years and might be ruling on marriage issues, or because Ian Binnie represented an anti-abortion group in its litigation in the 1970s?

### Distance and Silence

"Le devoir de réserve," the refusal of judges to comment on the judgments that they have handed down, has had a major impact on the ways in which stories are reported. It sets an entirely different dynamic into motion. For instance, because reporters are often unable to talk to judges, they are inevitably drawn to the antagonists and pressure groups. The vacuum created by the silence of the judges is filled by those who are clamouring to be heard. Small wonder then that reactions to the judgment, rather than an analysis of its meaning, often dominate news stories. Journalists simply go to where they can get the story. When judges complain that the "reasons" behind their judgments get little coverage and that this diminishes the way the court is perceived, they have, it can be argued, only themselves to blame. The court seems, in this case, to be trapped in the cement of its own customs and traditions.

Covering reactions from litigants and groups also fits into accepted journalistic norms and routines. Journalists often report stories in terms of binaries — pro and con, for and against, government versus opposition. This regime is so ingrained, so much a part of the DNA of modern journalism, that some news organizations will go as far as to drop stories if they can't get spokespeople for both sides to comment on the events that have taken place. Such practices are accepted because they supposedly provide proof of journalistic neutrality and that reporters have provided in-depth coverage. Interestingly enough, when journalists provide pro and con positions, they invariably turn to the protagonists in a case and not to the positions taken by the justices. They almost never, for instance, in a five-to-four or a six-to-three decision by the court, examine the divisions within the court or the positions taken by dissenting judges.

Not covering the judgment has its dangers. Perhaps the greatest danger is that the antagonists who are interviewed may not have fully understood the judgment or are willing to spin it in ways the judges didn't intend. This was certainly the case in the *Marshall* decision when Aboriginal spokespeople interpreted the decision as a victory that gave their fishers far-reaching rights. What occurred next was a chain reaction between Natives and non-Native fishers that quickly mushroomed out of control. Emotionally charged reactions to the decision dominated news coverage and drowned out what the court had actually said.

The *Little Sisters* case is another example of media coverage that seemed to rest on what the litigants had to say, rather than on a careful reading of the judgment. The gay and lesbian bookstore in Vancouver had been in an ongoing dispute with Customs and Revenue Canada about its importation of salacious materials. News reports were quick to proclaim a victory for Little Sister's despite that the judgment reiterated the government's right to carry out inspections.

A similar set of overheated reactions, it could be argued, occurred in response to the lower court rulings in the *Sharpe* case. Anti-pornography activists were quick to characterize the judgments as a blow against strict pornography laws rather than as rulings that made room for some privacy and freedom of expression. As Christopher Waddell (2001) remembers, the politicians were soon saying, "'Yikes – we don't want to be called soft on child pornography, we may lose votes.' They were responding to those who either wilfully or inadvertently, through lack of work or research, misrepresented the whole issue in the case. All of a sudden, you've got the government actually feeling that it's on the defensive, that it has to respond to something. And what's the truth in it all – nothing."

### The Debate on Whether Reporters Should Be Specialists or Generalists

Understanding and interpreting highly complex and abstract judicial decisions pose considerable problems for journalists. Judgments on tax law, torts, and constitutional issues can be dense and make tedious and even painful reading for practising lawyers, let alone unpractised reporters. Judgments are built on precedent and on principles of philosophy that often contain elusive and contradictory arguments. There are other reasons to be confused. In some cases, the justices use eloquent and passionate language in support of a particular principle but will choose remedies that do little to back up their strong language. Sometimes judgments suffer from the reverse: the court insists on strong remedies but the language used to make the case is tepid and cautious. Moreover, the justices can use relatively mundane cases to establish important legal principles, while high-profile cases may have little importance from a legal perspective.

The burning question for some justices is whether general or parliamentary reporters have the training necessary to properly cover the court. A significant number of justices believe that the beat requires reporters who have some legal education or are even lawyers. One of the classic comments on this topic was made by US justice Felix Frankfurter, who ventured that newspapers "would never send a reporter to cover the New York Yankees who had as little knowledge about baseball as Supreme Court reporters tended to have about the Court and the law" (Slotnick and Segal 1998, 23).

Former justice Frank Iacobucci (2001) contends that some legal training is necessary to do the job: "You need to have people who are trained in this kind of journalism. It's easy to go to an expert and get his or her two or three lines rather than put your nose into the case. I admire the genuine interest taken by the *New York Times* in the tradition of Anthony Lewis and Linda Greenhouse in getting into the guts of the decision as opposed to saying, well, the spokesman for the Aboriginal people said this, the spokesman for the government said this."

Michael Fitz-James, a lawyer by training, was even more biting in his criticism of those who don't believe that some legal training is necessary. According to Fitz-James (2002), who was an on-air legal columnist for CBC *Newsworld* for five years, "Media people don't have enough depth or training or knowledge of legal issues to really understand what's legally significant. The people who put together the media package always get it wrong, or they get it ass backwards, or they just emphasize the wrong thing or they don't really approach the story with any depth. I talk to a twenty-three-year-old producer who basically pitches a story to a twenty-five-year-old executive producer who basically says, 'Na! That's boring.'"

A former ELO, Robin Elliot was perhaps the most scathing in his evaluation of how unprepared a number of reporters were to do the job required. According to Elliot (2002),

> It's something of an irony, at least I view it as such, that a lot of the print media in their editorials will say that "judges have too much power" and "this is harmful to democracy" and "we've got to scrutinize appointments" and so on. But the court ranked very much at the bottom of their list of priorities in terms of institutions. The journalists with whom I would be dealing were very well meaning and were trying to do the best job that they could, but they were hampered by a lack of resources, a lack of time, and a lack of knowledge and experience. When I would try to explain what cases were about, I could often tell that for a number of these journalists this was just Greek. They just didn't have the knowledge and background that allowed them to assimilate a lot of cases. So of course the easy story was, you know, let's just talk about the gruesome facts – and just simplify it.

But most journalists take a far different tack, sharply rejecting the know-nothing critique. They believe that good journalism requires someone who has different skills and a different vantage point, someone who in effect comes from a different culture than those found in the legal community. The solution according to Don Newman of CBC *Newsworld* is for journalists to have a balance of skills and experience. According to Newman (2001), "If I wanted to be a sports reporter I wouldn't have to be a hockey player to cover hockey, but you'd sure have to understand the game and know the history of it and the strategies that are employed. But to say that you have to be a hockey player makes no sense." The journalists we interviewed often referred to the skills that were needed to be a good journalist: the ability to tell a story, to reduce complex details to their simplest elements, and to make issues and ideas understandable to the public. A good journalist is able to use these skills in any situation.

When asked if it was necessary for journalists to have legal training, Manon Cornellier of Le Devoir was strongly opposed: "Not at all. One must be rigorous but must also be able to popularize knowledge. Some people might be knowledgeable in the law but unable to explain it. This does not help. Someone who doesn't understand an issue but who is thorough will look for an explanation, will find out what it means. To sum up, one has to be rigorous, curious, and be able to make that knowledge accessible" (Cornellier 2003).[2]

Daniel Lessard of Radio-Canada believes that the downside of having court reporters with legal training is that they might have a tendency to talk to lawyers rather than to the antagonists, interest group representatives, or politicians when seeking out sources. They may also report in a manner that is too top heavy with legal interpretations and analysis to appeal to or be understood by ordinary citizens (Lessard 2001). For instance, there is some speculation that the reason Le Devoir dropped the column written by Alain-Robert Nadeau, who has a PhD in constitutional law, was because readers found his analysis too complex and difficult.

One question that is difficult to answer is whether parliamentary reporters who are used to seeing issues and events in political terms use a political lens when they report from the court. Instead of focusing on the legal or social implications of decisions, they inevitably revert to using a political frame. It is interesting to note that political reactions and repercussions were a main focus in all the major cases we reviewed in this book – Secession, Marshall, Vriend, and Sharpe. Although one can argue that historic cases will inevitably involve governments and political leaders, and that this is precisely why they are important cases, one can also speculate on whether this becomes a self-fulfilling prophecy – cases are considered to be important if they involve governments and politicians. Certainly, each of our great cases deserved the substantial coverage it received. The unanswered question is whether there were crucial cases that did not receive similar levels of coverage because their impact was primarily social or economic rather than capital-P political.

It can also be argued, however, that political reporters bring a strong set of skills that other reporters might not. Political reporters may have a better sense of the ramifications a particular judgment might have – how it will resonate among the politicians and even in the general public. The greater mistake perhaps would be to assign reporters who didn't have a strong grasp of the political world into which decisions of the court are almost inevitably thrust.

Susan Harada, a former parliamentary reporter, thinks that it's unfair to see parliamentary reporters as only having the ability to view issues in political terms. They are experienced enough and skilled enough to realize that there are social and legal dimensions as well (Harada 2003).

On the other hand, Kirk Makin (2003) thinks that "many of the parliamentary reporters *do* use a political lens rather than a heavily legal lens." He notes that "those who appear in their stories are more likely to be opposition justice critics than law professors. This is partly because of their worldview, but it's also editor-driven. Editors are always trying to 'move' stories forward these days, so as to not look as if their news angles are stale. This lends itself to reactions from politicians who criticize the ruling or vow action and to interest groups who fulminate about them."

There is also the broad question of whether journalists are stationed in the right places. The beat system is, in effect, a journalism of buildings that situates journalists at the places where decisions are being made. Hence, large news organizations establish almost a shadow government that allows them to monitor the activities of government leaders and officials. The argument can be made that news organizations are failing to reflect the new balance of power in Canadian public life because reporters are locked into their old locations. News organizations continue to cover even the smallest details of parliamentary warfare while largely ignoring an institution that many believe has the last word in settling the outstanding political and social issues in Canadian society. The criticism is that news organizations make much to do about nothing while making little of important developments. Others argue, however, that in Canadian public life, all roads eventually lead to Parliament Hill.

### Instant Everything: Time, Space, and News Values

The machinery of journalism has its own harsh imperatives. Journalists work within an organizational system that imposes tight guidelines and requirements. They operate according to distinct and rigid formulas, and they sometimes have little choice about if and how a story will be reported. News also has certain immutable characteristics; it must be immediate, dramatic, focus on conflict, and, in the case of TV, have compelling visuals. Most stories are about trouble of some kind – what went wrong, who is to blame, the suffering of innocent victims, and how order or safety can be restored. Most of all, stories must be able to pass the bar stool or coffee break test – they have to grab people's attention and be interesting enough to stir conversation. They have to be about events or situations that people will want to talk about. It is also noteworthy that much of the media's focus in our study of a year in the life of the court was on "celebrity villains" and on cases that involved moral dilemmas of some kind. The relationship between judges and journalists is dictated to a large degree by this basic grammar of contemporary journalism.

Perhaps the most difficult constraints on journalists are the limitations of time and space. Journalists are now caught in the vortex of a perpetual news cycle in which there is an insatiable and never-ending demand for new news. What was most apparent in Radio-Canada reporter Christine St-Pierre's coverage of the *Sharpe* decision were the deadlines and time constraints under which she had to operate. No one should underestimate the skill and intelligence that are needed to put a story together under such extraordinary pressures. First, she had only moments to absorb and analyze the decision before going live with her report. St-Pierre then had to keep track of reactions in Ottawa, follow a cross-country caravan of news conferences and reactions, and try to reach Robin Sharpe for an interview. In the end, a complicated and highly nuanced story was condensed into a report that was only two minutes and two seconds long. Admittedly, a great deal of information can be conveyed in two minutes, but a great deal is also left on the cutting room floor.

Christopher Waddell (2001) describes the difficulties of working under such stressful conditions: "You're trying to take a thirty- or forty-page document, read it in eighteen seconds, and effectively go on air and say what the court actually decided. And you make mistakes. But the demand for instant everything forces people into these situations."

There is little doubt that the demands for instant analysis can produce serious inaccuracies. One print reporter noted that the severe deadlines under which TV reporters have to operate has had an effect on her as well: "The way I look at it, take ten minutes and get it right. But I guess my editors didn't see it that way. If CBC has it, you have to have it at the exact same moment. That can be dangerous. I've seen them report inaccurately on TV. I've seen them get it wrong, get it backwards."[3]

These severe deadline pressures can also work their way down the information chain. Rainer Knopff, a political scientist at the University of Calgary, is frequently used as a source by journalists reporting on a decision. He has also felt the pressure of having to react almost instantly to judgments:

I arrive at my Calgary office in the morning. I'm booting up my computer, getting my e-mail running, and the e-mail flashes up saying the Supreme Court has just handed down the decision on whatever, the prisoner's voting rights case let's say. And just about the time that I'm doing that, seeing that the case has been handed down, the phone rings. A reporter is on the line wanting to interview me about the case. I say I haven't read it yet. The reporter conveys a sense of desperation. He hasn't read it either and prevails on me to talk anyway.

I'm pulling up the case as we are talking. I'm trying to get a sense of it. The next morning I read the paper and I find that I have been sound bitten in ways that I don't entirely approve. I mean it's the blind leading the blind. (Knopff 2002)

Kirk Makin of the *Globe and Mail* is always wary of the first reactions that come in after a decision is handed down: "It's at these moments when TV or a wire service is weakest and most vulnerable. I have full sympathy with the task that these reporters find themselves dealing with. So you've got to be really circumspect about those first impressions. Even the analysts that are being interviewed haven't had a chance to look at the decision themselves; they've read the summary, they've looked at the last couple of pages – and boom they're on TV" (Makin 2002b).

Even if the problem of immediate deadlines was solved or at least eased by lockups before important decisions are handed down, it can still be argued that the truncated length of stories inherently produces distortions and inaccuracies – how could it not? St-Pierre's story was largely a collage of descriptions, visuals, and clips from interviews that took place across the country. The judgment was explained in thirty to forty seconds, and each quote, each snippet, was between ten and twenty seconds in length. Highly abbreviated info-bites are natural for television. But they have also become natural for newspapers. As Kirk Makin (2003) explains, "If you only have 15 column inches or two minutes of airtime, you cannot even scratch the surface of the material lying within a judgment. You have too much material fighting for inclusion in too little space. I realize that all reporters feel they ought to have more space – it is part of the game. But I particularly feel the crunch when I have to tell a story, detail the history of litigation, show the divisions on the Court, get political and human interest content and give even a modest taste of the Court's reasoning – ALL IN THE SAME SHORT SPACE."

One exception to this trend was the *National Post*. When Conrad Black founded the *Post* in 1998 he envisioned it as a writer's paper. The *Post* hired a bevy of top writers, paid them high salaries, and encouraged them to write stories that were much longer than those found in other papers. It was an instance of European-style journalism being brought to Canada; writers were expected to be both highly partisan and long-winded. When the *Post* came under new ownership in 2000, lengthy articles and commentaries became a thing of the past.

Most reporters are guided by an internal gyroscope, an almost sixth sense, about what will make a good news story. Cases may be important from a judicial or legal perspective, but if they don't contain lively or dramatic elements, reporters will have difficulty persuading their desks – senior producers or editors – that the story is worth covering. In this, journalists are often guided by what they describe as an intrinsic feel about which stories they should cover. Global TV reporter David Vienneau (2001) described the instincts that drove him to cover one story and not another: "To me, there's an inherent instinct within some journalists that they know a story when they see it. I mean, Charter cases were certainly at the top of my list. Anything with crime, with police rights, police abuses. But I can't explain it. It's like something you're born with, and I think good journalists have that and they have the ability to see a story when nobody else can and say, I'm gonna get that in the paper come hell or high water."

The problem, however, is that there is sometimes little match, little overlap, between cases the judicial and legal communities think are important and the cases journalists think are important. Even if journalists are aware of the importance certain rulings may have within the law, they face limits in how far they can go in trying to convince media managers that these stories deserve time and space. One newspaper journalist describes a case involving a search and seizure that took place in lawyers' offices, a case that he considered important. Although he was aware that "you're not going to have little boys hawking papers on the street corner yelling, 'Read all about it, search and seizure in law offices,'" his editors bought the story based on their belief that "there's a purpose to the newspaper that goes beyond just being a comic book. They will ensure that a story like that gets in" (Makin 2002b). Of course, not all news managers share the same concerns, and TV newscasts and tabloid newspapers in particular have much smaller news holes.

Daniel Jutras had to deal with these contrasting agendas when he became the ELO:

Some of the cases are interesting to me as legal issues, but the cases that are interesting to me are not necessarily the ones that are interesting to them. I'll give you an example. Recently there was an Aboriginal rights case that I believed was a hugely significant case both in legal and in terms of public interest. But there was little media interest in it. It was too technical ... Another thing that is very characteristic is that very often the questions they ask are not law issues. Where did this happen? How old was he? Is he dead? These are not questions that a law professor would think of. For me the learning curve was fairly steep. I would come to the briefings and raise what I thought was important and they would say – is he on bail? There would be five or six questions that I couldn't answer. (Jutras 2003a)

TV stories are driven by fast-paced action. The camera cannot dwell on any face or action or thought for too long; TV has an incessant impatience. But by far the most important ingredient for TV reporters is whether there are exciting visuals. In television terms, reporting from the Supreme Court seems to follow a certain formula. In the four cases that we studied in depth, coverage on the day the decision was handed down always began with the man at the centre – Marshall, Sharpe, and Vriend. The story was to some degree wrapped around these individuals whether they were depicted as a hero or as a villain, though this was less true of the *Secession Reference,* where the importance of the issue superseded the fate of a particular person. However, "the man at the centre" would fade rapidly from view and was usually gone by the next day's coverage. The next visual would show the Supreme Court. Here there would be a specific sequence of shots moving from exterior to interior. In most cases the first shots showed the building's façade, followed by interior shots of the judges and the courtroom.

Most TV stories adopted a strategic frame depicting winners or losers in memorable visuals. There were shots taken of Delwin Vriend's victory speech and at his champagne-doused celebration. There was also the poignant image of a brochure showing a large gavel (the Supreme Court) smashing down on a drawing of the province of Alberta, that drawing filled with images of people. In contrast to Vriend, Robin Sharpe was depicted as a dangerous and freakish outcast. In one CBC report, which had used footage shot at the hearing, the camera focused on Sharpe's feet (white socks, dark brown shoes, and high-water pants) before slowly panning upward to show his face, using the old Hollywood technique of building up suspense before finally revealing the villain's identity. Two other visuals were also memorable. The first was of a group of women protestors who held up a sign reading: "Lord protect our children." The scene undoubtedly reinforced the notion that Sharpe was a threat. Most shocking, however, was a close-up of four publications authored by Sharpe. One publication featured a little boy with a missing eye and a grotesque deformity of some kind – either a burn or a scar. The images would no doubt have been unsettling to many viewers.

Interestingly, some of the cases that received the most coverage on TV during our year-long study of coverage of the court were also cases that contained potent visuals – *Latimer, Van de Perre,* and *Boucher.* Latimer was depicted as an ordinary "any" man caught in tragic circumstances. The scenes shot on his farm were reminiscent of the rustic man-versus-nature settings that many Canadians are familiar with. Latimer was depicted as any one of us. *Van de Perre v. Edwards* involved a star athlete who was locked in a custody dispute with his attractive former lover (described by one of the reporters who covered the story as being a "real babe"). The case focused on whether the child would be better off being raised in a black or white household. Glamour, race, and sports all intersected. And Maurice ("Mom") Boucher, the leader of the Hell's Angels, was the sinister celebrity villain par excellence. He had assumed almost mythic importance in the Quebec tabloid press, and he has a magnetic and malevolent presence that was made for TV.

The simple reality is that judgments that don't contain potent images are unlikely to become great TV stories even if they are crucial legal cases. Hence, the vast majority of cases will remain invisible, far below the waterline of public attention and knowledge.

## Conclusion

Judges and journalists are the products of two different cultures. The routines and imperatives that guide the two professions often work at cross-purposes. The complex nature of jurisprudence, the unavailability of judges to comment on cases, the instant nature of journalism, the lack of expertise of so many reporters, and television's requirement for compelling pictures all produce tensions and distortions. Although justices are sometimes disturbed by what they see as sensationalized coverage, errors of fact, and the lack of attention to the reasons behind a decision, they realize that there is little that they can do to affect changes in stories or alter the conditions under which journalists operate. To some degree, the relationship has settled into a polite world of live and let live, neither side believing that it can change the other or move the relationship forward in any real way. Indeed, most judges believe that they have gone as far as they can go in opening up the court to reporters and that further steps will bring more dangers than advantages.

Most importantly perhaps, there is a sense that the current system has worked to the advantage of the court. Despite the clash of institutional cultures and the often truncated nature of media coverage, the various gears and meshes of the court's communication system seem to be functioning well. In broad terms, the court's message seems to have reached the public in important ways. Canadians are far more conscious of their rights as citizens than they were twenty years ago, and the press is paying more attention to the court and its judgments than ever before. Moreover, the court and the Charter are sustained by a cushion of broad public support.

The key to the kingdom is that the court has created a communications system, based largely on the integrity and competence of the ELOs, which has won the confidence of journalists. To reporters, the ELOs are both the gateway to and the public face of the court. Their credibility is the hinge on which much of the court's relationship with journalists rests, and that credibility is largely unshaken and unchallenged.

Although reporters are handicapped by a lack of time and resources, few express discontent with the system. Part of the reason is that, for most journalists, reporting from the Supreme Court is not part of their main assignment and so they have little stake in developing greater expertise or in exploring issues in a substantial way. Their relationship with the court is sporadic. They go to the court only for the most sensational or controversial cases. For news organizations, the court is at best an afterthought. They invest little in reporting from the court and expect little in return.

Yet, a number of those whom we interviewed believe that there are structural problems that need addressing. The episodic nature of coverage, the lack of resources and training available to journalists, the heightened power of litigants and pressure groups resulting in part from the vacuum created by the silence of judges, and the emphasis on morality cases and celebrity villains at the expense of cases that might have a greater impact on citizens' lives and might in fact be no less interesting – all remain arthritic points. We also found journalists who are wary of becoming enmeshed in the court-media system and suspicious of the neutrality of the ELOs.

Clearly, both the justices and journalists have little incentive to change the system that now exists. Indeed, part of the reason for its evolution and durability is that the needs of both sides are largely being served. Unless the court finds itself at the centre of a crisis of authority and legitimacy, there are few reasons to expect changes. The question, however, is not whether justices and journalists are content with their current relationship but whether the interests of citizens are being served. The question is whether Canadians can be better informed about the world in which they live and their rights as citizens. We address these questions in the Conclusion.

## Notes

1 Interview 2003. The interview was conducted in confidentiality, and the name of the interviewee was withheld by mutual agreement.

2 Author translation. In French it was: "Non, pas du tout. Il faut avoir de la rigueur et la capacité de vulgariser, parce qu'il y a des gens qui ont des connaissances en droit et qui sont incapables de vulgariser et personne ne comprend ce qu'ils racontent. On n'est pas plus avancé. Mais si c'est quelqu'un qui a la rigueur et qu'il ne comprend pas, il va chercher l'explication. Il se le fait expliquer. Alors, il faut de la rigueur et de la curiosité et aussi une capacité de vulgariser, c'est surtout ça."

3 Interview with a reporter, 2001. The interview was conducted in confidentiality, and the name of the interviewee was withheld by mutual agreement.

## References

Anderson, Ellen. 2001. *Judging Bertha Wilson*. Toronto: University of Toronto Press.

Arbour, Louise. 2001. Interview by authors. Ottawa, 7 December.

Bindman, Stephen. 2001. Interview by authors. Ottawa, 1 December.

Binnie, Justice Ian. 2001. Interview by authors. Ottawa, 10 December.

Chwialkowska, Luiza. 2001. Interview by authors. Ottawa, 7 December.

Cornellier, Manon. 2003. Interview by authors. Ottawa, 21 March.

Cory, Peter. 2001. Interview by authors. Toronto, 26 July.

Dowd, Maureen. 2003. Nino's opera bouffe. *New York Times,* 29 June.

Elliot, Robin. 2002. Interview by authors. Ottawa, 11 September.

Ferland, Denis. 2001. Interview by authors. Ottawa, 11 December.

Fitz-James, Michael. 2002. Interview by authors. Ottawa, 16 September.

Harada, Susan. 2001. Interview by authors. Ottawa, 25 January.

—. 2003. Correspondence. 15 August.

Iacobucci, Frank. 2001. Interview by authors. Calgary, 26 October.

Jutras, Daniel. 2003a. Interview by authors. Ottawa, 24 March.

—. 2003b. Interview by authors. By phone, 3 December.

Knopff, Rainer. 2002. Comments. Media-Supreme Court Research Workshop, 7 November, Ottawa.

Lamer, Antonio. 1998. Remarks delivered at the Conference on the Media and the Law, 6 February, Toronto.

—. 2002. Interview by authors. Ottawa, 22 April.

LeBel, Louis. 2001. Interview by authors. Ottawa, 11 December.

L'Heureux, Daniel. 2001. Interview by authors. Ottawa, 11 December.

L'Heureux-Dubé, Claire. 2001. Interview by authors. Ottawa, 10 December.

Lessard, Daniel. 2001. Interview by authors. Ottawa, 11 December.

Levant, Ezra. 2002. Interview by authors. Calgary, 26 November.

Major, Justice John. 2001. Interview by authors. Ottawa, 7 December.

Makin, Kirk. 2002a. Lobbying hurt court, book says. *Globe and Mail,* 11 March, p. A9.

—. 2002b. Interview by authors. Ottawa, 13 September.

—. 2003. Correspondence. 7 August.

McLachlin, Justice Beverley. 2001. Interview by authors. Ottawa, 7 December.

Meehan, Eugene. 2002. Interview by authors. By phone, 16 September.

Meyrowitz, Joshua. 1985. *No sense of place.* New York: Oxford University Press.

Newman, Don. 2001. Interview by authors. Ottawa, 7 December.

Oliver, Craig, 2001. Interview by authors. Ottawa, 5 December.

O'Reilly, James. 2002. Interview by authors. Ottawa, 6 November.

Richer, Jules. 2003. Interview by authors. Montreal, 6 March.

Rubin, Sandra. 2001. Lawyers say judges not above media criticism. *National Post,* 16 August, p. A2.

Schmitz, Cristin. 2001. Bastarache explains dissents in one-third of SCC decisions. *Lawyers Weekly* (19 January), pp. 1 and 7.

Sharpe, Robert, and Kent Roach. 2003. *Brian Dickson: A judge's journey.* Toronto: University of Toronto Press.

Slotnick, Elliot, and Jennifer Segal. 1998. *Television and the Supreme Court.* Cambridge: Cambridge University Press.

Stewart, Edison. 1998. Judge wonders how to right twisted rulings: Should he speak out when wrong interpretations are made. *Toronto Star,* 24 August, p. A1.

Tibbetts, Janice. 2001. Interview by authors. Ottawa, 7 December.

Vienneau, David. 2001. Interview by authors. Ottawa, 5 December.

Waddell, Christopher. 2001. Interview by authors. Ottawa, 10 December.

—. 2003. Correspondence. 5 August.

# Conclusion:
# Reporting the Supreme Court
# through a Political Prism

*The Last Word* describes the contest over interpretive authority that exists between the Supreme Court and the news media. Although their power over legal interpretation is uncontested, judges do not have the last word in communicating the nature of their decisions to the public. Once a judgment is handed down, journalists rather than judges control the message. Journalists are the filters through which the court is seen and heard. Not surprisingly, an important part of the history of the court has been the creation of a communications environment that is intended to herald the messages and images the court wishes to convey. The media-court relationship that has been slowly constructed over time has both positive and negative aspects, but there can be little doubt that for the court, the Canadian news media, and the public, much is at stake. The most important question is whether current media routines and reporting work to the benefit of ordinary citizens. It is not clear that they do.

## The Dominance of Political Frames
There is a degree to which legal reporting from the Supreme Court simply does not exist. In the largest sense, coverage begins and ends with politics. Reporting is dictated almost entirely by the political importance of decisions and by the imperatives imposed by parliamentary reporters. This is evident in at least three ways: cases that involve political controversy receive by far the most coverage, the court is covered overwhelmingly by parliamentary reporters, and differences between English- and French-language reporting reflect the political values that predominate in Quebec and in English Canada.

First, our study of a year in the life of the court showed that while there was a steady patter of reporting at least in newspapers, in reality there were only a few brief instances when the court came into public view. These moments almost inevitably involved politicians in one way or another. The *Burns-Rafay, Latimer, Sharpe, Boucher,* and *Little Sisters* cases triggered or reflected important political controversies. Capital punishment, child pornography, biker gangs, and euthanasia are hot-button issues that arouse deep feelings. Not surprisingly, these high-profile cases became grist for the mill of politicians, and came to the attention of the Ottawa press gallery, one can argue, precisely because politicians had become involved.

It is also true, as we have emphasized in this book, that some of these cases involved celebrity villains, such as Robert Latimer and Robin Sharpe. Their very notoriety galvanized public interest and drew in the politicians. As Ericson and his colleagues have pointed out, much of what becomes news involves deviant behaviour and its punishment, and a battle over the moral boundaries of society (Ericson, Baranek, and Chan 1987, 7-8). Morality tales and politics go hand in hand.

The glaring reality, however, is that the legal aspects of decisions were buried beneath an avalanche of political reporting. The problem is particularly evident in the television media, where only a handful of cases are covered each year. The politics of the court and most of its ordinary work are rarely reported on. There is almost no coverage of dissenting opinions, splits in the court, the views and influence of individual judges, or the wider trends that are developing. The irony is that the journalists who cover the court almost never write about it. They cover the controversial cases and decisions without examining the larger institution. For instance, while American judges seem to have public profiles, to the point where their positions on issues are regularly talked about on TV talk shows, Canadian judges dwell in relative anonymity. They remain largely invisible to the public, and we suspect that they remain largely unknown to most of the country's journalists. Of course, too little exposure has just as many dangers as too much exposure.

Second, news is conditioned at least to some degree by where journalists are located, and Ottawa journalists are stationed almost exclusively on Parliament Hill. The one exception was when the *National Post* assigned Luiza Chwialkowska to cover the court as a major part of her responsibilities (Cobb 2004, 228). The *Post,* as we described in the Introduction, also devoted a great deal of attention to commenting – mostly negatively – on the court's judgments. But other news organizations never followed the *Post*'s lead in placing a reporter at the court.

The Supreme Court seems destined at least in the near future to be covered by parliamentary reporters who have little specialized knowledge and are assigned to cover cases on a temporary or helter-skelter basis. The journalists who cover a decision today may not be the same reporters who cover a judgment tomorrow. There are, of course, a handful of stalwarts who have covered the Supreme Court for years and have developed considerable expertise in the law and in the politics of the court. But the number is small. Journalists such as Kirk Makin and Yves Boisvert, who can be seen as genuine authorities on the court, are rare and, interestingly enough, they are not part of parliamentary bureaus. Makin works out of Toronto and is wary of being caught in the frenzy that often accompanies the handing down of major decisions; Boisvert is a columnist who covers a variety of subjects, including the court. Compared with their coverage of Parliament Hill, where even the most minor skirmishes can make headlines, news organizations treat the court as an afterthought, a sideshow that can never compete with the main event.

A number of those whom we interviewed expressed concern that senior producers and editors in parliamentary bureaus tend not only to cover, almost exclusively, highly charged political cases but view the importance and nature of judgments through a political lens. For instance, in our in-depth analysis of the four cases, strategic frames predominated. The emphasis was inevitably on the political battle and on often breathless attempts to determine the winners and losers among interest groups and politicians. The old horse race metaphor that is used in so much contemporary political reporting was invariably applied despite the reality that depicting winners and losers is often a difficult proposition at the Supreme Court, where judgments are often highly nuanced and give something to both sides in a dispute. Indeed, the rush to declare winners and losers is so great and so pronounced that, in some cases – *Marshall, Hudson,* and *Little Sisters,* for instance – the press clearly got it wrong.

One can argue that leaving Supreme Court reporting to parliamentary reporters has some advantages. Parliamentary reporters have a feel for the politics that surround cases, know how political parties will react to judgments, and can foresee the political repercussions of particular decisions. Defenders of the current system also contend that all roads do in fact lead back to Parliament Hill because it is parliamentarians who make the laws.

Those who believe that reporting is now too dominated by political frames and imperatives might counter by pointing out that in the dialogue between Parliament and the court, the politicians often leave the last word to the court. Most important, however, is that parliamentary reporters may miss cases that do not come within the range of fire of the politicians. Former justice Louise Arbour, for instance, was surprised that cases filled with human interest, and important societal problems often receive little attention. Arguably, there is as much human drama at the court as there is on Parliament Hill.

A third factor in the predominance of the political lens is the degree to which coverage of the Supreme Court mirrors the different political worlds of Quebec and English-Canadian journalism. News organizations in Quebec normally focus largely on the Quebec government and on politics in the National Assembly. Although there are some very good francophone reporters in Ottawa, the capital is sometimes seen as a faraway posting for aspiring journalists. For anglophone reporters, on the other hand, Ottawa is seen as a plum assignment, a step up the career ladder. It is interesting to note that aside from Radio-Canada and reporters from a host of news organizations assigned to Parliament Hill, there is only one French-language correspondent in the rest of Canada – a *La Presse* business reporter in Toronto. At the same time, the number of reporters from anglophone media organizations at the National Assembly has also declined over the years.

Language is also a factor. Litigants and interest group representatives are often unable to conduct interviews in French. This is the case as well with some federal and most provincial cabinet ministers. This makes it more difficult for TV and radio reporters who need sound bites to cover the story and presumably for audiences to identify with cases. Small wonder then that cases that received a great deal of coverage in English Canada, such as *Vriend* and *Van de Perre,* were barely reported in Quebec.

One of the goals of our study was to measure the differences between French- and English-language reporting. The suspicion in some quarters is that Quebec-based media portray federal institutions such as Parliament and the Supreme Court in a harsh light. Indeed, more than a few federal politicians, including a number of prime ministers, have railed against "separatist" reporters bent on depicting "evil" Ottawa. One need only recall the charges made by Jean Chrétien during the 1995 Quebec referendum that sovereignist leader Lucien Bouchard had received kid glove treatment from the Quebec media, and the threat made at the time by prominent Liberals to close Radio-Canada because it had become a "separatist nest" (Taras 2001, 158).

Our findings reveal two things. First, there is far more interest in the Supreme Court in the English-language media than in the French-language media. The old maxim that Quebec news organizations cover Ottawa only when Quebec interests or personalities are involved is to some degree supported by our study. Quebec journalists, some contend, cover Ottawa the way the American TV networks cover the Olympics – they are there only to report on the home team. Clearly, the Quebec press gave the most attention to Quebec cases.

Perhaps most crucial, however, is our second finding. When the court is the subject of reporting or commentary in the French-language media, they have viewed the court, on balance, in at least as favourable a light as have the English-language media. In portraying the court as an institution, Quebec journalists for the most part paint the Supreme Court in colours that are neutral or complimentary. A number of factors help to explain this generally positive portrayal, including perhaps a relatively less vibrant critique of the court in the Quebec scholarly community. But it may also be that major rulings have been favourably received because they were basically in accord with Quebec opinion. In cases such as *Vriend* and

*Sharpe,* the court's decisions stirred little controversy in Quebec because, it can be argued, these questions had been resolved by the court in ways that comported well with dominant opinion in Quebec. Matters might have been very different had key decisions gone against the grain of Quebec public opinion. In particular, the decision in the *Quebec Secession Reference* was critical in reinforcing the credibility of the court in Quebec. If the decision had been any more favourable to the federal government, the fallout in Quebec could have been considerable.

As discussed in the Introduction, one of the contentious debates within media studies is about whether media coverage is hegemonic or contingent. One school of thought sees media institutions as reflecting the power of the powerful and reinforcing established values and institutions. While opposing views can be normalized and absorbed, media coverage is inherently conservative and guards the gates of power. Other scholars point out that media reporting can be subversive and even radical, and that much depends on the factors at play in a given story. Our findings suggest that coverage of the Supreme Court was hardly deferential and certainly not automatic. While the court received laudatory coverage following its ruling on the *Quebec Secession Reference,* it was widely and sometimes savagely criticized in the aftermath of the *Marshall* decision. On *Vriend,* national coverage was supportive but coverage by the Alberta media was highly critical. Reporting seemed to vary from issue to issue, and much seemed to depend on the contingencies that might be at play in any given situation. The nature of the case, the swirl of public opinion, the ideology and political outlook of news organizations, and the frames chosen by reporters in covering their stories were all factors that could determine the nature of coverage.

The political nature of coverage means that other perspectives and angles are largely ignored. For instance, a reporter using a legal or rights frame in his or her reports would cast the net differently. The reporting of Charter cases, for instance, usually fails to explain how rights come to be defined by the court and how they can be limited by government. The limitations analysis has proved to be very important in Charter cases. The analysis rests on two assumptions: rationality and proportionality. First, there must be some rational connection between legislative objectives and the means employed. Second, that the means used infringe on Charter rights no more than is necessary to achieve the necessary objectives. Journalists, however, rarely explain the reasons why a legislative measure has failed or succeeded under this analysis. Framing stories in terms of rights might have greater explanatory power for viewers and readers. In this kind of analysis, majority and minority rulings would merit greater attention, and reasons for splits in the court might have to be explained.

A similar phenomenon was at work in the area of Aboriginal rights. Here our analyses of the two *Marshall* cases are instructive. The first case received little coverage, even though the lead litigant in the case was the renowned Donald Marshall Jr., who spent many years in prison for a crime he did not commit. It was only with the explosion of violence in the East Coast lobster fishery that its ramifications became apparent to journalists. Even then, no mention was made in news reports of the rules the court had handed down in prior cases that entitled government to abridge Aboriginal constitutional rights. Had the first news reports focused on the issue of rights rather than on what the two sides in the case were saying, reactions might have been different. Instead, media accounts incorrectly portrayed Aboriginal rights as being unlimited and the failure of the federal government to seek a negotiated solution may have reinforced this impression.

## The Problem of Specialized Reporting

To some degree, journalists who cover legal issues face problems similar to those faced by reporters with other specialized beats. Medical, science, environmental, and business reporters all enter worlds where they must translate often highly complex and rarefied knowledge into language that will be understandable to ordinary citizens. The question for news organizations and journalism schools is how to prepare journalists to enter and cope in these specialized worlds. The assumption of most news organizations about the Supreme Court is that little training is needed. Reporters schooled in general politics can be sent to the court without second thought.

The journalists we interviewed seemed to be divided on the issue. Most believed that journalistic skills and "feel" are the most important requirements for covering a story, and that these attributes can be transferred to any setting. Others felt that some level of knowledge is needed so that reporters don't become vulnerable to and dependent on the ELO or on litigants and pressure groups that have goods to sell. Without some knowledge, reporters can be easily spun.

Most journalism schools offer credit courses on media and the law. But these deal mostly with subjects like libel, defamation, and contempt of court, namely, they instruct journalists how to avoid problems in their encounters with the justice system. This, in our view, is insufficient. There is a strong argument that journalists covering the Supreme Court should have at least some knowledge of the Charter of Rights and Freedoms, Aboriginal rights, amending formulae, and the like, together with the foundations of the civil law, common law, and criminal law. News organizations might even consider hiring reporters who have some background in the law.

The issue, moreover, may be tied to the question of why there is relatively little coverage of the court compared with Parliament. Journalists who have little training in the law may not realize the importance of particular cases or see wider trends. In our chapter on judges and journalists, Chapter 6, we quoted one legal reporter who recalled that important stories were dismissed by young and inexperienced TV producers with little or no understanding of the court and its activities.

News organizations find themselves in something of a catch-22 situation. Although media managers feel that there is little need to put resources into a beat that provides stories only occasionally, the very absence of specialized reporters who cover the court on a regular basis, one can argue, creates little appetite for legal reporting. Indifference breeds indifference.

On one level, the solution is simply for news organizations to depoliticize their coverage. They could shift their gaze at least to some degree away from Parliament. The idea that viewers and readers are not interested in legal issues because they are too complex and abstract holds little water. Indeed, trials and legal issues have become a mainstay of news and entertainment programming, and audiences, one might contend, demonstrate a remarkable capacity to deal with legal complexity when celebrities or notorious villains are on trial. In the United States, audiences remain riveted by coverage of prominent court cases despite the numbing detail and arcane nature of the legal strategies used in many of the cases aired. Moreover, if attracting audiences is the determining factor, it should be apparent that parliamentary reporting in its current mode is not a great success story. If anything, interest in parliamentary news and in politics in general is plummeting (Taras 2001, 38-39).

The problem for journalists is to find ways to cover the court when there are no hot-button political cases. The model here may be medical and business reporters, who seem to do a far better job in reporting both details and major trends. They are specialized reporters with distinct domains, as compared with parliamentary reporters recruited for the day. They have established beats and are assured time and space. They are also expected to have developed considerable expertise. Business reporters can't afford to confuse class A and class B shares; medical reporters are expected to know how the West Nile virus spreads in addition to a whole lot more.

## Judges, Journalists, and Citizens

A number of judges interviewed for this study were generally pleased by media coverage and believe that the news media are doing a good job overall. They pointed out that Canadians are more aware of the Charter and their rights as citizens and that the court is held in high esteem at least compared with other institutions. Media coverage undoubtedly plays some role in this, but the court also benefits from the natural respect, even deference, that the public and many journalists have for judges. The court has also, some might argue, been a skilled and cautious interpreter of the public mood, never moving too quickly or getting too far ahead of public opinion, and careful, as was the case in the *Quebec Secession Reference,* to give something to both sides.

The justices, nevertheless, would like more attention paid to the work of the court, despite the fact that greater attention brings greater scrutiny. Miljan and Cooper (2003, 163-64) argue that lack of media coverage helps legitimize the court because the court is seldom held up to scrutiny. If this were correct, the justices might want to keep a lid on exposure. *La Presse* columnist Yves Boisvert (2002, 25) succinctly describes the dilemma: "Supreme Court judges say that they want more coverage and that they want to be better understood. But they also want less criticism and they have to realize that the two go hand in hand. It's a package deal. If you have more coverage, you'll have more interest and you're going to have more criticism as well." CBC journalist Rex Murphy likens the "publicity machine of the twentieth century" to a bridge that can be crossed only once: "If the judicial organs of this country decide that they are going to be part of the tumult of public exchange and hard opinion that goes on in every domain of society, remember that the decision to enter into it is a fundamental one, and cannot be retraced" (Canadian Judicial Council, 1999). Our study suggests, however, that there will be moments of intense scrutiny and then longer periods when the court receives little coverage.

There can be no doubt that the court by hesitant steps has entered this new world. Most of the judges whom we interviewed viewed media as something that exists on another plane, a plane beyond their control. Since there is little they can do to change it, there is little reason to expend time or energy on the subject. At the same time, whether calculated or not, the court has created a system of relationships that supports its attempts to convey its messages to the public. The expertise and objectivity of the court's executive legal officers (ELOs) and the general media environment that surrounds the court have undoubtedly provided judges with some shelter from the cold. Most critically, they have created a communications environment that for the most part seems to satisfy both their interests and those of journalists. The court-media system includes the pivotal role played by the ELO, who for journalists is the court's public face, the court-media relations committee, broadcasts on CPAC, the opening of the courthouse to reporters, and the numerous appearances and speaking engagements undertaken by judges each year. The system allows the judges to dwell in a netherworld between remoteness and availability.

One can argue that part of the reason for the predominance of political reporting is the age-old *devoir de réserve* that prevents justices from commenting on the judgments they have handed down. Commenting on or responding to questions about criticisms of their decisions or dissents on the court would open up the floodgates in ways that could only be damaging to the court. For instance, when Justice Bastarache criticized his colleagues in an interview with the *Lawyers Weekly*, it gave the impression that the court was divided and some decisions arbitrary. The problem, however, is that the silence of the judges creates a vacuum that is eagerly filled by others. As reporters rush to interview litigants, interest group representatives, and politicians, stories take on a political coloration. Legal issues are lost amid the drive to declare winners and losers.

Yet, there can be little doubt that justices are sometimes disturbed by what they see as sensationalized coverage, factual errors, and a lack of attention to the reasons behind a decision. In an interview with the *Globe and Mail* after his official retirement ceremony in June 2004, Frank Iacobucci reflected on his frustrations in dealing with the press. What was most distressing to Iacobucci was the degree to which the public misunderstood the court's rulings. He blamed "opinion 'brokers' who purposely take a judgment out of context" and "inaccurate newspaper headlines that precipitate a furor by misinforming those who read no further" (Makin 2004). Some of the criticism that judges received after the *Sharpe* decision caused Iacobucci particular anguish: "It's just awful. To say we were going out of our way to defend the rights of people doing those terrible things ... We really work very, very hard to be careful. It really does distress me when this happens" (Makin 2004).

Most upsetting to the judges and former judges that we interviewed was that the reasons behind a decision were mostly ignored or downplayed. This is evidence again that there is almost no legal reporting. To some degree the reasons for judgment are the cornerstone of the court's claims to objectivity and authority. If the reasons are omitted, decisions can look arbitrary or politically motivated rather than based on precedent and precise legal reasoning. This is not a situation the judges can take lightly. The justices must have been disturbed by the relish and vehemence with which they were attacked by Stephen Harper and the Conservatives during the 2004 federal election. Harper accused the justices of acting "unconstitutionally," ignoring the facts, and being "out of control" (*Globe and Mail* 2004). Harper went so far as to suggest that a Conservative government might be forced to use the notwithstanding clause to blunt the power of the judges.

Virtually all the judges we interviewed believed that the court has stretched as far as it can possibly stretch in meeting the needs of journalists. Most crucially, the judges are unwilling to comment on cases or on judgments that have been handed down because they believe that this would jeopardize the court's integrity in profound ways. Commenting on or responding to questions about criticisms of their decisions or dissenting opinions could create division and undermine the credibility of the court. It is a path that the judges do not want to take.

## Last Thoughts

As *The Last Word* was going to press in June 2005 the Supreme Court handed down its decision in the *Chaoulli* case. The judgment struck down two provisions of Quebec legislation that prohibited citizens from obtaining private health insurance. The case is considered pivotal because of the consequences that it could have for the future of the public health care system. But the decision was remarkable not only because of its extraordinary importance for Canadian public policy but because it rekindled all of the debates that surround the court and permeate this book. To begin, the judgment was a harsh awakening for those who thought that the court had retreated from playing a central role in Canadian life, that it had begun to tip its hat to the politicians and sought safer ground in terms of judicial activism. In fact, one of the crucial features of the judgment was the extent to which the judges had fiercely debated the role of the court among themselves.

But the case also exemplified both the power of media coverage and problems in the media-court relationship. Although the ruling produced glaring headlines across the country, and a veritable avalanche of editorials and commentaries, the familiar patterns of media coverage reasserted themselves. Faced with a long and complex judgment, TV reporters seemed hesitant and perplexed when first reporting the decision. There were long pauses and a reliance on the reactions of litigants and experts. Not surprisingly, the political lens again dominated coverage as the reactions of governments and interest groups were given the most play. Such coverage was only reasonable given that governments, particularly the Quebec government, were deeply affected by the decision. Yet it must be stressed that little attention was given to key issues, such as disagreements among judges, the emphasis placed by the judges on rights, and the legal battles that are likely to result from the decision.

Moreover, although a final evaluation will have to await further study, at first glance it would seem that there was more criticism of judicial activism in Quebec than there has been in years. Perhaps, as we have suggested, support for the court in Quebec may largely depend on whether judgments are aligned with prevailing public opinion.

This book represents the first major effort to examine the contours of a relationship that is critical to Canadian democracy. We hope that it will inspire further scholarly exploration and in fact stir serious debate and reflection among journalists and judges about how coverage can be improved. Our study found much that is commendable in the court-media relationship and we believe that other countries have something to learn from the Canadian example and experience. But to the extent that reporting sometimes short-changes citizens by giving them highly abbreviated, sporadic, sensationalized, and intensely political coverage, some rethinking is called for. The court has survived quite a number of media storms in recent years, but undoubtedly there are more to come.

## References

Boisvert, Yves. 2002. Comments. Media-Supreme Court Research Workshop, 7 November, Ottawa.

Canadian Judicial Council. 1999. *The judicial role in public information.*

Cobb, Chris. 2004. *Ego and ink: The inside story of Canada's national newspaper war.* Toronto: McClelland and Stewart.

*Chaoulli v. Quebec (Attorney General),* 2005 SCC 35.

Ericson, Richard, Patricia Baranek, and Janet Chan. 1987. *Visualizing deviance: A study of news organization.* Toronto: University of Toronto Press.

*Globe and Mail.* 2004. The Conservatives and the judges. Editorial, 21 June, p. A12.

Makin, Kirk. 2004. Iacobucci reflects on his Supreme Court trials. *Globe and Mail,* 22 June, p. A3.

Miljan, Lydia, and Barry Cooper. 2003. *Hidden agendas: How journalists influence the news.* Vancouver: UBC Press.

Taras, David. 2001. *Power and betrayal in the Canadian media.* Peterborough, ON: Broadview Press.

# Appendix A:
# Interview Questions

**Grid for Supreme Court Justices**

*Media Coverage*
- How would you describe current media coverage?
- How has media coverage evolved?
- How would you describe the way in which the media portray Supreme Court justices?
- What is an example of what you regard as excellent coverage of a decision? Of poor coverage?

*The Media and the Court*
- What is the role of the ELO? The role of the Supreme Court/Media Committee?
- How would you describe the relationship between yourself and members of the media?
- What would you regard as ideal coverage?
- From a legal point of view, what would you regard as the most significant decisions of the past year?

*The Public and the Court*
- What does the public need to know about the court?
- How could coverage affect public perception of the court?
- How has the role of the court in society changed since the Charter? Do you feel the media have a clear understanding of the new role of the court?

**Grid for Journalists/Editors**

*Media Coverage*
- Is coverage of the Supreme Court of Canada, a distinctive, specialized beat?
- What will or won't be covered? Who decides?
- What determines the extent and depth of the coverage?

- Does the Supreme Court journalist need particular skills?
- To what extent is the Supreme Court a different beat?
- What is the influence of his or her personal interests?
- What is the influence of other media?
- Which cases did you find difficult to cover?

### The Media and the Court

- What is your relationship with the Supreme Court justices?
- Comment on the ELO and a current system at the court.

### The Public and the Court

- What is the public's interest toward the Supreme Court of Canada?
- What is the role of the journalist in society? What is the role of the Supreme Court?
- What does the public want to know, and what does it need to know?

# Appendix B: Method of Analysis Coding Instructions and Sample Code Sheet

QUANTITATIVE CONTENT ANALYSIS assumes that the importance of an event, an idea, a symbol, or a speaker can be determined by factors such as frequency of the story and placement of a source within a story or on a page. Walizer and Weimer (1978) define quantitative content analysis as a "systematic way of examining the content of recorded information." As Hackett and Bailey (1997) write, content analysis can be used to assess the image of a particular person or group and to track trends in coverage. To better understand the nature of Supreme Court reporting, we developed variables to look at headlines, tone, story topics, sources, and frame.

Headlines were carefully scrutinized because they play a crucial role in readers' opinion formation. Often, headlines are the only part of the story read by the public. As noted media analyst Tuen van Dijk (1991) writes, headlines can also set the context in which story content is interpreted. Our headline variables included the main focus of the headline, which legal or political actor was mentioned in the headline, and what the tone of the headline was if the main topic of the headline was the Supreme Court or the decision handed down by the court.

The analysis of tone was an important part of our study. Our coders were instructed to measure tone by reflecting on the impact of the entire news story after the story had been read. News stories, editorials, and columns often contain both positive and negative references. This method of coding for tone gave us the advantage of being able to code as neutral those stories that contained equal measures of positive and negative information. And because most news stories and many editorials are neutral, we were able to capture that data.

The values in the story topic and source variables were determined by reading all stories before coding. Master lists for each variable were developed and refined. For frames we used the pre-established categories of conflict and issue for each decision. Other frames were added or deleted depending on the specifics of the case. For instance, both *Sharpe* and *Vriend* had moral-order categories because of the value-laden nature of these cases.

Because coder reliability can be a problem in social science research, we conducted inter-coder reliability tests. A computer generated a random sample of 20 percent of the total number of articles from each case. Coding decisions in this random sample were checked and any differences were reviewed and discussed by three trained coders until agreement was reached. This procedure was followed until we had an agreement level of over 85 percent in each case; an agreement level that is within acceptable limits established in social science research. Below is a sample code sheet and coding instructions.

Because the calculation of chi-square involves divisions by expected cell frequencies, its value can be greatly inflated if expected frequencies in individual cells are very small. In our cases, chi-square tests were run to determine significance, but, in most instances, more than 20 percent of the cells had an expected frequency below 5 and, thus, the chi-square was questionable.

## Coding Sheet for Secession

1.  Name of coder

2.  Case identification number

3.  Medium
    1   Television
    2   Newspaper

4.  Name of television network
    1   CTV
    2   CBC
    3   TVA
    4   Radio-Canada
    99  NA

5.  Name of newspaper
    1   *Globe and Mail*
    2   *National Post*
    3   *Le Journal de Montréal*
    4   *La Presse*
    5   *Le Devoir*
    6   Montreal *Gazette*
    7   *Le Droit*
    8   *Toronto Sun*
    99  NA

6. Date of story

7. Case status at time of article
   1 The hearing: 16, 17, 18, 19 February 1998
   2 The decision: 20 August 1998

8. Length of article (newspaper only)

9. Photo or illustration with article
   1 Yes
   2 No
   3 Don't know
   99 NA (television)

10. Time of segment in seconds (television only)

11. Location of print article in newspaper
    1 Front page (with or without inside turn)
    2 Front section
    3 Op-ed page
    4 Special section or page
    5 Other
    6 Don't know
    7 Tabloid inside page
    99 NA (television or magazine)

12. Section and page number (newspaper only)

13. Location of print article on page
    1 Main story on page, above the fold
    2 Main story on page, above and below the fold
    3 Above the fold, not main story
    4 Main story, below the fold
    5 Below fold, not main story
    6 Runs above and below fold, not main story
    7 Don't know
    99 NA (television/magazine)

*Headlines*

14. Main focus of headline

    1    Guy Bertrand
    2    Supreme Court's decision
    3    Supreme Court or Supreme Court justices
    4    Secession/Separatism
    5    Judicial activism
    6    Hearing or hearing arguments
    7    Canadian unity
    8    It's for Quebec to decide
    9    Alliances-Strategies
    10   Winners/Losers
    11   Standing head
    12   Other or unable to interpret (cite)
    99   NA (television)

15. First actor in principal head

    1    Supreme Court
    2    Guy Bertrand
    3    André Joli-Coeur, amicus curiae
    4    Prime Minister Jean Chrétien
    5    Federal government representative, including minister or lawyer, "Ottawa," Liberals, or Canada
    6    Representative of other federal parties, e.g., P. Manning or J. Charest
    7    Premier Lucien Bouchard
    8    Parti québécois government representative, including minister or "Quebec" as in the province of Quebec
    9    Representative of other Quebec provincial party
    10   Representative of any other provincial government
    11   Intervener
    12   Quebec sovereignist
    13   Academic or legal expert
    14   None
    15   Other (cite)
    16   Former Quebec politician
    17   Quebec nation or Peuple Québécois
    99   NA (television)

16. Second actor in principal head

    1    Supreme Court

2   Guy Bertrand
3   André Joli-Coeur, amicus curiae
4   Prime Minister Jean Chrétien
5   Federal government representative, including minister or lawyer, "Ottawa," Liberals, or Canada
6   Representative of other federal parties, e.g., P. Manning or J. Charest
7   Premier Lucien Bouchard
8   Parti québécois government representative, including minister, or "Quebec" as in the province of Quebec
9   Representative of other Quebec provincial party
10  Representative of any other provincial government
11  Intervener
12  Quebec sovereignist
13  Academic or legal expert
14  None
15  Other (cite)
16  Former Quebec politician
17  Quebec nation or Peuple Québécois
99  NA (television)

17. If court or decision is main focus of principal headline, what is its tone?
1   Positive
2   Negative
3   Neutral/Mixed
99  NA

18. Main topic of story
1   Details of arguments made or to be made
2   Focus or speculation on decision's details
3   Verbatim transcript of part of decision or hearing
4   Background, history, behind the scenes of the case
5   Clear majority on clear question means negotiation
6   Supreme Court should not hear case
7   It's a Quebec issue; Ottawa is interfering
8   Details of secession, partition, referendum, etc.
9   Judicial activism
10  Economic factors
11  Canadian unity
12  Political strategies employed by political actors
13  Other (cite)

14 Action taken by separatists, such as demonstrations
15 None
99 NA (television)

19. Second topic
    1 Details of arguments made or to be made
    2 Speculation on decision's details
    3 Verbatim transcript of part of decision or hearing
    4 Background, history, behind the scenes of the case
    5 Clear majority on clear question means negotiation
    6 Supreme Court should not hear case
    7 It's a Quebec issue; Ottawa is interfering
    8 Details of secession, partition, referendum, etc.
    9 Judicial activism
    10 Economic factors
    11 Canadian unity
    12 Political strategies employed by political actors
    13 Other (cite)
    14 Action taken by separatists, such as demonstrations
    15 None
    99 NA (television)

## Tone

20. Tone of references to Supreme Court
    1 Positive
    2 Negative
    3 Neutral/Mixed
    99 NA

21. Tone of references to Supreme Court decision
    1 Positive
    2 Negative
    3 Neutral/Mixed
    99 NA

22. Tone of references to Quebec government representatives
    1 Positive
    2 Negative
    3 Neutral/Mixed
    99 NA

23. Tone of references to federal government
    1   Positive
    2   Negative
    3   Neutral/Mixed
    99  NA

24. Genre
    1   Hard news
    2   Editorial
    3   News analysis
    4   Column, opinion piece, commentary
    5   Direct excerpt
    6   In brief
    7   Personality profile
    8   Feature
    9   Other (cite)

25. Are one or all three of the reference questions cited (paraphrased or direct quote)
    1   Yes
    2   No

## Sources (check all that apply)

26. Majority court (justice or decision)                          1 Yes      2 No

27. Prime Minister Jean Chrétien                                  1 Yes      2 No

28. Other federal Liberal                                         1 Yes      2 No

29. Premier Lucien Bouchard                                       1 Yes      2 No

30. Other Parti québécois member                                 1 Yes      2 No

31. Representative of other Quebec provincial party              1 Yes      2 No

32. Member of the Bloc Québécois                                 1 Yes      2 No

33. Representative of any other provincial government            1 Yes      2 No

34. Guy Bertrand     1 Yes     2 No

35. André Joli-Coeur     1 Yes     2 No

36. Yves Fortier     1 Yes     2 No

37. Member of Parliament who is not Liberal     1 Yes     2 No

38. Quebec sovereignist     1 Yes     2 No

39. General public     1 Yes     2 No

40. Intervener     1 Yes     2 No

41. Member of federalist organization     1 Yes     2 No

42. Academic or legal expert     1 Yes     2 No

43. Journalist or columnist     1 Yes     2 No

44. Other (cite)     1 Yes     2 No

45. Former Quebec politician     1 Yes     2 No

46. Number of sources in story
    1   0
    2   1-4
    3   5-9
    4   10-14
    5   Over 14
    99   NA

47. Source quoted first
    1   Court (justice or decision)
    2   Prime Minister Jean Chrétien
    3   Other federal Liberal
    4   Premier Lucien Bouchard
    5   Other Parti québécois member
    6   Representative of other Quebec provincial party
    7   Member of the Bloc Québécois

8   Representative of any other provincial government
9   Guy Bertrand
10  André Joli-Coeur
11  Yves Fortier
12  Member of Parliament who is not Liberal
13  Quebec sovereignist
14  Intervener
15  Member of federalist organization
16  Academic or legal expert
17  Journalist or columnist
18  Other
19  Former Quebec politician
99  NA or None

48. Source quoted second
1   Court (justice or decision)
2   Prime Minister Jean Chrétien
3   Other federal Liberal
4   Premier Lucien Bouchard
5   Other Parti québécois member
6   Representative of other Quebec provincial party
7   Member of the Bloc Québécois
8   Representative of any other provincial government
9   Guy Bertrand
10  André Joli-Coeur
11  Yves Fortier
12  Member of Parliament who is not Liberal
13  Quebec sovereignist
14  Intervener
15  Member of federalist organization
16  Academic or legal expert
17  Journalist or columnist
18  Other
19  Former Quebec politician
99  NA or none

49. Position of first journalist
1   Parliamentary bureau or Ottawa
2   Legal correspondent
3   Canadian Press or Presse canadienne correspondent

4   Freelance reporter, collaboration spéciale
5   Special correspondent, envoyé spéciale
6   Regional bureau correspondent
7   Regular staff, no position cited
8   Newspaper name only
9   Provincial affairs or Legislative/National Assembly reporter
10  Other
99  NA (TV or editorial/comment/opinion)

50. Position of second journalist
1   Parliamentary bureau or Ottawa
2   Legal correspondent
3   Canadian Press or Presse canadienne correspondent
4   Freelance reporter, collaboration spéciale
5   Special correspondent, envoyé spéciale
6   Regional bureau correspondent
7   Regular staff – no position cited
8   Newspaper name only
9   Provincial affairs or Legislative/National Assembly reporter
10  Other
99  NA (TV or editorial/comment/opinion or no second journalist)

51. Position of columnist/editorial/opinion writer
1   Staff member
2   Guest writer
3   Unable to tell
4   Regular contributor
5   Unsigned editorial
99  NA

52. Frame
1   Strategic
2   Issue
3   Human interest
4   Economic
5   Moral order
6   Other

## References

Hackett, R., and G. Bailey. 1997. Newswatcher's guide to content analysis. Burnaby, BC: NewsWatch Canada.

van Dijk, T.A. 1991. *Racism and the press.* London: Routledge.

Walizer, M., and P. Weiner. 1978. *Research methods and analysis.* New York: Harper and Row.

# About the Authors

**Florian Sauvageau** is Professor of Communications at Université Laval in Québec City and Director of the Centre d'études sur les médias / Centre for Media Studies. He has published and co-authored many books and numerous articles on journalism, the media, and public policies in communications. He was co-chair of the federal Task Force on Broadcasting Policy in 1985-86. Sauvageau has been a journalist for many years and is former managing editor of *Le Soleil,* one of Quebec's largest newspapers. He is also a member of the Quebec Bar.

**David Schneiderman** is Associate Professor of Law and Political Science at the Faculty of Law, University of Toronto. He has authored numerous articles on Canadian constitutional law and history, comparative constitutional law, and economic globalization. He has multiple volumes on these topics and is founding editor of the quarterly *Constitutional Forum Constitutionnel* as well as founding editor-in-chief of the journal *Review of Constitutional Studies.*

**David Taras** is University Professor and Professor in the Faculty of Communication and Culture at the University of Calgary. He is the author of *The Newsmakers: The Media's Influence on Canadian Politics* and *Power and Betrayal in the Canadian Media,* and co-editor of, among other works, *How Canadians Communicate.* He was a visiting professor at the University of Amsterdam in the Netherlands and served as an expert advisor to the House of Commons Standing Committee on Canadian Heritage during its two-year review of Canadian broadcasting policy from 2001 to 2003.

**Ruth Klinkhammer** is Assistant Professor in the Department of Professional Communication at Okanagan College. She has co-authored and authored articles on the media coverage of the courts and Aboriginal people. Klinkhammer was also a print journalist for many years and continues to write for a variety of publications.

**Pierre Trudel** is Professor at the Centre de recherche en droit public (CRDP) in the Faculté de droit at Université de Montréal, and L.R. Wilson Chair in Information Technology and Electronic Commerce Law. He has been a visiting professor at Université Laval, Université Paris 2, and Université Namur in Belgium. He teaches media law and cyberspace law. He has published books on radio and television law, privacy, cyberspace, and media law.

# Index

LAW AND
SOCIETY

Christopher N. Kendall
*Gay Male Pornography: An Issue of Sex Discrimination* (2004)

Roy B. Flemming
*Tournament of Appeals: Granting Judicial Review in Canada* (2004)

Constance Backhouse and Nancy L. Backhouse
*The Heiress vs the Establishment: Mrs. Campbell's Campaign for Legal Justice* (2004)

Christopher P. Manfredi
*Feminist Activism in the Supreme Court: Legal Mobilization and the Women's Legal Education and Action Fund* (2004)

Annalise Acorn
*Compulsory Compassion: A Critique of Restorative Justice* (2004)

Jonathan Swainger and Constance Backhouse (eds.)
*People and Place: Historical Influences on Legal Culture* (2003)

Jim Phillips and Rosemary Gartner
*Murdering Holiness: The Trials of Franz Creffield and George Mitchell* (2003)

David R. Boyd
*Unnatural Law: Rethinking Canadian Environmental Law and Policy* (2003)

Ikechi Mgbeoji
*Collective Insecurity: The Liberian Crisis, Unilateralism, and Global Order* (2003)

Rebecca Johnson
*Taxing Choices: The Intersection of Class, Gender, Parenthood, and the Law* (2002)

John McLaren, Robert Menzies, and Dorothy E. Chunn (eds.)
*Regulating Lives: Historical Essays on the State, Society, the Individual, and the Law* (2002)

Joan Brockman
*Gender in the Legal Profession: Fitting or Breaking the Mould* (2001)

Printed and bound in Canada by Friesens
Set in Perpetua by George Kirkpatrick
Copy editor: Judy Phillips
Indexer: Adrian Mather

"This is definitely the 'last word' in how the message of a Supreme Court decision is translated and conveyed to its broader publics; it explains the media to the court-watchers, and the Supreme Court to the media-watchers, in a readable, profound, and thoughtful way. Absolutely a must-read."
PETER McCORMICK, Political Science, University of Lethbridge

"*The Last Word* is one of the first books to examine the relationship between the media and the Supreme Court of Canada, and it should contribute to the very lively debate about the role and power of the court in our society. It's a pleasure to read and I expect it will find a wide audience among both the general public and scholars in a number of disciplines." ANDRÉE LAJOIE, Faculty of Law, Université de Montréal

Media coverage of the Supreme Court of Canada has emerged as a crucial factor not only for judges and journalists but also for the public. It's the media, after all, that decide which court rulings to cover and how. They translate highly complex judgments into concise and meaningful news stories that will appeal to, and be understood by, the general public. Thus, judges lose control of the message once they hand down decisions, and journalists have the last word.

To show how the Supreme Court has fared under the media spotlight, Sauvageau, Schneiderman, and Taras examine a year in the life of the court and then focus on the media coverage of four high-profile decisions: the *Marshall* case, about Aboriginal rights; the *Vriend* case, about gay rights; the *Quebec Secession Reference;* and the *Sharpe* child pornography case. They explore the differences between television and newspaper coverage, national and regional reporting, and the French- and English-language media. They also describe how judges and journalists understand and interact with one another amid often-clashing legal and journalistic cultures, offering a rich and detailed account of the relationship between two of the most important institutions in Canadian life.

**Florian Sauvageau** is Professor of Communications at Université Laval in Québec and Director of the Centre d'études sur les médias/Centre for Media Studies. **David Schneiderman** is Associate Professor in the Faculty of Law at the University of Toronto. **David Taras** is University Professor and Professor in the Faculty of Communication and Culture at the University of Calgary.

Printed in Canada
Cover design: David Drummond

**www.ubcpress.ca**

ISBN 0-7748-1244-3

9 780774 812443